.:FOR Dummies.

BESTSELLING
BOOK SERIES

Rome For Dummies,
1st Edition

Cheat
Sheet

St. Peter's Basilica

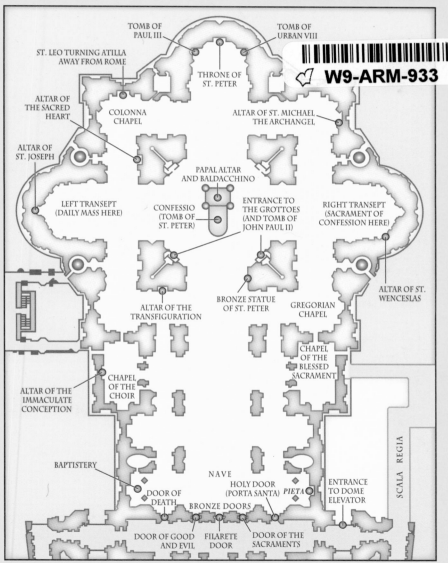

TOMB OF
PAUL III

TOMB OF
URBAN VIII

ST. LEO TURNING ATILLA
AWAY FROM ROME

THRONE OF
ST. PETER

W9-ARM-933

ALTAR OF
THE SACRED
HEART

COLONNA
CHAPEL

ALTAR OF ST. MICHAEL
THE ARCHANGEL

ALTAR OF
ST. JOSEPH

PAPAL ALTAR
AND BALDACCHINO

LEFT TRANSEPT
(DAILY MASS HERE)

CONFESSIO
(TOMB OF
ST. PETER)

ENTRANCE TO
THE GROTTOES
(AND TOMB OF
JOHN PAUL II)

RIGHT TRANSEPT
(SACRAMENT OF
CONFESSION HERE)

ALTAR OF ST.
WENCESLAS

ALTAR OF THE
TRANSFIGURATION

BRONZE STATUE
OF ST. PETER

GREGORIAN
CHAPEL

CHAPEL
OF THE
BLESSED
SACRAMENT

ALTAR OF THE
IMMACULATE
CONCEPTION

CHAPEL
OF THE
CHOIR

SCALA REGIA

BAPTISTERY

NAVE

HOLY DOOR
(PORTA SANTA)

PIETA

ENTRANCE
TO DOME
ELEVATOR

DOOR OF
DEATH

BRONZE DOORS

DOOR OF GOOD
AND EVIL

FILARETE
DOOR

DOOR OF THE
SACRAMENTS

Travel Tips

TELEPHONE TIPS

To call Italy from another country: Dial the international access code (U.S. or Canada 011, U.K., Ireland or New Zealand 00, Australia 0011) followed by the country code (39), and then the local number, which now includes the former city code (you must dial the initial zero).

To make a direct international call from Italy: Dial 00 followed by the country code (U.S. or Canada 1, U.K. 44, Ireland 353, Australia 61, New Zealand 64), the area code, and then the local number.

To charge international calls: Americans can reach an AT&T operator at 172-1011, MCI at 172-1022, or Sprint at 172-1877. Canadians can reach Teleglobe at 172-1001. Brits can reach British Telephone at 172-0044 or Mercury at 172-1061. New Zealanders can dial 172-1064. You can reach an international operator by dialing 170.

Directory assistance in English: 12 (national), 176 (Europe), or 1790 (beyond Europe).

International Operator in English: 170.

SIZE CONVERSIONS

WOMEN'S CLOTHING

American	8	10	12	14	16	18
Continental	38	40	42	44	46	48
British	10	12	14	16	18	20

WOMEN'S SHOES

American	5	6	7	8	9	10
Continental	36	37	38	39	40	41
British	4	5	6	7	8	9

CHILDREN'S CLOTHING

American	3	4	5	6	6X
Continental	98	104	110	116	122
British	18	20	22	24	26

CHILDREN'S SHOES

American	8	9	10	11	12	13	1	2	3
Continental	24	25	27	28	29	30	32	33	34
British	7	8	9	10	11	12	13	1	2

MEN'S SUITS

American	34	36	38	40	42	44	46	48
Continental	44	46	48	50	52	54	56	58
British	34	36	38	40	42	44	46	48

MEN'S SHIRTS

American	14$\frac{1}{2}$	15	15$\frac{1}{2}$	16	16$\frac{1}{2}$	17	17$\frac{1}{2}$	18
Continental	37	38	39	41	42	43	44	45
British	14$\frac{1}{2}$	15	15$\frac{1}{2}$	16	16$\frac{1}{2}$	17	17$\frac{1}{2}$	18

MEN'S SHOES

American	7	8	9	10	11	12	13
Continental	39$\frac{1}{2}$	41	42	43	44$\frac{1}{2}$	46	47
British	6	7	8	9	10	11	12

DISTANCE

To convert	multiply by
inches to centimeters	2.54
centimeters to inches	.39
feet to meters	.30
meters to feet	3.28
yards to meters	.91
meters to yards	1.09
miles to kilometers	1.61
kilometers to miles	.62

1 ft. = .30m   1 mile = 1.6km
1m = 3.3 ft.   1km = .62 mile

WEIGHT

To convert	multiply by
Ounces to grams	28.35
Grams to ounces	.035
Pounds to kilograms	.45
Kilograms to pounds	2.20

1 ounce = 28 grams
1 pound = .4555 kilogram
1 gram = .04 ounce
1 kilogram = 2.2 pounds

LIQUID VOLUME

To convert	multiply by
U.S. gallons to liters	3.8
Liters to U.S. gallons	.26
U.S. gallons to imperial gallons	.83
Imperial gallons to U.S. gallons	1.20
Imperial gallons to liters	4.55
Liters to imperial gallons	.22

1 liter = .26 U.S. gallon
1 U.S. gallon = 3.8 liters

FOR DUMMIES®

The fun and easy way™ to travel!

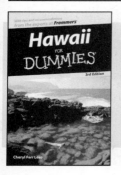
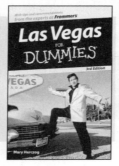

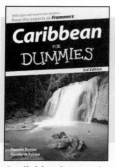
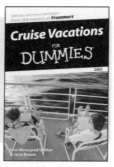

Rome

FOR

DUMMIES®

1ST EDITION

by Bruce Murphy and
Alessandra de Rosa

WILEY

Wiley Publishing, Inc.

Rome For Dummies® 1st Edition
Published by
Wiley Publishing, Inc.
111 River St.
Hoboken, NJ 07030-5774
www.wiley.com

Copyright © 2006 by Wiley Publishing, Inc., Indianapolis, Indiana

Published simultaneously in Canada

For general information on our other products and services, please contact our Customer Care Department within the U.S. at 800-762-2974, outside the U.S. at 317-572-3993, or fax 317-572-4002.

For technical support, please visit www.wiley.com/techsupport.

Wiley also publishes its books in a variety of electronic formats. Some content that appears in print may not be available in electronic books.

Library of Congress Control Number: 2005937355

ISBN-13: 978-0-7645-9950-7

ISBN-10: 0-7645-9950-X

Manufactured in the United States of America

10 9 8 7 6 5 4 3 2 1

1B/SR/QS/QW/IN

WILEY

About the Authors

Bruce Murphy has lived and worked in New York City, Boston, Chicago, Dublin, Rome, and Sicily. His work has appeared in magazines ranging from *Cruising World* to *Critical Inquiry*. In addition to guidebooks, he has published fiction, poetry, and criticism, most recently the *Encylopedia of Murder and Mystery* (St. Martin's Press).

Alessandra de Rosa was born in Rome and has lived and worked in Rome, Paris, and New York City. She did her first cross-Europe trip at age 2, from Rome to London by car. She has continued in that line ever since, exploring three out of five continents so far. Her beloved Italy remains her preferred destination and where she lives part of the year.

Authors' Acknowledgments

To San Nicola di Bari, Julia, Lily, and Eve.

We would like to thank our editors: Tim Ryan, for his enthusiasm and editing, and Naomi Black, for her patience and support. Thank you also to the cartographer, Roberta Stockwell. Finally, thank you to Rome and to Alessandra's parents, for choosing to live in this wonderful city. This book would not have been possible without all of them.

Publisher's Acknowledgments

We're proud of this book; please send us your comments through our Dummies online registration form located at www.dummies.com/register/.

Some of the people who helped bring this book to market include the following:

Editorial

Editors: Alexis Lipsitz, Project Editor; Melissa S. Bennett, Production Editor; and Jennifer Moore, Development Editor

Copy Editor: Elizabeth Kuball

Cartographer: Roberta Stockwell

Senior Photo Editor: Richard Fox

Cover Photos: *Front cover:* © Dallas and John Heaton/Corbis, *Back cover:* © Peter Barrett/Masterfile

Cartoons: Rich Tennant (www.the5thwave.com)

Composition Services

Project Coordinator: Ryan Steffen

Layout and Graphics: Denny Hager, Stephanie D. Jumper, Barry Offringa, Lynsey Osborn, Heather Ryan

Proofreaders: Leeann Harney, TECHBOOKS Production Services

Indexer: TECHBOOKS Production Services

Publishing and Editorial for Consumer Dummies

Diane Graves Steele, Vice President and Publisher, Consumer Dummies

Joyce Pepple, Acquisitions Director, Consumer Dummies

Kristin A. Cocks, Product Development Director, Consumer Dummies

Michael Spring, Vice President and Publisher, Travel

Kelly Regan, Editorial Director, Travel

Publishing for Technology Dummies

Andy Cummings, Vice President and Publisher, Dummies Technology/General User

Composition Services

Gerry Fahey, Vice President of Production Services

Debbie Stailey, Director of Composition Services

Contents at a Glance

Maps at a Glance

Table of Contents

Introduction

*R*ome, the Eternal City, the capital of the ancient Roman Empire and of the modern Italian state, is a city with many faces and myriad charms. Its history is epic — the city that vanquished Carthage and was itself sacked by barbarians — and is written in its monuments and ruins. Rome is also one of the most beautiful cities in the world, especially since the great refurbishing of its many monuments and revamping of its museums and attractions for the 2000 Papal Jubilee. More tourist friendly than ever, Rome can be bewildering, however, with its noise and traffic and its meandering streets. As an increasing number of people speak some English, the language barrier has slowly been receding, but don't expect everyone to understand English. Knowing a few key words and phrases in Italian will take you far; we list some of them throughout this book and especially in Chapter 17 and Appendix B.) You'll find Romans warm and welcoming, and ready to help ease you into *la dolce vita.*

About This Book

Whether you're a first-timer or making a repeat visit to see sights you missed the first go-round, *Rome For Dummies* is designed to give you all the information you need to help you make savvy, informed decisions about your trip, while also guiding you to the discovery of known and lesser-known facets of this exciting city.

You'll be able to use this guide as a reference book to look up exactly what you need at the time you need it. No need to read the whole thing from cover to cover — you can just dive in at any point. No need, either, to remember what you read: There are plenty of easy-to-find flags for quickly locating the bit of info you want.

Some people spend more time planning their trip than they do taking it. We know your time is valuable, so here, we happily do the work for you to help ease you into a memorable Roman holiday. Unlike some travel guides that read more like a phone book or directory, listing everything and anything, this book cuts to the chase. We've done the legwork for you, offering our expertise and not-so-humble opinions to help you make the right choices for your trip.

Please be advised that travel information is subject to change at any time — and this is especially true of prices. We therefore suggest that you write or call ahead for confirmation when making your travel plans. The authors, editors, and publisher cannot be held responsible for the experiences of readers while traveling. Your safety is important to us,

Dummies Post-it® Flags

As you're reading this book, you'll find information that you'll want to reference as you plan or enjoy your trip — whether it be a new hotel, a must-see attraction, or a must-try walking tour. Mark these pages with the handy Post-it® Flags included in this book to help make your trip planning easier!

however, so we encourage you to stay alert and be aware of your surroundings. Keep a close eye on cameras, purses, and wallets, all favorite targets of thieves and pickpockets.

Conventions Used in This Book

The structure of this book is nonlinear: You can open it at any point and delve into the subject at hand. We use icons to guide you toward particular kinds of tips and advice (see "Icons Used in This Book," later in this introduction).

We include lists of hotels, restaurants, and attractions, and for each we give you our frank evaluation. We divide the hotels into two categories: our personal favorites and those that don't quite make our preferred list but still get our hearty seal of approval. Don't be shy about considering these "runner-up" hotels if you're unable to get a room at one of our favorites, or if your preferences differ from ours — they're still excellent choices with above-average amenities and services.

We use this series of abbreviations for commonly used credit cards in our hotel and restaurant reviews:

AE: American Express

DC: Diners Club

MC: MasterCard

V: Visa

Note that Discover is not listed. The Discover Card is unknown in Italy, so carrying one or more of the big three — American Express, Visa, or MasterCard — is a good idea.

We also include some general pricing information to help you as you decide where to unpack your bags or dine on the local cuisine. We use a system of dollar signs to show a range of costs for one night in a hotel (the price refers to a double-occupancy room) or a full meal at a restaurant — including a pasta or appetizer, a *secondo* (main course

Follow the bouncing euro

Only a few years ago, the euro was worth about 90¢. Now it has bounced back strongly, and it costs around $1.30 to buy a euro. That's a 40-cent swing, which can make a huge difference. The 100€-per-night hotel that seemed like a bargain at $90 a couple years ago now costs $130 (if you can still find it; for more about price changes and increases, see Chapter 4). Obviously, keeping an eye on the euro while you're planning for your trip will be helpful.

or entree), a side dish, and a dessert (but no beverages). Note that within the restaurant listing info, we give you the price range of just the main courses, referred to as *secondi*. See Chapter 9 for a detailed chart telling you exactly what to expect in each hotel category. Here is a table to decipher the dollar signs:

Cost	Hotel	Restaurant
$	120€ ($156) or less	35€ ($46) or less
$$	121€–230€ ($157–$299)	36€–50€ ($47–$65)
$$$	231€–350€ ($300–$455)	51€–65€ ($66–$85)
$$$$	351€ ($456) and up	66€ ($86) and up

Prices are given in euros, with the U.S. dollar conversion; the exchange rate used is 1€ = $1.30. Although we give you definite prices, establishments sometimes change prices without notice. Also, there have been cases in which a price went down but because of exchange fluctuations, the cost went up. (See the "Follow the bouncing euro" sidebar for more on euro exchange rates.)

Another thing you'll find attached to each listing is contact information. Web sites are listed whenever possible. As for telephone numbers, don't be surprised if you see ☎ 06-93021877 just near ☎ 06-290831. The number of digits in Italian phone numbers is not standardized as it is in the United States. Area codes can have two, three, or four digits; the rest of the number could have as few as four or as many as eight digits.

For those hotels, restaurants, and attractions that are plotted on a map, a page reference is provided in the listing information. If a hotel, restaurant, or attraction is outside the city limits or in an out-of-the-way area, it may not be mapped.

Foolish Assumptions

We've made some assumptions about you and what your needs may be as a traveler. Here's what we assume about you:

✔ You may be an experienced traveler who hasn't had much time to explore Rome and wants expert advice when you finally do get a chance to enjoy the Eternal City.

✔ You may be an inexperienced traveler looking for guidance when determining whether to take a trip to Rome and how to plan for it.

✔ You're not looking for a book that provides all the information available about Rome or that lists every hotel, restaurant, or attraction available to you. Instead, you're looking for a book that focuses on the places that will give you the best or most unique experience in Rome.

If you fit any of this criteria, *Rome For Dummies* gives you the information you're looking for!

How This Book Is Organized

The book has six parts plus two appendixes. Each can be read independently if you want to zero in on a particular area or issue.

Part 1: Introducing Rome

This is where you find out more in-depth information about Rome. It begins with our rundown of the best of Rome in Chapter 1; continues in Chapter 2 with Rome's history, culture, people, architecture, and cuisine; and ends in Chapter 3 with climatic information and a calendar of special events.

Part II: Planning Your Trip to Rome

Here, we guide you through trip planning: budgeting (Chapter 4), deciding on escorted and package tours, and choosing whether you want to make the travel arrangements yourself or work through an agent (Chapter 5). We include Web sites throughout the section (and, indeed, the whole book), because that's where you often can find the best deals. We also address the special concerns of disabled travelers, families, seniors, and gays and lesbians (Chapter 6). Finally, we give you tips on all the other necessary details — from getting your passport to thinking about your health (Chapter 7).

Part III: Settling into Rome

Rome may be eternal, but it's far from dead. Here, we give you all the logistic info on how to get around this bustling city and where to find additional information (Chapter 8), as well as the lowdown on hotels (Chapter 9) and restaurants (Chapter 10).

Part IV: Exploring Rome

This section provides our selection of what are for us the best features and attractions of Rome (Chapter 11), its best shops and markets (Chapter 12), and a choice of guided tours and itineraries through its maze of ancient and modern treasures (Chapter 13). We also include side trips off the beaten track to great destinations on the outskirts of Rome (Chapter 14).

Part V: Living It Up After Dark: Rome's Nightlife

Here is where we give you tips on where to find the entertainment that best suits your mood, from classical concerts and opera (Chapter 15) to bars, pubs, and discos (Chapter 16).

Part VI: The Part of Tens

The Part of Tens allows us to squeeze in some extra stuff — Italian expressions worth knowing (Chapter 17), our favorite Italian artists (Chapter 18), and ideas for special souvenirs (Chapter 19) — that we believe will complement your vacation and make your trip complete.

In the back of this book, we've included two appendixes. The first — your Quick Concierge — contains lots of handy information you may need when traveling in Rome, like phone numbers and addresses of emergency personnel or area hospitals and pharmacies, lists of local newspapers and magazines, protocols for sending mail or finding taxis, and more. Check out this appendix when searching for answers to lots of little questions that may come up as you travel. You can find the Quick Concierge easily because it's printed on yellow paper.

Appendix B contains a glossary of Italian words that will earn you warm appreciation from the Italians.

Icons Used in This Book

We use icons throughout this book as signposts and flags for facts and information of a particular nature or interest. Following are the six types of icons we use:

Keep an eye out for the Bargain Alert icon as you seek out money-saving tips and/or great deals.

Best of the Best highlights the best Rome has to offer in all categories: hotels, restaurants, attractions, activities, shopping, and nightlife.

Watch for the Heads Up icon to identify annoying or potentially dangerous situations such as tourist traps, unsafe neighborhoods, budgetary rip-offs, and other things to beware.

Look to the Kid Friendly icon for attractions, hotels, restaurants, and activities that are particularly hospitable to children or people traveling with kids. When the icon is used in conjunction with a restaurant listing, it means that high chairs and *mezza porzione* (half portions) are available, and we spell out in the description what other special attention they provide. When we use the icon with a hotel listing, it means that the hotel can add a crib or an extra bed or two to your room (or the hotel has triples and quads available). It also means that the hotel might offer babysitting and/or amenities suitable for children, such as a garden, swimming pool, or play area.

 The Plan Ahead icon draws your attention to details or plans that you should take care of before you leave home.

 Find out useful advice on things to do and ways to schedule your time when you see the Tip icon.

Where to Go from Here

Now you can dig in wherever you want. Chapter 1 highlights the best of Rome, from museums to hotels to intangibles (experiences you might not want to miss). If you already have an itinerary in mind, you can jump ahead to the ins and outs of finding a flight and making a budget; or you can browse through sights and attractions you may want to visit. And if you've already visited Rome once or a score of times, you're sure to find something here you haven't seen before.

Part I
Introducing Rome

The 5th Wave   By Rich Tennant

"I insisted they learn some Italian.
I couldn't stand the idea of standing
in front of the Trevi Fountain and
hearing, 'gosh', 'wow', and 'far out'."

In this part . . .

*H*ere's where we give you a taste of Rome, offering up highlights without weighing you down with details. (Don't worry: We fill in all the blanks in the remainder of the book — we promise!)

Chapter 1 gives you the lowdown on the city's best bets, from ancient ruins and awe-inspiring churches to fantastic hotels and delicious restaurants; you can use this as a reservoir of suggestions when planning your trip. Chapter 2 delves into the city's rich history, culture, and architecture; tempts your taste buds with a discussion of Roman cuisine; and suggests interesting books and films about this most historic of cities. In Chapter 3, we describe the best seasons for visiting Rome and give you a calendar of the most important festivals and events, a number of which are attractions all on their own and may provide the focus for your trip.

Chapter 1

Discovering the Best of Rome

In This Chapter

▶ From picture galleries to ruins
▶ From frescoes to gelato
▶ From smart dining to picnic fare
▶ From hotels to nightclubs

*P*eople visit Rome for all sorts of reasons. Art lovers flock to its great museums; the faithful make pilgrimages to St. Peter's Basilica and the Vatican; and others come to soak up Italy's culture and atmosphere (or just the sun). In *Rome For Dummies,* we give you our opinions on the best Rome has to offer. In this chapter, we list our very favorites. The places in this chapter are marked with the Best of the Best icon throughout the rest of this book.

The Best Museums

Rome boasts numerous museums, some vast and famous, others small and catering to specialized audiences. Here is our short list of the not-to-be-missed museums that contain internationally renowned masterpieces and other mind-boggling beauties:

  ✔ The **Musei Vaticani (Vatican Museums)** top our list, for the monumental size of their collections and amazing number of masterpieces. They include dozens of rooms dedicated to Renaissance painting and sculpture, as well as a fantastic Egyptian section, an impressive ancient Roman collection, and ethnological art from all over the world. The museums are also home to the Sistine Chapel (mentioned in the next section). See Chapter 11.

  ✔ The **Galleria Borghese (Borghese Gallery)** isn't very big, but it is a triumph of Renaissance beauty. Caravaggio paintings and Bernini sculptures are only a few of its many treasures. See Chapter 11.

✔ The **Palazzo Massimo alle Terme (Massimo Palace by the Terme)** is a huge museum completely dedicated to Ancient Roman art. It contains hundreds of artifacts that have been found during the excavation of archaeological sites in Rome and surrounding areas, including a superb collection of sculptures and some breathtakingly beautiful Roman frescoes. See Chapter 11.

✔ The **Museo Nazionale Etrusco di Villa Giulia (National Etruscan Museum of Villa Giulia)** holds a wonderful collection completely dedicated to the Etruscans, the mysterious predecessors of the Romans. This is a unique treasure trove of Etruscan artifacts and jewelry. See Chapter 11.

✔ The **Museo Nazionale degli Strumenti Musicali (National Museum of Musical Instruments)** has recently reopened its doors after a major reorganization. Its splendid collection of rare and marvelous instruments is a wonderful surprise for anyone, but it especially delights music lovers. See Chapter 11.

The Best Churches

Among Rome's hundreds of churches, we considered not only the architecture of the church itself and the importance of the artwork inside, but also the individual charm and personality of each. Here are our top picks:

✔ **Basilica di San Pietro (St. Peter's Basilica)** in Rome is the most famous church in a city filled with magnificent churches. Its majestic colonnade and soaring dome are a symbol of Rome as well as of the Catholic Church; treasures inside include Michelangelo's *Pietà*. See Chapter 11.

✔ **Santa Maria sopra Minerva** is the only Gothic church in Rome and is filled with artistic delights such as Michelangelo's sculpture *Cristo Portacroce*. See Chapter 11.

✔ The **Cappella Sistina (Sistine Chapel)** contains the most famous artwork in all of Italy, and after the *Mona Lisa,* the ceiling of the chapel is probably the most famous single piece of art in the world. Decorated with Michelangelo's frescoes, it is accessible from the Vatican Museums. Don't forget your binoculars. See Chapter 11.

✔ The little chapel of the **Basilica di Santa Prassede (St. Prassede Basilica)** will take your breath away. It is one of the oldest churches in Rome and completely covered with gilded mosaics. See Chapter 11.

✔ The church of **Santa Maria in Trastevere** is a splendid example of Medieval and Byzantine art, which is rare in Rome after the general Baroque overhaul. It is also an excellent excuse to visit Trastevere, a delightful neighborhood. See Chapter 11.

The Best Ruins

Considering that Rome is the site of the world's largest collection of ancient Roman archaeological remains, deciding which places to visit can be a trying affair. Here's a list of our favorite and most atmospheric sites:

- ✔ The majestic and austere **Colosseo (Colosseum),** where the Romans watched "sports" (as in fights to the death) and chariot races, is Rome's most famous ruin and an impressive work of architecture. See Chapter 11.

- ✔ The **Foro Romano (Roman Forum)** and the **Palatino (Palatine Hill),** containing the remains of temples, public buildings, villas, and triumphal arches, will take you back in time. They are particularly evocative on romantic Roman nights. See Chapter 11.

- ✔ The **Appia Antica (Appian Way),** the first road built by the ancient Romans, has been transformed into an archaeological park that you can visit on foot or by bicycle. Along the way are the remains of tombs and villas that make the trip well worth the exercise. See Chapter 11.

- ✔ The **Terme di Caracalla (Caracalla Baths)** were among the largest in Rome and are still an impressive sight. They also become the site for opera performances during the Roman summers. See Chapters 11 and 15.

- ✔ The **Villa Adriana** near Tivoli, outside Rome, is more than just a villa. It is a huge complex of buildings, gardens, reflecting pools, and theaters built by the Emperor Hadrian in the second century A.D. In the mountains above Rome where Hadrian and a few hundred friends could get away from it all, the villa remains an atmospheric retreat. See Chapter 14.

The Best Hotels

We picked our favorite luxury hotels as well as our preferred moderately priced and inexpensive accommodations. For good measure, we've also thrown in a few places that have a particularly special atmosphere or are a good deal for families:

- ✔ Presidents and stars stay at the **Hotel de Russie,** positively one of the most elegant and classiest hotels in the world. Contemporary design and exquisite good taste are coupled with excellent service and antique beauty. See Chapter 9.

- ✔ The **Hotel Arenula** is the best of the less-expensive hotels in Rome for service, quality of the rooms' furnishings, and location. See Chapter 9.

✔ The **Albergo Santa Chiara** is one of the oldest hotels in Rome and our favorite. The beauty of the palace and the quality of the service make it a great value. See Chapter 9.

✔ If you have your children with you, the best hotel for you might be the **Hotel Britannia,** where children under 10 stay for free in their parents' room and where triples are available. See Chapter 9.

✔ If you want to fully immerse yourself in historical Rome, check in at the **Hotel Celio,** where frescoed walls and mosaic floors create a truly special atmosphere. See Chapter 9.

The Best Restaurants

Here is a short list of our favorite restaurants in Rome. We love many more than what we describe here, and you'll find all those we left behind in Chapter 10:

✔ For fantastic views over the Eternal City, with wonderful food to match, try **La Pergola.** This elegant restaurant will be one of your most romantic experiences in Rome. See Chapter 10.

✔ For a truly Roman outing — vetted by Alessandra, a Rome native — nothing can beat **Checchino dal 1887,** a historical restaurant in Monte Testaccio. See Chapter 10.

✔ For the best *enoteca* (restaurant winery) in town, head to **Enoteca Capranica.** Not only will you love the food, the wine, and the atmosphere, but you'll also get to enter one of the most charming Roman palaces in the historical center. See Chapter 10.

✔ If you're a gourmet, you should not miss **Il Convivio Troiani,** the best restaurant in Rome. The dining rooms are extremely welcoming and pleasant, and the food is a delight. See Chapter 10.

✔ If you have only one night in Rome, make your reservations at **La Casina Valadier;** this *La Dolce Vita* hangout has finally reopened its doors after a lengthy restoration and offers great food, a great location, and sweeping views. See Chapter 10.

The Best Buys in Rome

Shopping in Rome is great fun and a perfect excuse to stroll the labyrinthine streets. You can also find some unique treasures, including the following souvenirs:

✔ Select a pair of **socks fit for a cardinal** — or any other religious item you might think of — from one of the shops in the center of Rome. These historical vendors showcase a variety of items from apparel to artwork. See Chapter 12.

✔ Give yourself the pleasure of a handmade piece of **gold jewelry.** The ancient tradition of goldsmiths is well alive in Rome, and you'll find craftspeople working in a variety of styles, from reproductions of ancient techniques to contemporary design. See Chapter 12.

✔ An **antique print** makes a wonderful gift — for yourself or a loved one. This traditional Roman craft has been maintained since the Renaissance. See Chapter 12.

✔ Get a **picture of the pope** from the huge collection at the Vatican gift shop. See Chapter 11.

✔ Take your pick of **fashion accessories** — scarves, leather gloves, handbags, wallets, watches, sunglasses — from the many local designers in Rome. See Chapter 12.

The Best Daytime and Nighttime Outings

In our opinion, you shouldn't leave Rome before having taken part in at least a few of the following adventures:

✔ Take a **hot-air balloon** ride over the city. From its base in Villa Borghese, the anchored balloon — the largest in the world — soars high into the sky, affording breathtaking views. See Chapter 11.

✔ Go for a **river cruise along the Tiber.** The Compagnia di Navigazione Ponte San Angelo organizes both romantic dinner cruises and day excursions, including a great one to Ostia Antica. See Chapter 11.

✔ Book tickets for an **opera performance** at the Terme di Caracalla (Caracalla Baths), the summer location of the Teatro dell'Opera. See Chapter 15.

✔ Listen to a concert or watch a dance performance at the **Parco della Musica,** the recently opened state-of-the-art performing-arts center in Rome. See Chapter 15.

✔ Go for a drink at one of the historical cafes in Rome, the best being the **Caffè Greco** in Via Condotti, near the Spanish Steps. It still has its original 19th-century furnishings and decoration. See Chapter 16.

Chapter 2

Digging Deeper into Rome

*U*nder the Roman Empire, all roads really did lead to Rome, which was the cosmopolitan heart of the Roman civilization. In spite of some passionate attempts by Milan to steal her role, Rome still is the cosmopolitan heart of the Italian civilization and culture. For thousands of years, artists have come to Rome to work; visitors have come to Rome to see the grandiose monuments; and since the city was made the seat of the *Holy See* (the official papal seat), pilgrims have come to Rome for spiritual enlightenment.

Artists and scholars were drawn to the city during the Renaissance, and their contributions exist today in Rome's churches, buildings, and public squares. In the 19th century, young aristocrats from all over Europe and the United States flocked here to absorb the classical world and admire Renaissance art in that rite of passage that was the *Grand Tour* (the months-long European tour enjoyed by the rich and satirized by Mark Twain in *The Innocents Abroad*). Rome was maybe the single most important stop then, and it remains so today.

Here we try to draw a quick picture of the most striking cultural features of this historically and culturally rich city.

History 101: The Main Events

As legend has it, Rome was founded by Romolo, one of two semigod twins (the other one was Remo) fathered by Mars on the daughter of a local king, Rea Silvia. After a close escape from death — they were saved by a wolf who nursed them — the twins grew up and set about establishing a new town. After a dispute, Romolo took over and marked on the ground the limits of his new town. The date was April 21, 753 B.C. The city grew to be a beacon of civilization, absorbing and borrowing any good features from all other cultures it encountered (or conquered), and creating a set of rules, principles, and laws that are still the bedrock of modern Western values and institutions.

Rome started as a collection of shepherds' huts, a small town populated by the local Italic tribe. These people were descended from the Villanova tribes, which had settled in the region of Rome around 1,000 B.C. on the Palatino (Palatine Hill). The town was deeply influenced by the **Etruscans,** a people famed for their seafaring, gold and metal work, and trading. The Etruscans probably came from Asia Minor, but they established themselves in Tuscany and then expanded southward. They gave Rome its name, drained the swamps, built sewers, and introduced writing. At that time, Rome had kings, and the chasing out of the last king coincided with the loss of influence by the Etruscans. Weakened by their struggles with the Greeks, who were colonizing southern Italy, the Etruscans lost their power over Rome near the beginning of the fifth century B.C.

The **Roman Republic** was founded in 509 B.C., when the last of Rome's kings was overthrown. The republic was headed by two consuls and the senate, all controlled by the upper or *patrician* (aristocratic) class. The *plebeians* (the working class) later obtained their own council and were represented by tribunes. It took hundreds of years for Rome to gain control over the Italian peninsula; in the meantime, it suffered many reverses, including the destruction of the city by the Gauls in 390 B.C.

Gradually, Roman military supremacy was established. The Romans have been called the "Prussians of the ancient world" for their militarism. They first showed their might in decades of bloody war against the city of Carthage, whose empire spread across North Africa and into Spain. Known as the Punic Wars, these conflicts began in 264 B.C. It took the Carthagian general Hannibal six months to make his famous march over the Alps to attack the Romans from behind in 218 B.C., which marked the start of the Second Punic War. Hannibal's army inflicted crushing defeats on the Roman armies, but eventually, the Punic Wars ended with the Romans erasing Carthage from the map in 146 B.C. The door was then open for Rome to spread its influence across the Mediterranean. It ruled its provinces through governors and allowed subject countries to retain local government and customs — though betrayal of Rome was brutally avenged. The republic became fantastically rich, and Hellenic and Eastern art, wealth, and cultural influences flowed into Rome. Recent archaeological finds have shown a Roman presence as far away as the borders of China.

The end of the Roman Republic and the beginning of the **Roman Empire** arrived largely through the antagonism of two great generals, **Pompey** and **Julius Caesar.** Caesar became a tyrant after his defeat of Pompey. Following Caesar's murder on the Ides of March (March 15) in 44 B.C., civil war ensued and was won by Caesar's grandnephew and adopted son, Octavian, who became the first emperor, **Caesar Augustus.** His regime turned Rome into a glowing marble city the likes of which the world had never seen, but he was followed by a string of mostly debauched and even

The Roman Empire at a glance

1500 B.C.	Bronze Age peoples settle the site of Rome.
c. 753 B.C.	Rome is officially founded.
c. 509 B.C.	The last of the Roman kings is overthrown, and the Republic is born.
264 B.C.	The Punic Wars with Carthage begin.
216 B.C.	In the worst defeat in Roman history, more than 50,000 Romans fall at the battle of Cannae against Hannibal's smaller force.
146 B.C.	Carthage is destroyed, and all human habitation of the site is forbidden.
44 B.C.	Julius Caesar is assassinated.
31 B.C.	Octavian (Augustus) defeats Mark Antony and Cleopatra at the battle of Actium. He reigns as emperor for the next 40 years.
27 B.C.–A.D.180	The famous *Pax Romana* (Roman peace), dated from the ascension of Augustus to the death of Marcus Aurelius. There is plenty of war during the *pax,* but Rome brings the whole Mediterranean world under its administrative control.
27 B.C.	Marcus Agrippa, friend of Augustus, builds the Pantheon.
A.D. 64	Great Fire of Rome, blamed by history on Nero (and by Nero, on Christians)
A.D. 69	Due to a power struggle after Nero's death, Rome has four emperors in one year.
A.D. 79	Pompeii and Herculaneum are destroyed.
A.D. 80	The Colosseum is completed.
A.D. 98	Ascension of Trajan, the second of the so-called "good" emperors.
A.D. 148	Rome celebrates its 900th anniversary.
A.D. 161	The reign of the humanistic Marcus Aurelius begins.
A.D. 395	Emperor Constantine builds Constantinople. The empire splits into eastern and western factions.
A.D. 410	Rome is sacked by the Visigoths.
A.D. 441	The Romans get behind in their payments to Attila the Hun, who begins his attacks on the empire.
A.D. 455	The Vandals sack Rome.
A.D. 476	Western emperor Julius Nepos is executed, and the German warrior Odoacer is proclaimed king, effectively ending the Roman Empire.

insane rulers: **Tiberius, Caligula, Claudius,** and **Nero.** Thanks to Robert Graves's historical novel *I, Claudius* (and the subsequent television miniseries based on the book), Claudius is popularly considered a partial exception (even though his third wife, Nero's mother, was also his niece, and Claudius also had 40 senators put to death during his reign — he was by no means a model of enlightened statesmanship). And then there was **Nero,** whose very name is a synonym for cruelty — he had his own mother put to death in A.D. 59. Rome also famously burned in A.D. 64, under Nero's reign (though not, perhaps, by his own hand).

The last hurrah, so to speak, for the Roman Empire came in the second century, when it enjoyed a string of "good" emperors who brought order, stable succession, and civility — instead of madness and corruption — to the state. They were **Nerva, Trajan, Hadrian, Antoninus Pius,** and the philosopher–emperor **Marcus Aurelius.** With the ascension of Marcus's 19-year-old son **Commodus** (the villain of the hugely popular but fictionalized film *Gladiator*), the empire was headed once again for trouble. The corrupt and arrogant Commodus even had the senate recognize him as divine. With his assassination in A.D. 192, the empire plunged once more into chaos.

At its height, the empire extended from the Caspian Sea to Scotland. However, a chaotic period of war, plague, barbarian invasions, and inflation spelled the beginning of the bitter end. When **Emperor Constantine** converted to Christianity and founded Constantinople in A.D. 330, Rome's wealth shifted east. The western empire began to crumble under barbarian pressure: The **Goths** sacked Rome in A.D. 410; the Huns came next under **Attila;** and they were followed by the **Vandals** of North Africa. In A.D. 476, the German chief Odoacer deposed the western Roman emperor, in effect signaling the end of the once-invincible Roman Empire.

Almost 80 years passed before Rome was reconquered by the Byzantines of the Roman Oriental Empire at the end of a long and destructive war against the Goths. The city had suffered terrible destruction, and its population had dwindled from over 2 million at the height of the Roman Empire to about 35,000. After the church's right to have a political state was recognized and the Vatican state was established under the aegis of the Franks, Rome settled back into being a small provincial town. The French king **Charlemagne** had the pope crown him emperor in A.D. 800, hoping to revive the western Roman Empire. He instead ended up founding the **Holy Roman Empire.**

This historical oddity profoundly affected Roman politics during the Middle Ages and Renaissance. The German emperor was elected by the German princes, but only the pope could crown him Holy Roman Emperor. For the next 1,000 years, the pope became a key element in the struggle for power among the Holy Roman Emperor (who was German), Spain, and France (aspiring to the imperial crown). In spite of the troubles that such a system brought to Rome — the city was under siege between 1081 and 1084, before being won by the Normans — the papacy grew stronger and richer, allowing it to become a leading force in Italy.

From the Byzantines to modern Rome

A.D. 552   Narsete — the General of Justinian, emperor in Constantinople — occupies Rome after the long war against the Goths. The Byzantine domination of Rome begins, together with the slow rise of the temporal power of the church.

A.D. 756   In the famous "donation of Pepin," the Carolingian ruler Pepin III (predecessor of Charlemagne) recognizes the papacy's right to its own state and territory, in exchange for being crowned king by the pope. The Vatican State has formally begun.

A.D. 800   Charlemagne is crowned emperor in St. Peter's Basilica by Pope Leo III.

1084   Robert Guiscard, the Norman, overcomes the resistance of the city after a three-year siege.

1309   The popes, with Clement V, move to Avignon, France, at the urging of the French crown. They will not be back until 1377, when Gregory XI returns to Rome.

1526   First reliable census: Rome counts 55,000 inhabitants.

1527   The sack of Rome by Holy Roman Emperor Charles V.

1600   The pope and Rome's most important families start lavishing artwork on the Eternal City: New churches and palaces and great redecorations of existing buildings are undertaken.

1798   Rome is occupied by the French, who proclaim a "Jacobite" Roman republic.

1800   The census calculates the city's population at 150,000.

1815   Restoration of Pope Pio VII after the fall of Napoleon.

1849   Mazzini and Garibaldi proclaim a new Roman Republic, but the French help the pope regain his power over the city.

1870   Rome is occupied by Victor Emanuel II's troops; it will be proclaimed capital of the kingdom in 1871.

1881   A new census counts the city's population at 273,952. Twenty years later, in 1901, the population reaches 422,411 inhabitants.

1922   After the "march on Rome," Benito Mussolini obtains from the king the right to form a new government. He will rapidly transform it into a dictatorship.

1929   The Vatican signs the Lateran Pacts, agreeing to relinquish all of Rome except its churches and the territory of the Vatican.

1943   Rome, occupied by the Germans in spite of the resistance of Italian troops, is later heavily bombed by the Allies.

1944	Rome is liberated by the Allies on June 4.
1961	Rome reaches over 2 million inhabitants, returning to ancient levels.
1995	In preparation for the millennium celebrations and the Papal Jubilee, a great campaign of restorations, reorganizations, and renovations is launched.

The popes, usually coming from the leading families in Rome, attracted the best artists from all over Italy and Europe to decorate the city's ever-increasing number of religious and secular buildings. They would give great influence to the artistic side of the **Renaissance** — the rediscovery of classical learning and culture — as they sought to make their city and its churches more and more splendid with works of art and architectural masterpieces.

But in many ways, Rome was very backward. Unfortunately, the popes were not very interested in commerce, and they imposed a reactionary and stultifying rule that killed the economy and stopped the city's development, making them quite unpopular. This state of affairs lasted for hundreds of years. Rome was also caught up in international politics and war, as well as in the struggle for power in Europe between the Germans and the French. The German troops of the Holy Roman Emperor Charles V sacked the holy city on May 6, 1527, one of Rome's darkest days. Peace was restored in 1529, and the popes kept their control over the city until the 19th century.

When the *Risorgimento* (resurgence) movement, which envisioned a unified Italy, started developing, Rome was the designated capital for the unified country, and local patriots started working toward that aim. In 1848, when revolution swept Europe, Romans seemed to have a somewhat sympathetic ruler in Pius IX, who granted many concessions. However, after a democratic republic was declared the following year, Pius fled, and entreated France, Austria, Spain, and the Kingdom of Naples to help him regain his temporal power. Romans, obviously, could not defeat several great empires at once, and papal rule was restored.

In fact, Rome was the last piece of the Italian puzzle to fall to the nationalist movement, because the pope continued to receive help from the French. In 1870, almost ten years after the unification of the rest of Italy, Rome was finally wrested from papal–French control and made into the capital of the Italian Kingdom — the parliamentary monarchy of the Savoy house — thus completing the unification.

After **World War I,** discontent and economic depression helped **Mussolini** rise to power in Rome and in the rest of the country. One of his first actions was to reach an agreement with the Vatican, the issue of whose political role had continued to divide the people of Rome ever since the unification of Italy in 1870. With the Lateran Pacts of 1929, the pope agreed to have a much reduced state, and Rome relinquished the territory of the Vatican while recognizing the pope's authority on church ground. Mussolini's imperialist adventures abroad were matched by repression at home, and his alliance with the Nazis was disastrous. Italians turned against him in 1943, and his puppet government was overthrown. Under the king's rule, Italy continued in **World War II** on the Allied side while suffering under German occupation. Rome was bombed repeatedly during the German occupation and suffered much destruction. It was finally liberated on June 4, 1944, by the Allies — only two days before D-day.

After the war, Rome voted against the monarchy and was established as the capital of the new Italian republic. Economic recovery was slow, but Rome emerged from the process as a thriving modern city and seat of the Italian government on the one hand, and an ancient archaeological site badly in need of preservation on the other. This contrast set up the tension between modernization and preservation of the city's unique historical endowment that persists to this day. (Rome has been building its subway system for over a century but still has only two lines because of the innumerable archaeological treasures hidden underground.) Traffic — a Roman problem since antiquity — continues to top the list of local priorities, together with the management of the massive influxes of illegal immigrants and refugees that has been a factor since the 1990s.

Architecture: From Ruins to Rococo

Rome offers an almost complete compendium of architectural styles — Ancient Roman, Romanesque, medieval, Gothic, Renaissance, baroque, rococo, neoclassical, modern, and so on. Roman architecture was deeply influenced by Greek culture, as can be seen in column-capital styles around the city:

- ✔ The **Doric** style is most easily spotted in the simple rectilinear capitals at the tops of columns.

- ✔ The **Ionic** capital is like a scroll.

- ✔ The **Corinthian** is the most ornate capital, decorated with a profusion of leaves.

The **Colosseum** demonstrates all three styles, or *orders*. Roman architects added enormously to the Greek heritage with the invention of the **arch** and the vault. The dome of the **Pantheon** is the apogee of such art, a model that has been copied over the centuries, not least by Michelangelo for the cupola in **St. Peter's Basilica.**

Of the country's Christian-era churches, the earliest to be found are in the **Romanesque** style, which as its name suggests drew inspiration from Roman architecture and particularly the use of the rounded arch.

These churches have thick walls and massive piers that support the superstructure of the building, as well as bell towers with arched openings. The Romanesque style has an appealing simplicity (especially in comparison with some gaudy later developments in church architecture), as you can admire in many churches in Rome, including **Santa Maria in Trastevere.**

With the **Gothic** style, lines become longer and arches pointed, giving a feeling of soaring toward the sky. Rome's only card-carrying Gothic church, **Santa Maria sopra Minerva,** is a less obvious version of the style, much restored (and, alas, mutilated) over the centuries.

With the **Renaissance** style, ancient architecture is rediscovered, and proportion and balance are stressed. The classical orders have a comeback, with the Doric in the first story of the building, the Ionic in the middle, and the Corinthian at the top. Michelangelo's **Palazzo Farnese** in Rome is a classic example of the Renaissance style.

Eventually, the Renaissance style evolved into the more elaborate **baroque.** The sweeping colonnade in front of St. Peter's, designed by Bernini, is considered baroque. Rome went through a huge face-lift during the baroque period, when popes and all the important families in the city poured money into new palaces and churches and lavish decorations. If baroque was an elaboration of the Renaissance style, **rococo** — the addition of all sorts of baubles and flourishes to the underlying structure — was overkill. Perhaps the best word to describe rococo is *busy.* With its twisting columns and encrusting of gold, Bernini's *baldacchino* (baldaquin, or canopy) inside St. Peter's shows the baroque starting to get out of hand.

A Taste of Rome: Eating Locally

Although some snobbish Italian gourmands look down on Rome as a dining center, we think that assessment is both unfair and out of date. Although landmark upscale restaurants used to be few in number and not particularly good, hundreds of excellent trattorie and *osterie* — small eateries, simple (if not basic) in décor, offering typical Roman cuisine — and *pizzerie* serving pizza and little else have always existed in Rome.

Some of the best food in Rome is still served by mom-and-pop operations that may not have a sign but serve authentic homemade cuisine. If you poke around *il centro* (the historic center) or just try some of our picks, you can find your own favorite hangout. And if you're into upscale eating, you'll be happy to learn that the dining landscape has changed dramatically in the past decade, and new gourmet restaurants have opened all over town. You'll find something to satisfy even the most demanding of gourmets.

As in the rest of Italy, meals are divided among *primi, secondi,* and *contorni* (first courses, second courses, and side dishes), with fruit or cheese at the end. *Antipasti* (appetizers) to open the meal and *dolci* (sweets) or *gelato* (ice cream) are special treats to be had on special occasions (though we think you should indulge any time you want — every day's a special day on vacation).

Roman cuisine is just one style of Italian cuisine, with a number of local characteristics that make it unique. You'll find many of the staples of Italian food — all kinds of pasta, plenty of veggies, olive oil, fresh herbs — but also a lot of specific and traditional ingredients and preparations that you won't find elsewhere in Italy. The leitmotif of Roman cuisine is simplicity, with dishes based on few and fresh ingredients.

Food is always cooked with olive oil. Butter and cream don't belong to traditional Roman cuisine — although, of course, you'll find those in dishes from other Italian regions (the north in particular), which have become common also in Rome. Parmesan cheese (the best being *Parmigiano Reggiano,* the original thing from Reggio, which makes the commercial stuff taste like sawdust) is widely used, but you'll also find the savory *Pecorino Romano* grated on traditional pasta dishes; it is the local sheep cheese from the Roman countryside and has a sharp, distinctive flavor. Vegetarian dishes are common both as main dishes (pasta dishes and *secondi*) and as side dishes and salads.

A little oddity in traditional restaurants and trattorie is that each day of the week comes with a few specialties that are traditionally prepared for that day. For example, Thursday is the day for gnocchi, and Friday is the day for *seppie coi piselli* and *baccalà* (see "Secondo," later in this chapter). The underlying reason is that many of these dishes require lengthy preparations, and because in the best restaurants everything is strictly homemade, these operations are performed only once a week. Be adventurous, and try the local specialties when you can.

Antipasto

The tradition of antipasto is relatively recent and refers to the "munchies" brought out to while away the time before the real meal is served. We aren't talking about a bowl of peanuts or potato chips, either. In regular meals, pasta dishes (or *risotto*) are the appetizer, but on special occasions, a large spread is brought out before the *primo* (of course, you can choose to have antipasti instead of a *primo* if you want). With current concern about carbs, many will chose to have antipasto instead of a carb-loaded *primo.*

Traditional Roman antipasti usually include a choice of the best local cured meats — salami, ham, and cured sausages from the area around Rome — but also some of the best specialties from the rest of Italy, such as the incomparable *prosciutto di Parma* (air-cured ham) and the *lardo di Colonnata* (a cholesterol-free lard cured in marble vats). Other typical appetizers include *insalata di mare* (sliced octopus seasoned with olive oil, vinegar, and herbs), olives, and *carciofini* (pickled artichokes). In *pizzeria* restaurants, you may also be offered *bruschetta* (slices of toasted peasant-style bread dressed with olive oil, garlic, and sometimes tomatoes), *supplì* (egg-shaped balls of seasoned rice filled with cheese and deep fried), *olive Ascolane* (large green olives filled with meat and cheese, battered and deep fried), or *fiori di zucca* (zucchini flowers filled with cheese and anchovy and deep fried).

Primo

As everywhere in Italy, in Rome you'll find spaghetti, penne, tagliatelle, and innumerable other varieties of fresh pasta. The most traditional dishes, though, are spaghetti *con le vongole* (with clams, no tomato), bucatini or rigatoni *all'amatriciana* (a spicy tomato sauce with lard and onions served with pecorino cheese), and pasta *all'arrabbiata* (tomato and lots of hot red pepper). Another delicious traditional pasta seasoning is *gricia* (lard, onions, and pecorino). You'll also find fresh filled pasta — particularly ravioli filled with ricotta and spinach, *agnolotti* (filled with meat), *cannelloni* (large rolls of fresh pasta filled with meat or fish, and baked with tomato sauce and cheese), and *lasagne* — the richest pasta specialties of all.

In Rome, fresh filled pasta is usually reserved for special days — Sundays and holidays — but it's always on offer for the visitor. A beloved specialty traditionally served on Thursdays is *gnocchi* (potato dumplings, usually in a tomato-based sauce). You'll also usually find at least one kind of *risotto* on the menu, a typical dish of somewhat sticky but very tasty seasoned Italian rice. In seafood restaurants, you'll find risotto *alla pescatora* (with fresh shellfish and a bit of tomato); in other restaurants, you'll find vegetable-based risotto of various kinds depending on the season — with artichokes, asparagus, or radicchio, among others. Soups are also present on the menu, especially in the traditional dishes of *minestrone* (a thick vegetable and bean soup) and *pasta e ceci* (a thick savory soup of pasta and chickpeas, usually served on Thursdays).

Secondo

Tradition holds that Romans eat fish on Tuesdays and Fridays, and meat the other days of the week, with vegetarian dishes always acceptable. Although few Romans still observe these traditions at home, you'll find that they are more than happy that Roman trattorie do, and you'll find them gaily eating the daily specials — so much so that if you arrive too late, the specials will be gone.

Although most trattorie offer fish every day, you'll find a greater variety of seafood dishes offered on Tuesdays and Fridays, especially those traditional seafood dishes such as *seppie coi piselli* (cuttlefish stewed with peas) and *baccalà* (salted cod prepared in a stew with potatoes). Among the best traditional meat dishes are the *abbacchio arrosto* (young lamb roasted with herbs), *scottadito* (literally "finger burning" — thin grilled lamb cutlets), and *saltimbocca alla romana* (literally "jump in your mouth

Roman style" — thin slices of veal or beef rolled with ham and sage and sautéed with a bit of wine). For the more adventurous, there is *trippa alla romana* (tripe Roman style, stewed with a light tomato sauce) or *coda alla vaccinara* (oxtail stew).

Contorno and salads

When you order a *secondo* in a restaurant, it will come without a side dish; you'll have to order that separately — convenient for vegetarians who can always have the full choice of vegetables prepared for the day. Cooked greens are very common, and you'll always find a choice of *cicoria* (dandelions), spinach, or *bieda* (swiss chard); they'll offer them *all'agro* (seasoned with oil and lemon juice) or *ripassati* (sautéed with garlic and hot pepper). Other traditional *contorni* are *patate arrosto* (roasted potatoes deliciously prepared with fresh herbs), *patate fritte* (french fries), and *fagiolini* (green beans — but beware; they are well cooked and seasoned with olive oil and lemon juice). When in season — from January through March — you'll find the unique *carciofi Romani* (wonderful artichokes you can eat in their entirety — no spines, woody leaves, or barbs inside to contend with).

You'll also always find salad, usually a simple affair of plain lettuce, but you can usually ask for tomatoes; sometimes it's more elaborate, with thinly sliced carrots and fennel in addition to sliced tomatoes and lettuce leaves. A special kind of salad that's very common in the summer (lots of people with their swimsuit size in mind order it as a main course) is the *Caprese,* made of fresh mozzarella, tomatoes, and basil; sometimes it will be made with the famous *mozzarella di bufala* (buffalo mozzarella) imported from nearby Campania. All these salads are served unseasoned, with olive oil and vinegar on the side.

Last but not least is *puntarelle,* our favorite *contorno.* It's a specialty in early spring in Rome. This side dish is made from the stalks of the *cicoria* plant, which are peeled and served (uncooked) with garlic, anchovy, and olive oil.

Dolci and desserts

Most working people will end their meal with a piece of fresh fruit or a piece of cheese (usually, local *pecorino*), and indeed, Rome is not particularly famous for its sweets. You'll also find *macedonia* (fruit cut in small pieces and served with sugar syrup) and, when in season, fresh strawberries with whipped cream.

This doesn't mean your sweet tooth will go unsatisfied — not by a long shot. Among the most common desserts are *creme caramel* and the traditional *crostata* (tart) in two main versions: *crostata alla marmellata* (tart with homemade jam) and *crostata della nonna* (tart filled with pastry cream and pine nuts). Other desserts include *bignè alla crema* (puff-pastry balls filled with cream, covered with dark chocolate, and

The etiquette of drinking

Don't expect to order a martini before dinner — in many restaurants, and more par-ticularly in trattorie, *osterie*, and *pizzerie*, you probably won't find a full bar, because Romans simply don't drink liquor before dinner. And unless they're in a pub, Italians don't drink alcohol at all without eating something (you won't see a waiter bring out wine before putting some food on the table). You're likely to find liquor in larger, more touristy restaurants, where you can ask for a scotch and water and won't be rewarded with a perplexed stare. Elsewhere, follow the "when in Rome" rule: Have an *aperitivo* at a bar; follow with wine over dinner; and have a grappa (a clear brandy) or an *amaro* (a 60- to 80-proof bitter drink, made with herbs) *after* your meal.

served with whipped cream) and *tiramisù* (layers of mascarpone cheese and espresso-soaked ladyfingers).

You'll also always find ice cream (gelato), but it will rarely be homemade in a restaurant, and you're definitely better off waiting and having your ice cream at a proper ice-cream parlor. There, you'll also find *granita* (frozen coffee or lemon ice), which is very refreshing and low in calories (unless you add real whipped cream to your coffee *granita,* which is deli-cious). The main attraction, gelato, comes in a variety of fruit and cream flavors (see Chapter 10), but one of our favorites is *zabaglione* (a cream made with sugar, egg yolks, and Marsala wine, similar in taste to eggnog).

Wines

The best-known Roman wines come from the nearby Castelli Romani (hill towns to the east of the city; see Chapter 14). Among these, the white vari-eties — such as the *Frascati* — are especially good, very dry and treacher-ously refreshing. Other excellent wines come from the region of Viterbo, near Tarquinia and the Lago di Vico (see Chapter 14), such as the famous *Est, Est, Est!* and the dessert muscat wine *Aleatico di Gradoli.*

Word to the Wise: The Local Language

Italian is Rome's primary language; however, if you know it a bit, or if your ear is particularly good, you'll notice that in Rome people speak differ-ently than in other parts of Italy. Roman is the local dialect, a very colorful lingo that has given life to a rich heritage of poetry — Trilussa is the most famous poet writing in Roman dialect — and popular sayings, often full of a witty philosophy, which are sometimes quite untranslatable.

The other language you can resort to is sign language. Actually, other Italians make fun of Romans for using their hands so much. In Rome, your hands talk — both to emphasize your words and to convey further mean-ing. If you don't speak any Italian, many Romans will go out of their way to try to understand you and help you out, and signs will be of great help. See the glossary of Italian words in Appendix B for some key words and phrases. Also see Chapter 17, where we list what we deem are the ten most useful Italian expressions to know before your trip. If you're more adventurous, devote some time to *Italian For Dummies,* by Francesca Romana Onofri and Karen Antje Möller (Wiley), and become a pro.

Background Check: Recommended Books and Movies

Rome has been the subject or the background of innumerable works, both of fiction and nonfiction. We have excluded guidebooks from the suggestions in this section — you'll find those recommended in Appendix A. Whether you want to bone up on history or be entertained by sights of the Eternal City, here are a few surefire choices.

True stories

The following nonfiction favorites will not only expand your knowledge of Rome, but also will be pure reading pleasure:

- **Polybius** was a Greek hostage in Rome for 16 years in the second century B.C., during which he wrote his *Histories* (reprinted by Regnery/Gateway as *Polybius on Roman Imperialism* and by Penguin as *The Rise of the Roman Empire*) to explain "by what means and under what kind of constitution, almost the whole inhabited world was conquered and brought under the dominion of the single city of Rome, and that, too, within a period of not quite fifty-three years" (219–167 B.C.).

- The Roman historian **Tacitus** is one of our primary sources of information — and lurid stories — about the early emperors, including Augustus, Tiberius, Caligula, and Nero. His *Annals* have been published in the Penguin Classics series as *The Annals of Imperial Rome* and reprinted many times since.

- If you read 25 pages a day, it'll take you only about four months to get through Edward Gibbon's *History of the Decline and Fall of the Roman Empire* (begun in 1776), a monument of English prose in several volumes. (You can find a less monumental Penguin abridged version in paperback.)

- **Johann Wolfgang von Goethe** was the first great modern literary visitor to Italy, and his wonderful *Italian Journey* (1816) contains a few great pages on Rome as it was at the time of his visit.

- Shortly following Goethe, **Stendhal** — the famous author of *The Red and the Black* and *The Charterhouse of Parma* — visited Rome and fell deeply in love with the city. You can read his impressions in *Three Italian Chronicles* (1826–1829).

Art history

When you visit Rome, you will see art, and in particular Renaissance art, everywhere you look. Here are a few books to help you brush up on the subject of Roman art:

✔ Italian **Giorgio Vasari** was a painter, architect, and (literally) Renaissance man. His *Lives of the Most Eminent Painters and Sculptors* (1550; expanded in 1568) has been criticized for inaccuracy but is full of interesting information about the great painters of the Renaissance. The Oxford edition (1998) is one of the many abridgements in translation of this huge work.

✔ **Benvenuto Cellini's** famous *Autobiography* (1728) presents a vivid picture of Cellini's time in Renaissance Florence and Rome.

✔ **Karl Ludwig Gallwitz**'s recent *Handbook of Italian Renaissance Painters* (1999) gives you an at-a-glance guide to 1,200 Italian painters; it also has some nice reproductions, brief essays on the major schools of painting, and some weird charts that show who influenced whom. You may want to peruse it before you go if you're really into art — it's softcover and not very thick, so you may even want to bring it along.

Works of fiction

A good novel is often one of the best ways to acquaint yourself with a place, allowing you to immerse yourself in its culture. Our choices include excellent books on both modern and ancient Rome:

✔ **Alberto Moravia**, one of the great Italian writers of the 20th century, wrote many novels and short stories but none as famous as *The Conformist* (1951), a study of the Fascist personality. He also wrote two novels about Rome and Romans: *Roman Tales* (1954) and *The Woman of Rome* (1949).

✔ **Robert Graves** wrote two novels — *I, Claudius* (1934) and its sequel, *Claudius the God* (1934) — about the best of Augustus's Claudian successors. Although they're works of fiction, they're a highly entertaining way to learn about the glory and decadence of Imperial Rome.

✔ **Henry James**'s great novel *The Portrait of a Lady* (1881) — recently turned into a movie (see the next section) — unveils the heart of Rome as seen by a young American woman in the 19th century.

✔ Polish writer **Henryk Sienkiewicz** won the Nobel Prize in 1905 largely on the strength of his monumental *Quo Vadis?* (1896), set in Rome during the time of Nero and concerning the relationship between a Christian woman and a Roman soldier.

✔ **Carlo Emilio Gadda**'s novel *That Horrible Mess in Via Merulana* (1954) is a wonderful Italian thriller; it was also adapted on the screen in Pietro Germi's film *The Facts of Murder* (1959).

The moving image

Rome has been the subject or the setting of several hit films over the years. Of course, Roman and Italian directors have used Rome as the background for many of their masterpieces. Fellini is the author of one of the most famous Italian films of all time, *La Dolce Vita* (1960), but his beloved Rome figures in many of his other movies, including *The Nights of Cabiria* (1957), a touching story showing unusual views of the city. Vittorio De Sica got his second Oscar with *The Bicycle Thief* (1948) and kept going with *Umberto D.* (1952) and *Yesterday Today and Tomorrow* (1963). Rossellini's *Open City* (1945) is another masterpiece, as is Pasolini's *Mamma Roma* (1962). Bernardo Bertolucci gained fame with *The Conformist* (1970), an adaptation of Moravia's novel (see the preceding section), but Rome appears in other of his great movies, such as the psychological *Luna* (1979) and the dramatic *Besieged* (1998).

International directors have also loved Rome, beginning with the many movies that re-created the grandeur of Imperial Rome: William Wyler's *Ben-Hur* (1959); Mervyn LeRoy's *Quo Vadis* (1951); Joseph L. Mankiewicz's *Cleopatra* (1963); Anthony Mann's *The Fall of the Roman Empire* (1964); and *Spartacus* (1960), the Oscar-winning Kirk Douglas movie about a slave revolt in ancient Rome (Spartacus's story actually took place in Capua). It was a precursor to Ridley Scott's *Gladiator* (2000), which also gives a visceral feel for the brutal side of the empire. Also treading the paths of ancient Rome is Julie Taymor, in her *Titus* (1999), an adaptation from Shakespeare's *Titus Andronicus*.

Innumerable movies have been set in Rome, both oldies and recent successes. William Wyler's famous *Roman Holiday* (1953), the Gregory Peck–Audrey Hepburn romance, is said to have caused a surge in tourism to Rome. Jean Negulesco's *Three Coins in the Fountain* (1954) was a great hit, followed by Vincent Minnelli's *Two Weeks in Another Town* (1962) and Jean-Luc Goddard's *Contempt* (1963). More recently, Rome has been portrayed or appears in cameo in an increasing number of movies: from Peter Greenaway's *Belly of an Architect* (1987) to Michael Lehmann's madcap art-theft caper *Hudson Hawk* (1990). Rome even turns up in Gus Van Sant's *My Own Private Idaho* (1991), as well as in Norman Jewison's *Only You* (1996), Anthony Mingella's *The Talented Mr. Ripley* (1999), and the final scene of Neil Labute's *Nurse Betty* (2000). Rome was used more extensively in Jane Campion's *The Portrait of a Lady* (1996), based on Henry James's novel.

Chapter 3

Deciding When to Go

● ●

In This Chapter

▶ Knowing the right time to visit
▶ Scanning a calendar of the best festivals and events

● ●

*R*ome has offered unending surprises and pleasures to its visitors for over 2,000 years, and the large wave of restorations and reorganization that started in the 1990s in preparation for the Millennium celebrations and the Papal Jubilee in 2000 — and still ongoing — have brought back the splendor to many long-neglected monuments and sights, like the soot-blackened **Palazzo Farnese** and the long-closed **Palazzo Senatorio,** now part of the completely restructured **Capitoline Museums.** Also, many hotels and restaurants got face-lifts, but perhaps more important, the tourist industry and the art and cultural management have started thinking in a modern way that makes things easier for international tourists: longer opening hours, Web sites, information hotlines, cumulative tickets, air-conditioning, shuttle services, and so on. More than ever, tourists are welcome in the Eternal City, and the added benefit of the euro makes things a lot easier for visitors used to dollars or pounds — no more 3,500-lire ice-cream cones or shoes costing a cool quarter million.

Rome, though, is also a large metropolis, with its very own cultural and logistic quirks that can make your visit more or less pleasant depending on when you go. Here, we give you tips to plan what we hope will be your own best trip ever.

Revealing the Secrets of the Seasons

Rome has a warm, dry climate with well-defined seasons. Winters are mild, and what Romans call "bitter cold" is temperatures around 30°F (−4°C), which rarely happen during the day. In summer the weather is hot, but not as humid as it gets in, say, Washington, D.C.; however, the sun will beat down on you in August in the Roman Forum, making things rather unpleasant if you're sensitive to heat.

You know your limits. If the idea of waiting in line for two hours in the hot sun to get into the Vatican Museums sounds unendurable, don't come to Rome in July or August. Check the average temperatures we list in Table 3-1 before you plan your trip.

Most of the rain usually falls in the late fall and winter (it rarely snows in Rome — maybe once every ten years), with November usually being the most rainy month. However, heavy and short-lasting thunderstorms are common, not only during the fall and winter, but also in the spring and summer (particularly in August), and the occasional rainy day — rarely more than two in a row — can happen all year around but particularly from fall to spring.

Table 3-1 Average Temperatures and Precipitation in Rome

	Jan	Feb	Mar	Apr	May	June	July	Aug	Sept	Oct	Nov	Dec
High (°C/°F)	12/ 53	13/ 55	15/ 59	18/ 65	23/ 73	27/ 81	30/ 87	30/ 87	27/ 80	22/ 71	16/ 61	13/ 55
Low (°C/°F)	3/ 37	4/ 38	5/ 41	8/ 46	11/ 52	14/ 58	17/ 63	18/ 64	15/ 59	11/ 51	7/ 44	4/ 39
Rainfall (cm/in.)	10.3/ 4	9.8/ 4	6.8/ 3	6.5/ 3	4.8/ 3	3.4/ 1	2.3/ 1	3.3/ 1	6.8/ 3	9.4/ 4	13/ 5	11.1/ 4

The once well-defined **high season** for tourism has become somewhat blurred and variable. As more and more people travel to Italy at all times, the off season is shrinking. Currently, hotels in Rome consider high season mid-March to June, September to mid-October, and December 24 to January 6. Low season is July and August, as well as January and February. The rest is shoulder season, during which the application of higher rates depends on the hotel. As a general guideline, high season starts earlier and lasts longer for smaller and cheaper hotels (which tend to fill faster). The reverse is true for more expensive hotels.

Here are what we consider to be the pros and cons for traveling in each season.

April through June

In our opinion, spring and early summer are the most pleasant time to visit Rome:

✔ Temperatures are moderate, and the weather is mild, making it a pleasure to walk through the city both during the day and at night.

✔ Limited rainfall allows you to get out and enjoy the outdoor activities — without worrying about excess heat and sunstroke.

But keep in mind:

- ✔ Everybody knows this is a great season — including hotels and airlines, which jack up their prices. Make your reservations as early as possible, particularly for small, highly desirable hotels.

- ✔ Around Easter time, vast numbers of Catholic pilgrims and large groups of *very* noisy schoolchildren from all around the world descend on Rome. Plan your museum visits carefully, and definitely make reservations.

- ✔ May 1 is Labor Day in Italy, and all workers in Rome have the day off, including waiters in restaurants, shopkeepers, and bus drivers. Everything shuts down, even public transportation.

July and August

Summertime is when most people take their vacations, and there are many upsides:

- ✔ The weather is beautiful, and outdoor life — especially in the sweet evenings — is at its max.

- ✔ You can get discount rates in most hotels.

- ✔ There is little traffic because residents tend to escape to the seashore, especially on weekends.

On the other hand, it might also be the worst time to come to Rome:

- ✔ Airfares are high.

- ✔ You can expect long lines for major attractions, because many tourists visit in this period.

- ✔ The heat can make things quite uncomfortable — temperatures during the day often soar into the 90s, and Roman ruins turn into ovens (also, Rome is still mostly non-air-conditioned).

- ✔ Many shops and restaurants close during August, most definitely on August 15, the Italian holiday of Ferragosto.

September and October

Next to spring, fall is our favorite time to travel to Italy. Here's why:

- ✔ The weather is still fairly mild and pleasant.

- ✔ With school back in session, crowds are relatively sparse.

On the other hand:

- ✔ Hotel prices are high.

- ✔ You have to watch for the rain, which typically starts falling in October.

November through March

More and more vacationers are reaping the benefits of traveling to Italy in the winter; if you can put up with rain and occasional cold spells, this is an excellent time for traveling to Rome:

✔ The relatively mild weather keeps the city pleasant for touring. Rain is at its heaviest in November and December but is usually manageable, with short-lived heavy rainfalls followed by periods of calm.

✔ You can enjoy your visits more, because there are fewer crowds at the prime attractions, and you often receive better and more attentive service.

✔ Except for the Christmas–New Year period, airfares and hotel rates are at their lowest.

✔ On a rainy day in November, we once found the Pantheon almost *empty*.

But keep in mind:

✔ Although average temperatures are mild, and cold spells tend to be short lived, it can get quite chilly. Depending on how resistant you are to colder temperatures, you may not be able to enjoy some of the outdoor attractions.

✔ Traffic is at its worst because most people take their cars to go to work and shopping when it gets nippy; correspondingly, air- and noise-pollution levels rise.

Perusing a Calendar of Events

Rome has many events worth planning a holiday around. Alternatively, you can use the following calendar to *avoid* big events and their attendant crowds.

Most Christian holidays — not just Christmas and Easter, but also saints' days and **Tutti Santi** (**All Saints' Day**, Nov 1) — are marked by some kind of celebration and often by processions and special foods.

January

Celebrate the **new year** with your children in **Piazza del Popolo,** and watch the clowns, acrobats, papier-mâché masks, and other fun attractions. Contact the tourist info line for a schedule of events at ☎ **06-36004399.** January 1.

The religious holiday **Epifania (Feast of the Epiphany)** takes a secular turn in Rome, and children receive special gifts on this day — more than on Christmas. The open-air fair in Piazza Navona selling children's toys and gifts stays open until the wee hours of the morning. January 6.

February

In Rome, as everywhere else in Italy, **Carnevale** swallows up the week before Ash Wednesday, culminating on Fat Tuesday or *Martedì Grasso.* During this former pagan rite of the coming of spring, people — especially children — dress up in costumes and participate in masked parties. Everyone celebrates Carnevale to one degree or another — at least by eating *frappe* (thin slices of crunchy fried dough with powdered sugar) and *castagnole* (deep-fried balls of dough, often filled with custard). In Rome, you can find concerts and organized events, as well as lots of people parading around the city (particularly along Via Veneto) in costume on Fat Tuesday evening. Call the tourist office at ☎ **06-4889991** or check www.comune.roma.it for details. Tuesday before Ash Wednesday.

March and April

Every year, more than 40 directors from over 25 countries participate in **RIFF,** the **Roma Independent Film Festival** (☎ **06-45425050;** www.riff.it). One week in March or April.

On the high holy day of **Venerdì Santo (Good Friday),** the Catholic rite of the procession of the stations of the cross *(Via Crucis)* is presented in most Roman churches, sometimes as a reenactment with costumes. The Vatican's procession takes place at night, led by the pope, between the Colosseum and Palatine Hill. Friday before Easter Sunday.

The pope gives his traditional **Benedizione Pasquale (Easter Benediction)** in Piazza San Pietro. Easter Sunday, between the end of March and mid-April.

During the **Mostra delle Azalee (Exhibition of Azaleas),** more than 700 azalea plants are exhibited on the Spanish Steps in Rome to celebrate the beginning of spring. Concerts are held in Trinità dei Monti at the head of the steps. Call ☎ **06-4889991** for more information. The period of the festival has recently been extended. Mid-April through July, weather dependent.

Tradition has it that Romulus founded Rome — by tracing its original limits on the ground — on April 21 in the year 753 B.C. The day, **Rome's Birthday (Natale di Roma),** is still warmly celebrated in Rome with a series of cultural events. Contact the tourist info line at ☎ **06-36004399** for more information. April 21.

May

For **Labor Day (Festa del Lavoro),** everything shuts down except in Piazza San Giovanni, where the holiday is celebrated with a great pop-music festival (check the tourist info line for a program of events at ☎ **06-36004399**). May 1.

Rome's **Concorso Ippico Internazionale (International Horse Show)** attracts the best riders and mounts from all over the world to Villa Borghese's beautiful Piazza di Siena. You can buy tickets at the gate. For details, contact the ticket agent of the Piazza di Siena at ☎ **06-6383818** or visit www.piazzadisiena.com. Near the end of May.

June

The **Estate Romana (Roman Summer)** is a multifarious festival with an extremely rich program of concerts, theater, special exhibits, and other events throughout Rome lasting into September. Performances held inside Roman ruins are particularly dramatic. See Chapters 15 and 16 for details, or call ☎ **06-4889991** or visit www.estateromana.comune. roma.it. Mid- to late June through early September.

July

An aside of the **Estate Romana** festival (see preceding section), **Fiesta!** (Ippodromo delle Capannelle, Via Appia Nuova 1245; ☎ **06-7182139**) celebrates Latin American music and culture by featuring concerts, films, theater, and children's activities. Late June to mid-August.

Another offshoot of the **Estate Romana** festival is the **Villa Celimontana Jazz** (Via della Navicella; ☎ **06-77208423**; www.villacelimontana jazz.com), where jazz concerts by international and national musicians are held in the picturesque setting of the Villa Celimontana park. June through August.

August

A section of the Testaccio neighborhood becomes **Gay Village** (☎ 340-5423008; www.gayvillage.it), a small town of tolerance and culture where gay and straight mingle to enjoy dining, music, and a variety of artistic performances for all age groups. Late June to early September.

The pagan holiday of **Ferragosto** — and the religious holy day of the Assumption — celebrates the culmination of the summer. Romans vacation on the seashore and in the mountains. Most businesses are closed, so call ahead to make sure your destination is open. August 15.

September

The **Romaeuropa Festival** (☎ 800-795525; www.romaeuropa.net) is a cultural extravaganza, presenting the best innovative and experimental European dance, music, and theater performances. It celebrated its 20th season in 2005, and its success continues unabated. End of September to end of November.

October

The **Festa di San Francesco d'Assisi (Feast of St. Francis of Assisi),** a celebration for the patron saint of Italy, is observed with processions, special masses, and other religious events. October 4.

November

One hundred artists are selected for the **Cento Pittori Via Margutta** exhibit, which turns scenic Via Margutta into an open-air gallery twice a year. Contact the tourist info line at ☎ **06-36004399** for precise dates. November and April/May.

December

For Rome's **Crèche Exhibit,** more than 50 nativity scenes are displayed in the Villa Giulia, and many others are on view in churches around the city. Particularly nice are the ones in the Basilica di Santa Maria Maggiore, Santa Maria d'Aracoeli (see Chapter 11), Santa Maria del Popolo (Piazza del Popolo 12; ☎ **06-3610487**), and Chiesa del Gesù (Piazza del Gesù, off Via del Plebiscito; ☎ **06-6795131**). Don't miss the life-size nativity scene in front of St. Peter's, either. The three weeks leading up to Christmas.

Piazza Navona becomes the seat of the **Mercatino di Natale (Christmas Market),** with toys and candy sellers. The market starts three weeks before Christmas and stays open all night on its last day, January 5, the night of the Epiphany. Beginning of December through January 6 at dawn.

If you don't mind crowds or getting up early, you can witness the pope giving a special **Christmas Blessing** to Rome and the world from St. Peter's Square at noon on Christmas Day. For a chance of being *in* the square, you should get there by 9 a.m. December 25.

Romans love **New Year's Eve,** and partying reaches its climax at midnight, when the city explodes — literally — with fireworks. The Vatican puts on its own fiery show, and there's an organized concert–cum–fireworks show in Piazza del Popolo, but everybody gets into the act, shooting fireworks from every window and roof. By tradition, fireworks are accompanied by the symbolic throwing away of something old to mark the end of the old year. Although the tradition has been outlawed, some people still get carried away, so watch out for falling UFOs if you take a stroll shortly after midnight! December 31.

Part II
Planning Your Trip to Rome

The 5th Wave   By Rich Tennant

"And how shall I book your flight to Italy — First Class, Coach, or Medieval?"

In this part . . .

*1*t's time to delve into the nitty-gritty of trip planning: all those details that are necessary to make your vacation as perfect as possible. We give you some tips on budgeting — how to save a few euro here and there — and tell you what to expect in terms of banks and currency exchange. We also lay out the different ways you can get to Rome, including various travel packages, and offer suggestions on buying travel insurance, staying healthy, and staying in contact with those who didn't get to make the trip. And so everyone has a good time, we also offer advice to those people who have special travel needs or interests — disabled travelers, families, seniors, and gays and lesbians.

Chapter 4

Managing Your Money

• •

In This Chapter

▶ Devising a realistic budget
▶ Determining travel, lodging, and dining expenses
▶ Remembering the extras: Shopping and entertainment
▶ Saving money

• •

*W*hen it comes to planning a vacation budget, you usually deal with two different numbers: what you'd *like* to spend and what you *can* spend. In this chapter, we give you some pointers to help you decide where to trim on the incidentals and splurge just on the things that really matter to you, so that you can design a terrific vacation without breaking the bank.

Planning Your Budget

Budgeting your vacation dollars is easy; it's the choices — and the mistakes — that hurt. We figure there are six major elements that eat up your vacation budget: transportation, lodging, dining, sightseeing, shopping, and nightlife. How well in advance you plan certain elements can make or break your budget.

Consider transportation: If you wait until mid-June to reserve a flight to Rome for July, you'll be lucky to pay $1,000 — if you can find a seat at all. Book ahead, and you might save a couple hundred bucks that you could put toward a shopping splurge.

Lodging is another big-ticket item. You can save on lodging and get the cost down around $120 a night if you're willing to forgo amenities and put up with a certain amount of inconvenience (less-central location, shared bath, and so on). How elastic your budget is will depend on how flexible you are. And if you book all your hotels in advance, you'll know that piece of the budget before you leave.

In Rome, dining is a great place to save money because the food is so good everywhere, even in the cheapest eateries. Pizza is cheap, and so is a bowl of pasta, though it may be the best you ever tasted. Armed with a corkscrew and a plastic fork, you can assemble a fine picnic lunch from the supermarket, using ingredients you won't find anywhere in your local grocery.

The following sections provide more tips and consideration as you plan your budget. Table 4-1 gives you a sampling of costs that you may encounter on your trip. Oh, yes, and don't forget taxes — we cover that topic in Appendix A.

Table 4-1	What Things Cost in Rome
Item	*Cost*
A metro or city bus ride	1€ ($1.30)
Can of soda	1€–2€ ($1.30–$2.60)
Pay-phone call	0.10€ (13¢)
Movie ticket	6€–8€ ($7.80–$10.40)
Caffè lungo (American-style espresso)	0.65€ (85¢)
Cappuccino (or something similar)	.80€ ($1)
Ticket to the Galleria Borghese (including reservation)	8.50€ ($11)
Gasoline	1.26€ ($1.64) per liter = 5.04€ ($6.55) per gallon
Average hotel room	200€ ($260)
Liter of house wine in a restaurant	6€ ($7.80)
Individual pizza in a pizzeria	8€–12€ ($10–$16)
First-class letter to United States (or any overseas country)	0.80€ ($1)

Transportation

Airfare is one of the biggest components of your budget. Keeping it low gives you a sort of cushion for the rest of your expenses. The actual cost depends on the time that you travel (but booking in advance helps, too). In high season, you're lucky to find a round-trip ticket for less than $850; other times, though, you may find tickets for half that much. Make sure that you check out our money-saving tips before buying an airline ticket (see Chapter 5).

Moving within Rome after you're there is quite inexpensive — for example, a three-day public transportation pass is only 11€ ($14). Out-of-town trips are cheap, too, if you use public transportation. You have to budget more if you're planning to take a tour, hire a limousine, or rent a car — a rather expensive proposition in Rome.

Keep in mind that in Rome you absolutely don't need a car, and if you arrive there with one, you have to keep it garaged during your entire stay. Rome has too many roads and drivers for you to want to deal with, plus it bans nonresidents from driving in *il centro* (the historic center), which is the part of the city where most of the attractions lie. Also, organized thieves steal cars and from cars, and you don't want the risk. If you feel you need a car for a day trip — and a thrilling adventure that might turn into a nightmare — rent one for the occasion by all means, but expect to pay a minimum of 70€ ($91) per day for an economy car and about 5.05€ ($6.55) per gallon of gas.

Lodging

Accommodations in Rome probably aren't much like the hotel or motel in your hometown. For one thing, your lodging is likely to be in a building that went up when your hometown was still a big empty spot on the map. And originally, the building may have been a princely *palazzo,* a grand townhouse, or a spartan monastery. Hotel bathrooms are often tiny, and it's easy to see why. Buildings are much older than in the United States, and private bathrooms were added to existing rooms, creating sometimes-funky results. Be aware that in many smaller hotels, rooms still exist with a shared bath down the hall and just a sink (or nothing) in the room itself.

We list many renovated hotels in this book, but keep in mind that space is at a premium in Rome, especially in the city historical center (see Chapter 9 for a detailed discussion of what you can expect in Rome's hotel rooms), and that if you want spacious accommodations — both in the room and the bathroom — you have to be willing to fork over extra euro. On the other hand, you can save a lot of money if you don't mind smaller private facilities and a simpler room.

Prices also vary depending on which area of Rome you choose for your lodgings. Figure that 150€ ($195) buys you a decent double room with private bath anywhere in Rome, but 230€ ($299) buys you a nice room in the historical center. From 350€ ($455) and up, you're buying a luxury room, probably close to the most famous attractions. Of course, the amounts that these estimates represent in dollars constantly vary according to the current currency exchange rates.

You can save money if you renounce the breakfast that your hotel serves unless it's included with your room rate (which we indicate in our reviews in Chapter 9). Breakfast is worth paying for only at the more expensive hotels ($$$ and above), where you find a buffet with a variety of foods, usually including eggs, sausage, cheese, cold cuts, yogurt, fruit, and cereal. This kind of breakfast may run about 20€ ($26), so you have to decide if what you get is worth the money.

In all the hotel reviews in this guide, we supply the *rack rate,* which in Rome is the highest rate the hotel will charge you (at the peak of high season and when the hotel is completely full). You should be able to do better than that in most cases. See Chapter 9 for a table indicating what the $ symbols in our writeups ($–$$$$) mean.

Dining

As in any destination, you can spend a lot or a little when it comes to dining in Rome. For example, less-formal restaurants (called *pizzerie, trattorie, osterie,* and *rosticcerie*) often offer the best combination of quality and price. You can generally count on all of these having traditional fare served in simple surroundings. *Pizzerie* (obviously) specialize in pizza; **trattorie** and **osterie** are casual, often family-run restaurants serving full, hearty meals at relatively inexpensive prices; and ***rosticcerie*** are cafeterias with pre-prepared hot dishes and roasting chickens in the window. Of course, you can find some famous ***ristorante*** (restaurants) that are both elegant and pricey and serve fantastic food, but the equation *high price = good food* is not at all a certain bet in Rome — which is good news if you want to save a bit of money in this area.

To confuse the issue even further, the names of the different eateries are not as descriptive as they once were. Many high-priced joints take the name trattoria for its homey, feel-good vibe, and smaller places anoint themselves as *ristorante* to try to class up the place. When in doubt, always go for the simpler option. Chances are you'll get homemade cooking for only a few dollars.

Pranzo (lunch) used to be the big meal in Rome, where the lunch "hour" was more like one-and-a-half to two hours, but things are changing, and you can have a small lunch in any restaurant now. Lunch prices may also be cheaper than dinner, so in most places, two people can eat a nice lunch with a half-liter of wine for about 40€ to 50€ ($52–$65) or a smaller meal for about 30€ ($39). Dinner in the same type of place will be 60€ ($78) and up for two.

Most restaurants impose a basic **table-and-bread charge,** called *pane e coperto,* of about 2€ to 4€ ($2.60–$5.20), and service is usually included (look for the words *servizio incluso* on the menu) unless otherwise noted. If it's not, leave a 10 to 15 percent tip on the table if service was satisfactory.

We give you our restaurant recommendations in Chapter 10, and just as with the hotels, we use a dollar-sign system to alert you to the prices of restaurants. See the table near the beginning of Chapter 10 for an explanation of the $ symbols ($–$$$$). These prices reflect a per-person charge for a meal consisting of a pasta or appetizer, a main course (*secondi*), a side dish (called a *contorno* in Italy), and dessert. It does not include wine or alcoholic drinks, the prices of which can vary widely. Within the listing information we give you the price range of just the main course, listed as *secondi.*

More and more Roman restaurants are adding a side dish to the entree. It used to be that if you ordered grilled salmon as your main course, that's what you got — just grilled salmon. Now you may find a side dish such as a vegetable sharing the plate.

 On a tight budget? Try our splurge-and-save approach to dining: If we really want to try a particular expensive restaurant, we make up for the extra outlay by eating a lunch or dinner of fresh bread, locally cured prosciutto, regional cheeses, raw or cooked vegetables, and local wine or mineral water, all of which you can find at a local supermarket or food store, or by buying a pound or so of just-out-of-the-oven pizza to go at a local *rosticceria* or *pizza a taglio* shop (see Chapter 10 for our recommendations). A picnic lunch is also a great way to visit some of the outdoor sights.

Sightseeing

Museums and other attractions charge anywhere from 2€ to 12€ ($2.60–$16) for admission. Most churches are free (avoid visiting during services unless you're attending the service, however). Frankly, sightseeing isn't an area where you can save a lot of money, and you'll probably be sorry if you try. On the other hand, entrance fees for most attractions aren't that expensive to begin with (with some notable exceptions), so your budget won't be stretched to its limits by daily sightseeing expenditures.

 In Chapter 11, we note all the special combination discount tickets and special discount cards, which can represent a great savings.

Beware that many special discounts are available based on reciprocity between countries. Therefore, many discounts — senior and children discounts especially — aren't available to Americans but are available to British and other residents of European Union (EU) countries.

 Because of the long lines at times of great tourist influx, many major attractions in Rome have started offering advance ticketing. You can now make reservations before you leave home, thus bypassing waits of up to three hours. The list of attractions for which you can make reservations includes the **Galleria Borghese** and the **Colosseum.** We indicate in the reviews in Chapter 11 whether an attraction offers advance ticketing.

Shopping

Shopping is the one expenditure that is totally within your control: You can shop 'til you drop, spending hundreds or even thousands of dollars, or you can limit yourself to window shopping. In Chapter 12, we give you our recommendations for the best shops and items that each neighborhood offers. Rome is famous for its artwork, design, and crafts — antique prints, handmade paper, plaster works, pottery, leather, gold, and lace, among many other fine wares. And the city isn't half bad for Italian fashion — Valentino, Versace, Dolce & Gabbana, and Armani are

Don't sit to sip

Be aware that any time you sit down in a *caffè* or bar in Italy, things cost more. Coffee at an outside table in Piazza del Popolo or Piazza Navona, for example, may cost the same as lunch elsewhere. Most Italians stand at the bar while they have a coffee or a beer.

a few of the world-famous Italian firms located in Rome, to which you can add the local designers.

Depending on exchange rates, you may actually save by buying Italian goods in Rome. More important, though, being in Rome gives you a chance to buy things that simply aren't available, or not in such variety, back home. Use your trip as a chance to pick up that special something you have an irresistible craving for — maybe a print of the Pantheon, a handmade golden necklace, a Gucci handbag, or even a nice used Ferrari (just kidding). Remember to plan in your budget enough shopping money for the kind of goods you think you might want to buy, and remember also that you can get back the value-added tax (VAT) for large purchases (see Chapter 12).

Nightlife

Visiting the opera, going out for a drink, listening to music in a jazz club, and dancing the night away are all extra pleasures that will make your time in Rome that much more memorable. You can spend big bucks in this department, or you can cut your costs by enjoying those serendipitous little things that are free or nearly so, such as people-watching on a beautiful floodlit piazza or ordering a coffee or drink in a classic *caffè* and soaking in the atmosphere.

Ticket prices for performances can vary a good deal, from 10€ ($13) for a concert at a small venue to 120€ ($156) for the best seat at the opera. Nightclubs in Rome are about as expensive as anywhere else, but you may be able to avoid a cover charge by sitting or standing at the bar rather than taking a table or by arriving before a certain hour. If you happen to be in Rome during a public holiday or festival, you may enjoy abundant free entertainment, much of it in the streets.

Cutting Costs — but Not the Fun

Don't feel like taking out a second mortgage on your house so you can afford a vacation to Rome? Well, you know the saying: "When in Rome . . . ." Start thinking like a Roman. Romans have relatively less disposable income than Americans; the closer you mirror the way they live and move about town, the cheaper your trip will be — and the closer you get to the Romans themselves. Staying in a huge hotel designed for foreign tourists with all the fixings will cost you a lot, as will the luxury of renting a big car. Tack on a few five-star-restaurant experiences, and your budget flies out the window.

Instead, try to live for a week without your own private bathroom. Make big, healthy sandwiches from the delicious stuff you bought in a market. Pass on the postcards, trinkets, and other things that you pick up just to say that you've been to Rome — you may even save enough for a splurge here and there.

But remember that sometimes, paying more makes sense. For example, if you're facing sightseeing overload and are dead tired, you may not want to take an hourlong bus ride to the other side of town to your hotel. Take a cab instead. And why not grab a bite to eat in the more expensive cafe near your hotel rather than deal with crossing town to an extra-cheap restaurant? Plus there are areas where you shouldn't make cuts: Not seeing Rome's Vatican Museums and Sistine Chapel, or the Colosseum, or the Galleria Borghese, or some other major sight just because they cost more would be a tragedy. We'd rather skip lunch and take the opportunity to go to one of these must-sees twice. Who knows when you'll be back that way again?

 Throughout this book, we use the Bargain Alert icon to identify money-saving tips and/or great deals. Here are some additional cost-cutting strategies:

- ✔ **Go off season.** If you can travel at nonpeak times (Nov–Mar, with the exception of the Christmas/New Year's holidays), you can find airfares and hotel prices as much as 30 percent less than during peak months.

- ✔ **Travel during off-peak days of the week.** Airfares vary depending not only on the time of the year, but also on the day of the week. International flights tend to be cheaper midweek. When you inquire about airfares, ask whether you can obtain a cheaper rate by flying on a different day. (See Chapter 5 for more tips on getting a good fare.)

- ✔ **Try a package tour.** For popular destinations like Rome, you can book airfare, hotel, ground transportation, and even some sight-seeing by making just one call to a travel agent or packager, and you may pay a lot less than if you tried to put the trip together yourself. But always work out the prices that you'd pay if you arranged the pieces of your trip yourself, just to double-check. See the section on package tours in Chapter 5 for specific suggestions.

- ✔ **Pack light.** Packing light enables you to carry your own bags and not worry about finding a porter (don't forget to tip yourself). Likewise, if you're carrying only one or two bags, you can take a bus or a train rather than a cab from the airport, saving yourself quite a few more euro.

✔ **Reserve a room with a refrigerator and coffeemaker.** You don't have to slave over a hot stove to cut a few costs; most hotels have minifridges, and some have coffeemakers. Buying supplies for breakfast will save you money — and probably calories.

✔ **Always ask for discount rates.** Membership in AAA, frequent-flier plans, trade unions, AARP, or other groups may qualify you for discounts on plane tickets and some rooms in international chain hotels (see Appendix A for a list of international hotel chains in Rome). Ask about everything — you may be pleasantly surprised by the answer you receive.

✔ **Get out of the center of town.** In Rome, you'll find that staying in hotels just outside *il centro* (the historic center) isn't quite as convenient but is a great bargain. You may need to do only a little more walking or take a short commute. Don't overdo it, though: If you pick a hotel too far out of the way, you'll waste hours of precious time in transportation, and you may well ruin your trip. The key is always to stay only a short commute from the attractions you want to visit. See Chapter 9 for more hotel information.

✔ **Ask whether your kids can stay in your room with you.** Many hotels won't charge you the additional-person rate if your extra person is pint-size and related to you. Even if you have to pay $20 or $30 extra for a rollaway bed, you'll save hundreds by not taking two rooms.

✔ **Try expensive restaurants at lunch instead of dinner.** At most top restaurants, prices at lunch are usually considerably less than those at dinner, and the menu often offers many of the same specialties.

✔ **Have a picnic.** You can put together some delicious and inexpensive meals at a Roman grocery store and then enjoy your feast in a garden or park.

✔ **Use public transportation.** In Rome, using the local bus system may be a little complicated at times, but it's also a great way to see the city the way locals do.

✔ **Don't rent a gas guzzler.** If you absolutely need to rent a car to get yourself out of town, renting a smaller car is cheaper, and you save on gas to boot. Unless you're traveling with kids and need lots of space, don't go beyond economy size.

✔ **Walk a lot.** A good pair of walking shoes can save you money in taxis and other local transportation. As a bonus, you'll get to know your destination more intimately as you explore at a slower pace. Rome's historic center is quite large, but you'll want to visit it in sections, so that you can actually walk almost anywhere you need to go for that part of the day.

✔ **Skip the souvenirs.** Your photographs and your memories could be the best mementos of your trip. If you're concerned about money, you can do without the T-shirts, key chains, salt-and-pepper shakers, and other trinkets.

Handling Money

You're the best judge of how much cash you feel comfortable carrying or what alternative form of currency is your favorite. That's not going to change much on your vacation. True, you'll probably be moving around more and incurring more expenses than you generally do (unless you happen to eat out every meal when you're at home), and you may let your mind slip into vacation gear and not be as vigilant about your safety as when you're in work mode. But those factors aside, the only type of payment that won't be quite as available to you away from home is your personal checkbook.

Making sense of the euro

Italy's currency, the *euro* (the plural is also *euro,* and it's abbreviated as € in this guide), was introduced in January 2002 in Italy and in 11 other European countries. You can use the same currency in Austria, Belgium, Finland, France, Germany, Greece, Ireland, Italy, Luxembourg, the Netherlands, Portugal, and Spain.

The transformation to the euro has made things much easier for Americans, because 1€ exchanges in a range nearer $1 (the exchange rate used in this book is 1€ = $1.30; we round off all dollar values above $10). Many Web sites present the latest exchange rates, but one of the best is www.ex-rates.com, where you can get up-to-date (and historical) comparisons between the euro and your currency, whether it is the U.S. or Canadian dollar, the British pound, or something else. Another excellent Web site is www.xe.com/ucc. At press time, the British pound exchanged at 1£ = 1.51€. These were the rates of exchange used to calculate the values in Table 4-2.

Table 4-2 Foreign Currencies vs. the U.S. Dollar

Euro €	U.S. $	U.K. £	Euro €	U.S. $	U.K. £
1.00	1.30	0.66	75.00	97.50	49.50
2.00	2.60	1.32	100.00	130.00	66.00
3.00	3.90	1.98	125.00	162.50	82.50
4.00	5.20	2.64	150.00	195.00	99.00
5.00	6.50	3.30	175.00	227.50	115.50
6.00	7.80	3.96	200.00	260.00	132.00
7.00	9.10	4.62	225.00	292.50	148.50
8.00	10.40	5.28	250.00	325.00	165.00

(continued)

Table 4-2 *(continued)*

Euro €	U.S. $	U.K. £	Euro €	U.S. $	U.K. £
9.00	11.70	5.94	275.00	316.25	181.50
10.00	13.00	6.60	300.00	390.00	198.00
15.00	19.50	9.90	350.00	455.00	231.00
20.00	26.00	13.20	400.00	520.00	264.00
25.00	32.50	16.50	500.00	650.00	330.00
50.00	65.00	33.00	1000.00	1300.00	660.00

Note that in the word *euro,* Italians pronounce all three vowels, so it's *ay-ur-oh,* not *yurr-oh.*

All did not go smoothly with the transition to the euro from the old lira. In many cases, Italian businesses, museums, and other attractions set their prices in euro as an *exact* equivalent to former prices in lire. The result was a lot of funny-looking prices like 14.03€, 18.61€, and so on — and a lot of annoyed Italians searching through fistfuls of change. As they became more comfortable with the new currency, businesses started rounding up their prices. At first, this caused a wild increase in prices, but the Italian government stepped in and demanded that price increases be justifiable. Now, after a couple of years, the situation is much more under control. It's true that a number of prices have increased, but you also usually get more.

For example, some museum admissions have increased, but the opening hours have also been extended to be more in line with opening hours in the rest of Europe and the world. In other cases, prices have *decreased* because they've been rounded off to the lower whole-euro amount. In Rome, the Palazzo Altemps admission went from 5.16€ to 5€, for example.

Similarly, some hotel prices have gone up considerably, but more and more hotels now offer a level of amenities comparable with U.S. hotels.

Of course, from the U.S. standpoint, Italian prices have increased, and quite a lot. This is due to the loss of value suffered by the U.S. dollar on international currency markets. For example, although that admission to Palazzo Altemps we just mentioned went down from 5.16€ in 2003 to 5€ in 2005, in dollars, the price went up from $4.70 to $6, because at press time, the dollar can buy fewer euro than two years ago. By the time you read this, the two currencies may be closer to parity, but then again, maybe not. It's all the more important, then, to plan ahead and get the best deals you can.

You can exchange money at the airport in Rome — where you'll also find an automated teller machine (ATM), as well as at banks and exchange bureaus in town. These usually display multilingual signs (CHANGE/CAMBIO/WECHSEL). Rates may vary to some degree. For example, some bureaus advertise "no fee" but then give you a lower rate so you come out the same anyway. Arriving in Rome with a small supply of euro, at least enough to pay for a cab to your hotel, is a good idea in case the ATM machine at the airport doesn't work or the lines are unbearably long.

Nowadays, you don't even need to go to your bank to buy euro: You can get foreign currencies delivered to your door before you leave. The **OANDA** Web site (www.oanda.com) provides everything you ever wanted to know about currency (including the euro's most recent value against your own country's currency). The minimum purchase is $200, and the maximum is $1,500; shipping is free if you buy over $500, and you'll probably want to pay by debit card. (If you pay by credit card, you're charged as you would be for a cash advance, with the consequent fees.)

Using ATMs and carrying cash

The easiest and best way to get cash away from home is from an ATM. The **Cirrus** network (☎ 800/424-7787; www.mastercard.com) is the most common international network in Rome. **PLUS** (☎ 800/843-7587; www.visa.com) exists in Rome but is less common. The Banca Nationale del Lavoro (BNL) is one bank that does offer PLUS in its ATMs; you can find several BNL branches in Rome.

The euro look

Paper bills come in 5€, 10€, 20€, 50€, 100€, 200€, and 500€ denominations. All bills are brightly colored and have a different shade for each denomination. In addition, the higher the value, the larger the physical size of the bill. A 50€ bill is bigger than a dollar bill, and even the smaller denominations are taller than U.S. dollars; if you have a bunch, you'll find stuffing them in your wallet a bit difficult. Remember that shops are always short of change, and breaking those large bills to buy a soft drink is sometimes difficult. Think ahead, and try to have enough 10€ bills with you as you travel in Italy.

Coins come in 1€ and 2€ (both thin and brass-colored); 10-cent, 20-cent, and 50-cent (all brass colored); and 1-cent, 2-cent, and 5-cent (all copper-colored) denominations.

For more information and pictures of the currency, check online at the official Web site of the **European Union** (http://europa.eu.int/euro) or at the site of the **European Central Bank** (www.euro.ecb.int).

Don't be surprised to see different country names on euro bills and coins: One face is the European side, common to each of the 12 participating countries, and the reverse face is the national side, where each country has printed its own design. All are valid and accepted in each of the countries.

Before leaving for Rome, make sure that you check the daily withdrawal limit for your ATM card, and ask whether you need a new personal identification number (PIN). (You need a four-digit PIN for Europe, so if you currently have a six-digit PIN, you must get a new one before you go.)

Not all ATM keypads in Rome display letters as well as numbers. Some have only numbers. Therefore, if your PIN is "SPOT," you need to know how it translates into numbers. (Check this before you leave home!)

Look at the back of your bank card to see which network you're on; then call or check online for ATM locations at your destination. Be sure to find out your daily withdrawal limit before you depart. Also keep in mind that many banks impose a fee every time your card is used at a different bank's ATM, and that fee can be higher for international transactions (up to $5 or more) than for domestic ones (where they're rarely more than $1.50). On top of this, the bank from which you withdraw cash may charge its own fee. For international withdrawal fees, ask your bank.

In Rome, ATMs are never far away, so you can walk around with 100€ ($115) in your wallet, and you should be set to dine and pay your museum admissions (but not your hotel bill). Before going off on a driving tour of the countryside, however, make sure that you have a good stock of cash in your wallet; banks and ATMs are rarer outside the big cities, and lots of small businesses don't accept credit cards.

If you have linked checking and savings accounts and you're in the habit of moving relatively small amounts of money from savings to checking as you need it, beware: Italian ATMs won't show you the transfer-between-accounts option, and they won't allow you to withdraw money directly from your savings account. If your checking account runs dry, you must call or write your bank to move money from savings to checking. (We did so, and our bank charged us $30. Ouch!)

Charging ahead with credit cards

Credit cards are a safe way to carry money: They also provide a convenient record of all your expenses, and they generally offer relatively good exchange rates. You can also withdraw cash advances from your credit cards at banks or ATMs, as long as you know your PIN. If you've forgotten yours or didn't even know you had one, call the number on the back of your credit card, and ask the bank to send it to you. It usually takes five to seven business days, though some banks will provide the number over the phone if you tell them your mother's maiden name or some other personal information.

Keep in mind that when you use your credit card abroad, most banks assess a 2 percent fee above the 1 percent fee charged by Visa or MasterCard or American Express for currency conversion on credit charges. But credit cards still may be the smart way to go when you factor in things like exorbitant ATM fees and higher traveler's check exchange rates (and service fees).

Some credit-card companies recommend that you notify them of any upcoming trip abroad so that they don't become suspicious when the card is used numerous times in a foreign destination and block your charges. Even if you don't call your credit-card company in advance, you can always call the card's toll-free emergency number if a charge is refused — a good reason to carry the phone number with you. But perhaps the most important lesson here is to carry more than one card with you on your trip; a card may not work for any number of reasons, so having a backup is the smart way to go.

Toting traveler's checks

These days, traveler's checks are less necessary because 24-hour ATMs allow you to withdraw small amounts of cash as needed. However, keep in mind that you'll likely be charged an ATM withdrawal fee if the bank is not your own (in Rome, it won't be), so if you're withdrawing money every day, you might be better off with traveler's checks — as long as you don't mind showing identification every time you want to cash one. Traveler's checks are widely accepted in Rome, especially at large tourist stores and at hotels.

You can get traveler's checks at almost any bank. **American Express** offers denominations of $20, $50, $100, $500, and (for cardholders only) $1,000. You'll pay a service charge ranging from 1 to 4 percent. You can also get American Express traveler's checks over the phone by calling ☎ **800/221-7282;** AMEX gold and platinum cardholders who use this number are exempt from the 1 percent fee.

Visa offers traveler's checks at Citibank locations nationwide, as well as at several other banks. The service charge ranges between 1.5 and 2 percent; checks come in denominations of $20, $50, $100, $500, and $1,000. Call ☎ **800/732-1322** for information. AAA members can obtain Visa checks without a fee at most AAA offices or by calling ☎ **866/339-3378.** **MasterCard** also offers traveler's checks. Call ☎ **800/223-9920** for a location near you.

 If you choose to carry traveler's checks, be sure to keep a record of their serial numbers separate from your checks in case they're stolen or lost. You'll get a refund faster if you know the numbers.

Dealing with a Lost or Stolen Wallet

Being on vacation is a blissful time of distraction and discovery. Unfortunately, this makes a tourist a ripe target for pickpockets. In Italy, violent crime is rare; most wallets that are stolen are lost to pickpockets, not muggers.

If you discover that your wallet has been lost or stolen, contact all of your credit-card companies right away. You'll also want to file a report at the nearest police precinct. Your credit-card company or insurer may require a police-report number or record of the loss. Most credit-card companies have an emergency toll-free number to call if your card is lost or stolen; they may be able to wire you a cash advance immediately or deliver an emergency credit card in a day or two. Call the following emergency numbers in the United States:

- ✔ **American Express** ☎ **800/221-7282** (for cardholders and traveler's check holders)
- ✔ **MasterCard** ☎ **800/307-7309** or 636-722-7111
- ✔ **Visa** ☎ **800/847-2911** or 410-581-9994

For other credit cards, call the toll-free-number directory at ☎ **800-555-1212.**

In Rome, contact these offices:

- ✔ **American Express** (☎ **06-7220348** or 06-72282 or 06-72461; www.americanexpress.it)
- ✔ **Diners Club** (☎ **800-864064866** toll-free within Italy; www.diners club.com)
- ✔ **MasterCard** (☎ **800-870866** toll-free within Italy; www.mastercard.com)
- ✔ **Visa** (☎ **800-819014** toll-free within Italy; www.visaeu.com)

If you need emergency cash over the weekend, when all banks and American Express offices are closed, you can have money wired to you via Western Union (☎ **800-325-6000;** www.westernunion.com).

Identity theft or fraud are potential complications of losing your wallet, especially if you've lost your driver's license or passport along with your cash and credit cards. Notify the major credit-reporting bureaus immediately; placing a fraud alert on your records may protect you against liability for criminal activity. The three major U.S. credit-reporting agencies are **Equifax** (☎ **800-766-0008;** www.equifax.com), **Experian** (☎ **888-397-3742;** www.experian.com), and **TransUnion** (☎ **800-680-7289;** www.transunion.com). Finally, if you've lost all forms of photo ID, call your airline, and explain the situation; it may allow you to board the plane if you have a copy of your passport or birth certificate and a copy of the police report you've filed.

 Watch your purse, wallet, briefcase, or backpack in any public place. And when walking on the streets, keep your purse on the side away from traffic, so a thief on a motor scooter can't speed by and grab it from you. Better yet, carry your money, credit cards, and passport in an interior pocket, where pickpockets won't be able to snatch them.

Chapter 5

Getting to Rome

· ·

In This Chapter
▶ Checking out the major airlines flying into Rome
▶ Getting to Rome by train, ship, bus, or car
▶ Sorting out packages and escorted tours

· ·

Although most visitors fly to Rome, you could also arrive by train or by ship. Technically, you could even drive from another European city, although we don't recommend it. This chapter outlines your options for getting to Rome as effortlessly as possible.

Flying to Rome

Rome is one of the only two Italian cities to which you can fly nonstop from North America — Milan is the other one. If you live near a major airport, flying to Rome may be even easier than reaching another destination in your own country — but it won't be cheaper. Airfares to Rome are significantly higher than those from the United States to London, for example, and a round-trip ticket during peak times can run between $800 and $1,200. Of course, with the cutthroat competition among airlines, you may be able to lock in a much better deal — especially if you book well in advance and have a flexible itinerary.

Finding out which airlines fly there
Alitalia (☎ 800/223-5730 in the United States; 800/361-8336 in Canada; 020/7602-7111 in London or 0990/448-259 in the rest of the United Kingdom; 1300/653-747 or 1300/653-757 in Australia; toll-free 1478-65643 or 06-65643 in Italy; www.alitalia.it), the Italian national airline, offers direct or one-stop flights to Rome from most major cities in the world. Alitalia also offers daily flights to all European capitals. Direct daily flights are scheduled from a number of U.S. cities, as well as Toronto and Montréal. Likewise, Alitalia offers direct service between Sydney and Italy, but not every day.

Among the U.S. airlines, **American Airlines** (☎ 800/433-7300; www. aa.com), **Delta** (☎ 800-241-4141; www.delta.com), **United** (☎ 800/ 538-2929; www.united.com), **US Airways** (☎ 800/428-4322; www.us airways.com), **Continental** (☎ 800/525-0280; www.continental.com), and **Northwest/KLM Airlines** (☎ 800-447-4747; www.nwa.com) all usually offer direct nonstop flights to Rome or Milan from the United States, at least during peak season.

From Britain, your best bet is **British Airways** (☎ 0845/773-3377 in the United Kingdom; www.britishairways.com), though smaller charter companies also offer flights. **Alitalia** (☎ 020/8745-8200 in the United Kingdom; www.alitalia.it) is another possibility. Innovative options include **Ryanair** (☎ 0871/246-0000; www.ryanair.com) and **EasyJet** (www.easyjet.com), which fit the old no-frills or discount airline slot.

From Australia and New Zealand, there is **Alitalia** (☎ 02/9922-1555 in Australia and New Zealand; www.alitalia.it). **Cathay Pacific** (☎ 1-300/361-060 in Australia; 0800/800-454 in New Zealand; www. cathaypacific.com) offers three flights a week to Rome from Melbourne and Sydney, connecting through Hong Kong. The airline also offers two flights from Perth and Cairns, connecting through Hong Kong, and one flight from Brisbane, connecting through Hong Kong. Auckland is also served thrice weekly, also with a connection through Hong Kong. Another option is **Qantas** (☎ 13-13-13; www.qantas.com), which offers some direct flights — daily from Melbourne to Rome and several days a week from Sydney. **Air New Zealand** (☎ 0800/737-000; www.airnz. com) doesn't fly directly to Italy. You have to change in another European city to a national carrier.

On any day of the week, you can get a connecting flight through a major European capital, where you switch to the national carrier — for example, connecting through London with British Airways or through Paris with Air France. European airlines include **British Airways** (☎ 800/ 247-297; www.britishairways.com), **Air France** (☎ 800/237-2747; www.airfrance.com), **KLM** (☎ 800/374-7747; www.klm.nl), and **Lufthansa** (☎ 800/645-3880; www.lufthansa-usa.com).

Getting the best deal on your airfare

Competition among the major U.S. airlines is unlike that in any other industry. Every airline offers virtually the same product (basically, a coach seat is a coach seat is a . . .), yet prices can vary by hundreds of dollars.

Business travelers who need the flexibility to buy their tickets at the last minute and change their itineraries at a moment's notice — and who want to get home before the weekend — pay (or at least their companies pay) the premium rate, known as the *full fare*. But if you can book your ticket far in advance, stay over Saturday night, and are willing to travel midweek (Tues, Wed, or Thurs), you can qualify for the least expensive price — usually a fraction of the full fare. For example, a flight from New York to Rome on two days' notice is a gruesome $3,000. But make it a seven-day advance-purchase ticket, and the price immediately drops to $1,100. Make it 14-day advance-purchase, and it drops further, and so on.

The airlines also periodically hold sales, in which they lower the prices on their most popular routes. These fares have advance-purchase requirements and date-of-travel restrictions, but you can't beat the prices. As you plan your vacation, keep your eyes open for these sales, which tend to take place in seasons of low travel volume — for Rome, that means the dead of winter. You almost never see a sale for travel from around mid-May through the peak summer vacation months of July and August and into September for Rome; you also pay top dollar at Thanksgiving and Christmas, when many people fly regardless of the fare they have to pay.

Consolidators, also known as *bucket shops,* are great sources for international tickets, although they usually can't beat the Internet on fares within North America. Start by looking in Sunday newspaper travel sections; U.S. travelers should focus on the *New York Times, Los Angeles Times,* and *Miami Herald.*

Bucket-shop tickets are usually nonrefundable or rigged with stiff cancellation penalties, often as high as 50 to 75 percent of the ticket price, and some put you on charter airlines with questionable safety records.

Several reliable consolidators are worldwide and available on the Net. **STA Travel** (☎ **800-781-4040;** www.statravel.com), the world's leader in student travel, offers good fares for travelers of all ages. **ELTExpress** (☎ **800-TRAV-800;** www.flights.com) started in Europe and has excellent fares worldwide. Flights.com also has "local" Web sites in 12 countries. FlyCheap, an industry leader, has become **Lowestfare.com** (www.lowestfare.com) and is owned by Priceline (see later in this chapter). **Air Tickets Direct** (☎ **800-778-3447;** www.airticketsdirect.com) is based in Montréal and leverages the currently weak Canadian dollar for low fares. **The TravelHub** (☎ **888-AIR-FARE;** www.travelhub.com) represents nearly 1,000 travel agencies, many of which offer consolidator and discount fares.

Booking your flight online

The "big three" online travel agencies — **Expedia** (www.expedia.com), **Travelocity** (www.travelocity.com), and **Orbitz** (www.orbitz.com) — sell most of the air tickets bought on the Internet. (Canadian travelers should try www.expedia.ca and www.travelocity.ca; U.K. residents can go for expedia.co.uk and opodo.co.uk.) Each has different business deals with the airlines and may offer different fares on the same flights, so shopping around is wise. Expedia and Travelocity will also send you an **e-mail notification** when a cheap fare becomes available to your favorite destination. Of the smaller travel-agency Web sites,

SideStep (www.sidestep.com) receives good reviews from users. It's a browser add-on that purports to "search 140 sites at once" but in reality beats competitors' fares only as often as other sites do.

Great **last-minute deals** are available through free weekly e-mail services provided directly by the airlines. Most of these deals are announced on Tuesday or Wednesday and must be purchased online. Most are valid for travel only that weekend, but some can be booked weeks or months in advance. Sign up for weekly e-mail alerts at airline Web sites, or check megasites that compile comprehensive lists of last-minute specials, such as **Smarter Living** (www.smarterliving.com). For last-minute trips, www.site59.com in the United States and www.lastminute.com in Europe often have better deals than the major-label sites.

If you're willing to give up some control over your flight details, use an *opaque fare service* like **Priceline** (www.priceline.com) or **Hotwire** (www.hotwire.com). Both offer rock-bottom prices in exchange for travel on a "mystery airline" at a mysterious time of day, often with a mysterious change of planes en route. The mystery airlines are all major, well-known carriers — and the possibility of being sent hither and yon before you arrive in Italy is remote. But your chances of getting a 6 a.m. or 11 p.m. flight are pretty high. For example, Hotwire has a "no red-eye" option, but be aware that it thinks that a 6 a.m. flight for which you have to be at the airport two hours in advance (it's hardly worth putting on your jammies, is it?) is *not* a red-eye. Hotwire tells you flight prices before you buy; Priceline usually has better deals than Hotwire, but you have to play its "name our price" game — and with each try, you have to change something besides your bid, which is to prevent people from making endless iterations starting at 20 bucks. If you have fixed travel dates, better make a realistic bid to start, or you'll have to change them or look elsewhere. In order to cover all the bases, Priceline now owns **Lowestfare.com** (www.lowestfare.com), on which you don't have to bid for seats.

Great last-minute deals are also available directly from the airlines themselves through a free e-mail service called *E-savers*. Each week, the airline sends you a list of discounted flights, usually leaving the upcoming Friday or Saturday and returning the following Monday or Tuesday. You can sign up for all the major airlines at one time by logging on to **Smarter Living** (www.smarterliving.com), or you can go to each individual airline's Web site. Airline sites also offer schedules, flight booking, and information on late-breaking bargains.

Keep in mind that European national airlines (Alitalia, Lufthansa, Air France, and so on) may cost more, but they also seem to have more legroom and better service. This may be an important consideration, given that the flight from New York to Rome is about eight hours, compared with five hours to London.

Arriving by Other Means

You may be adding Rome to a larger European vacation, or perhaps you live in Britain or Ireland (if you are in Britain and are tempted to drive your own car to Rome, don't — we did it once, and it was *long* and exhausting). Flying to Rome and renting a car there — or skipping the car altogether — will be cheaper. So you may be looking for other ways to get to Rome. If so, check out the following list of alternative ways to get to Italy.

Train

Paris is connected to Italy by high-speed TGV trains to Torino–Novara–Milan. From Paris, you can also take the famous *Palatino,* the overnight train to Rome. You can also catch overnight trains from Germany (Hanover, Düsseldorf, Köln, Bonn, and Frankfurt). International trains usually arrive at **Stazione Termini,** in the heart of Rome. Contact **Trenitalia** (☎ **892021** from anywhere in Italy; www.trenitalia.it), the Italian railroad company, for fares and information.

Ship and ferry

Cruise ships and ferries headed for Rome land at the harbor of Civitavecchia, about one hour north of Rome and easily connected by very frequent train and bus service, as well as car service. A number of ferry companies service Civitavecchia from several countries in the Mediterranean.

Bus

Eurolines (☎ **0990/143-219;** www.eurolines.com) is the leading operator of scheduled coach services across Europe, and it offers service from London's Victoria Coach Station to Rome.

Joining an Escorted Tour

You may be one of the many people who love escorted tours: The tour company takes care of all the details; it tells you what to expect at each leg of your journey. You know your costs up front, and you don't get many surprises. Escorted tours can take you to the maximum number of sights in the minimum amount of time with the least amount of hassle.

 If you decide to take an escorted tour, we strongly recommend buying travel insurance, especially if the tour operator asks to you pay up front. Buying travel insurance through an independent agency is wise (more about the ins and outs of travel insurance in Chapter 7).

When choosing an escorted tour, along with finding out whether you have to put down a deposit and when final payment is due, ask a few simple questions before you buy:

✔ **What is the cancellation policy?** Can the tour operator cancel the trip if it doesn't get enough people? How late can you cancel if you're unable to go? Do you get a refund if you cancel? If the tour operator cancels?

✔ **How jam-packed is the schedule?** Do tour organizers try to fit 25 hours into a 24-hour day, or is there ample time for relaxing and/ or shopping? If getting up at 7 a.m. every day and not returning to your hotel until 6 or 7 p.m. sounds like a grind, certain escorted tours may not be for you.

✔ **How big is the group?** The smaller the group, the less time you spend waiting for people to get on and off the bus. Tour operators may be evasive about this, because they may not know the exact size of the group until everybody has made reservations, but they should be able to give you a rough estimate.

✔ **Is there a minimum group size?** Some tours have a minimum group size, and operators may cancel the tour if they don't book enough people. If a quota exists, find out what it is and how close the tour is to reaching it.

✔ **What is included?** Don't assume anything. You may have to pay to get yourself to and from the airport. A box lunch may be included in an excursion, but drinks may be extra. How much flexibility do you have? Can you opt out of certain activities, or does the bus leave once a day, with no exceptions? Are all your meals planned in advance? Can you choose your entree at dinner, or does everybody get the same chicken cutlet?

Most companies specializing in escorted tours for Italy include Rome as part of a larger tour. Escorted tours focusing exclusively on Rome are more difficult to find, and most companies offer packages (see the following section), with the possibility of adding specific guided excursions of your choice. Here are a few of the best Italian operators (prices quoted include airfare except as noted; remember that packages and prices change all the time):

✔ **Italiatour** (www.italiatour.com), a company associated with Alitalia, offers great flexibility and native expertise. It maintains information offices in most countries, and you can contact it in the United States (☎ 800/845-3365 or 212/675-2183; www.italia tourusa.com), as well as in the United Kingdom (☎ 1883-623363; www.italiatour.co.uk), in Canada (☎ 905/673-3623; www. cittours-canada.com), and in Australia (Concorde Leisure, ☎ 3-99203825; www.italiatour.com.au). Italiatour always has great packages for Rome, to which you can add guided tours and excursions of your choice from a large menu. The prices are always competitive, and all excursions and guided tours are priced 10 to 30 percent less than what you could do if you booked directly on your own.

✔ **Perillo Tours** (577 Chestnut Ridge Rd., Woodcliff Lake, NJ 07675-9888; ☎ **800/431-1515** or 201-307-1234; www.perillotours.com) has been in business for more than half a century. It also offers packages to which you can add guided tours and excursions of the Eternal City.

✔ **Central Holidays** (☎ **800/935-5000**; www.centralholidays.com) offers fully escorted tours in addition to its packages. Several levels of tours — and levels of "escort" — are offered. "Romantic Rome," a six-night tour, is priced between $891 (in Nov) and $1,697 (in spring and early Sept).

Choosing a Package Tour

For Rome, package tours are definitely a smart way to go. In many cases, a package tour that includes airfare, hotel, and transportation to and from the airport costs less than the hotel alone on a tour you book yourself. That's because packages are sold in bulk to tour operators, which resell them to the public.

Package tours can vary widely. Some offer a better class of hotels than others; others provide the same hotels for lower prices. Some book flights on scheduled airlines; others sell charters. In some packages, your choice of accommodations and travel days may be limited. Some let you choose between escorted vacations and independent vacations; others allow you to add on just a few excursions or escorted day trips (also at discounted prices) without booking an entirely escorted tour.

Remember that the **escorted tour** operators discussed earlier also offer packages. **Italiatour** is one of the best, offering packages with your choice of guided tours and excursions that you can tailor to your specific needs and interests, with accommodations at a discounted rate. Some of its tours offer very competitive prices: In the late spring season, you can get a five-night Rome package for $1,199, including airfare. The afore-mentioned **Perillo Tours** and **Central Holidays** also have good packages for Rome. (See the preceding section for contact information for all three tour companies.) Another recommended packager is **Kemwell** (☎ **800-678-0678**; www.kemwell.com).

Another good source of package deals is the airlines themselves. Most major airlines offer air/land packages, including **American Airlines Vacations** (☎ 800/321-2121; www.aavacations.com), **Delta Vacations** (☎ 800/221-6666; www.deltavacations.com), **Continental Airlines Vacations** (☎ 800/301-3800; www.coolvacations.com), and **United Vacations** (☎ 888/854-3899; www.unitedvacations.com).

If you search for a package on an airline Web site, be prepared to spend a long time playing around with the variables. A dozen or more outbound- and return-flight options may pop up, each of which will affect the price. Your selected departure city matters, too. At the

American Airlines Vacations site, we came up with a whopping $5,822 for a five-day air/hotel package to Florence in July, flying from Boston. Change the departure airport to New York's JFK, and the price for the same trip plummets to $2,081. This is not unique to American; with any of these airline sites, you need to do a lot fiddling to get the best price. And always look first for the specials and last-minute deals they're running.

The travel section of your local Sunday newspaper or the ads in the back of travel magazines such as *Travel + Leisure, National Geographic Traveler,* and *Condé Nast Traveler* are also a good source of information on packagers. **Liberty Travel (☎ 888/271-1584;** www.libertytravel. com) is one of the biggest packagers in the Northeast and usually has a full-page ad in Sunday papers.

Several big **online travel agencies** — Expedia, Travelocity, Orbitz, Site59, and Lastminute.com — also do a brisk business in packages. If you're unsure about the pedigree of a smaller packager, check with the Better Business Bureau in the city where the company is based, or go to www. bbb.org. If a packager won't tell you where it's based, don't fly with that company.

Chapter 6

Catering to Special Travel Needs or Interests

In This Chapter

▶ Traveling with kids

▶ Making the most of senior advantages

▶ Rising to the challenge: Disabled travelers

▶ Finding gay and lesbian communities and special events

*E*very traveler is a special traveler, but bringing kids along on your trip to Rome, traveling alone as a single woman, or trying to find wheelchair-accessible accommodations and attractions all require extra care and thought. Seniors may be interested in special programs and activities; gays and lesbians may wonder how friendly and welcoming Rome will be. We consider all these issues in this chapter.

Traveling with the Brood: Advice for Families

 If you have enough trouble getting your kids out of the house in the morning, dragging them thousands of miles away may seem like an insurmountable challenge. But family travel can be immensely rewarding, allowing you to see the world in new ways, through smaller pairs of eyes.

Families with kids can have a great time in Rome. It helps if you talk to your kids before the trip, preparing them for special things in store for them. Involve your children in planning for the trip. Go over the list of sights and activities in the areas that you plan to visit, particularly noting those labeled with the Kid Friendly icon in this book. Let your kids make their own list of things they want to do. Encourage older children to research Rome on the Internet (see Appendix A for a list of Web sites worth checking out).

Romans are very family oriented, and Romans of all age love children, which makes traveling here with your kids much easier. People rarely get annoyed at children, and you'll find that people will often talk to or inquire about your child(ren) in stores and restaurants or even as you walk in the street. Romans love their children so much that they can hardly imagine leaving their children behind, and they bring them along nearly everywhere. So although businesses and service providers are used to dealing with children and ready to meet their basic needs, few businesses cater especially to families with kids in ways that you might be used to in the United States.

Basically all restaurants provide high chairs and *mezza porzione* (half-portions) and are ready to prepare a simple dish (spaghetti with plain tomato sauce, for example) even if it isn't on the menu. Also, all hotels will add to your room a crib or a small child bed, often for free, and most will have triples and sometimes quads available for families with older children; at a minimum, they'll have adjoining rooms with a communicating door to turn your hotel room into a suite. However, only rarely will you find special children's menus in restaurants — Italian children usually eat what their parents eat — and you'll find even less often special kids' treats such as crayons and paper. Similarly, you'll almost never see a child-care or play area at museums, and hotels don't provide nurseries or a playroom for day-care service. Hotels in the more expensive categories offer babysitting on request and call in professional baby sitters from a reputable agency, but they rarely offer a children's program or structured activities for your kids (see Appendix A for details on babysitting services).

What this all boils down to is that Italians in general expect children to be well behaved (act politely like little adults in museums and other public places) and parents to know how to keep them happy. When tantrums, whining, and other outbursts occur, Romans frown upon the parent(s), not the child, whom Romans look at understandingly with a smile, as if to ask, "What is this mother or father of yours putting you through, poor thing?" Be prepared for a lot of well-meaning interference when your child misbehaves.

Fortunately, several organizations exist whose aim is to make traveling with the brood an enjoyable experience. One of the best, **Familyhostel** (☎ **800-733-9753;** www.learn.unh.edu/familyhostel), takes the whole family, including kids ages 8 to 15, on moderately priced domestic and international learning vacations. Lectures, field trips, and sightseeing are guided by a team of academics.

You can find good family-oriented vacation advice on the Internet from sites like **Family Travel Forum** (www.familytravelforum.com), a comprehensive site that offers customized trip planning; **Family Travel Network** (www.familytravelnetwork.com), an award-winning site that offers travel features, deals, and tips; **Traveling Internationally with Your Kids** (www.travelwithyourkids.com), a comprehensive site that offers customized trip planning; and **Family Travel Files** (www.thefamily travelfiles.com), which offers an online magazine and a directory of off-the-beaten-path tours and tour operators for families.

How to Take Great Trips with Your Kids (The Harvard Common Press) is full of good general advice that can apply to travel anywhere. *Family Travel Times,* another good resource, is published six times a year (☎ 888/822-4FTT or 212/477-5524; www.familytraveltimes.com) and includes a weekly call-in service for subscribers. Subscriptions are $39 per year for quarterly editions.

Making Age Work for You: Tips for Seniors

In general, Romans accord older people a great deal of respect, probably because of the Roman embrace of extended family as well as the culture and nature of the Italian language (polite forms of address are to be used when speaking with someone older than yourself). Therefore, you're unlikely to encounter ageism.

Members of **AARP** (formerly known as the American Association of Retired Persons), 601 E St. NW, Washington, DC 20049 (☎ **888/687-2277** or 202/434-2277; www.aarp.org), get discounts on international chain hotels, airfares, and car rentals. AARP offers members a wide range of benefits, including *AARP: The Magazine* and a monthly newsletter. Anyone over 50 can join.

Being a senior entitles you to some terrific travel bargains. Many reliable agencies and organizations target the 50-plus market and offer trips to Rome. **Elderhostel** (☎ **877/426-8056;** www.elderhostel.org) arranges study programs for those age 55 and over (and a spouse or companion of any age) in the United States and in more than 80 countries around the world. Most courses last five to seven days in the United States (two to four weeks abroad), and many include airfare, accommodations in university dormitories or modest inns, meals, and tuition. **ElderTreks** (☎ **800/741-7956;** www.eldertreks.com) offers small-group tours to off-the-beaten-path or adventure-travel locations, restricted to travelers 50 and older.

Recommended publications offering travel resources and discounts for seniors include the quarterly magazine *Travel 50 & Beyond* (www.travel50andbeyond.com); *Travel Unlimited: Uncommon Adventures for the Mature Traveler* (Avalon); *101 Tips for Mature Travelers,* available from Grand Circle Travel (☎ **800/221-2610** or 617/350-7500; www.gct.com); *The 50+ Traveler's Guidebook* (St. Martin's Press); and *Unbelievably Good Deals and Great Adventures That You Absolutely Can't Get Unless You're Over 50* (McGraw-Hill).

 Senior discounts on admission at theaters, museums, and public transportation are subject to reciprocity between countries. Because the United States hasn't signed the bilateral agreement (you discount us, and we'll discount you), Americans aren't eligible for senior discounts in Italy. (The same rule applies to the under-17 discount.) All discounts apply to citizens of European Union countries.

Accessing Rome: Advice for Travelers with Disabilities

Most disabilities shouldn't stop anybody from traveling, and more options and resources are available than ever before. Rome is working to make its treasures more accessible, but it's a slow process.

Although Italy may not be as advanced as some other countries in its accessibility, Rome, as the country's capital, is more in step with the times than other destinations in Italy. But keep in mind that the age of the housing stock and the difficulty of retrofitting medieval buildings with elevators or ramps pose serious limits to accessibility. Some of the major buildings and institutions have been converted; others have not or cannot. Calling ahead is always best, especially because, although special entrances may exist for the disabled, you may need to arrange to have an attendant meet you there. Public transportation reserves spaces for the disabled, and the Roman transportation authority has recently introduced new kneeling busses that make getting in and out quite easy. Some train stations and bus lines, though, can prove difficult, even impossible, if you're in a wheelchair.

You can avoid some of these problems by joining a tour that caters specifically to your needs. Many travel agencies offer customized tours and itineraries for travelers with disabilities. **Flying Wheels Travel** (☎ 507/451-5005; www.flyingwheelstravel.com) offers escorted tours and cruises that emphasize sports and private tours in minivans with lifts. **Access-Able Travel Source** (☎ 303/232-2979; www.access-able.com) offers extensive access information and advice for traveling around the world with disabilities. **Accessible Journeys** (☎ 800/846-4537 or 610/521-0339; www.disabilitytravel.com) caters to wheelchair travelers and their families and friends.

Avis Rent a Car's "Avis Access" program offers such services as a dedicated 24-hour toll-free number (☎ 888/879-4273) for customers with special travel needs; special car features such as swivel seats, spinner knobs, and hand controls; and accessible bus service.

Organizations that offer assistance to disabled travelers include **Moss Rehab Hospital** (www.mossresourcenet.org), which provides a library of accessible-travel resources online; and **SATH**, the **Society for Accessible Travel and Hospitality** (☎ 212/447-7284; www.sath.org; annual membership fees: $45 adults, $30 seniors and students), which offers a wealth of travel resources for all types of disabilities and informed recommendations on destinations, access guides, travel agents, tour operators, vehicle rentals, and companion services. The **American Foundation for the Blind** (☎ 800/232-5463; www.afb.org) provides information on traveling with Seeing Eye dogs.

For more information specifically targeted to travelers with disabilities, the community Web site **iCan** (www.icanonline.net/channels/travel/index.cfm) has destination guides and several regular columns on accessible travel. Also check out the quarterly magazine *Emerging Horizons* ($14.95 per year, $19.95 outside the U.S.; www.emerging horizons.com), and *Open World Magazine,* published by SATH (see preceding paragraph; subscription: $13 per year, $21 outside the U.S.).

Following the Rainbow: Resources for Gay and Lesbian Travelers

Rome is a very tolerant city in a fairly tolerant country, and violent displays of intolerance such as gay bashing are quite unheard of. However, as in the United States, an active gay and lesbian movement is trying to raise public consciousness about prejudice and discrimination.

Rome has an active gay life, and you can check out the local branch of **ARCI-Gay/ARCI-Lesbica** (www.arcigay.it/roma), the country's leading gay organization. Its Web site has an English-language version. The Eternal City can boast of having held the first-ever World Pride event in Italy in July 2000, to coincide with the Jubilee celebrations. During the summer, in parallel with the **Estate Romana** festival, a whole neighborhood of Rome turns into **Gay Village** (www.gayvillage.it), a town within the town, where tolerance is the leitmotif and gay and straight mingle while enjoying a variety of cultural events (see Chapters 15 and 16).

The **International Gay & Lesbian Travel Association (IGLTA)** (☎ 800/448-8550 or 954/776-2626; www.iglta.org) is the trade association for the gay-and-lesbian travel industry and offers an online directory of gay-and lesbian-friendly travel businesses; go to its Web site, and click Members.

Chapter 7

Taking Care of the Remaining Details

*E*ven if you have a destination, an itinerary, and a ticket in hand, you aren't going anywhere until you get a passport. You also need to figure out whether you need a rental car, whether to get traveler's insurance, and how you want to stay in touch with the folks back home. In this chapter, we help you tie up all the loose ends.

Getting a Passport

A valid passport is the only legal form of identification accepted around the world. You can't cross an international border without it. Getting a passport is easy, but the process takes some time. For an up-to-date, country-by-country listing of passport requirements around the world, visit the Foreign Entry Requirement Web page of the U.S. State Department at http://travel.state.gov/foreignentryreqs.html.

Applying for a U.S. passport

If you're applying for a first-time passport, follow these steps:

1. **Complete a passport application in person at a U.S. passport office; a federal, state, or probate court; or a major post office.**

   To find your regional passport office, either check the U.S. State Department Web site (http://travel.state.gov) or call the National Passport Information Center (☎ 202/647-0518).

2. Present a certified birth certificate as proof of citizenship.

Bringing along your driver's license, state or military ID, or Social Security card is also a good idea.

3. Submit two identical passport-size photos, measuring 2 x 2 inches.

You often find businesses that take these photos near a passport office. *Note:* You can't use a strip from a photo-vending machine because the pictures aren't identical.

4. Pay a fee.

For people 16 and over, a passport is valid for ten years and costs $85. For those 15 and under, a passport is valid for five years and costs $70.

Allow plenty of time before your trip to apply for a passport; processing normally takes three weeks but can take longer during busy periods (especially spring).

If you have a passport in your current name that was issued within the past 15 years (and you were over age 16 when it was issued), you can renew the passport by mail for $55. Whether you're applying in person or by mail, you can download passport applications from the U.S. State Department Web site at http://travel.state.gov. For general information, call the **National Passport Agency** (☎ 202/647-0518). To find your regional passport office, either check the U.S. State Department Web site or call the **National Passport Information Center** toll-free number (☎ 877/487-2778) for automated information.

Losing your passport may be worse than losing your money. Why? Because a passport shows (and proves to authorities) that you are you. Safeguard your passport in an inconspicuous, inaccessible place like a money belt. Always carry a photocopy of your passport with you, and keep it in a separate pocket or purse. If you lose your passport, visit the nearest consulate of your native country as soon as possible for a replacement.

Applying for other passports

Australians can visit a local post office or passport office, call the **Australia Passport Information Service** (☎ 131/232 toll-free from Australia), or log on to www.passports.gov.au for details on how and where to apply.

Canadians can pick up applications at passport offices throughout Canada; at post offices; or from the central **Passport Office, Department of Foreign Affairs and International Trade,** Ottawa, ON K1A 0G3 (☎ 800/567-6868; www.ppt.gc.ca). Applications must be accompanied by two identical passport-size photographs and proof of Canadian citizenship. Processing takes five to ten days if you apply in person or about three weeks by mail.

New Zealanders can pick up a passport application at any New Zealand Passports Office or download it from the agency's Web site. Contact the **Passports Office** at ☎ **0800/225-050** in New Zealand or 04-474-8100, or log on to www.passports.govt.nz for more information.

United Kingdom residents can pick up applications for a standard ten-year passport (five-year passport for children under 16) at passport offices, major post offices, or a travel agency. For information, contact the **United Kingdom Passport Service** (☎ **0870/521-0410;** www.ukpa.gov.uk).

When you get your passport photos taken, ask for six to eight total photos if you're planning to also apply for an International Driving Permit and an international student or teacher ID, which may entitle you to discounts at museums. Take the extra photos with you. You may need one for random reasons on the road, and if — heaven forbid — you ever lose your passport, you can use them for a replacement request.

Renting a Car — Not!

To start with, nonresidents are not allowed to drive within the city center — basically within the city walls. You can't even drive in the forbidden area just to drop your luggage at your hotel. If you arrive by car, you must either get a hotel outside the city center or park your car outside the city walls and take a taxi to your hotel.

Even if you were allowed to drive in Rome, we would still strongly discourage you from doing so. Rome's streets are notoriously congested. The Roman way to deal with the nightmarish traffic situation is to ride mopeds and motorscooters, and *thousands* of them seem to swarm at every intersection. Because of the snarl of cars and mopeds, crossing the street on foot is a dangerous enough activity — and driving is almost suicidal!

Making matters worse, secure parking garages are few and far between — and expensive! (about 30€/$39 per day) — and you certainly don't want to park in the street, where your car can be broken into. Factor in the high cost of fuel (about 5€/$6.50 a gallon), and you see why it's best to leave the driving to someone else. See Chapter 8 for details on transportation within the city.

Playing It Safe with Travel and Medical Insurance

Three kinds of travel insurance are available: trip-cancellation insurance, medical insurance, and lost-luggage insurance. The cost of travel insurance varies widely, but expect to pay between 5 and 8 percent of the vacation itself. Here is our advice on all three:

✔ **Trip-cancellation insurance** helps you get your money back if you have to back out of a trip or go home early, or if your travel supplier goes bankrupt. Allowed reasons for cancellation can range from sickness to natural disasters to the State Department's declaring your destination unsafe for travel. (Insurers usually won't cover vague fears, though, as many travelers discovered who tried to cancel their trips in October 2001 because they were wary of flying.)

A good resource is **"Travel Guard Alerts,"** a list of companies considered high-risk by Travel Guard International (www.travel insured.com). Protect yourself further by paying for the insurance with a credit card — by law, consumers can get their money back on goods and services not received if they report the loss within 60 days after the charge is listed on their credit-card statement.

Note: Some experts suggest that you avoid buying insurance from the tour or cruise company you're traveling with, saying it's better to buy from a third-party insurer than to put all your money in one place.

✔ For travel overseas, most health plans (including Medicare and Medicaid) do not provide **medical insurance** coverage, and the ones that do often require you to pay for services up front and reimburse you only after you return home. Even if your plan does cover over- seas treatment, most out-of-country hospitals make you pay your bills up front and send you a refund only after you've returned home and filed the necessary paperwork with your insurance company. As a safety net, you may want to buy travel medical insurance. If you require additional medical insurance, try **MEDEX Assistance** (☎ **410-453-6300;** www.medexassist.com) or **Travel Assistance International** (☎ **800-821-2828;** www.travelassistance.com; for general information on services, call the company's Worldwide Assistance Services, Inc., at ☎ **800-777-8710**).

✔ **Lost-luggage insurance** is not necessary for most travelers. On international flights (including U.S. portions of international trips), baggage coverage is limited to approximately $9.07 per pound, up to approximately $635 per checked bag. If you plan to check items more valuable than the standard liability, see whether your valu- ables are covered by your homeowner's policy, get baggage insur- ance as part of your comprehensive travel-insurance package, or buy Travel Guard's "BagTrak" product. Don't buy insurance at the airport — it's usually overpriced. Be sure to take any valuables or irreplaceable items with you in your carry-on luggage, because many valuables (including books, money, and electronics) aren't covered by airline policies.

If your luggage is lost, immediately file a lost-luggage claim at the airport, detailing the luggage contents. For most airlines, you must report delayed, damaged, or lost baggage within four hours of arrival. The airlines are required to deliver luggage, once found, directly to your house or destination free of charge.

For more information on travel insurance, contact one of the following recommended insurers: **Access America** (☎ 866-807-3982; www.access america.com), **Travel Guard International** (☎ 800-826-4919; www. travelguard.com), **Travel Insured International** (☎ 800-243-3174; www.travelinsured.com), and **Travelex Insurance Services** (☎ 888-457-4602; www.travelex-insurance.com).

Staying Healthy When You Travel

For travel abroad, you may have to pay all medical costs up front and be reimbursed by your health-care plan later. For information on purchasing additional medical insurance for your trip, see the previous section.

Talk to your doctor before leaving on a trip if you have a serious and/or chronic illness. For conditions such as epilepsy, diabetes, or heart problems, wear a **MedicAlert identification tag** (☎ 888/633-4298; www. medicalert.org), which immediately alerts doctors to your condition and gives them access to your records through MedicAlert's 24-hour hotline. Contact the **International Association for Medical Assistance to Travelers (IAMAT)** (☎ 716/754-4883 or, in Canada, 416/652-0137; www.iamat.org) for tips on travel and health concerns in the countries you're visiting, as well as lists of local, English-speaking doctors. The U.S. **Centers for Disease Control and Prevention** (☎ 800/311-3435; www.cdc.gov) provides up-to-date information on health hazards by region or country and offers tips on food safety.

If you do get sick in Rome, ask the concierge at your hotel to recommend a local doctor — even his or her own doctor, if necessary. If you can't locate a doctor, try contacting your embassy or consulate — they maintain lists of English-speaking doctors. In an emergency, dial ☎ 113 for the police or ☎ 112 for the *Carabinieri* (army police corps): They can call an ambulance and help you in many other ways. If your situation is life threatening, call ☎ 118 for immediate medical help such as an ambulance or even a helicopter ambulance if needed. If you can move

Avoiding "economy-class syndrome"

Deep vein thrombosis or, as it's known in the world of flying, "economy-class syndrome," is a blood clot that develops in a deep vein. It's a potentially deadly condition that can be caused by sitting in cramped conditions — such as an airplane cabin — for too long. During a flight (especially a long-haul flight), get up, walk around, and stretch your legs every 60 to 90 minutes to keep your blood flowing. Other preventive measures include frequent flexing of the legs while sitting, drinking lots of water, and avoiding alcohol and sleeping pills.

by your own means and are not far from a hospital, get yourself to the *pronto soccorso* (emergency department) at the nearest hospital (check Appendix A for addresses).

Under the Italian national health-care system, you're eligible only for free *emergency* care. If you're admitted to a hospital as an inpatient, even from an accident and through an emergency department, you're required to pay (unless you're a resident of the European Economic Area). You're also required to pay for follow-up care. For the names, addresses, and phone numbers of hospitals offering 24-hour emergency care, see the "Fast Facts" section in Appendix A.

Staying Connected by Cellphone or E-Mail

If you're from Europe, you're lucky: Your phone already works in Rome. If you're from another continent, things are a little complicated.

Using a cellphone outside the United States

The three letters that define much of the world's **wireless capabilities** are GSM (Global System for Mobiles), a big, seamless network that makes for easy cross-border cellphone use throughout Europe and dozens of other countries worldwide. In the United States, T-Mobile and Cingular use this quasi-universal system; in Canada, Microcell and some Rogers customers are GSM; and all Europeans and most Australians use GSM.

If your cellphone is on a GSM system, and you have a world-capable multiband phone such as many Sony Ericsson, Motorola, or Samsung models, you can make and receive calls across civilized areas on much of the globe. Just call your wireless operator, and ask for "international roaming" to be activated on your account. Unfortunately, per-minute charges can be high — usually $1 to $1.50 in Western Europe.

 For many, **renting a phone** is the way to go. In Rome, you don't have to look for a place to rent a phone; you can make the phone come to you. **Rentacell** (☎ 877-736-8355 in the U.S.; 02-86337799 in Italy; www.rentacell.com) will deliver a phone to you anywhere for free. You can also pick it up in the United States before you leave. The kit rental is 8€ ($10) per day (less for longer periods), and incoming calls are free, while outgoing calls range from .76€ (98¢) within Italy to 1.22€ ($1.60) to other countries, including the United States. If you need only a SimCard (the chip to put in your own phone), the rental is free, and you pay only for outgoing calls. **Easyline** (☎ 800-010600 in Italy) also delivers phones for free and applies similar charges.

Accessing the Internet away from home

You have any number of ways to check your e-mail and access the Internet on the road. Of course, using your own laptop — or even a personal digital assistant (PDA) or electronic organizer with a modem — gives you the most flexibility. But even if you don't have a computer, you can still access your e-mail from Rome. Your hotel is most likely to have an **Internet point** free for its guests or even to offer full Internet access in your room through a multimedia TV.

Rome also has a great number of **cybercafes.** Although there's no definitive directory of cybercafes — these are independent businesses, after all — two places to start looking are www.cybercaptive.com and www.cybercafe.com. **Easy Everything** (www.easyeverything.com), a global Internet-cafe company, currently has two franchises in Rome, but the company is rapidly expanding, and by the time you read this, there may well be more — check the Web site for other locations. **Internet Train** (www.internettrain.it), another franchise, already has multiple sites in Rome.

To retrieve your e-mail, ask your **Internet service provider (ISP)** if it has a Web-based interface tied to your existing e-mail account. If your ISP doesn't have such an interface, you can use the free **mail2web** service (www.mail2web.com) to view and reply to your home e-mail. For more flexibility, you may want to open a free, Web-based e-mail account with **Yahoo! Mail** (http://mail.yahoo.com). (Microsoft's Hotmail is another popular option, but Hotmail has severe spam problems.) Your home ISP may be able to forward your e-mail to the Web-based account automatically.

If you're bringing your own computer, the buzzword in computer access to familiarize yourself with is **Wi-Fi** (wireless fidelity), and more and more hotels, cafes, and retailers are signing on as wireless "hotspots" from where you can get high-speed connection without cable wires, networking hardware, or a phone line. You can get a Wi-Fi connection in one of several ways. Many laptops sold in the past year have built-in Wi-Fi capability (an 802.11b wireless Ethernet connection). Mac owners have their own networking technology: Apple AirPort. If you have an older computer, you can buy an 802.11b/**Wi-Fi card** (around $50) and plug it into your laptop.

You sign up for wireless access service much as you do cellphone service, through a plan offered by one of several commercial companies that have made wireless service available in airports, hotel lobbies, and coffee shops, primarily in the United States (followed by the U.K. and Japan). **T-Mobile Hotspot** (www.t-mobile.com/hotspot) serves up wireless connections in many hotel lobbies and other points in Rome. **Boingo** (www.boingo.com) and **Wayport** (www.wayport.com) have set up networks in airports and high-class hotel lobbies. iPass providers also give you access to a few hundred wireless hotel lobby setups. Best of all, you don't need to be staying at the hotel to use its network; just set yourself up on a nice couch in the lobby. The companies' pricing policies can be byzantine, with a variety of monthly, per-connection, and per-minute plans, but in general, you pay around $30 a month for limited access — and as more and more companies jump on the wireless bandwagon, prices are likely to get even more competitive.

There are also places that provide **free wireless networks** in cities around the world. To locate these free hotspots, go to www.personal telco.net/index.cgi/WirelessCommunities.

If Wi-Fi is not available at your destination, most business-class hotels throughout the world offer dataports for laptop modems, and a few thousand hotels in the United States and Europe now offer free high-speed Internet access using an Ethernet network cable. You can bring your own cables, but most hotels rent them for around $10. **Call your hotel in advance** to see what your options are.

In addition, major ISPs have **local access numbers** around the world, allowing you to go online by simply placing a local call. Check your ISP's Web site, or call its toll-free number and ask how you can use your current account away from home and how much it will cost. If you're traveling outside the reach of your ISP, the **iPass** network has dial-up numbers in most of the world's countries. You'll have to sign up with an iPass provider, which will then tell you how to set up your computer for your destination(s). For a list of iPass providers, go to www.ipass.com, and click Individual Purchase. One solid provider is **i2roam** (www.i2roam. com; ☎ **866/811-6209** or 920/235-0475).

 Wherever you go, bring a **connection kit** for Italy, including a phone-plug adapter, a spare phone cord, and a spare Ethernet network cable — or find out whether your hotel supplies them to guests. For information on the electric current in Rome, see the "Fast Facts" section in Appendix A.

Keeping Up with Airline Security

With the federalization of airport security, security procedures at U.S. airports are more stable and consistent than ever. Generally, you'll be fine if you arrive at the airport **one hour** before a domestic flight and **two hours** before an international flight; if you show up late, tell an airline employee, and she'll probably whisk you to the front of the line.

Bring a **current, government-issued photo ID** such as a driver's license or passport. Keep your ID at the ready to show at check-in, the security checkpoint, and sometimes even the gate. (Children under 18 do not need government-issued photo IDs for domestic flights, but they do for international flights to most countries.)

In 2003, the TSA phased out **gate check-in** at all U.S. airports. And **E-tickets** have made paper tickets nearly obsolete. If you have an E-ticket, you can beat the ticket-counter lines by using airport **electronic**

kiosks or even **online check-in** from your home computer. Online check-in involves logging on to your airline's Web site, accessing your reservation, and printing out your boarding pass — and the airline may even offer you bonus miles to do so! If you're using a kiosk at the airport, bring the credit card you used to book the ticket or your frequent-flier card. Print out your boarding pass from the kiosk, and simply proceed to the security checkpoint with your pass and a photo ID. If you're checking bags or looking to snag an exit-row seat, you'll be able to do so using most airline kiosks. Even the smaller airlines are employing the kiosk system, but always call your airline to make sure these alternatives are available. **Curbside check-in** is also a good way to avoid lines, although a few airlines still ban curbside check-in; call before you go.

Security checkpoint lines are getting shorter than they were during 2001 and 2002, but some doozies remain. If you have trouble standing for long periods of time, tell an airline employee; the airline will provide a wheelchair. Speed up security by **not wearing metal objects** such as big belt buckles. If you have metallic body parts, a note from your doctor can prevent a long chat with the security screeners. Keep in mind that only **ticketed passengers** are allowed past security except for folks escorting disabled passengers or children.

Federalization has stabilized **what you can carry on** and **what you can't.** The general rule is that nail clippers and small scissors and tools, are okay, and food and beverages must be passed through the X-ray machine — but that security screeners can't make you drink from your coffee cup. Bring food in your carry-on bag instead of checking it, because explosive-detection machines used on checked luggage have been known to mistake food (especially chocolate, for some reason) for bombs. Travelers in the United States are allowed one carry-on bag plus a "personal item" such as a purse, briefcase, or laptop bag. Carry-on hoarders can stuff all sorts of things into a laptop bag; as long as it has a laptop in it, it's still considered a personal item. The Transportation Security Administration (TSA) has issued a list of restricted items; check its Web site (www.tsa.gov/public/index.jsp) for details.

Airport screeners may decide that your checked luggage needs to be searched by hand. Travel Sentry certified locks (available at luggage and travel shops, as well as at Brookstone stores or online at www.brookstone.com) are approved by the TSA and can be opened by inspectors with a special code or key. If you use something other than TSA-approved locks, your lock will be cut off your suitcase if a hand-search is required.

Part III
Settling into Rome

The 5th Wave   By Rich Tennant

©RICHTENNANT

"I appreciate that our room looks out onto several baroque fountains, but I had to get up 6 times last night to go to the bathroom."

In this part . . .

This is where we provide all the logistical information you'll need to make your way around the city, find a comfortable bed, and eat a delicious meal.

In Chapter 8, we give you a few tips about Rome's airports and other entry points, and how to get from there to your accommodations. We also provide a detailed description of the city's neighborhoods and suggest the best ways to get around in Rome. In Chapter 9, we recommend our favorite Roman hotels — in a number of price categories and locations — and offer tips for reserving the best room at the best rate. In Chapter 10, we tell you what to expect from Roman restaurants and offer extensive reviews of our favorite choices, as well as provide handy lists of restaurants by neighborhood, price, and cuisine. And because you'll need some snacks to keep you going between meals, we give you the scoop on snacks such as pizza and gelato.

Chapter 8

Arriving and Getting Oriented

In This Chapter

▶ Arriving in Rome

▶ Acquainting yourself with the neighborhoods

▶ Finding information after you arrive

▶ Getting from place to place

*A*rriving in a foreign city is always a challenge, and although Rome isn't one of the largest cities in the world, it is large enough to be confusing; the narrow and winding streets of *il centro storico* (the historic center) are a maze even for Romans! In this chapter, we give you all the information you need to negotiate the Eternal City like a native.

Navigating Your Way through Passport Control and Customs

To enter Italy, you need a passport. Because Italy is now part of the group of European countries that have unified their passport and Customs procedures (under the Schengen agreement), your passport is checked as soon as you enter European or Italian territory, whichever comes first. If you've already landed in a European country that is part of the Schengen area, chances are that you won't need to show your passport again — only spot checks are performed at the Italian border. If Rome is your first port of call in Europe, you'll have to line up for passport control; often, you'll find two lines, one for European Union citizens and one for everyone else. If everything is okay with your passport, you'll be allowed in — but don't expect your passport to be stamped.

While you're in Italy, you're required to have your passport with you at all times, and you can be asked to produce it at any time to prove your identity and your legal status. All hotels will ask to see your passport when you check in. Carry your passport in a safe place on your person (such as a document pouch worn under your clothes), or leave the original in the safe at your hotel and carry a photocopy.

After having your passport checked and collecting your luggage, you must pass through Customs. Items for personal use enter duty free up to 175€ ($228) for each adult and 90€ ($117) for each child under 15. In addition, adults can import a maximum of 200 cigarettes (50 cigars), 1 liter (slightly more that 1 quart) of liquor or 2 liters of wine, 50 grams of perfume, 500 grams (1 pound) of coffee, and 100 grams (3 ounces) of tea; children are allowed only perfume. Also, you cannot bring currency in excess of 10,329€ (at press time $13,428, though the dollar amount will depend on the conversion rate on the day you travel). See Chapter 12 for Customs regulations regarding what you can bring home. You can find more-detailed information at the Italian Customs Web site (www.agenziadogane.it).

Making Your Way to Your Hotel

It's still true that "all roads lead to Rome," but nowadays, so do all planes, trains, coaches, and even ferries.

Arriving by plane

Rome's main airport, Leonardo da Vinci, is located in **Fiumicino,** and this is where you're likely to land if you come by plane. However, charter flights and some European companies also arrive in the smaller airport of **Ciampino.**

If you arrive at Fiumicino airport

Though officially named after Leonardo, everybody refers to this airport as Fiumicino (☎ **06-65951;** www.adr.it), after the name of the nearby town. The airport is compact and very well organized (but ever expanding), with three terminals connected by a long corridor: Terminal A handles domestic travel; Terminal B handles domestic and Schengen European Community flights (that is, internal flights to the countries of the European Community that have signed a special agreement to waive Customs controls); and Terminal C manages all other international flights. If you're flying direct from a U.S. airport, Terminal C is your likely point of entry. Terminal C is connected to a newer set of gates by a cool monorail.

While at the airport, you may notice the high level of security. Don't be concerned if you see police officers with submachine guns walking around — due to recent world tensions, it's now routine procedure and one you should be glad of.

Be aware that the security forces at Fiumicino have terrorists in mind, not common thieves — that means you still have to watch your belongings like a hawk, and don't leave anything precious in your checked luggage.

After exiting passport control and Customs, you enter the main concourse, a long hall that connects all three terminals. There, you'll find ATMs (one per terminal), as well as 24-hour currency exchange machines and a *cambio* (change) office, open from 8:30 a.m. to 7:30 p.m. and located just outside Customs in the international arrivals area.

If you're using traveler's checks, you may want to change them at the *cambio* office — its rates are usually the best in town.

On your way out to ground transportation, you find a very good **tourist information desk** (☎ 06-65956074) providing information on Rome at one end and on the rest of Italy at the other. Nearby is a help desk for **last-minute hotel reservations** — the service, however, doesn't cover all hotels in Rome.

Public transportation, including taxis and car-rental shuttle buses, is just outside along the sidewalk; the train station is on the second floor of a building attached to the international terminal.

Fiumicino lies about 30km (18 miles) from Rome and is well connected by highway, train, shuttle, and bus.

The easiest way to get to your hotel is by taking a **taxi.** The line forms on the curb just outside the terminals and is marked by a sign; taxis are white and have a meter. For three adult passengers — sometimes, taxis accept four — expect to pay about 45€ ($58) for the 50-minute ride (well over an hour at rush hour), plus a luggage fee of 1€ ($1.30) per item for *everything* that goes in the trunk, so keep your purse or any small bags with you inside the car. Expect a night surcharge (10 p.m.–6 a.m.) of 2.60€ ($3.40) and a Sunday and holiday surcharge of 1€ ($1.30).

Although they have almost disappeared, beware of gypsy cab drivers who approach you as you exit the arrival gate. They don't have meters and charge you a lot more than the regulated cab rates.

Taking the **train-shuttle** into Rome is equally simple — and a lot faster during rush hour. If you have a lot of luggage, you can hire help at the baggage-claim area for 2€ ($2.60) per item; they'll take your bags to the train. The railroad terminal is connected to the air terminal through a corridor on the second floor, just outside arrivals (follow the sign marked TRENI). The best train is the **Leonardo Express,** a 35-minute shuttle ride to **Termini** (Rome's central rail station), which runs daily every 30 minutes from 6:37 a.m. to 11:37 p.m. and costs 9.50€ ($12). There also is a cheaper local commuter train (look for trains with final destination Orte or Fara Sabina), which makes various stops along the way and within Rome but doesn't stop at Termini. It takes about 40 minutes, depending on your stop, and runs every 15 minutes Monday through Saturday and every 30 minutes on Sunday for about 5€ ($6.50). Get off at **Roma Ostiense** if your hotel is in the area of the Aventino or the Colosseum; **Roma Trastevere** if it is in the area of Trastevere, San Pietro, or Prati; and at **Roma Tiburtina** if your hotel is in the Porta Pia or Villa Borghese area. Tickets for both trains are sold at the ticket booth in the terminal. Remember to stamp your ticket at one of the small yellow validation boxes before you board the train.

If you're planning to use public transportation in Rome, consider buying a day pass or a tourist three-day ticket (see "Getting Around Rome," later in this chapter) at the tobacconist in the railroad terminal. *Definitely* do so if you're planning to use the commuter train from the airport to Rome, because the ride is included in either of those passes (only for the regular commuter train, though, not for the Leonardo Express).

Whichever train you take, a taxi stand is located immediately outside the train stations upon your arrival. You can also take public transportation. Ranks of buses, with signs indicating their numbers and routes, stop in the area in front of the train station; the subway is underneath the station.

Finally, you can take a **bus shuttle** into Rome. **Terravision** (☎ 06-79494572; www.terravision.it) runs a shuttle to Termini station and to Tiburtina station, with stops at a few major hotels for 9€ ($12) and 5€ ($6.50) for children ages 2 to 12.

Note: We do not recommend renting a car at the airport and driving it into Rome. See Chapter 7 for additional information.

If you arrive at Ciampino airport

A number of international charter flights and some companies that mainly serve Europe arrive at **Ciampino** (☎ 06-794941 or 06-79340297), 16km (10 miles) from the center of Rome. This airport has few structures or services; it's almost like an American civil-aviation airport.

Taxis are by far the easiest way to get to town from Ciampino. Expect to pay about 35€ ($45) for the 45-minute trip. You can also take a **shuttle bus; Terravision** (☎ 06-79494572. www.terravision.it) runs a shuttle service in concert with Ryanair flights, and **Schiaffini** runs a shuttle coinciding with EasyJet flights. Both take you to Termini station for 8€ ($10); tickets are sold at the Hotel Royal Santina or at the Hotel Stromboli on Via Marsala, just across from the Termini train station.

Arriving by ship

If you're coming by sea, your ocean liner will dock in the harbor of **Civitavecchia** (about 80 km/50 miles north of Rome). There, you can catch one of the frequent coaches and trains for Rome arriving at Termini station or Tiburtina station. Trains leave every about 20 minutes for the hourlong ride to Rome, with direct coaches departing every hour.

You can call a taxi from either the harbor or the train station, dialing ☎ **0766-26121** or 0766 24251 should none be available at the taxi stand. You can also arrange for limousine service from the harbor. The best no-frills service is **Rome Shuttle Limousine** (☎ **348-5141804** or 06-61969084; www.romeshuttlelimousine.com); it offers a Civitavecchia-to-Rome transfer for 110€ ($143) for a maximum of four people. Also good, **Best Limos in Rome** (☎ **338-4289389**; www.bestlimosinrome.com) is an English-speaking company based in Rome and specializing on seaport services. Another good company is **Romalimo** (☎ **800-999669** or 06-5414663; www.romalimo.com).

Arriving by train

Rome is a major railroad hub, offering service to every domestic and international destination. Italy's **Trenitalia** train service (☎ **892021**; www.trenitalia.it) is excellent: cheap, reliable, and frequent. No fewer than six railway stations are located in the center of Rome, but the central and largest is **Termini** (☎ **800/431784**), the second-busiest is **Tiburtina.** Trains usually stop at one or the other.

After you get off the train at Termini station, make your way to the main concourse by exits located near platforms 1 and 22. The concourse is a long commercial gallery with a bar at the north end and a pharmacy at the south end; in between are many newsstands, a tobacconist, a travel agency, ATMs, and a *cambio* office, as well as information booths. You can exit to the street at either end of the gallery, although if you plan to catch a taxi, take the north exit, where you find a small taxi stand. From the gallery, you can go one floor below to the lower concourse, a mall complete with a large bookstore, supermarket, cosmetics store, shoe-repair shop, and ATMs. Continuing in a straight line across the gallery, you reach the main hall, where train tickets are sold at the windows and at automatic machines. Public toilets and luggage check are at either end of the platform area.

Outside the main hall is Piazza dei Cinquecento, the largest bus terminal in Rome. Termini is the major public transportation hub of the city, with many bus lines starting here, and with the two Roman subway lines crossing underneath (see "Getting Around Rome," later in this chapter). The main taxi stand is just outside the main hall near the metro sign on the right. For some mysterious reason, the line forms at the end farthest from the exit of the train station, so depending on how many people are waiting, you may have to walk a bit. Take your cab from the line of taxis (taxis are white, with a yellow-and-black checkered line on the side and a taxi sign on the roof).

Although they've virtually disappeared, a few gypsy cabbies hang around the station and approach people as they walk from the train to the taxi line. Reject their offers; be firm; and get in line for a regulation ride.

Figuring Out the Neighborhoods

Rome started outgrowing its Ancient Roman and medieval walls (the medieval city walls were built on top of the Roman walls, some of which are still standing in places) in the 20th century and has seen an immense urban sprawl over the past two decades. The city is divided by the river **Tevere** (Tiber), which meanders southward, leaving about a third of the city on its western bank and the rest on its eastern bank. The historic center of Rome within the walls, called *il centro,* remains the heart of the city and the area you most want to visit.

Il Centro

The western bank of the Tevere holds the **Vatican,** the tiny city-state that is the base of the Catholic religion, with the pope as both a religious and administrative leader; its major feature is the basilica of **San Pietro.** North of the Vatican is the largish area called **Prati,** crossed by the busy **Via Cola di Rienzo.** Also on the western bank in *il centro* are the **Gianicolo** hill and **Trastevere.**

On the eastern bank of the Tevere is the political, cultural, commercial, and tourist heart of the city. About three millennia of consecutive layers of urban development have created a confused layout of streets, with tiny medieval roads crossed by larger and more recent avenues. At the east end on **Piazza dei Cinquecento** is Termini — Rome's main train station and major public transportation hub. Branching out of Piazza dei Cinquecento (and the connected Piazza della Repubblica to the west) are three major downhill avenues: The central one is **Via Nazionale,** leading to Piazza Venezia, continuing along Via del Plebiscito and Corso Vittorio Emanuele II all the way to the River Tiber, and across it to St. Peter's and the Vatican. The two other avenues are **Via Cavour,** heading toward the Colosseum, and **Via Barberini,** which leads into Via Veneto and Via del Tritone. The major cross streets are **Via del Corso** and **Via dei Fori Imperiali,** joining Piazza del Popolo at one end and, through Piazza Venezia, the Colosseum at the other. Beyond the Colosseum, you find the start of **Via Appia,** the first highway created by the Ancient Romans. A section of it — still showing the ancient pavement — has been transformed into an archaeological and natural park (see Chapter 11).

Because *il centro* is so large, we have divided it into several smaller neighborhoods. All neighborhoods in *il centro* are desirable places to stay, with lively nightlife, restaurants, and cafes nearby. The neighborhoods are identified on the "Rome Orientation" map in this chapter.

Aventino

This elegant residential neighborhood is one of the original seven hills of Rome, where a number of monasteries were built in the Middle Ages. It has known very little urban development since, and today, it's a unique island of quiet, where small restaurants and a few hotels are surrounded by greenery and peaceful streets. It is well connected through public transportation to all other destinations in Rome.

Campo de' Fiori

In the southern area of *il centro* along the left bank of the Tiber, this authentic neighborhood is mostly residential but is made very lively by the market square and the connected commercial strip of **Via dei Giubbonari.** Here, you'll find plenty of restaurants and an active nightlife. Among the attractions is the beautiful **Palazzo Farnese.**

Colosseo

The Colosseum was at the heart of ancient Rome, and the area around it is a romantic mix of residential buildings and ruins. The Colosseo is home to the most illustrious monuments of ancient Rome, including the **Palatino;** the **Roman Forum;** the **Campidoglio;** and, of course, the **Colosseum** itself. To the north, in an area sloping up along Via Cavour, is a very authentic and residential neighborhood. Although not elegant, it is experiencing new life with the opening of trendy restaurants, small hotels, and bars. To the east is another small residential and very Roman neighborhood, with a few hotels and some nice neighborhood restaurants.

Navona/Pantheon

At the hearth of *il centro* on the southwestern side of the **Corso,** this lively neighborhood is a mix of elegant Renaissance and medieval buildings, including the beautiful palaces that house the government and the two chambers of the Italian Parliament (the **Parlamento** and **Senato**). Many hotels occupy this area, and several nice restaurants and bars can be found along **Via del Governo Vecchio.** Some of Rome's best antiques shops line the **Via dei Coronari.** Graced by two of Rome's greatest attractions — **Piazza Navona** and the **Pantheon** — at its heart, this is one of the most desirable areas to stay; its popularity means that you have to put up with crowds, especially in summer.

Parioli

Beyond the city walls and north of the **Villa Borghese** park, this residential neighborhood, with some hotels and restaurants, is among the most elegant in the city. Its many trees perfume the air and provide a beautiful (and, more important, shady) place for a quiet stroll. Though the prices match the area's exclusivity, this is a great place to be — you're just a short ride from many attractions, yet far from the madding crowd.

Piazza del Popolo

At the north edge of *il centro,* around one of the most beautiful squares of Rome, this lively neighborhood has a lot of trendy new restaurants and bars in the area extending west of the **Corso.**

Rome Orientation

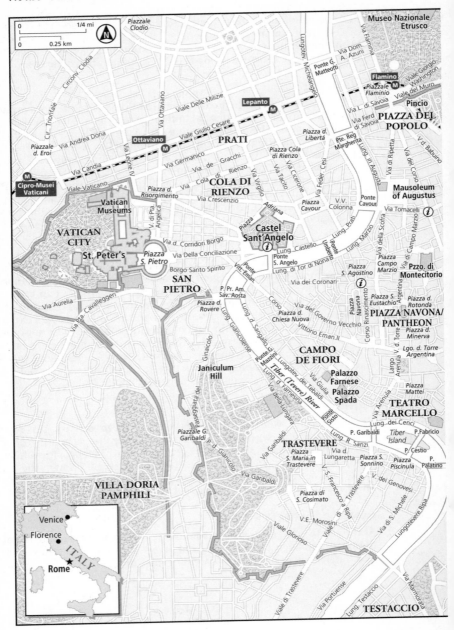

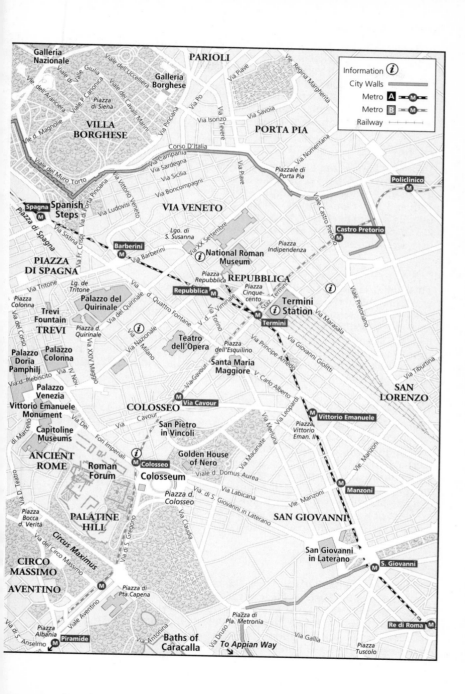

Galleria Nazionale

PARIOLI

Viale di Giulia

Viale dell'Uccelliera

Galleria Borghese

Via Piave

Vle. Regina Margherita

Vle. dell'Aranciera

Viale P. Canonica

Viale dei Cavalli Marini

Piazza di Siena

Via Po

Via Pinciana

Via Isonzo

Via Savoia

Information (i)

City Walls

Metro A ═M═

Metro B ═M═

Railway +—+—+—+

VILLA BORGHESE

Vle. d. Magnolie

PORTA PIA

Via Tevere

Corso D'Italia

Viale del Muro Torto

Via Campania

Via Sardegna

Via Sicilia

Via Boncompagni

Via Vittorio Veneto

Via di Porta Pinciana

Corso D'Italia

Via Nomentana

Piazzale di Porta Pia

Via Piave

Viale C. Castro Pretorio

Policlinico M

Spagna M Spanish Steps

Piazza di Spagna

Via Sistina

Via Ludovisi Veneto

VIA VENETO

Lgo. di S. Susanna

Via XX Settembre

Piazza Indipendenza

Castro Pretorio M

PIAZZA DI SPAGNA

Via Fr. Crispi

Barberini M

Via Barberini

(i) National Roman Museum

Piazza Repubblica

REPUBBLICA

Piazza Cinque-cento

(i)

Viale Pretoriano

Via Tritone

Lg. de Tritone

Palazzo del Quirinale

Via d. Quattro Fontane

Repubblica M

Via Viminale

Termini (i) Station

Via Marsala

Piazza Colonna

Trevi Fountain

TREVI

Piazza d. Quirinale

Via del Quirinale

(i)

Via Nazionale

Via del Corso

V. d. Torino

Via Milano

Teatro dell'Opera

Via Principe Amedeo

Termini M

Via Giovanni Giolitti

SAN LORENZO

Palazzo Doria Pamphilj

Palazzo Colonna

Via XXIV Maggio

Santa Maria Maggiore

Piazza dell'Esquilino

V. Carlo Alberto

Via di Plebiscito

Via 'N Nov.

Palazzo Venezia

Vittorio Emanuele Monument

Via Dei

COLOSSEO M Via Cavour

Cavour

Via Merulana

Via Leopardi

Vittorio Emanuele M

Piazza Vittorio Eman. II

Via Tiburtina

Capitoline Museums

Via di Marcello

Fori Imperiali

Via

San Pietro in Vincoli

ANCIENT ROME

Roman Forum

(i) Colosseo M

Golden House of Nero

Viale d. Domus Aurea

Via Macanate

Via d. Teatro

Colosseum

Piazza d. Colosseo

Via Labicana

Via di S. Giovanni in Laterano

Vle. Manzoni

Manzoni M

Piazza Bocca d. Verità

PALATINE HILL

Via d. S. Gregorio

SAN GIOVANNI

Via Claudia

CIRCO MASSIMO

Circus Maximus

Via del Circo Massimo

AVENTINO

M

Piazza di Pta. Capena

Viale Aventino

San Giovanni in Laterano

S. Giovanni M

Via di S. Anselmo

Piazza Albania

Piramide M

Via Antonina

Via Druso

Baths of Caracalla

↘ To Appian Way

Piazza di Pla. Metronia

Via Gallia

Piazza Tuscolo

Re di Roma M

Piazza di Spagna

In *il centro*, on the east side of the **Corso**, this former residential neighborhood has been almost completely taken over by the fashion and tourist industries. It is the best shopping neighborhood in Rome, home to all the great names of Italian couture, plus a lot of other tony shops. It has many hotels, including some of the city's best. The shopping streets get a bit deserted at night, and if you're seeking some nightlife, you have to edge toward **Fontana di Trevi** or cross over the Corso.

Porta Pia

Taking its name from a gate in the city walls at the northeast corner of *il centro*, this well-to-do residential area is almost as upscale as the Parioli. It's an interesting mix of beautiful villas and elegant buildings from the 18th and 19th centuries and middle-class dwellings. Very well connected by public transportation, it has many places to eat, hang out, and relax. It's an excellent choice for quieter, moderately priced accommodations that are still quite central to the big attractions.

Prati

This "new" residential neighborhood (it is not part of *il centro*) on the western bank of the Tiber takes its name from the fields, or *prati*, that still existed here at the end of the 19th century. It stretches north from **St. Peter's Basilica** and **Castel Sant'Angelo** along the Tiber. Reflecting its late-19th-century origin, streets are wide and straight, and lined with trees. The area is pleasant and close to *il centro*; it has a relatively active, if subdued, nightlife, with restaurants, jazz clubs, and an important shopping area along **Via Cola di Rienzo.**

Repubblica

Piazza della Repubblica is a gorgeous square created over what was the main hall of Diocletian's thermal baths, a few steps west of Piazza dei Cinquecento and the Termini train station. The areas along Via Cernaia on one side of the square and Via Nazionale on the other are lively during the day because of the numerous shops and offices, but not particularly happening at night, when it turns into a quiet residential neighborhood with a few hotels and restaurants. Very convenient to most of Rome's attractions and very well connected by public transportation, this is a good alternative to the more glamorous and pricey areas of *il centro*.

San Pietro

On the western bank of the Tiber, this area is mainly occupied by the walled city of the **Vatican** (seat of the Holy See and site of the Vatican Museums and the Sistine Chapel). It is dominated, of course, by the grandiose **Basilica di San Pietro (St. Peter's Basilica).** Flanking the basilica are two ancient and picturesque residential neighborhoods that are home to a few hotels and restaurants.

Teatro Marcello

This area covers what is still commonly referred to as the Ghetto, the old Jewish neighborhood at the edge of ancient Rome. It is among the most authentic of the neighborhoods in *il centro* and remains very residential. Some nice restaurants are tucked away in its small streets, along with pubs, local shops, and a few archaeological treasures.

Testaccio

This neighborhood is named for Monte Testaccio, which is not a mountain but actually a heap of broken pots collected in A.D. 55 after Emperor Nero whimsically ordered that the shards *(testae)* be gathered and dumped here. Though the top of this dangerously shifting mountain is closed to visitors (the stack, now covered with dirt and grass, is 200 feet high), dwellings that were dug into its lower slopes over the centuries still exist. Many of them now house restaurants and jazz clubs. Testaccio is a real Roman neighborhood, famous for its nightlife; big crowds of people flock here after dark, particularly in summer. During the day, it is quieter, though livened by an open-air food market.

Trastevere

Located on the western bank of the Tiber at the foot of the **Gianicolo** hill, this neighborhood is just across the river from the Aventino. Literally meaning "on the other side of the Tiber," during ancient Roman times, this was the traditional (and rather seedy) residence of poorer artisans and workers. Its character was preserved during the Middle Ages and the Renaissance, and to some extent up to the last century. In recent times, though, it has been largely transformed into an artsy, cultured neighborhood, famous for its restaurants, street life, and nightlife, appealing to younger and not-so-young Romans and visitors.

Trevi

At the heart of *il centro* on the east side of the **Corso,** this neighborhood slopes up the Quirinale hill with the magnificent Renaissance presidential (formerly papal) residence as its centerpiece. Aside from the tourist hubbub around its famous fountain — always surrounded by a sea of humanity — it's a relatively unspoiled neighborhood with many small restaurants and shops.

Via Veneto

Made famous by Fellini as the heart of *La Dolce Vita,* this elegant street is lined by famous hotels and a few upscale stores. The environs are very quiet at night and have a number of nice hotels in the side streets but relatively few restaurants and nightspots. Well connected by public transportation, the areas behind the glitzy strip of Via Veneto are actually a good alternative to the glamorous and expensive parts of *il centro,* especially if you go toward **Via XX Settembre** (at the southeastern edge of this neighborhood).

Finding information after you arrive

The main tourist information office is at Via Parigi 5, off Piazza della Repubblica (☎ 06-488991; www.romaturismo.it; Mon–Sat 9 a.m.– 7 p.m.); it offers plenty of literature on Rome and on side trips from the city, plus a free map and a monthly calendar of events. You'll also find a tourist information desk at the international arrivals in the Terminal B of Fiumicino Airport (☎ 06-65956074; daily 8 a.m.–7 p.m.) and several information kiosks around the city near major attractions (daily 9 a.m.– 6 p.m.):

- ✔ **Castel Sant'Angelo,** Piazza Pia, to the west of the Castel Sant'Angelo (☎ 06-68809707; Metro: Ottaviano–San Pietro)

- ✔ **Largo Goldoni,** on Via del Corso at Via Condotti (☎ 06-68136061; Metro: Piazza di Spagna)

- ✔ **Piazza delle Cinque Lune,** off Piazza Navona to the north (☎ 06-68809240; Minibus: 116)

- ✔ **Fori Imperiali,** Piazza Tempio della Pace on Via dei Fori Imperiali (☎ 06-69924307; Metro: Colosseo)

- ✔ **Santa Maria Maggiore,** Via dell'Olmata, on the southeastern side of the church (☎ 06-4740955; Metro: Termini)

- ✔ **Stazione Termini,** Piazza dei Cinquecento, in front of the railroad station (☎ 06-47825194; Metro: Termini)

- ✔ **Stazione Termini,** inside the gallery (☎ 06-48906300; Metro: Termini)

- ✔ **Trastevere,** Piazza Sonnino (☎ 06-58333457; Tram: 8)

- ✔ **San Giovanni,** Piazza San Giovanni in Laterano (☎ 06-77203535; Metro: San Giovanni)

- ✔ **Fontana di Trevi,** Via Minghetti, off Via del Corso (☎ 06-6782988; Minibus: 117, 119)

- ✔ **Palazzo delle Esposizioni,** Via Nazionale (☎ 06-47824525; Bus: 64)

Usually, the staff at the info points in or near Termini station are the most overwhelmed; elsewhere, you'll find people more available to assist you.

The **Holy See,** as a separate state, maintains its own tourist office. It is located in Piazza San Pietro (☎ 06-69884466; Mon–Sat 8:30 a.m.–6 p.m.), just left of the entrance to the Basilica di San Pietro. The office has information on the Vatican and on its tourist attractions and religious events. You may also make reservations for a visit to the Vatican gardens or fill out the form to participate in a papal audience — but we recommend you make a reservation to do so before you leave home (see Chapter 11 for more information).

Getting Around Rome

Rome's historic hills are no myth: They are real — and sometimes even steep. The one myth is that there are only seven of them. Rome may look flat on a map, but it's very hilly — you'll soon understand why locals use mopeds (or cars, unfortunately) and public transportation, and why you see so few bicycles around.

Remember also that the city is thousands of years old, meaning that much of it isn't designed for any mode of conveyance other than the human foot. There are times, however, when you'll welcome public transportation. Taxis, for example, are a great convenience at night when crossing large sections of the city.

Rome is generally very safe, especially in the center, though you should follow all the usual big-city precautions. The most common form of crime is pickpocketing, which is practiced extensively and with great skill at crowded locations, such as on buses and at markets. Roving gangs of gypsy children are now less common than they once were; they virtually surround you, creating distraction and confusion, while some artful dodger picks your pocket. Hold tight to your wallet and purse, and brush your way past with a stern "no." In addition, don't walk on the edge of the sidewalk near the curb — thieves on motor scooters sometimes yank bags or purses from people's shoulders.

Getting a ticket to ride

ATAC (☎ 800-431784 or 06-46952027; www.atac.roma.it), Rome's transport authority, runs all metros, trams, and buses in the city, and one ticket is valid for all public transportation in Rome. You need to buy tickets **before boarding** any mode of transportation, and you must **stamp** them upon boarding, or they aren't valid (on subway and trains, the stamping machines — little yellow boxes — are at the entrance gates; on buses and trams, they're onboard). A regular *biglietto* (ticket) for the bus/metro is valid for 75 minutes and costs 1€ ($1.30). Within the 75 minutes of validity, you can take as many buses and trams as you want, but you can take only one subway ride. If you're on a different bus from the one you stamped your ticket on when you approach the expiration of the 75 minutes of validity, stamp your ticket again at its other end; this will show that you boarded the bus during the period of validity of your ticket and not after it expired, so you'll be in the clear if a ticket inspector boards the bus. You can also get a daily pass called **BIG** and costing 4€ ($5.20), a three-day ticket called **BTI** for 11€ ($14), and a weekly pass called **CIS** for 16€ ($21). All passes give you unlimited rides on bus, metro, and urban trains. You can buy tickets at most bars, tobacconist shops (signed TABACCHI or by a white *T* on a black background), and newsstands. Tickets and passes are also sold at the ticket booths in the metro, at the ATAC bus information booth in front of Stazione Termini (near Platform C), and from machines at many locations (but machines usually take only exact change).

By subway (metropolitana)

Although the Metropolitana, or metro for short, has only two lines, it is the best way to get around because the underground routes don't suffer from the terrible city traffic. In addition, the routes naturally stay the same — unlike the city bus system, which is under constant reorganization. **Line A** and **Line B** cross at the Termini station, which is also the head of many bus lines. A big red *M* marks all metro entrances. Metro A runs near San Pietro, passing Piazza di Spagna and the Palazzo Barberini (Via Veneto) on one side and San Giovanni on the other. Take Line B to get to the Colosseum. The metro runs Sunday through Friday from 5:30 a.m. to 11:30 p.m. and Saturday from 5:30 a.m. to 12:30 a.m.

The Colosseum, Circus Maximus, and Cavour stops on Line B don't offer full elevator/lift service and aren't disabled accessible. (For tips for travelers with disabilities, see Chapter 6.)

By bus (autobus)

The ATAC bus system is large and under continuous improvement. However, Rome's ancient layout resists any real modernization, so things don't always go smoothly: Buses are very crowded at rush hour, and traffic jams are endemic. Still, buses remain an excellent resource because they go absolutely everywhere in Rome, especially the diminutive **electric buses** that are the only vehicles allowed in the tiny, narrow streets of the historical heart of the city. These electric buses are the ones you'll be using most often: **115** in Trastevere and on the Gianicolo; **116, 116T, 117,** and **119** in *il centro*. Of the large number of regular bus lines that service Rome — and many of them overlap in the center of town — the bus you're most likely to use is **64** (Stazione Termini–Vatican). Most buses run daily from 5:30 a.m. to 12:30 a.m., but some stop at 8.30 p.m. A few night lines are marked with an *N* for *notturno* (night); they usually run every hour, leaving the ends of the line on the hour.

When you arrive in Rome, one of the first things you should do is pick up an updated bus map from the bus information booth outside the Termini station in Piazza dei Cinquecento, provided that it has one — there is such a demand that the government can never print enough. Routes we mention in this book may have changed.

On foot

Walking is by far the best way to experience Rome, because you see the most as you wander the curving streets that merge, narrow to almost shoulder width, change names, and meander among beautiful old buildings. Wear very comfortable shoes, and be ready to switch to another form of transportation — usually handy — when you get tired.

Rome's Metropolitana (Subway)

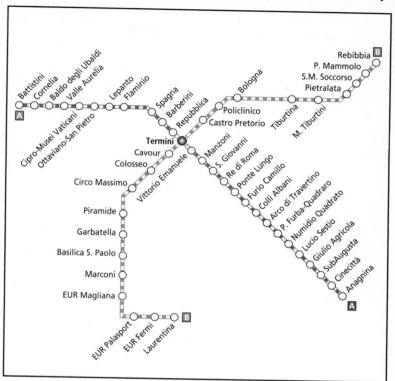

 To enjoy Rome's delightful labyrinth, you need a good map. The free tourist-office map is quite good, but it doesn't have a *stradario* (street directory), which is essential for locating addresses. You can buy a detailed city map with a *stradario* at any newsstand and many bookstores.

By tram

Rome still has a few tram lines, which belong to the same system as the buses. They aren't as spectacular as the cable cars in San Francisco, but they're fun to ride. Also, trams have a separate lane to themselves, so they're less frequently stopped by traffic. The routes are long, however, and you may have an extended — though scenic — ride on your way to your destination. A line we like a lot is the **3**, which passes by the Basilica di San Giovanni and the Colosseum. Another line that you're likely to use is number **8** to Trastevere. Trams are indicated on the free ATAC bus map by a green line.

Rome's Electric Buses

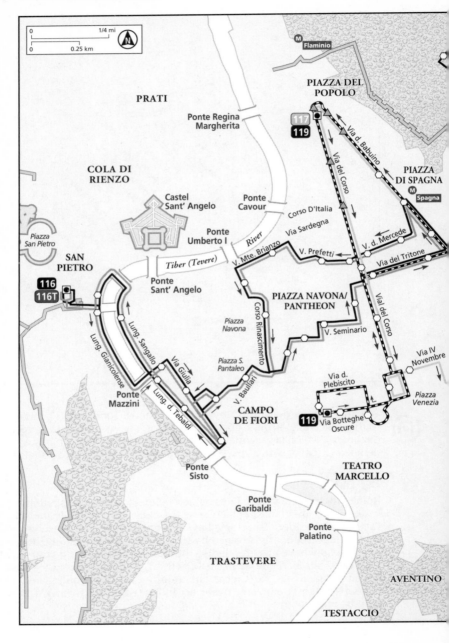

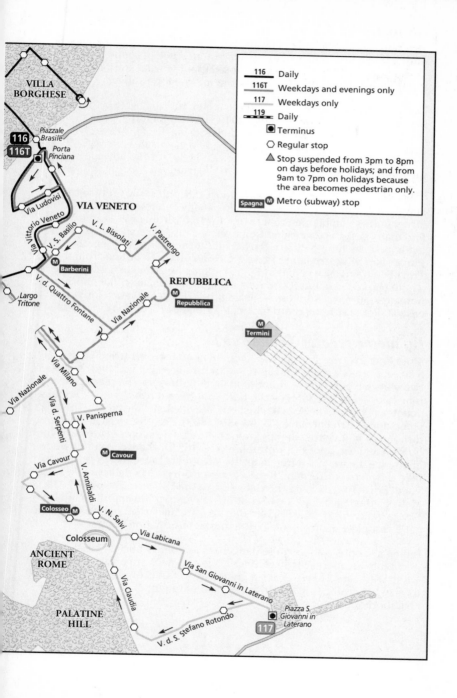

116 — Daily
116T — Weekdays and evenings only
117 — Weekdays only
119 — Daily
● Terminus
○ Regular stop
▲ Stop suspended from 3pm to 8pm on days before holidays; and from 9am to 7pm on holidays because the area becomes pedestrian only.
Spagna Ⓜ Metro (subway) stop

VILLA BORGHESE

Piazzale Brasile
116
116T
Porta Pinciana
Via Ludovisi
VIA VENETO
Via Vittorio Veneto
V. L. Bissolati
V. Pastrengo
V. S. Basilio
Ⓜ Barberini
V. d. Quattro Fontane
Largo Tritone
Via Nazionale
REPUBBLICA
Ⓜ Repubblica
Ⓜ Termini
Via Milano
Via Nazionale
Via d. Serpenti
V. Panisperna
Ⓜ Cavour
V. Annibaldi
Via Cavour
Colosseo Ⓜ
V. N. Salvi
Via Labicana
Colosseum
ANCIENT ROME
Via San Giovanni in Laterano
Via Claudia
PALATINE HILL
V. d. S. Stefano Rotondo
117
Piazza S. Giovanni in Laterano

By taxi

Taxi rates are reasonable in Rome, but taking a taxi can be expensive during those busy times of day when you're stuck in traffic. They're a great resource for getting to your hotel from the train station and traveling around at night after the buses and metro stop running.

Taxi fare starts at 2.35€ ($3), and the meter adds 0.80€ ($1) for every kilometer (⅗ mile) if you're moving at least 20kmph (12 mph); if you're stuck in traffic, the meter racks up a charge of .10€ (13¢) every 19 seconds. Don't forget the night surcharge (10 p.m.–6 a.m.) of 2.60€ ($3.40), the Sunday and holiday surcharge of 1€ ($1.30), or the luggage supplement of 1€ ($1.30) for each bag put in the trunk.

Taxis don't cruise the streets, as in most U.S. cities; they return to taxi stands and wait for a call. Hence, you usually cannot hail a taxi on the street unless you happen to find one that's returning to a stand. You'll find many taxi stands around Rome, especially in *il centro* near major landmarks, including **Piazza Barberini** (at the foot of Via Veneto), **Piazza San Silvestro,** and **Piazza SS. Apostoli** (both not far from the Trevi Fountain). You can identify taxi stands by a smallish telephone on a pole marked TAXI. But if you're starting from a place with a phone — a hotel, restaurant, and so on — asking the staff to call a taxi for you is easiest. For a **24-hour radio taxi,** call ☎ **06-88177,** 06-6645, or 06-4994.

By motor scooter (motorino)

Most Romans travel around via moped, or so it seems when you're on a street corner waiting for the signal to turn green. If you have some two-wheel experience — Rome is most definitely *not* the place to learn how to operate a scooter — the best spot to rent a *motorino* is **Treno e Scooter (TeS)** on Via Marsala, just outside Stazione Termini by the taxi stand and metro entrance (☎ **06-48905823**). TeS gives you a 10 percent discount if you've traveled by train that day. The scooters are very good quality, and the prices (for example, 52€/$68 for the weekend) include insurance, taxes, and a free map; TeS also rents bicycles. To get there, take the metro to Termini. **Rent a Scooter Borgo,** Via delle Grazie 2, off Via di Porta Angelica, on the right side of the Vatican (☎ **06-6877239;** Metro: Ottaviano), and **New Scooter,** Via Quattro Novembre 96, up from Piazza Venezia (☎ **06-6790300;** Bus: 64), are also good options. You can get a complete list from one of the tourist information points.

Riding a scooter can be quite dangerous in Rome's busiest areas. Accidents are increasingly common, and scooters are pretty flimsy compared with cars. However, it's a great way to travel on Sundays and holidays, when traffic is light and fewer buses are out, or to explore quiet neighborhoods.

Chapter 9

Checking In at Rome's Best Hotels

*R*ome has been a magnet for travelers for literally thousands of years. More than a few inns can claim several centuries of service, and as the flow of visitors remains strong, new hotels keep opening every year. This creates an enormous variety in Rome's hotels and gives lodging in Rome a different character from that of, say, the United States. Although the hotel industry in Rome has made enormous progress toward standardization and upgrading of lodging in line with the expectations of international travelers, there are cultural differences that are hard to iron out — and why not, because traveling also means experiencing a different culture? That's not to say you shouldn't be comfortable. This chapter gives important tips on choosing among a wide, and in some cases unfamiliar, variety of choices.

Knowing Your Roman Hotels: What to Expect

Destination to some 20 million tourists every year, Rome offers a huge choice of accommodations, from very basic to supremely elegant, from family-run historical hotels to international chains, and from mom-and-pop places to the haunts of jet setters. Most hotels are private businesses, not belonging to a chain. Some may belong to a hotel association — which fixes standards, gives a common approach, or simply allows some economies of scale. With such a variety, you'll certainly find what you need, but keep in mind that in general, rooms — especially bathrooms — and beds tend to be smaller than what you're used at home. Space is at a premium, especially in the historical palaces within *il centro storico* (the historic center) — which is where you want to be — and only the most expensive hotels can offer sizable rooms and bathrooms.

Because medieval and Renaissance buildings were not designed for elevators, they are rare — absent in the cheaper hotels — and often start from a landing above street level. Steps are ubiquitous, so if they're a problem for you, make sure to call and ask. When you do, be very specific, and ask how many steps you have to climb *from the street*. Even in the most expensive hotels, there might be a short flight of steps to reach the lobby from the street and another to reach the elevator. The street level of Renaissance and baroque *palazzi* was not a living floor (imagine the stench of those times), and the main stairwell usually starts from an internal alcove or courtyard. Elevators have commonly been constructed inside the narrow stairwell enclosed by the staircases — the only space available — and this is why they often can't be accessed from curbside.

Then there are amenities: Some that are commonplace in the United States — big ice machines, for instance — are virtually unknown in Italy. But others, such as air-conditioning and satellite TV — necessary to view English-language programs — are now more the rule than the exception, although you may have to pay extra for them in smaller and cheaper hotels (we spell this out in our write-ups). By the way, regular TVs are standard except in the cheapest accommodations, but they don't offer English-language programs. Then again, you didn't go to Italy to watch TV, did you? And you can always step out of your hotel and sit at the terrace of a nearby cafe for that iced drink. . . .

Fortunately, soundproofed rooms are commonplace — and even in the cheaper hotels, the thickness of the old walls helps protect you from noisy neighbors and the roar of the traffic outside. Street noise, by the way, is a problem that soundproofed windows cannot eliminate if you like to sleep with your window open. If that is the case, ask for an inner room.

Smoking has recently been banned from public places in Rome, so all hotel lobbies and breakfast rooms are smoke free. Rooms, though, are considered private; hence, you are allowed to smoke there. Make sure to specify whether you want a smoke-free room when you make your reservation.

Another big difference is breakfast: Although this important meal is generally included in your room rate, and although an increasing number of hotels offer a buffet, eggs and hot dishes are served only at the most expensive hotels. The usual continental buffet includes a choice of breads, jams, and fruit; sometimes cakes; and usually cereals, yogurt, cheese, and cold cuts. Sometimes you can order — and pay extra for — eggs and bacon if they aren't on the spread.

One more thing: When you make a hotel reservation back home, you probably don't ask about the flooring. In Rome, you'll often find tile or marble floors, sometimes wood, and only rarely carpeting. So bring slippers to get around the room and go to the bathroom in the cooler months if you don't want to get cold feet!

Finding the Best Room at the Best Rate

Getting the room you want at the right price is the name of the game. Many hotels have been refurbished recently, and several new ones have opened, but prices have risen sharply in recent years. A weak dollar and poor exchange rate haven't helped. Rome is a capital city, and capital cities the world over are expensive. The best way to get a deal is to plan well in advance.

Finding the best rate

The **rack rate** is the maximum rate a hotel can charge for a room. That's the rate you get if you walk in off the street at the peak of high season and ask for a room for the night when the hotel is almost full. You see these rates printed on the fire/emergency-exit diagrams posted on the back of your hotel-room door.

In Rome, where most hotels don't belong to chains, you'll rarely be charged the rack rate. Chains are happy to charge you the rack rate, but you can almost always do better. Perhaps the best way to avoid paying the rack rate is surprisingly simple: Just ask for a cheaper or discounted rate. You may be pleasantly surprised.

The rate you pay for a room usually depends on many factors — chief among them being how you make your reservation. In Rome, a travel agent may be able to negotiate a better price than you can get by yourself, but only with those hotels belonging to a chain. (That's because the hotel often gives the agent a discount in exchange for steering his or her business toward that hotel.) Exploring package tours, in which both airline fares and hotel rooms are priced at a discount, is also worthwhile. (See Chapter 5 for more on this.)

 With hotel chains, reserving a room through the central reservation toll-free number may result in a lower rate than calling the hotel directly. On the other hand, the central reservation number may not know about discount rates for special events at specific locations. Your best bet is to call both the local number and the toll-free number, and see which one gives you a better deal.

As a general rule, nonchain hotels in Rome will give you their lowest price when you make your reservation directly. Room rates change with the season and with occupancy: If a hotel is half-empty, you'll likely get a better rate than if it has only one room available — but the rates they agree on with agents are based on seasons, not occupancy, and therefore tend to be higher. Refer to Chapter 3 for more details on high and low seasons in Rome.

Most hotels in Rome offer special-event deals — such as Easter, the big shopping sales in January, or a special art exhibition (see Chapter 3 for a calendar of events). They may also offer a special rate for a two- or three-night stay and sometimes a weekend rate (which you may see abbreviated *WE* elsewhere). Always ask if there are any specials when you make your reservation. Also, always check the hotel's Web site — it often offers special Internet deals (see "Surfing the Web for hotel deals," later in this chapter).

Finally, if you're Irish or British, be sure to mention membership in any automobile clubs, which may have reciprocity with Automobile Club d'Italia or the Touring Club Italiano; you may get a 10 percent discount. Frequent-flier programs with Alitalia and sometimes other European carriers also may get you some points. Unfortunately, U.S. associations such as AARP and AAA usually have nothing to do with private Italian businesses, although some international chains offer discounts for these associations.

Surfing the Web for hotel deals

Shopping online for hotels is generally done one of two ways: through the hotel's own Web site or through an independent booking agency (or a fare-service agency like Priceline.com). Booking through the **hotel's own Web site** is definitely the way to go in Rome: Many private hotels have started to offer special online rates, which are often cheaper even than what an agency can get you for the same place. Some also offer significant discounts for advance booking, provided that you also pay in advance. Another method is to narrow your options via one of the Internet agencies listed later in this section and then check the Web site of the hotel you selected directly. You'll often find that you can do better on the hotel's site — the hotel doesn't have to pay any agency fees.

Internet hotel agencies have multiplied in mind-boggling numbers lately, competing for the business of millions of consumers surfing for accommodations around the world. This competitiveness can be a boon to consumers who have the patience and time to shop and compare the online sites for good deals — but shop you must, because prices can vary considerably from site to site. And keep in mind that hotels at the top of a site's listing may be there for no other reason than it paid money to get the placement. Among the many sites existing for Rome, we recommend **Venere Net** (www.venere.com), which is very comprehensive and user friendly, as well as **Roma Hotels** (www.roma-hotels.com) and the **Cooperativa Il Sogno** (www.romeguide.it), which is also comprehensive and has good descriptions of the hotels (with pictures). Among the intercontinental agencies, **hoteldiscount!com** (www.180096hotel.com), which lists bargain room rates at many hotels in Rome, is good, as is **Late Rooms.com** (www.it.laterooms.com) — excellent for last-minute deals on hotels and B&Bs. Other sites to check are **Italyhotelink.com** (www.italyhotelink.com), **ITWG.com** (www.itwg.com), **Welcome to Italy** (www.wel.it), **Europa Hotels** (www.europa-hotels.com), and **Italy Hotels** (www.hotels-in-italy.com).

Most intercontinental sites tend to list only a few hotels in Rome. Still, some may offer good deals, and it is worth checking just in case.

Expedia offers special deals and "virtual tours" or photos of available rooms so you can see what you're paying for (a feature that helps counter the claims that the best rooms are often held back from bargain-booking Web sites). **Travelocity** posts frank customer reviews and ranks its properties according to the AAA rating system. Also reliable and easy to use is **Hotels.com**. **InnSite** (`www.innsite.com`) is a good source for locating B&Bs in Rome — you can see pictures of the rooms and check prices and availability, though keep in mind that the descriptions are written by the innkeepers (and getting an inn listed is free).

In the opaque Web site category, **Priceline** and **Hotwire** are even better for hotels than for airfares; with both, you're allowed to pick the neighborhood and quality level of your hotel — but that's all — before offering up your money. Priceline's hotel product is much better at getting five-star lodging for three-star prices than at finding anything at the bottom of the scale. On the downside, many hotels stick Priceline guests in their least desirable rooms. Be sure to go to the **BiddingforTravel** Web site (`www.biddingfortravel.com`) before bidding on a hotel room on Priceline; it features a fairly up-to-date list of hotels that Priceline uses in major cities, including Rome. For both Priceline and Hotwire, you pay up front, and the fee is nonrefundable. *Note:* Some hotels don't provide loyalty-program credits or points or other frequent-stay amenities when you book a room through opaque online services.

 If you book your room through one of these online services, always **get a confirmation number,** and **make a printout** of any online booking transaction in case your reservation is lost. Actually, after you've reserved your rooms, it doesn't hurt to contact your hotel and request a confirmation via fax or e-mail, to eliminate the chance of your arriving at a hotel that has no record of your reservation. Make sure that you bring this confirmation fax/e-mail with you to Italy.

Reserving the best room

First and foremost, make your reservations well ahead of time, especially if you decide to stay in a small hotel: The best rooms are the first to go.

 After you make your reservation, asking one or two more pointed questions can go a long way toward making sure you get the best room in the house. Ask for a corner room. Corner rooms are usually larger, quieter, and have more windows and light than standard rooms, and they don't always cost more. (This may not be true, though, if the hotel occupies only part of a historical building, where corner rooms may actually be smaller and darker.) Always ask if the hotel is renovating; if it is, request a room away from the renovation work. Inquire, too, about the location of elevators, restaurants, and bars in the hotel — all sources of annoying noise. And if you aren't happy with your room when you arrive, talk to the front desk. If the hotel has another room, it should be happy to accommodate you, within reason.

Finding Alternative Accommodations: Apartments to Convents

Rome offers several accommodation options beyond hotels. If you plan to stay for a week or more, you may want to consider renting an apartment. Another option is to stay at one of the many convents and other religious houses that rent out rooms; they allow couples, and although the rooms aren't monastic cells, they don't offer many frills. In this book, we don't list religious houses that accept guests, because they usually have curfews (10 or 11 p.m., sometimes even earlier), and we don't think that you want to deal with that, especially if your trip is relatively short. If you're interested, however, the **Cooperativa Il Sogno** (www.romeguide.it) is probably your best resource.

If you want to rent an apartment, consult an organization that specializes in such arrangements. **Vacation Rentals by Owner** (www.vrbo.com) lists hundreds of homes for rent (listings are in English). Each listing contains pictures, prices, and descriptions of the area where the house or apartment is located. Usually, you deal directly with the owner, so you may save considerably over the rates that would be charged for the same property by a broker.

B&Bs are also an option, but don't expect romantic getaways: In Rome, a B&B is often just a one-room operation in somebody's home where you also get breakfast. Most of the Italy-based Internet agencies also maintain apartment and B&Bs listings (see the section "Surfing the Web for hotel deals," earlier in this chapter). Other agencies to try are **Hideaways International** (767 Islington St., Portsmouth, NH 03801; ☎ 800/843-4433; www.hideaways.com), **At Home Abroad** (405 E. 56th St., Suite 6H, New York, NY 10022; ☎ 212/421-9165), and **Rentals in Italy** (700 East Main St., Ventura, CA 93001; ☎ 800/726-6702 or 805/641-1650; www.rentvillas.com).

Arriving without a Reservation

In Rome, arriving without a room reservation is usually not a problem: You will find *something*, although you may have to compromise with location and price. The hotel desks at the airport and in the train station Termini are the best place to start. The staff will call around town and find you a room, if one is available. (In the high season, there's always the risk that rooms aren't available — or at least not in your price range.) Sometimes this service is free, and sometimes you have to pay a small fee.

Rome's Best Hotels

In selecting our favorite hotels, we use cleanliness, comfort, and the most amenities at the best prices as essential criteria. All the hotels we list in this section are conveniently located in the center of Rome, have private bathrooms, and offer basic amenities. We always specify in the description if a hotel has no elevator, satellite TV, or air-conditioning. In addition to giving you exact prices, we use a system of dollar signs ($) to show a range of costs for hotels (see Table 9-1). The dollar signs correspond to rack rates (nondiscounted, standard rates) for a double room. If the hotel offers triples, quads, or suites, we also give rack rates for those. To help you further with the selection, we've created quick-reference indexes at the end of this chapter that list all the hotels by neighborhood and by dollar sign.

Table 9-1	Key to Hotel Dollar Signs	
Dollar Sign(s)	**Price Range**	**What to Expect**
$	120€ ($156) or less	No frills but dignified; usually family-run small hotels housed in oldish buildings. Rooms tend to be small; televisions are not necessarily provided; and you may have to pay extra for air-conditioning. These hotels may not accept credit cards and may not have an elevator.
$$	121€–230€ ($157–$299)	These are middle-range hotels: All guest rooms have air-conditioning and a good level of amenities and service. Bathrooms tend to be small at the bottom end of the scale, but bedrooms are always roomy and pleasantly furnished. The category also includes some of the higher-end hotels that are located in less glamorous areas.
$$$	231€–350€ ($300–$455)	These are superior hotels where you get a bathroom that's really a room, not a corner, and bedrooms that are spacious and have a number of amenities; they may even be luxurious in the less expensive neighborhoods. Service is excellent, and a nice buffet breakfast is usually included.
$$$$	351€ ($456) and up	These are deluxe hotels, sometimes owned by international interests. They offer lots of space; attentive professional staff; and top amenities, ranging from antique furnishings and fine linen to lavish bathrooms, free parking (a luxury in Rome), gyms, spas, terraces, and often gardens with pools. Usually, an American-style breakfast is included. Hotels in this category occupy new or very historic buildings, such as former aristocratic *palazzos* or villas.

Important note: Very few hotels in Rome have a garage or their own parking lot; instead, they usually have some kind of agreement with a nearby facility for somewhat reduced rates. If you plan to bring a car (which we warmly discourage — see Chapter 7), ask your hotel for the rates when you book your room, but expect to pay between 15€ and 30€ ($20–$39) per day.

Bernini Bristol
$$$$ Via Veneto

One of the best hotels in Rome, we particularly appreciate it for its great position — just at the foot of Via Veneto — and its impeccable service, provided at (relatively) moderate rates. Opened in 1874, it served as the background location for many scenes of Dan Brown's novel *Angels and Demons.* Its guest rooms are classically furnished with fine linen and elegant marble baths; some of them offer great views over *il centro.* From the splendid rooftop restaurant, the Olympus, you can enjoy a 360-degree view over Rome; the hotel also has a spa and gym for its guests. It sometimes has great Internet specials.

See map p. 104. Piazza Barberini 23. ☎ *06-488931. Fax: 06-4824266.* www.bernini bristol.com. *Metro: Line A to Barberini. Rack rates: 530€ ($689) double; suites 785€ ($1,026) and up. AE, DC, MC, V.*

Casa Kolbe
$ Teatro Marcello

Near the Jewish Ghetto, steps from the major classical sites — the Capitoline Hill, Palatine Hill, Roman Forum, and Colosseum — this is an old-fashioned hotel in a former convent. The guest rooms are clean but a little worn, and the furnishings are simple. For the price, however, you can't beat it. This is a peaceful area, and the quietest rooms overlook the small inner garden. Many tour groups book here, so reserve in advance. A number of rooms are disabled-accessible, but there is no air-conditioning. Room-and-board combinations are available.

See map p. 104. Via San Teodoro 44. ☎ *06-6794974. Fax: 06-69941550. Bus: 60 or 81 to Bocca della Verità; then walk east to Via San Teodoro. Rack rates: 90€ ($117) double. Rates include breakfast. AE, DC, MC, V.*

Casa Valdese
$ Prati

Located on the Vatican side of the river, near Castel Sant'Angelo and the shopping district of Cola di Rienzo, this small hotel offers a great value. The name "Valdese" refers to the Protestant group of Swiss origin, and the hotel reflects this in its simple but spotlessly clean and pleasant rooms. The very moderate prices and the excellent location — basically across the river from Piazza del Popolo — are other pluses.

See map p. 104. Via A. Farnese 18, off Via Cola di Rienzo. ☎ **06-3218222.** *Fax: 06-3211843. Metro: Lepanto. Via Farnese is the first right as you walk toward the river on Via Giulio Cesare. Rack rates: 103€–135€ ($134–$176) double. Rates include breakfast. AE, V.*

City Hotel
$$ Piazza di Spagna/Via Veneto

Located on the third floor of a nice *palazzo* (with an elevator from street level), this hotel offers comfortable rooms, well appointed and recently renovated, and decent-size marble and tile bathrooms, all at moderate prices. Nice woodwork and bright spaces add to the atmosphere. The furnishings are tasteful, and the service, excellent. It also has the great advantage of a perfect location, walking distance from the Piazza di Spagna (Spanish Steps) and the Fontana di Trevi (Trevi Fountain), and very well connected to public transportation — a rare advantage in *il centro*.

See map p. 104. Via Due Macelli 97. ☎ **06-6784037.** *Fax: 06-6797972.* www.paginegialle.it/cityhotel. *Metro: Barberini; then take the fifth right as you walk downhill on Via del Tritone: 200€ ($260) double; 225€ ($293) junior suite. Rates include buffet breakfast. AE, DC, MC, V.*

Grand Hotel de la Minerve
$$$$ Navona/Pantheon

This very elegant hotel is located in one of our preferred small squares in the center of Rome and offers magnificent accommodations and service. Housed in a 17th-century palace, the spacious guest rooms are elegantly appointed with stylish contemporary furnishings whispering of comfort and excellent taste; some of the rooms have beautifully decorated ceilings with fine moldings. The marble bathrooms are spacious and with all manner of amenities. In the warm season, the hotel's restaurant moves to the roof garden, where you can enjoy a gorgeous view over the dome-studded skyline. You can enjoy live music in the bar every evening. A very nice gym is located on the premises.

See map p. 104. Piazza della Minerva 69. ☎ **06-695201.** *Fax: 06-6794165.* www.grandhoteldelaminerve.it. *Bus: 116 to Pantheon; 64 or 70 to Largo Argentina. Rack rates: 420€–550€ double ($546–$710); suites 580€ ($754) and up. AE, DC, MC, V.*

Hotel Andreotti
$$ Repubblica

This quietly elegant hotel is within walking distance of many attractions and very accessible to public transportation. Its location, in a somewhat less glamorous area of the center, means that you get better service and amenities for a lower price. Guest rooms are large and comfortable, each differently furnished but all in classic style, and bathrooms are good size and modern; some rooms have ceilings decorated with original moldings. The courteous service is a plus.

Rome Accommodations

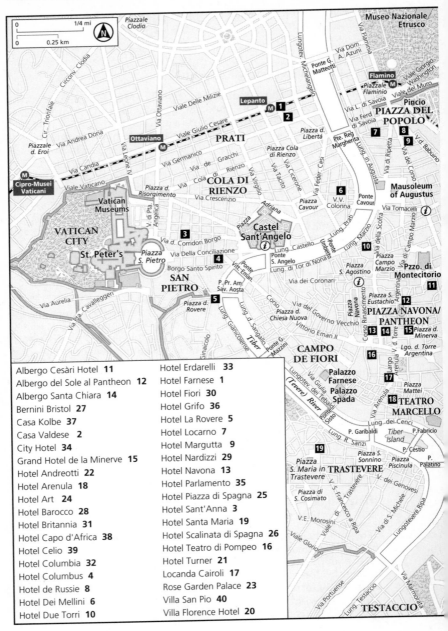

Albergo Cesàri Hotel **11**	Hotel Erdarelli **33**
Albergo del Sole al Pantheon **12**	Hotel Farnese **1**
Albergo Santa Chiara **14**	Hotel Fiori **30**
Bernini Bristol **27**	Hotel Grifo **36**
Casa Kolbe **37**	Hotel La Rovere **5**
Casa Valdese **2**	Hotel Locarno **7**
City Hotel **34**	Hotel Margutta **9**
Grand Hotel de la Minerve **15**	Hotel Nardizzi **29**
Hotel Andreotti **22**	Hotel Navona **13**
Hotel Arenula **18**	Hotel Parlamento **35**
Hotel Art **24**	Hotel Piazza di Spagna **25**
Hotel Barocco **28**	Hotel Sant'Anna **3**
Hotel Britannia **31**	Hotel Santa Maria **19**
Hotel Capo d'Africa **38**	Hotel Scalinata di Spagna **26**
Hotel Celio **39**	Hotel Teatro di Pompeo **16**
Hotel Columbia **32**	Hotel Turner **21**
Hotel Columbus **4**	Locanda Cairoli **17**
Hotel de Russie **8**	Rose Garden Palace **23**
Hotel Dei Mellini **6**	Villa San Pio **40**
Hotel Due Torri **10**	Villa Florence Hotel **20**

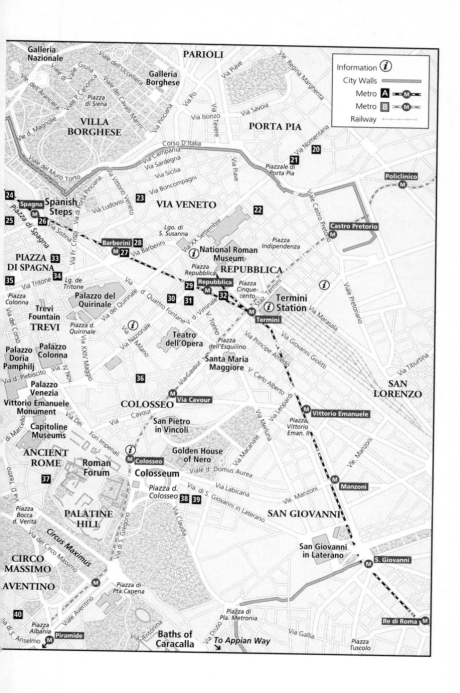

See map p. 104. Via Castelfidardo 55, at the corner of Via Cernaia. ☎ *06-4441006. Fax: 06-4453777.* www.hotelandreotti.it. *Metro: Repubblica. Walk east on Via Cernaia for 4 short blocks. Rack rates: 215€ ($280) double; 300€ ($390) triple. Rates include breakfast. AE, DC, MC, V.*

Hotel Arenula
$ Campo de' Fiori/Teatro Marcello

This hotel offers large and well-appointed guest rooms at moderate prices. Above all, you can't beat the location. On the second floor of a nice *palazzo*, with a beautiful marble spiral staircase leading to it (but be warned — there is no elevator), it lies within walking distance of many of the center's main attractions and to buses and trams that will take you to the others. The nearby Campo is busy with a market during the day and dining and nightlife after dark. The hotel's guest rooms are simple but bright, with decent-size bathrooms and showers, and good amenities.

See map p. 104. Via Santa Maria de' Calderari 47, off Via Arenula. ☎ *06-6879454. Fax: 06-6896188.* www.hotelarenula.com. *Bus: 64, 70, 170, 492, 40 to Largo Argentina. Walk south on Via Arenula, and take the fourth street on your left. Rack rates: 125€ double ($163). Rates include buffet breakfast. AE, DC, MC, V.*

Hotel Art
$$$$ Piazza di Spagna

This new hotel, located in one of the most desirable areas of Rome, edges beyond modern into the realm of postmodern. If you don't get a room here, go just to see the hall and the court, with its crystal staircase and designer-contemporary furnishings, and the bar — created in the columned and frescoed chapel of a palace. All these striking features illustrate the artistic "eclecticism" on which the hotel prides itself. Each floor is color coordinated with the details of the rooms (even down to the stationery and pens), and much of the furniture is made of fine hardwoods. Hotel Art has much the feel of the boutique hotels you find in all the great cities of the world. The accent is on comfort; service; and, of course, style. Check its Web site for Internet specials.

See map p. 104. Via Margutta 56, next to via del Babuino. ☎ *06-328711. Fax: 06-36003995.* www.hotelart.it. *Metro: Piazza di Spagna. Walk on Via del Babuino; take the first right and then the first left. Rack rates: 387€–490€ ($503–$637) double; 930€ ($1,209) suite. Rates include breakfast. AE, DC, MC, V.*

Hotel Britannia
$$–$$$ Repubblica

This recently renovated hotel offers nicely appointed rooms at moderate prices and is within walking distance of attractions and transportation. The elegant guest rooms are furnished in neoclassical style and are large; some have private terraces or vaulted ceilings and other architectural details. The marble bathrooms include a sun-tanning lamp. Children under 10 stay free in parents' room.

See map p. 104. Via Napoli 64, off Via Nazionale. ☎ *06-4883153. Fax: 06-4882343.* www.hotelbritannia.it. *Metro: Repubblica. Walk 2 blocks on Via Nazional, and turn left. Rack rates: 233€ ($303) double; 285€ ($371) triple. Rates include buffet breakfast. AE, DC. MC, V.*

Hotel Capo d'Africa
$$$ Colosseo

This elegant new hotel is located on an atmospheric street between the Colosseum and San Giovanni, close to most of the sights of Ancient Rome. Run by the same owners as the Hotel Dei Mellini (see review later in this chapter) and known for its excellent service, the Capo d'Africa offers comfortable rooms furnished in a warm, modern-ethnic style. The marble bathrooms are good size and nicely fitted out. The hotel also offers some suites and wheelchair-accessible rooms. Don't miss the roof terrace and its splendid views.

See map p. 104. Via Capo d'Africa 54. ☎ *06-772801. Fax: 06-77280801.* www.hotel capodafrica.com. *Metro: Colosseo. Walk southeast across Piazza del Colosseo to Via Capo d'Africa. Rack rates: 320€ ($416) double; suites 500€ ($650) and up. Rates include buffet breakfast. AE, DC, MC, V.*

Hotel Celio
$$$ Colosseo

This small hotel is a real jewel, housed in an 1870 building just steps from some of the city's most famous monuments. Rooms are individually decorated in Renaissance and Ancient Roman style, with mosaic floors and frescoed walls. The beautiful bathrooms are done in marble and mosaics. The decoration and the furnishings — fine modern reproductions and some antiques — are the essence of what people mean by "old-world charm." The roof terrace, where breakfast is served in the fine weather, enjoys gorgeous views over Ancient Rome — as do the three private terraces of the Pompeian suite.

See map p. 104. Via dei Santissimi Quattro 35/c. ☎ *06-70495333. Fax: 06 7096377.* www.hotelcelio.com. *Metro: Colosseo. Walk east across Piazza del Colosseo to Via dei Santissimi Quattro. Rack rates: 290€–310€ ($377–$403) double; 390€ ($507) triple; 420€ ($546) quad; 580€–680€ ($754–$884) suite. Rates include buffet breakfast. AE, DC, MC, V.*

Hotel Columbia
$$ Repubblica

This refined hotel, recently renovated, has been under the same family management since 1900. This part of *il centro* offers excellent value and convenience. Guest rooms are spacious and bright, many with beamed ceilings, some with arched windows or Murano chandeliers. All rooms are individually furnished with modern beds and antiques or quality reproductions. Bathrooms are good size and modern. The hotel also has a pleasant roof garden with a bar, where breakfast is served.

See map p. 104. Via Viminale 15. ☎ *06-4744289. Fax: 06-4740209.* www.hotel columbia.com. *Metro: Line A to Repubblica; then walk toward Stazione Termini. Rack rates: 225€ ($293) double; 290€ ($377) triple. Rates include buffet breakfast. AE, DC, MC, V.*

Hotel de Russie
$$$$ Piazza di Spagna

Making the lists of the world's top hotels ever since it opened in 2000, the Russie is the most elegant place to stay in Rome, offering superb location, service, and accommodations. If you stay here, you'll follow the steps of the rich and famous — Bill and Chelsea Clinton, among others. Housed in a beautiful *palazzo* enclosing a delightful terrace garden, the hotel is furnished in extremely tasteful and classy contemporary Italian style, and guest rooms have all kinds of amenities. You'll also find a spa with sauna; a health club; and, amazingly enough, a swimming pool. The restaurant on the premises, Le Jardin du Russie, gets excellent reviews.

See map p. 104. Via del Babuino 9. ☎ *06-328881. Fax: 06-32888888.* www.hotelde russie.it. *Metro: Piazza di Spagna. Rack rates: 677€–825€ ($879–$1,076) double; 920€ ($1,196) studio; suites 1,210€ ($1,560) and up. AE, DC, MC, V.*

Hotel Dei Mellini
$$$ Prati

Walking distance from Piazza del Popolo and Castel Sant'Angelo, this new hotel has a sophisticated atmosphere, with a relaxing internal garden and a contemporary-art collection in the public areas. Guest rooms are pleasantly furnished in modern-classic style with marble bathrooms; some rooms have private terraces. Children up to age 12 stay free in parents' room.

See map p. 104. Via Muzio Clementi 81, off Via Colonna. ☎ *06-324771. Fax: 06-32477801.* www.hotelmellini.com. *Bus: 30, 70, 81, 87, 186, 492 to Via Colonna. Rack rates: 350€ ($455) double; 450€–550€ ($585–$715) suite. AE, DC, MC, V.*

Hotel Due Torri
$$$ Navona/Pantheon

This small hotel, located in one of the most romantic areas of *il centro*, offers elegant and stylish accommodations. Once the residence of cardinals and bishops, it has been completely restored. The beautiful original floors *alla veneziana* (marble and colored cement mosaic) or in parquet, the antiques and quality reproduction furnishings, and the handsome bathrooms all contribute to a pleasant stay. Make your reservations early — the hotel doesn't have many rooms.

See map p. 104. Vicolo del Leonetto 23. ☎ **06-68806956** *or 06-6876983. Fax: 06-6865442.* www.hotelduetorriroma.com. *Minibus: 116. Bus: 30, 70, 81, 87, 186, 492 to Largo Nicosia. Walk 1 short block south on Via Campana. Vicolo del Leonetto is to your right. Rack rates: 235€ ($306) double; 315€ ($410) apartment-suite. Rates include breakfast. AE, DC, MC, V.*

Hotel Fiori
$$ **Repubblica**

This small family-run hotel offers a central location, kindly service, and comfortable accommodations at a moderate (for Rome) price. Guest rooms are large and bright, with wooden or tiled floors and with good-size bathrooms and showers. Furnishings are tasteful and of high quality in reproduction style.

See map p. 104. Via Nazionale 163. ☎ **06-6797212.** *Fax: 06-6795433.* www.travel. it/roma/hotelfiori. *Minibus: 117. Bus: 40, 60, 64, 70, 170 to Via Nazionale. Rack rates: 180€ ($234) double; 230€ ($299) triple; 250€ ($325) quad. AE, DC, MC, V.*

Hotel Farnese
$$$ **Prati**

Tucked behind Castel Sant'Angelo in a quiet neighborhood and across the Tiber from Piazza del Popolo, this hospitable hotel occupies a 1906 patrician *palazzo,* which has been completely renovated. Quiet and off the tourist path, it is elegantly decorated. The guest rooms are spacious — the largest ones geared for families — and the bathrooms are particularly nice, clad in marble and tile and with new modern fixtures. The Farnese is steps from one of Rome's best shopping streets — Via Cola di Rienzo — and within walking distance of the Vatican and the historic center. The hotel also has a roof garden.

See map p. 104. Via Alessandro Farnese 30. ☎ **06-3212553.** *Fax: 06-3215129.* www. hotelfarnese.com. *Metro: Line A to Lepanto; then walk northeast on Via degli Scipioni to Via Farnese. Rack rates: 280€–310€ ($364–$403) double; 360€ ($468) triple; 370€ ($481) junior suite. Rates include buffet breakfast. AE, MC, V.*

Hotel La Rovere
$$ **San Pietro**

Set on the lower slope of the Gianicolo on a quaint side street, the Rovere is close to Trastevere and the Vatican. Housed in a small *palazzo,* it's quiet, with comfortable rooms, some of them with beamed ceilings or windows opening on the roofs of Rome. The rooms on the top floor have delightful private terraces. Each guest room is individually furnished with quality modern furniture and carpeting; public spaces are decorated with antiques and quality reproductions.

See map p. 104. Vicolo Sant'Onofrio 4, off Piazza della Rovere and Via del Gianicolo. **06-68806739.** *Fax: 06-68807062.* www.hotellarovere.com. *Minibus: 115, 116, or 116T to Via del Gianicolo. Bus: 64 to Via del Gianicolo. Rack rates: 190€–210€*

($247–$273) double; 210€–310€ ($273–$403) triple. Rates include buffet breakfast. AE, DC, MC, V.

Hotel Locarno
$$–$$$ Piazza del Popolo

This family-run hotel is a peaceful and elegant retreat but only steps from Piazza del Popolo. Opened in 1925, the hotel earned international fame in 1978, when it became the set and subject of the movie *Hotel Locarno*. Always beloved by actors and other personalities of the movie industry, it offers charming guest rooms furnished with antiques or reproductions. (Those in the newer wing are better.) Many Liberty-style (Italian Art Nouveau) details recall the origin of the building. The attentive service includes nice extras such as free bicycles and free Internet access.

See map p. 104. Via della Penna 22. ☎ *06-3610841. Fax: 06-3215249.* www.hotel locarno.com. *Metro: Flaminio. Walk across Piazza del Popolo; turn right on Via dell'Oca, which becomes Via della Penna after 1 block. Rack rates: 190€–310€ ($247–$403) double; 510€ ($663) suite. Rates include breakfast. AE, DC, MC, V.*

Hotel Margutta
$ Piazza di Spagna

This small hotel is a great find — often booked solid — offering accommodations at a very moderate price in the most glamorous area of *il centro*. Guest rooms are not large, but they're bright and pleasant, with whitewashed walls, tiled floors, and simple furniture. The tiled bathrooms are small but functional. Of the three rooms on the top floor, two share a terrace, and one has a private terrace. Note that there is no elevator.

See map p. 104. Via Laurina 34, from Via del Corso to Via del Babuino. ☎ **06-3223674.** *Fax: 06-3200395.* www.hotelmargutta.it. *Metro: Flaminio. Cross Piazza del Popolo, and take the second street on your left from Via del Corso. Rack rates: 160€ double ($208). AE, DC, MC, V.*

Hotel Navona
$ Navona/Pantheon

A great location and modest prices make this family-run hotel always in demand. Guest rooms are individually furnished with quality modern or period furniture, with tiled floors and small bathrooms. The rooms tend to be good size, and some have beautiful coffered ceilings. Air-conditioning is available on request and for an extra fee of 15€ ($19) per day.

See map p. 104. Via dei Sediari 8, off Corso Rinascimento. ☎ **06-6864203.** *Fax: 06-68803802.* www.hotelnavona.com. *Bus: 64 to Piazza Sant'Andrea della Valle. Walk on Corso Rinascimento, and take the first right. Rack rates: 140€ ($182) double; 185€ ($240) triple. AE, DC, MC, V.*

Hotel Parlamento
$$ Navona/Pantheon

Located right in the heart of Rome, this hotel is housed in a 15th-century building and offers great accommodations at excellent prices (off-season prices can be half the rack rate). Rooms are bright and spacious, with tiled floors; large beds; and comfortable bathrooms, some of them with tubs. Weather permitting, breakfast is served on the pleasant roof terrace. Guests have free Internet access, but air-conditioning is an extra charge of 12€ ($16) per day.

See map p. 104. Via delle Convertite 5, off Piazza San Silvestro. ☎/fax: **06-69921000.** www.hotelparlamento.it. *Bus: 492 or 116 to Piazza San Silvestro. Rack rates: 158€ ($205) double; 185€ ($240) triple; 230€ ($299) quad. Rates include breakfast. MC, V.*

Hotel Sant'Anna
$$ San Pietro

In a charming and authentic neighborhood a stone's throw from the Vatican, this hotel is housed in a 16th-century building that surrounds a garden–courtyard (where breakfast is served in nice weather). The rooms are large and have elegant modern furnishings, carpeting, and good-size marble bathrooms; a number of rooms have coffered ceilings. The vaulted breakfast room has bright fresco decorations. The hotel offers wheelchair access and allows pets.

See map p. 104. Via Borgo Pio 133. ☎ **06-68801602.** *Fax: 06-68308717.* www.hotel santanna.com. *Bus: 62 to Borgo Sant'Angelo. Take Via Mascherino, and turn right on Via Borgo Pio. Rack rates: 220€ ($286) double; 230€ ($299) triple. Rates include buffet breakfast. AE, MC, V.*

Hotel Santa Maria
$$ Trastevere

This small hotel occupies a block of low buildings surrounding a romantic garden–courtyard lined by a portico. Most of the guest rooms are on the first floor and open directly on the courtyard (except one garret suite on the second floor). Rooms are cozy and welcoming, decorated with terra-cotta–tiled floors, whitewashed walls, and dark-wood furniture; however, they can be a bit dark on rainy days, as all light natural comes from the portico. The courtyard, though, is a pleasant place to take breakfast on a sunny morning; in the afternoon and early evening, guests can have a glass of wine from the wine bar. The suites are on two levels and are designed for families with children (up to six beds).

See map p. 104. Vicolo del Piede 2, off Piazza Santa Maria in Trastevere. ☎ **06-5894626.** *Fax: 06-5894815.* www.htlsantamaria.com. *Tram: 8 to Piazza Sonnino. Take Via della Lungaretta to Piazza Santa Maria in Trastevere; cross the square, and turn right. Rack rates: 210€ ($273) double; 250€ ($325) triple; suites 280€ ($364) and up. Rates include buffet breakfast. AE, MC, V.*

Hotel Scalinata di Spagna
$$$ Piazza di Spagna

This is a charming small hotel located just above the Spanish Steps (there is a public elevator if you're too tired to negotiated this tourist-clogged attraction). The guest rooms are smallish but cheery and nicely appointed; some may have exposed beams, and two have a private small terrace. Free Internet TV is available in every room. The marble bathrooms are fair size but not large by any means. This place feels more like a country inn on a hill — the view from the roof garden is spectacular — than a hotel in the congested *centro*.

See map p. 104. Piazza Trinità dei Monti 17. ☎ 06-6793006. Fax: 06-69940598. www. hotelscalinata.com. *Metro: Line A to Spagna; then up the Spanish Steps (or elevator). Rack rates: 320€–350€ ($416–$455) double; 380€ ($494) triple; 400€ ($520) quad; and 420€ ($546) junior suite. Rates include buffet breakfast. AE, MC, V.*

Hotel Teatro di Pompeo
$$ Campo de' Fiori

The name of this hotel comes from a 55 B.C. Roman theater that lies beneath the hotel — some of it can still be seen in the breakfast room. The rest of the building is much newer — that is, from the 15th century — as you see by the beamed ceilings in some of the rooms. The rooms are spacious for this ancient area of Rome, and the white plaster walls and simple furnishings give it an old-fashioned charm. The hotel is small, so reserve your room early.

See map p. 104. Largo del Pallaro 8. ☎ 06-68300170. Fax: 06-68805531. E-mail: hotel.teatrodipompeo@tiscalinet.it. *Bus: 64 to Sant'Andrea della Valle; then walk east on Via dei Chiavari, and turn right. Rack rates: 190€ ($247) double; 220€ ($286) triple. Rates include breakfast. AE, DC, MC, V.*

Hotel Turner
$$ Porta Pia

With large rooms and elegant, almost gaudy furnishings, Hotel Turner is an excellent value. Located at the beginning of the Via Nomentana, it is outside *il centro* but closely connected by transportation and within walking distance of Via Veneto. All guest rooms are decorated with fine wall fabrics and quality furniture, and the best rooms have marble baths with Jacuzzis and Turkish baths. Contact the hotel directly for its specials.

See map p. 104. Via Nomentana 27, by Porta Pia. ☎ 06-44250077. Fax: 06-44250165. E-mail: info@hotelturner.com. *Bus: 60, 62. Rack rates: 268€ ($348) double; 354€ ($460) triple; suites 423€ ($550) and up. Rates include buffet breakfast. AE, MC, V.*

Locanda Cairoli
$$$ Campo de' Fiori

This small hotel offers elegance and perfect service with a self-consciously clubby, British feeling. Guest rooms are furnished with antiques and original artwork from contemporary artists, which contribute to create a refined yet warm and relaxing surrounding. You need to book well in advance to snag one of the 15 well-appointed rooms.

See map p. 104. Piazza Benedetto Cairoli 2, off Via Arenula. ☎ *06-68809278. Fax: 06-68892937.* www.locandacairoli.it. *Bus: 64, 70, 170, 492, 40 to Largo Argentina; then walk south on Via Arenula. Rack rates: 240€ ($312) double. Rates include breakfast. AE, DC, MC, V.*

Rose Garden Palace
$$$–$$$$ Via Veneto

In the exclusive area around Via Veneto, this is a new hotel housed in a Liberty (Italian Art Nouveau) building from the beginning of the 20th century. The eponymous rose garden is a lovely inner garden perfect for a private stroll. Charm isn't the only thing you'll find here, however; the amenities are top notch. The marble bathrooms have both showers and bathtubs; the rooms themselves are large; and the entire hotel is furnished with very sleek yet inviting modern décor. A new health club and even a swimming pool are on site.

See map p. 104. Via Bonconpagni 19. ☎ *06-421741. Fax: 06-4815608.* www.rose gardenpalace.com. *Bus: 116 to Via Boncompagni; then walk north 1 block. Rack rates: 300€–440€ ($390–$572) double; 473€–524€ ($615–$681) suite. Rates include buffet breakfast. AE, DC, MC, V.*

Villa Mangili
$$$ Parioli

This small family-run hotel is a pearl hidden on a quiet street of this elegant, residential area of Rome — one that few tourists, as yet, have discovered. Well connected to the major attractions, Villa Mangili offers elegant guest rooms, modern furnishings, and a relaxing atmosphere. Each room is uniquely decorated — we particularly like the red room — and has a comfortable marble bathroom. The public areas house ongoing exhibits of contemporary art. The beautiful garden surrounding the villa is a perfect private retreat where breakfast is served in the good season.

Via G. Mangili 31, off Via Ulisse Aldrovandi. ☎ *06-3217130. Fax: 06-3224313.* www. hotelvillamangili.it. *Tram: 19 to Via Mangili. Rack rates: 240€ ($312) double. Rates include buffet breakfast. AE, DC, MC, V.*

Villa San Pio
$$$ Aventino

This is the best of a group of three beautifully located and family-run hotels on the Aventino. It is a peaceful spot, surrounded by a private garden, yet only steps from attractions and transportation. Guest rooms are large and elegantly decorated, with period furniture and delicate frescoes and moldings on the walls. Good-size marble bathrooms add to the value. If this hotel is full, an employee will suggest that you reserve at one of the nearby sister hotels — each with its own personality, and which we also recommend (**Hotel Sant'Anselmo,** located at Piazza Sant'Anselmo 2, and **Hotel Aventino,** located at Via San Domenico 10).

See map p. 104. Via Santa Melania 19. ☎ *06-5745231. Fax: 06-5741112.* www. aventinohotels.com. *Tram: 3 to Piazza Albania; then take Via di Sant'Anselmo, and turn right. Metro: Circo Massimo; walk up Viale Aventino to Piazza Albania, and follow directions for Tram. Metro: Piramide. Rack rates: 240€ ($312) double; 260€ ($338) triple; 270€ ($351) quad. Rates include breakfast. AE, DC, MC, V.*

Runner-Up Accommodations

Albergo Cesàri Hotel

$$ Navona/Pantheon   A historic hotel, still family run, with renovated guest rooms (some with modern furnishings; others with quality reproduction beds and armoirs) and a fantastic location. For families or small groups, inquire about the triple and quad rooms. *See map p. 104. Via di Pietra 89a.* ☎ *06-6749701.* www.albergocesari.it.

Albergo del Sole al Pantheon

$$$$ Navona/Pantheon   Claiming to be Rome's oldest hotel (since 1467), the Albergo is right across from the Pantheon and has some rooms with spectacular views. Individually decorated guest rooms feature original hand-painted coffered ceilings. Suites offer baths with hydromassage. Check the Web site for specials, which can mean considerable savings. *See map p. 104. Piazza della Rotonda 63.* ☎ *06-6780441.* www.hotelsole alpantheon.com.

Albergo Santa Chiara

$$$ Navona/Pantheon   Operated since 1838 by the Corteggiani family, this hotel offers a great value. Inside is a chapel built in the room where St. Clare (St. Francis's spiritual sister) lived her last years. Some guest rooms feature beamed ceilings; there are also some triples, quads, and three garret suites with private terraces. *See map p. 104. Via Santa Chiara 21.* ☎ *06-6872979.* www.albergosantachiara.com.

Hotel Barocco

$$$ Via Veneto   Right off Piazza Barberini, this charming small hotel offers tastefully furnished guest rooms, in dark woods and fine fabrics, with marble bathrooms; some rooms have a balcony or a terrace. The refined ambience is pleasant without being stuffy. *See map p. 104. Via della Purificazione 4, off Piazza Barberini.* ☎ *06-4872001.* www.hotelbarocco.com.

Hotel Columbus

$$$ San Pietro This spacious hotel is housed in the beautiful 15th-century Palazzo della Rovere. Decorated with frescoes (some by Pinturicchio) and preserving the feeling of a dignified aristocrat's palace, it offers large and commodious rooms. La Veranda restaurant (see Chapter 10) opens on the delightful inner garden courtyard. The hotel is disabled-accessible. *See map p. 104. Via della Conciliazione 33.* ☎ *06-6865435.* www.hotelcolumbus.net.

 ## Hotel Erdarelli

$ Piazza di Spagna   This small hotel, family run since 1935, is a great value. Guest rooms are large, with parquet floors, quality modern furniture, and good-size bathrooms. Some rooms have balconies. *See map p. 104. Via Due Macelli 28.* ☎ *06-6791265.* www.venere.com/it/roma/erdarelli.

Hotel Grifo

$$ Colosseo   With large, bright rooms with white walls and modern wood furniture, the Hotel Grifo offers simplicity, value, and a central location. The hotel also has a roof garden and some triples and quads. *See map p. 104. Via del Boschetto 144.* ☎ *06-4871395.* www.hotelgrifo.com.

 ## Hotel Nardizzi

$$ Repubblica This family-run hotel offers an excellent value and a good location. Guest rooms are simply furnished, and some enjoy a good view, but the tiled bathrooms are a bit cramped. The hotel offers triples and quads, and has a roof terrace. Check its interesting Internet specials. *See map p. 104. Via Firenze 38, off Via Nazionale.* ☎ *06-48903916.* www.hotelnardizzi.it.

Hotel Piazza di Spagna

$$$ Piazza di Spagna   A family-run hotel now in its third generation, Hotel Piazza di Spagna offers welcoming accommodations near the Spanish Steps. Guest rooms are small but comfortable, with wrought-iron bedsteads and bright tiled bathrooms; some have small private terraces. Triples and quads are available. It books up fast — make your reservations well in advance. *See map p. 104. Via Mario de' Fiori 61.* ☎ *06-6796412.* www.hotelpiazzadispagna.it.

Villa Florence Hotel

$$ Porta Pia Housed in an 1860 patrician villa in Liberty style (Italian Art Nouveau) with its own garden, this hotel offers quiet and elegance at moderate prices. The large, individually furnished guest rooms are decorated with quality furniture and have large tiled bathrooms. Some rooms have private terraces, and some bathrooms have a Jacuzzi. *See map p. 104. Via Nomentana 28.* ☎ *06-4403036* or *06-4402966. E-mail:* villa.florence@flashnet.it.

Index of Accommodations by Neighborhood

Aventino
Villa San Pio ($$$)

Campo de' Fiori
Hotel Arenula ($)
Hotel Teatro di Pompeo ($$)
Locanda Cairoli ($$$)

Colosseo
Casa Kolbe ($)
Hotel Capo d'Africa ($$$)
Hotel Celio ($$$)
Hotel Grifo ($$)

Navona/Pantheon
Albergo Cesàri Hotel ($$)
Albergo del Sole al Pantheon ($$$$)
Albergo Santa Chiara ($$$)
Grand Hotel de la Minerve ($$$$)
Hotel Due Torri ($$$)
Hotel Navona ($)
Hotel Parlamento ($$)

Parioli
Villa Mangili ($$$)

Piazza del Popolo
Hotel Locarno ($$–$$$)

Piazza di Spagna
City Hotel ($$)
Hotel Art ($$$$)
Hotel de Russie ($$$$)
Hotel Erdarelli ($)
Hotel Margutta ($)
Hotel Piazza di Spagna ($$$)
Hotel Scalinata di Spagna ($$$)

Porta Pia
Hotel Turner ($$)
Villa Florence Hotel ($$)

Prati
Casa Valdese ($)
Hotel Dei Mellini ($$$)
Hotel Farnese ($$$)

Repubblica
Hotel Andreotti ($$)
Hotel Britannia ($$–$$$)
Hotel Columbia ($$)
Hotel Fiori ($$)
Hotel Nardizzi ($$)

San Pietro
Hotel Columbus ($$$)
Hotel La Rovere ($$)
Hotel Sant'Anna ($$)

Trastevere
Hotel Santa Maria ($$)

Via Veneto
Bernini Bristol ($$$$)
City Hotel ($$)
Hotel Barocco ($$$)
Rose Garden Palace ($$$–$$$$)

Index of Accommodations by Price

$

Casa Kolbe (Teatro Marcello)
Casa Valdese (Prati)
Hotel Arenula (Campo de' Fiori/Teatro Marcello)
Hotel Erdarelli (Piazza di Spagna)
Hotel Margutta (Piazza di Spagna)
Hotel Navona (Piazza Navona/Pantheon)

$$

Albergo Cesàri Hotel (Navona/Pantheon)
City Hotel (Piazza di Spagna/Via Veneto)
Hotel Andreotti (Repubblica)
Hotel Britannia (Repubblica)
Hotel Columbia (Repubblica)
Hotel Fiori (Repubblica)
Hotel Grifo (Colosseo)
Hotel La Rovere (San Pietro)
Hotel Locarno (Piazza del Popolo)
Hotel Nardizzi (Repubblica)
Hotel Parlamento (Navona/Pantheon)
Hotel Sant'Anna (San Pietro)
Hotel Santa Maria (Trastevere)
Hotel Teatro di Pompeo (Campo de' Fiori)
Hotel Turner (Porta Pia)
Villa Florence Hotel (Porta Pia)

$$$

Albergo Santa Chiara (Navona/Pantheon)
Hotel Barocco (Via Veneto)
Hotel Britannia (Repubblica)
Hotel Capo d'Africa (Colosseo)
Hotel Celio (Colosseo)
Hotel Columbus (San Pietro)
Hotel Dei Mellini (Prati)
Hotel Due Torri (Navona/Pantheon)
Hotel Farnese (Prati)
Hotel Locarno (Piazza del Popolo)
Hotel Piazza di Spagna (Piazza di Spagna)
Hotel Scalinata di Spagna (Piazza di Spagna)
Locanda Cairoli (Campo de' Fiori)
Rose Garden Palace (Via Veneto)
Villa Mangili (Parioli)
Villa San Pio (Aventino)

$$$$

Albergo del Sole al Pantheon (Navona/Pantheon)
Bernini Bristol (Via Veneto)
Grand Hotel de la Minerve (Navona/Pantheon)
Hotel Art (Piazza di Spagna)
Hotel de Russie (Piazza di Spagna)
Rose Garden Palace (Via Veneto)

Chapter 10

Dining and Snacking in Rome

*I*talian gourmands long maintained that there wasn't a really good restaurant in Rome — but they can't say that any longer. Rome has hundreds of good little trattorie, *osterie,* and *pizzerie* offering traditional local food (see Chapter 2 for more on Roman specialties and cuisine). In addition, thanks to fresh trends sweeping the dining scene, lots of new quality restaurants in the middle and upper-end range have appeared and continue to appear. As a result, Romans are dining out more, both for lunch and dinner, even during the week — which used to be a rarity in more traditional days, when people would go out mostly on Saturday night and Sunday lunch, and for special occasions.

Getting the Dish on the Local Scene

Traditional Roman cuisine is based on pasta, fresh seasonal vegetables, seafood, and meat — especially organ meat and smaller animals such as pork, chicken, rabbit, lamb, and goat. Preparations are usually simple and flavorful, and a number of "established" dishes remain great favorites with the locals (see Chapter 2). Although like other Italians, Romans are attached to their culinary tradition, they don't seem to despise innovation, and the many new restaurants, revisiting traditional dishes as well as new combinations of traditional ingredients, have been very successful.

The accent in these new restaurants is always on the lightness of the dish as well as on the quality of the ingredients — their freshness and natural preparation. Many of them have integrated ethnic elements into their cuisine, such as French and Mediterranean at **Bric** and Middle Eastern at **Gusto** (both are reviewed in this chapter). One of the newest trends is what Romans are calling *crudi* — Italian-style sashimi. Italians have always eaten *carpaccio* (thinly sliced raw beef served with oil and Parmesan cheese) or fish made in the *ceviche* style (prepared with lemon juice, which in effect "cooks" the fish), but the trend toward raw fish is completely new. You can sample it at the **Enoteca Capranica** or at **Presidente,** both reviewed in this chapter.

The best (and most convenient) areas to eat are still in *il centro* (the historic center) — especially the little streets off Via di Ripetta in the Piazza del Popolo area and the circuitous byways around the Pantheon, around Fontana di Trevi, and around Campo de' Fiori, where new restaurants are constantly cropping up. Another famed dining area is Trastevere, a destination dear to many Romans.

A steady flow of locals — from government offices and the numerous businesses in these areas, but also from everywhere in Rome — feeds this constant renewal and ensures good quality. Feel free to try one of the small restaurants in these neighborhoods even if we don't specifically recommend it: It would be impossible to list all the good places in Rome. Just follow your nose.

There are, however, some less likely areas for dining that have, in fact, been developing in recent times — in residential neighborhoods such as Parioli along Viale Liegi and the little streets off Via Nomentana, near Porta Pia.

Dining hours are later than in the United States. Romans sit down to dinner between 8:30 and 10:30 p.m.; lunch is between 1 and 3 p.m. However, restaurants in *il centro* and in Trastevere open around noon for lunch and 7:30 p.m. for dinner to accommodate tourists — only pubs and tourist joints will open any earlier than that. Nonsmokers and gourmets will be pleased to hear that **smoking has been outlawed in public places,** but it's still allowed in separate rooms. Although a 10 to 15 percent charge for *servizio* (service) is often included in the price of each dish (check for this on the menu; if it is not specified, it means that it is not included), an extra 5 to 10 percent is expected for good service.

If you're visiting in the summer, remember that Roman men tend to dress in what may look rather formal to American eyes (no shorts and rarely jeans), even during the day, and as a man, you might unpleasantly stick out with your shorts and tank top, and may not be able to have lunch except in the most informal eateries. Shorts and tank tops (except for really stylish and elegant ones) are not a good choice for women, either, but women may pass more easily.

Trimming the Fat from Your Budget

Thanks to Rome's dining boom, it gets easier and easier to find nice restaurants but harder and harder to find really cheap (and good) ones, which were once very common. However, having a good meal in Rome remains very affordable, and you don't need to make big sacrifices to save a little.

A common strategy is to have a bite on the go at a bar or *rosticceria* for lunch (see "Dining and Snacking on the Go," later in this chapter) and save your lunch money for dinner. Be prepared to stand, though, because few bars offer sitting. Bars (what Romans call *cafes,* although they serve alcohol) do, but the price surcharge for sitting at a table *(à tavola)* rather than eating at the counter *(al banco)* is so high that you may be better off with a small restaurant. In restaurants, you can easily spend less by having fewer courses. The classic Roman meal includes appetizer, pasta, *secondo* (meat or fish), *contorno* (salad, vegetables, or potatoes), and dessert, together with copious wine and an espresso to finish, but this kind of meal — usually stretching for a couple of hours — is only for special occasions and on weekends. Consuming anaconda-size meals also takes some getting used to. For lunch or a light dinner, most Romans eat a *secondo* with a *contorno,* or even just a pasta dish with a *contorno,* or a pizza (round; individual size). Dining in this fashion will keep your expenses down.

Another thing to watch is drinks. A bottle of wine will considerably increase your bill, but most restaurants offer *vino della casa,* sold by volume (minimum *un quarto* — a quarter liter, or about 9 ounces), and many have a few choices by the glass. What may surprise you is that wine may be less expensive than soft drinks, which are a very unusual thing to have with dinner and might significantly increase your bill. If you're a group or a family, agree on one kind of soda, and ask for a large bottle (liter size) — it's much cheaper than individual cans. Beer is also sold in large bottles in pizzerias. Cocktails are basically unknown — in Italy, you take your *aperitivo* before dinner at a bar or club, not at your restaurant table, so it's an expensive addition to your bill.

Rome's Best Restaurants

We have reviewed what we feel are the best restaurants in Rome — of course, there are many more than we have room for here, but these are our preferred ones. Each listing is marked with dollar signs to give an idea of the cost of a full meal, including a pasta or appetizer, a *secondo* (main course or entree), a side dish, and dessert. Beverages are not included. Note that within the restaurant listing, the numbers we give you are the price range of the main courses, listed as *secondi.*

Here is a table explaining what the dollar signs translate to in terms of cost:

Cost	Restaurant
$	35€ ($46) or less
$$	36€–50€ ($47–$65)
$$$	51€–65€ ($66–$85)
$$$$	66€ ($86) and up

At the end of this chapter, you'll find indexes of all the restaurants we recommend: by location, by cuisine, and by $ sign. See the "Rome Snacking and Dining" map in this chapter for the locations of all eateries we review in this chapter.

Italy recently instituted one of Europe's toughest laws against smoking in public places. All restaurants and bars come under the ruling except those with ventilated smoking rooms. Smokers face steep fines if caught lighting up. Only 10 percent of Italian restaurants currently have separate smoking areas.

Al Regno di Re Ferdinando II
$$–$$$ Testaccio   NEAPOLITAN/FISH

In one of the historic cellars of Monte Testaccio — the hill of discarded pottery shards collected during Emperor Nero's reign — this restaurant offers excellent Neapolitan food. The choice of fresh pasta is superb, and the *Sfizietto del Re* (a huge portion of linguine with a mountain of shellfish from the nearby Tirrenian Sea) delights any palate and leaves an everlasting memory after you finish — *if* you can finish. The other seafood dishes are excellent as well. This restaurant also makes pizza — the Neapolitan specialty — but the pasta is much better. If you visit in the summer, bring a jacket — the place isn't air-conditioned, but the cellar maintains an icy temperature inside.

See map p. 122. Via di Monte Testaccio 39. ☎ *06-5783725. Reservations recommended. Metro: Line B to Piramide, but taking a cab is best. Secondi: 15€–30€ ($20–$39). AE, DC, MC, V. Open: Tues–Sat noon to 2:30 p.m.; Mon–Sat 7–11:30 p.m.*

Arcangelo
$$ Prati   ROMAN/CREATIVE ITALIAN/FISH

The chefs at this new restaurant are among those who've taken to the trend of enlivening Italian cuisine with new combinations that Grandma never imagined. Here, the experiments are subtle and delicious — though the chefs keep your options open with more traditional offerings, too. The *maccheroni all'amatriciana* (pasta in a spicy tomato and bacon sauce) is excellent, but so are the less usual *spaghetti aglio olio e mazzancolle* (spaghetti with garlic, olive oil, and local crayfish), the *tonno arrosto con melanzane* (baked tuna with eggplant), and the *anatra in salsa di frutta secca* (duck in dried fruit sauce).

See map p. 122. Via G.G. Belli 59, off Via Cicerone, 1 block from Piazza Cavour. ☎ *06-3210992. Reservations recommended. Bus: 30, 70, 81. Secondi: 13€–21€ ($17–$27). AE, DC, V. Open: Mon–Sat 12:30–3 p.m. and 7:30–10:30 p.m. Closed Aug.*

Bolognese
$$ Piazza del Popolo   BOLOGNESE

Elegant and hip, this restaurant serves well-prepared food at moderate prices in a nicely appointed dining room or, in good weather, on the outdoor

Rome Dining and Snacking

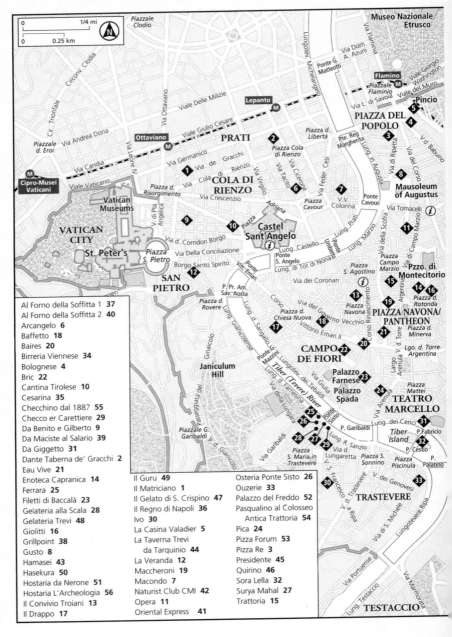

Al Forno della Soffitta 1 **37**
Al Forno della Soffitta 2 **40**
Arcangelo **6**
Baffetto **18**
Baires **20**
Birreria Viennese **34**
Bolognese **4**
Bric **22**
Cantina Tirolese **10**
Cesarina **35**
Checchino dal 1887 **55**
Checco er Carettiere **29**
Da Benito e Gilberto **9**
Da Maciste al Salario **39**
Da Giggetto **31**
Dante Taberna de' Gracchi **2**
Eau Vive **21**
Enoteca Capranica **14**
Ferrara **25**
Filetti di Baccalà **23**
Gelateria alla Scala **28**
Gelateria Trevi **48**
Giolitti **16**
Grillpoint **38**
Gusto **8**
Hamasei **43**
Hasekura **50**
Hostaria da Nerone **51**
Hostaria L'Archeologia **56**
Il Convivio Troiani **13**
Il Drappo **17**

Il Guru **49**
Il Matriciano **1**
Il Gelato di S. Crispino **47**
Il Regno di Napoli **36**
Ivo **30**
La Casina Valadier **5**
La Taverna Trevi
   da Tarquinio **44**
La Veranda **12**
Maccheroni **19**
Macondo **7**
Naturist Club CMI **42**
Opera **11**
Oriental Express **41**

Osteria Ponte Sisto **26**
Ouzerie **33**
Palazzo del Freddo **52**
Pasqualino al Colosseo
   Antica Trattoria **54**
Pica **24**
Pizza Forum **53**
Pizza Re **3**
Presidente **45**
Quirino **46**
Sora Lella **32**
Surya Mahal **27**
Trattoria **15**

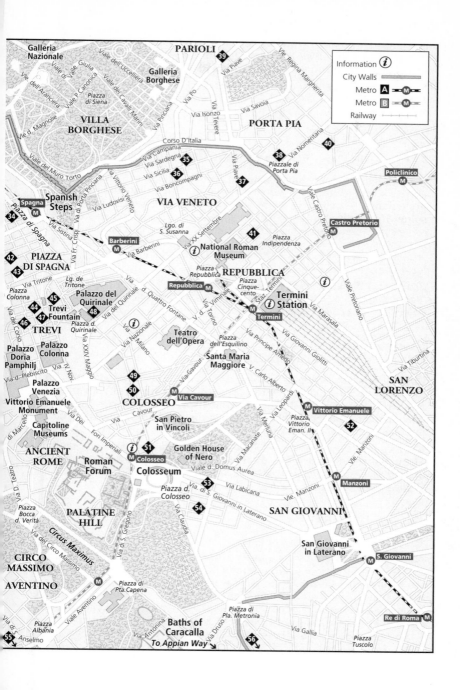

terrace. Even Romans admit that Bologna has produced some good dishes, like the lasagna prepared so well here; the *tagliatelle alla Bolognese* (homemade pasta with tomato and meat sauce) and the *fritto di verdure e agnello* (tempura of vegetables and lamb tidbits) are mouthwatering. End with something from the unusually large selection of delicious desserts.

See map p. 122. Piazza del Popolo 1. ☎ 06-3611426. Reservations required. Bus: 117, 119. Secondi: 14€–29€ ($18–$38). AE, DC, MC, V. Open: Daily 12:30–3 p.m. and Tues–Sun 8:15 p.m. to midnight. Closed Aug.

Bric

$ Campo de' Fiori   ROMAN/FRENCH/MEDITERRANEAN

In this pleasant, informal restaurant, you can relax with some wine and cheese selected from an extensive list — of both Italian and international provenance — or have a more substantial meal from the inventive and somewhat "fusion" menu. Try the *charlotte di carciofi con guanciale croccante e pecorino* (molded layers of artichokes, bacon and pecorino cheese) or the *abbacchio alla parmigiana* (lamb in Parmesan sauce). Bric is a great stop in the trendy but authentic area of Campo de' Fiori, a perfect setting for dinner.

See map p. 122. Via del Pellegrino 51, off Campo de' Fiori. ☎ 06-6879533. Reservations recommended. Bus: 116 to Campo de' Fiori. Secondi: 9€–19€ ($12–$25). DC, MC, V. Open: Tues–Sun 7:30–11 p.m. Closed 10 days in Aug.

Cesarina

$$$ Via Veneto   ROMAN/BOLOGNESE

Offering a nice selection of specialties from Rome and Bologna, this restaurant is an excellent choice in the residential area north of Via Veneto and away from the crowds. The food is wonderful — go for the tasting menu of homemade pastas or the choice of meat dishes. The *bollito misto* (variety of boiled meats) is delicious.

See map p. 122. Via Piemonte 109. ☎ 06-4880828. Reservations recommended. Metro: Line A to Barberini. Bus: 56 or 58 to Via Piemonte (the fourth street off Via Boncompagni coming from Via Veneto). Secondi: 17€–28€ ($22–$36). AE, DC, MC, V. Open: Mon–Sat 12:30–3 p.m. and 7:30–11 p.m.

Checchino dal 1887

$$ Testaccio   ROMAN

An elegant restaurant with a lively atmosphere, Checchino is the best of several restaurants housed in Monte Testaccio (the Ancient Roman pottery dump) and certainly the most traditional. It serves real Roman specialties such as *lingua con salsa verde* (tongue in a green sauce of garlic, parsley, and olive oil) and the classic *coda alla vaccinara* (oxtail with pinoli nuts and raisins), as well as excellent pasta dishes, including *penne con broccoletti strascinati al pecorino romano* (short pasta with broccoli rabe

Ethnic dining

"When in Rome do as Romans do" goes the adage, and indeed, you'll find that although Rome has become quite cosmopolitan, with residents from around the globe, people of all nationalities appear to enjoy eating in the local *pizzerie* and trattorie of old Roman tradition. Ethnic restaurants are rare and often tucked away in residential neighborhoods out of *il centro,* and they serve dishes that often have taken on some of the local culinary culture.

These restaurants are also not cheap, or at least not cheaper than trattorie and *pizzerie.* Actually, besides the ubiquitous Chinese restaurants — about one per neighborhood and none to write home about — where you will spend the same as in the local trattoria, the others are fancy places where Romans go for something special or exotic, and they have prices to match. Romans love Japanese, which is available at **Hasekura** (Via dei Serpenti 27; ☎ 06-483648; open daily) and **Hamasei** (Via della Mercede 35; ☎ 06-6792134; closed Mon). Another Asian cuisine with a growing following is Indian, found, for example, at **Il Guru** (Via Cimarra 4; ☎ 06-4744110; closed Sun), where you can eat at moderate prices, and the more upscale **Surya Mahal** (Piazza Trilussa 50; ☎ 06-5894554; closed Sun).

A few other interesting choices are South American cuisine at **Baires** (Corso Rinascimento 1; ☎ 06-6861293; open daily), Caribbean at **Macondo** (Via Marianna Dionigi 37; ☎ 06-3212601; closed Sun), Greek at **Ouzerie** (Via dei Salumi 2; ☎ 06-5816378; closed Sun; live music Fri and Sat), and French Colonial at **Eau Vive** (Via Monterone 86; ☎ 06-68801095; closed Sun). For a taste of "Mittel Europe" and more moderate prices, try **Birreria Viennese** (Via della Croce, 21, off Piazza di Spagna; ☎ 06-6795569; open daily) or **Cantina Tirolese** (Via Vitelleschi 23, off Castel Sant'Angelo to the west; ☎ 06-6869994; closed Mon).

Not really an ethnic restaurant, **Naturist Club CMI** (Via della Vite 14 on the fifth floor; ☎ 06-6792509; closed Sun) offers organic vegetarian meals with a menu that changes daily and is more extensive at dinner. Finally, not a restaurant at all but a fast-food place is **Oriental Express** (Via Calatafimi 7; ☎ 06-4818791; open daily lunch only), which serves excellent Arab fare.

sautéed with pecorino cheese), and a large variety of meat and fish choices. On the extensive wine list, you'll also find wine by the glass.

See map p. 122. Via di Monte Testaccio 30. ☎ 06-5743816. Reservations recommended. Metro: Piramide, but taking a cab is best. Secondi: 14€–25€ ($18–$33). AE, DC, MC, V. Open: Tues–Sat 12:30–3 p.m. and 8 p.m. to midnight; closed Aug and Dec 23–Jan 1.

Checco er Carrettiere
$$ Trastevere ROMAN

This traditional trattoria is still faithful to the old Italian-cuisine values of fresh ingredients and professional service. It even prepares the fish for you at your table. The *bombolotti all'amatriciana* (pasta in spicy tomato sauce with bacon) is excellent, and so are the *abbacchi scottadito* (grilled lamb chops) and the *coda alla vaccinara* (oxtail stew). Homemade desserts round out the menu nicely.

See map p. 122. Via Benedetta, 10 near Piazza Trilussa. ☎ 06-5800985. Reservations recommended. Bus: 23, 115 to Piazza Trilussa. Secondi: 13€–18€ ($17–$23). AE, DC, MC, V. Open: Daily 12:30–3 p.m., Mon–Sat 7:30–11 p.m.

Da Benito e Gilberto
$$ San Pietro   FISH

Don't expect a written menu and a lot of time to make up your mind in this informal restaurant; you'll have to listen to the daily offerings and recommendations of your waiter, and go for it. Don't worry; you won't regret it: The quality of the ingredients and the preparation of the food are outstanding. The *pasta e fagioli con frutti di mare* (bean and seafood soup) is warm and satisfying; the *tagliolini alla pescatora* (homemade pasta with seafood), delicate; and the *fritto di paranza* (fried small fish), delicious. Also try the grilled daily catch.

See map p. 122. Via del Falco 19, at Borgo Pio. ☎ 06-6867769. Reservations required several days in advance. Bus: 23 and 81 to Via S. Porcari. Secondi: 12€–18€ ($16–$23). AE, MC, V. Open: Tues–Sat 7:30–11:30 p.m. Closed Aug.

Da Giggetto
$$ Teatro Marcello   JEWISH ROMAN

This famous restaurant has for decades been the destination of Romans who want to taste some of the specialties of Jewish Roman cuisine. Some Romans say Giggetto is a little past its prime, but we think it's still a good place to sample such specialties as *carciofi alla giudia* (crispy fried artichokes), as well as traditional Roman dishes such as *fettuccine all'amatriciana* (pasta with a tomato-and-bacon sauce) and *saltimbocca alla romana* (sauteed veal with ham and sage).

See map p. 122. Via del Portico d'Ottavia 21. ☎ 06-6861105. Reservations recommended. Bus: 63, 23; then walk north behind the synagogue. Secondi: 12€–18€ ($16–$23). AE, DC, MC, V. Open: Tues–Sun noon to 3 p.m.; Tues–Sat 7:30–11 p.m. Closed 2 weeks in Aug.

Dante Taberna de' Gracchi
$–$$ San Pietro   ROMAN

This classic Roman restaurant comprises several small (and air-conditioned) dining rooms. Among the specialties are *spaghetti alla vongole* (spaghetti with clams), *scaloppine al vino bianco* (veal cutlets sauteed in white wine), and a daily soup with choice of various *sfizi fritti* (fried tidbits).

See map p. 122. Via dei Gracchi 266, between Via M. Colonna and Via Etzio. ☎ 06-3213126. Reservations required. Metro: Line A to Lepanto; walk on Via Colonna for

3 blocks, and turn right. Secondi: 12€–16€ ($16–$21). AE, DC, MC, V. Open: Tues–Sat 12:30–3 p.m., Mon–Sat 7:30–11 p.m. Closed Christmas and 3 weeks in Aug.

Enoteca Capranica
$$$ Navona/Pantheon   CREATIVE ITALIAN/WINERY

This elegant historic *enoteca* (wine bar) is housed in the beautiful Palazzo Capranica. It offers a wonderful wine list with hundreds of Italian and foreign labels, accompanied by creative cuisine, including such flavorful forays as *crudo di spigola di mare agli agrumi con finocchio selvatico* (raw sea bass with citrus fruits and wild fennel) and *paccheri di Gragnano con asparagi, cipollotti e pecorino di fossa* (homemade pasta with asparagus, small onions, and specially aged pecorino cheese). It also has two tasting menus and extensive choices of cheese.

See map p. 122. Piazza Capranica 99/100. ☎ 06-69940992. Reservations recommended. Bus: 117, 119. Secondi: 21€–32€ ($27–$42). AE, DC, MC, V. Open: Daily 8 p.m. to midnight.

Ferrara
$$$ Trastevere   CREATIVE ITALIAN/WINERY

A seasonal menu with many interesting flavors served in warm and picturesque surroundings — as well as one of the best wine cellars in Rome — have made this restaurant a favorite in spite of steepish prices. If it's on offer, we recommend the *brandade di baccalà con uova di quaglia e fiori di zucca* (salted cod concoction with quail eggs and zucchini flowers) or the *minestra di primavera con legumi e quenelle di ricotta di bufala* (bean-and-vegetable soup with buffalo ricotta *quenelle,* which is sort of like sausages). Leave room for such desserts as *mousse di cioccolato bianco con fragoline di Nemi* (white chocolate mousse with local strawberries). Wine and food are also offered in the wine bar; the adjacent store sells wine and specialties.

See map p. 122. Piazza Trilussa 41, at Ponte Sisto. ☎ 06-58333920. Reservations recommended. Bus: 23 or 115 to Piazza Trilussa. Secondi: 16€–28€ ($21–$36). DC, V. Open: Daily 8 p.m. to midnight.

Gusto
$$ Piazza del Popolo   CREATIVE ITALIAN/PIZZA

If an establishment can be all things to all people, this is it: a restaurant, an *enoteca* (wine bar), a pizzeria, a cigar club — and a kitchenware store. The pasta dishes are tasty — if it's on the menu, try the *carbonara di maccheroncini con fave* (carbonara with homemade pasta and fava beans) or *trancio di tonno alla cajun con finocchi e olio di agrumi* (Cajun tuna steak with fennel and citrus oil). As for the pizzas, we are partial to *cicoria e funghi* (with dandelion greens and mushrooms). The menu ranges to couscous, wok-prepared Asian dishes, and continental recipes. Popular with workers during the day and young people at night, the restaurant keeps late hours. The wine bar in back offers a large choice of drinks, whiskies, and grappas (Italian brandy). A great brunch buffet is served on Saturday and Sunday.

See map p. 122. Piazza Augusto Imperatore 9. ☎ *06-3226273. Reservations recommended for dinner. Bus: 117 or 119 from Piazza del Popolo to Via della Frezza/Piazza Augusto Imperatore. Secondi: 11€–21€ ($14–$27). AE, MC, DC, V. Open: noon to 3 p.m. and 7 p.m. to midnight.*

Hostaria da Nerone
$ Colosseo   ROMAN

This old family *trattoria* lies near the ruins of Nero's palace — but you don't need the budget of an emperor to enjoy the great view from the terrace (or the good food). We like it especially for the heartier Roman specialties, like *osso buco* (stewed veal shank) and even *trippa alla Romana* (tripe, with a light tomato sauce) — an acquired taste.

See map p. 122. Via Terme di Tito 96, off Via Nicola Salvi uphill from the Colosseum. ☎ *06-4817952. Reservations necessary Sat only. Metro: Colosseo. Secondi: 9€–14€ ($12–$18). AE, MC, V. Open: Mon–Sat noon to 2:30 p.m. and 7–11 p.m.*

Hostaria L'Archeologia
$$ Appian Way   ROMAN

This old *trattoria* is decorated like a country tavern, with beamed ceilings and rustic decorations — the kind of place Romans like to visit on a weekend outing. If you're visiting the nearby catacombs, of course, it's very convenient. The hearty Roman fare includes *vitello alla massenzio* (veal with mushrooms, artichokes, and olives), *tagliatelle al ragu di scorfano* (homemade pasta with tomato sauce and rockfish), grilled meats, and homemade gnocchi on Thursday — the traditional day for making this Roman potato-dumpling dish.

See map p. 122. Via Appia Antica 139. ☎ *06-4880828. Reservations recommended on weekends. Bus: 218 to Appia Antica. Secondi: 12€–21€ ($16–$27). AE, DC, MC, V. Open: Wed–Mon 12:30–3 p.m. and 7:30–11 p.m.*

Il Convivio Troiani
$$$–$$$$ Navona/Pantheon   CREATIVE ROMAN

This is the best restaurant in Rome, provided that what you're after is excellent food and not magical ambience — the exclusive and lavish La Pergola (reviewed later in this chapter) is unforgettable, but here, you get better value: You'll spend half as much and get superb cuisine. Chef Angelo Troiani concocts wonderful and innovative combinations of traditional ingredients as his own rendition of great Roman classics. The menu varies, but you'll probably find the intriguing and delicious *sorbetto di pomodoro* (tomato savory sherbet) and the excellent *saltimbocca alla Romana* (thin slices of veal with bacon and sage). Leave enough room for dessert, because the desserts are fabulous — one of us still dreams of the ginger crème brûlée with chocolate ice cream. . . . The wine list is extensive and well priced.

See map p. 122. Vicolo dei Soldati 31, steps from Piazza Navona to the north. ☎ *06-6869432. Reservations recommended. Bus: 116 or 116T to Piazza di Ponte Umberto I. Secondi: 29€–31€ ($38–$40). AE, DC, MC, V. Open: Mon–Sat 1–2:30 p.m. and 8–11 p.m.*

Il Drappo
$ Campo de' Fiori   SARDINIAN

The subdued atmosphere of Drappo is a perfect setting for serious cuisine at moderate prices. The *malloreddus con vongole pomodorini e basilico* (homemade pasta with clams, cherry tomatoes, and basil) and the *fettuccine con fiori di zucca* (homemade pasta with zucchini flowers) contain wonderful bursts of flavors. Other typical dishes are *maialino al mirto* (suckling pig) and *anatra alle mele* (duck with apples).

See map p. 122. Vicolo del Malpasso 9, off Via Giulia. ☎ *06-6877365. Reservations recommended. Bus: 116, 117 to Lungotevere Sangallo. Secondi: 11€–16€ ($14–$21). AE, DC, MC, V. Open: Mon–Sat 12:30–3 p.m. and 7:30–11 p.m. Closed 4 weeks in Aug/Sept.*

Il Matriciano
$$ San Pietro   ROMAN

This family-run restaurant is a wonderful place to eat outside in summer, but you must have a reservation, because it's well known and popular. The name reflects one of the specialties, *bucatini all'Amatriciana* (*bucatini* is a kind of thick spaghetti with a hollow center). You can also find excellent versions of other typical specialties of Roman cuisine, such as *abbacchio al forno* (roasted lamb).

See map p. 122. Via dei Gracchi 55 ☎ *06-3212327. Reservations required. Metro: Ottaviano/San Pietro. Walk south on Via Ottaviano; the third left is Via dei Gracchi. Secondi: 12€–18€ ($16–$23). AE, DC, MC, V. Winter Thurs–Tues noon to 3 p.m. and 7:30–11 p.m.; summer Sun–Fri noon to 3 p.m. and 7:30–11 p.m.. Closed 3 weeks in Aug.*

La Casina Valadier
$$$–$$$$ Piazza del Popolo   CREATIVE ROMAN

Beautifully located by the Pincio, one of the most romantic spots of Rome, this elegant restaurant offers great views, sophisticated service, and surprisingly good food. Closed for decades, this early-19th-century building opened its doors again after 23 months of restoration to an expectant Roman audience, which had grown up with memories of this chic hot spot of the era of *La Dolce Vita*. On the first floor, you'll find a wine bar (not yet open at press time); on the second floor, a bar with a terrace; on the third floor, a large restaurant; and in the fourth-floor tower, an even more exclusive restaurant with a famous panoramic terrace. The menu is simpler at lunch than dinner; you may find *ricotta infornata con pesto di olive e pistacchi* (warm ricotta with olive-and-pistachio-nut pesto), *fricelli alle erbe con ragout d'anatra e funghi porcini* (homemade green pasta with a duck ragout and porcini mushrooms), or *costolette d'agnello con purea di melanzane al timo* (lamb cutlets with thyme eggplant puree). For dessert, try one — or several — of the specialty sherbets.

See map p. 122. Piazza Bucarest, Villa Borghese. ☎ 06-69922090. Reservations required for dinner. Bus: 116 to Piazza del Popolo. Secondi: 18€–32€ ($23–$42). AE, DC, MC, V. Open: Tues–Sun 12:30–3 p.m. and Tues–Sat 8–11 p.m. Closed 10 days in Aug.

La Pergola
$$$$ Monte Mario   CREATIVE ITALIAN

No doubt about it, this restaurant, located inside the Rome Cavalieri Hilton on the Monte Mario (a steep hill overlooking Prati), is a hike. There's also no doubt that it's one of the best restaurants in Italy. The site is breathtaking, with the whole panorama of Rome laid out at your feet, and the elegance of the furnishings and the professionalism of the service — both kind and discreet — add even more to the experience. Chef Heinz Beck, a master of Italian cuisine, is known for concocting unexpected combinations, such as *tortellini verdi con vongole e calamaretti* (green tortellini with clams and squid) and *triglia su ragout di carciofi* (red mullet served over a ragout of artichokes). The tasting menu is a great way to sample several inventions at once (there's even a tasting menu of seven desserts). Finding your way here by public transportation would be impressive but laborious; take a taxi.

Via A. Cadlolo 101, up the Monte Mario hill. ☎ 06-35092152. Reservations necessary. Secondi: 36€–54€ ($47–$70). AE, DC, MC, V. Open: Tues–Sat 7:30–11 p.m.; closed 3 weeks in Jan and 2 weeks in Aug.

La Taverna Trevi da Tarquinio
$ Trevi   ABRUZZESE/ROMAN

Opening into a courtyard-size square shared with another restaurant — Il Chianti — the Taverna is a great spot to dine outdoors in nice weather. Given its location, you'd expect one of those touristy prix-fixe places, but Romans love the center as much as visitors do, and this restaurant has so far maintained its standards. The food is good traditional Abruzzese and Roman, with a variety of delicious homemade pastas, *abbacchio* (lamb roast), and a choice of grilled meats.

See map p. 122. Via del Lavatore 82. ☎ 06-6792470. Reservations recommended. Bus: 116 to Via del Tritone; then turn right on Via Poli, pass in front of the Fontana di Trevi, and turn right on Via del Lavatore. Secondi: 11€–17€ ($14–$22). MC, V. Open: Mon–Sat noon to 3 p.m. and 7–11 p.m.

La Veranda
$$$ San Pietro   ROMAN/CREATIVE ITALIAN

This restaurant is in the Palazzo della Rovere (which also houses the Hotel Columbus; see Chapter 9), and when the weather is fine, you can dine in one of Rome's nicest garden courtyards. But the draw is not just location;

it's also the interesting and even surprising cuisine. In addition to the *piatti della storia* (dishes made from recipes from Renaissance Rome), La Veranda has branched out into experiments like *ravioli al rosmarino e cavalfiore con ragout di tonno* (ravioli with rosemary and cauliflower with a tuna ragout). Even more adventurous is the dessert *millefoglie con melanzane al ciccolato* — a napoleon with eggplant and chocolate, which works, strangely enough.

See map p. 122. Borgo Santo Spirito 73. ☎ **06-6872973.** *Reservations recommended on weekends. Bus: 62 to San Pietro; then turn right on Borgo Santo Spirito. Secondi: 16€–28€ ($21–$36), including* contorno *(side dish). AE, MC, V. Open: Daily noon to 3 p.m. and 7–11 p.m.*

Maccheroni
$ **Pantheon   ROMAN**

This clean, bright, nouveau trattoria has great food, including excellent pastas and wines, and a wonderful location only steps from the Pantheon but out of the hubbub. The focus is on pasta, and it specializes in traditional Roman recipes, among which the *gricia* (sautéed bacon and onions and pecorino cheese) is queen. The trattoria also has a few *secondi*, including excellent steaks, and we recommend the *contorni* (vegetables) and the appetizers, including excellent cold cuts and cheese. The house wine is very good.

See map p. 122. Piazza delle Coppelle 44. ☎ **06-68307895.** *Bus: 64, 70, 75, or 116. Secondi: 9€–16€ ($12–$21). AE, MC, V. Open: Daily noon to 3 p.m. and 8–11:30 p.m.*

Osteria Ponte Sisto
$ **Trastevere   ROMAN**

Offering traditional Roman fare, this famous *osteria* has been a longstanding destination for locals and tourists alike. Try the delicious *risotto al gorgonzola* (Italian rice cooked with Gorgonzola cheese) or, if you dare, some truly Roman specialties such as *trippa alla romana* (tripe in a light tomato sauce) or beef roasted on a charcoal grill.

See map p. 122. Via Ponte Sisto 80, off Piazza Trilussa. ☎ **06-5883411.** *Reservations recommended. Bus: 23 or 115 to Piazza Trilussa. Secondi: 9€–16€ ($12–$21). AE, MC, V. Open: Thurs–Tues noon to 3 p.m. and 7–10:30 p.m. Closed Aug.*

Pasqualino al Colosseo Antica Trattoria
$ **Colosseo   ROMAN**

This is a traditional Roman restaurant, with large dining rooms to accommodate feasting Romans on weekends and for special occasions, and cozier ones for everyday eating; it has a terrace for use in the good season. The food is well prepared and, of course, traditional; the service is attentive. Besides a comprehensive menu, you'll find daily specials: the traditional Roman ones of *gnocchi* (potato dumplings) on Thursdays, *baccalà* (salted cod) and chickpea soup on Fridays, and so on.

See map p. 122. Via Santissimi Quattro 66. ☎ 06-7004576. Reservations recommended on weekends. Metro: Colosseo. Secondi: 9€–18€ ($12–$23). AE, MC, DC, V. Open: Tues–Sun 11:30 a.m.–3:30 p.m. and 7–11 p.m.

Presidente
$$$ Trevi   FISH

Looking rather nondescript from the outside — if anything, a bit touristy — this restaurant is a hidden pearl where you can taste excellent fish dishes accompanied by fine wines. To a comfortable interior, it adds in the good season a small and pleasant terrace. The four tasting menus are definitely recommended and include a satisfying selection of dishes following one of four themes: Traditional Roman, fish, meat, or the restaurant's own recipe (called *al Presidente*). The menu changes often, but you might find the wonderful *fettuccine con calamaretti bottarga e pomodori* (homemade pasta with squid, fish roe, and fresh tomatoes) or the exquisite *millefoglie di pesce e verdure* (fish and vegetable napoleon).

See map p. 122. Via in Arcione 95, off Piazza Fontana di Trevi. ☎ 06-6797342. Reservations recommended. Bus: 116, 117, 119 to Largo del Tritone; walk 1 block toward underpass, and turn right. Secondi: 15€–28€ ($20–$36). MC, V. Open: Tues–Sun 7:30–11:30 p.m.

Quirino
$$ Trevi   ROMAN/SICILIAN

A traditional Roman restaurant with some Sicilian influence, Quirino's focus is on seafood — for example, *fritto di paranza* (mixed, deep-fried small fish and calamari), which is made to perfection. The seafood also gets worked into the homemade fresh pasta dishes, such as the classic *spaghetti alle vongole* (spaghetti with clams) or the more venturesome *tagliatelle ai porcini e alle vongole* (fresh pasta with porcini mushrooms and clams). A variety of grilled fish, meat, and vegetarian pastas completes the menu. For dessert, you can't go wrong with the homemade *cannoli* (sweet ricotta-filled tubes).

See map p. 122. Via delle Muratte 84, off Via del Corso. ☎ 06-6794108. Reservations recommended. Bus: 116, 117, 119 to Via del Corso. Secondi: 11€–18€ ($14–$23). AE, MC, V. Open: Mon–Sat 12:30–3:30 p.m. and 6:30–11:30 p.m. Closed 3 weeks in Aug.

Sora Lella
$$ Trastevere   ROMAN

This family-run restaurant — created by the sister of the famous Roman actor Aldo Fabrizi and run today by his son and grandsons — was already a Roman institution, but with the recent renovations both in the dining room and on the menu, it has won new admirers. The gnocchi are superb, and complementing the solid traditional menu are many new dishes, such as the delicious *polpettine al vino* (small meatballs in a wine sauce). Tasting menus and a vegetarian menu are available, and the traditional Roman *contorni,* such as *cicoria* (dandelion greens) and *carciofi* (artichokes), are exceptional. *See map p. 122. Via di Ponte Quattro Capi 16, on Isola Tiberina, in the river between the center and Trastevere.* ☎ *06-6861601. Reservations recommended. Bus: 23, 63, and 115 to Isola Tiberina. Secondi: 14€–20€ ($18–$26). AE, DC, V. Open: Mon–Sat noon to 2 p.m. and 7–11 p.m. Closed Aug.*

Trattoria
$$ Navona/Pantheon CREATIVE SICILIAN

This pleasant, lively restaurant may have a generic name, but names can be deceptive. You can have your *aperitivo* (predinner drink) on the first floor with a choice of savory — and delicious — tidbits and then move upstairs to your table for dinner. The new chef is Sicilian, and so is the menu, including many classics and a number of original creations. Among the classics, the *caponata* (sautée of cubed eggplants with pinoli nuts and raisins) is a standout, as is the *pasta alla Norma.* The other offerings change, but you might find *scottata di capesante con verdurine* (sautée of scallops and vegetables). Do not miss the desserts: delicious baby *cannoli* (sweet ricotta filled tubes) and the *cassata* (a sweet Sicilian ricotta con-coction covered with a thin layer of almond paste). The wine list includes wine by the glass.

See map p. 122. Via del Pozzo delle Cornacchie 25. ☎ *06-68301427.* www. ristorantetrattoria.it. *Reservations recommended. Bus: 64, 70, 75, or 116. Secondi: 14€–20€ ($18–$26). AE, DC, V. Open: Mon–Sat 12:30–3 p.m. and 7:30–11 p.m. Closed Aug.*

Dining and Snacking on the Go

Americans may be surprised to discover that fast food was invented in Rome more than 2,000 years ago: Street food was sold at carts and small shops in the Forum, and a quick bite to eat could be had at any *caupona* (the Ancient Roman word for *eatery*), standing or perched on a high stool at the counter. Although times have changed, you'll see many Romans still doing the same — having a sandwich standing up in a bar or eating a square of pizza from a take-away *rosticceria.* Here is the low-down on Roman fast food — quite different, as you'll see, from what you're used to.

Bars

Roman cafes are called *bars;* they rarely have more than a few seats and do most of their business at the counters — also because there is a sur-charge for sitting down. Romans basically live in the bar during the day. This is where they come for breakfast before going to work, espresso and *cornetto* (sweet croissant, often filled with cream or jam) being the typical fare; for coffee break; and for lunch. They return in the evening for *aperitivo,* a predinner drink (with or without alcohol) accompanied by small tidbits to eat. For lunch, bars prepare a large variety of sandwiches. The *rosetta* is the typical Roman bread roll, which can be filled with *frittata* (omelet), mozzarella and tomatoes, or cheese and cold cuts; the *tramezzino* is slices of crustless American-style bread filled with a variety of mayo-based salads; and the *pizza Romana* — often our preferred — is a square of savory focaccia filled with ham and cheese, which can be eaten cold or warmed up. Many bars also double as ice cream parlors. For some of the trendiest bars, see Chapter 16, but any bar will provide a basic, good-quality breakfast or lunch.

Picnics

In fine weather, a nice, inexpensive option — and one greatly favored by children — is to get some sandwiches and head to one of Rome's great public parks, such as Villa Borghese or the Gianicolo (see Chapter 11), and have a picnic; even smaller neighborhood parks are a good option.

Keep in mind, however, that sitting on public fountains and monuments to have your lunch is forbidden, and you'll be asked to move. You may even be heavily fined if you're found littering.

An excellent place to buy farm-fresh food for your picnic is the **Fattoria la Parrina** (Largo Toniolo 3, between Piazza Navona and the Pantheon; ☎ 06-68300111), which offers wonderful farm bread, cold cuts, cheese, wine, and veggies, all organically produced on its farm in nearby southern Tuscany. Another good place is **L'Antico Forno di Piazza Trevi** (Via delle Muratte 8; ☎ 06-6792866), selling one of the best *pizza bianca* (focaccia) in Rome, as well as a large variety of bread, cheese, cold cuts, olives, and wine to go with it. This is an old-fashioned grocer, the ancestor of supermarkets, where you can find everything — including sodas, cookies, and paper napkins — to round out your picnic. If you don't like the idea of preparing your own sandwiches, pick up some already made or some hot pizza to go from one of the places described in the "Pizza a taglio" section, below.

Pizza a taglio

The single most common snack for Romans — and one that all kids seem to love — is a square of pizza from one of the ubiquitous hot-pizza counters around Rome. These joints — usually a glass counter with a few ovens in the background — bake pizza all day long (usually Mon–Sat 8 a.m.–8 p.m.) in large, oblong, metal pans, with a variety of toppings, from the simple *rossa* (tomato and oregano) and *bianca* (focaccia) to *con i funghi* (mushrooms with tomato sauce or with cheese), *con la mozzarella* (tomato and mozzarella), *con le patate* (with thin slices of crispy potatoes), and *ripiena* (filled with ham and cheese). Some of the fancier places will have a larger variety, but novelty is not necessarily a sign of quality; look instead for steaming-hot pans, which means that they sell so much, they have to prepare new pizzas often. (At the best places, you'll see Romans waiting for the next slab of their favorite flavor to roll out.) Good addresses are too many to list, and many of the best don't even have names, but here are a few of our favorites: **Pizza** (Via del Leoncino 28; ☎ 06-6867757), **Pizza a Taglio** (Via della Frezza 40; ☎ 06-3227116), **Pizza** (Via della Penna 14; ☎ 06-7234596), **Pizza Rustica** (Via del Portico d'Ottavia, ☎ 06-6879262; and Via dei Pastini 116, ☎ 06-6782468), **Il Tempio del Buongustaio** (Piazza del Risorgimento 50; ☎ 06-6833709), **Pizza Al Taglio** (Via Cavour 307; ☎ 06-6784042), and **Pizzabuona** (Corso Vittorio Emanuele II 165; ☎ 06-6893229).

Pizzerie

For a fast — and cheaper — lunch or dinner without giving up on the pleasure of sitting down to a good table, Romans choose a *pizzeria*. These are simple restaurants specializing in pizza — strictly individual-size, round pizzas — and go from the more fancy (with tablecloths and fashionable dining rooms) to the more rustic (a piece of paper on a wooden table). They offer pizza with a variety of established toppings, most of which have been defined by name in a longstanding tradition, such as *margherita* (tomato and mozzarella), *napoletana* (tomato, mozzarella, and anchovies), *capricciosa* (tomato, mozzarella, mushrooms, artichoke hearts, olives, ham, and an egg), and *funghi* (mushrooms, tomato, and mozzarella). You'll also find more-modern and sometimes original combinations on the menu, such as *rugola, bresaola, e parmigiano* (fresh arugula and thin slices of cured beef and Parmesan cheese on a simple tomato sauce), *quattro formaggi* (four kinds of cheese), *broccoletti e salsicce* (broccoli rabe and Italian sausages), and so on. In addition, *pizzerie* typically serve a choice of savory and delicious appetizers, starting with *bruschetta* (toasted peasant-style bread topped with oil and garlic and, on request, tomatoes, olives, ham, and so on), but also *supplì* (rice balls stuffed with a small piece of mozzarella and deep fried), *filetti di baccalà* (deep-fried salt cod), *olive ascolane* (large green olives stuffed with meat and cheese and then deep fried), and *fiori di zucca* (zucchini flowers stuffed with a small piece of anchovy and mozzarella and then deep fried). If you like *filetti di baccalà,* the best in Rome are fried at **Filetti di Baccalà** (Largo dei Librari 88, off Via dei Giubbonari at Campo de' Fiori; ☎ **06-6864018;** open Mon–Sat dinner only), a small restaurant where you can take out or sit down — it also serves a few *contorni* and desserts, but lines are epic.

For real Neapolitan pizza that has received the seal of honor from the organization that guards the quality of Neapolitan pizza (a bit like D.O.C. for wine), try **Al Forno della Soffitta 1** (Via Piave 62; ☎ **06-42011164**) and **Al Forno della Soffitta 2** (Via dei Villini, 1/f; ☎ **06-4404642;** closed Sun) or **Pizza Re** (Via di Ripetta 14; ☎ **06-3211468;** closed Sun). The pizza is also excellent at the elegant **Il Regno di Napoli** (Via Romagna 22; ☎ **06-4745025;** closed Sat–Sun lunch only), which is also a full-scale restaurant and therefore a bit more expensive, and at **Pizza Forum** (Via San Giovanni in Laterano 34; ☎ **06-7002515**), with large and modern dining rooms and fast service.

For Roman-style pizza (thinner than the Neapolitan version and less bready but more savory), try **Baffetto** (Via del Governo Vecchio 114;

☎ 06-6861617); **Ivo** (Via di San Francesco a Ripa 158; ☎ 06-5817082; closed Tues); or **Opera** (Via del Leone 23; ☎ 06-68809927), which offers 30 types of pizza.

Really good coffee

Even if you're on the go, the proper way to finish a meal is with a good coffee — at least that's what Romans believe. Note, however, that many smaller trattorie and pizzerias don't make coffee. What better reason to remove to a famous coffee shop after your meal? If you're a coffee aficionado, you should not miss the **Caffè Sant'Eustachio** (Piazza Sant'Eustachio 82; ☎ 06-68802048; Bus: Minibus 116), a traditional Italian bar that has been serving Rome's best espresso since 1938, made with water still carried into the city on the Ancient Roman aqueduct. Another excellent temple of coffee is **Tazza d'Oro,** just by the Pantheon (☎ 06-6789792; Bus: Minibus 116 to Pantheon); its coffee is very good, and you haven't lived until you've tried its *granita di caffè* (a concoction of frozen espresso served with whipped cream).

Snack bars, tavola calda, and rosticcerie

A delicate nuance differentiates each of these typical Roman fast-food eateries. They correspond to your local diner or deli — if not in look and kind of food served, at least in purpose. This is where you can have a simple lunch at a fraction of the price you would pay in a restaurant and where harrassed working parents and singles who don't feel like cooking come for takeout in the evening. They present the food behind glass counters and sell it by weight or by the piece. Sometimes, they're organized as cafeterias, and you take your food on a tray to a sitting place; others have only standing room at a counter and are mostly takeout. *Snack bars* usually have fewer offerings than a *tavola calda,* and *rosticcerie* focus on roasted chickens and pizza, although often with an array of side dishes. Some are obviously better than others, and although in the simplest snack bar, you'll find little more than sandwiches, in the best *tavola calda,* you'll have an ample choice of tasty and well-prepared hot and cold dishes, including pasta, *secondi,* and *contorni* — in short, all you need for a full meal. Always look carefully at the food before ordering to check that it isn't dried out; in mediocre places, you'll be much worse off than at the local bar, where sandwiches are usually freshly prepared. The clientele will also help you: Crowds at mealtime (especially Romans) are an excellent sign.

Midway between a snack bar and a restaurant, **Grillpoint** (Piazzale di Porta Pia 122; ☎ 06-44236435; open daily noon to 2:30 p.m.) provides an elegant dining room and a wide choice of well-prepared dishes, including pizza. **Da Maciste al Salario, Pizza, Vino e Cucina** (Via Salaria 179/a, at Via Metauro; ☎ 06-8848267; closed Mon dinner and Sun lunch) serves its excellent food cafeteria style and provides ample seating. There is a long line for lunch, and if you arrive too late, the best will be gone. In *il centro,* there's the crowded **Taverna del Campo** snack stop with *crostini, panini,* and beer (Campo de' Fiori 16; ☎ 06-6874402).

Sweet endings: Gelato

Italian ice cream (gelato) is among the best in the world and has nothing to do with what is often called in America "Italian ice." It is creamy without being heavy, and even the fruit flavors have little in common with icy sherbet. Serious gelato comes in a variety of flavors and is sold by the size of the cone or cup you choose. It's served with a special spatula and not by the ball; hence, you can have up to three flavors even in the smallest size. Romans like to top it with whipped cream, so you'll be asked if you care for *panna* or not; our answer is usually "Yes, plenty!" Flavors are divided between *frutta* (fruit) — *limone* (lemon), *arancio* (orange), *melone* (melon), *pesca* (peach), *mora* (blackberry), *frutti di bosco* (mixed wild berries), the list is endless — and *creme* (creams). The best cream flavors for us are *zabaglione* (a rum-and-egg combo, reminiscent of eggnog), *bacio* (hazelnut chocolate), and *stracciatella* (vanilla with chocolate chips), but even plain *crema* (egg cream) and *cioccolato* (chocolate) can be fabulous when well prepared.

You'll see prepackaged, commercial gelati, which you can choose from the signs nailed on the wall or pasted on the cooler where they're sold. Although any bar will have the prepackaged kind in a white cooler somewhere inside, unless you're dying for any old ice cream *now,* wait to find a bar that also says GELATERIA outside, and look for the sign PRODUZIONE PROPRIA: It means they make their own ice cream, and it will be fresh and delicious.

The oldest gelato parlor in Rome is **Giolitti** (Via Uffici del Vicario 40; ☎ 06-699-1243; Bus: Minibus 116), which offers a huge selection of flavors — the fruit and chocolate flavors are excellent. The second-oldest is the **Palazzo del Freddo di G. Fassi** (Via Principe Eugenio 65; ☎ 06-4464740; Metro: Piazza Vittorio). In Trastevere, try the **Gelateria alla Scala** (Via della Scala 5; ☎ 06 5813174; Tram: 8), for rich homemade ice cream that could almost be described as pungent. Near Campo de' Fiori, go to **Pica** (Via della Seggiola 12, off Via Arenula; ☎ 06-68803275; Tram: 8), which prepares one of the best ice creams in Rome. Near the Fontana di Trevi, the **Gelateria Trevi** (Via del Lavatore 84–85; ☎ 06-6792060; Bus: 116 or 492) serves a nicely sized, good ice cream, and there is the famous **Il Gelato di S. Crispino** (Via della Panetteria 42; ☎ 06-6793924), for gourmet ice cream served in small cups (exclusively — no cones) and prepared with the freshest fruits — often uncommon ones, such as the *susina* (a local fruit between a plum and a litche) — and ranging to the outright extravagant, such as *funghi* (mushrooms), which is surprisingly tasty.

On the light side, Romans love a sort of frappe/shake/smoothie made with real fresh yogurt and fruit. The refreshment is served in several bars, but you can find some of Rome's best at **Yogobar,** with several locations, including Via Lucania 23, off Via Boncompagni, near Via Veneto (☎ 06-42883001; Bus: Minibus 116), and Viale Regina Margherita 83b, off Via Nomentana to the west (☎ 06-8551374; Bus: 63 or tram 3).

Index of Establishments by Neighborhood

Appian Way
Hostaria L'Archeologia (Roman, $$)

Campo de' Fiori
Bric (Roman/French/Mediterranean, $)
Il Drappo (Sardinian, $)
Filetti di Baccalà (Fish, $)
Pica (Gelato, $)

Colosseo
Hasekura (Japanese, $$)
Hostaria Nerone (Italian, $)
Il Guru (Indian, $$)
Pasqualino al Colosseo Antica
Trattoria (Roman, $$)
Pizza Forum (Pizza, $)

Monte Mario
La Pergola (Creative Italian, $$$$)

Navona/Pantheon
Baffetto (Pizza, $)
Baires (SouthAmerican, $$)
Enoteca Capranica (Creative
Italian/Winery, $$$)
Giolitti (Gelato, $)
Il Convivio Troiani (Creative Roman,
$$$–$$$$)
Maccheroni (Roman, $)
Trattoria (Creative Sicilian, $$)

Parioli
Da Maciste al Salario, Pizza, Vino e
Cucina (Roman/Pizza, $)

Piazza del Popolo
Bolognese (Bolognese, $$)
Gusto (Creative Italian/Pizza, $$)
La Casina Valadier (Creative Roman,
$$$–$$$$)
Pizza Re (Pizza, $)

Piazza di Spagna
Birreria Viennese (Mittel Europe, $$)
Hamasei (Japanese, $$)
Naturist Club CMI (Vegetarian, $)

Porta Pia
Al Forno della Soffitta 2 (Pizza, $)
Grillpoint (Roman/Pizza, $)
Opera (Pizza, $)

Prati
Arcangelo (Roman/Creative
Italian/Fish, $$)
Macondo (Caribbean, $$)

Repubblica
Al Forno della Soffitta 1 (Pizza, $)
Opera (Pizza, $)
Oriental Express (Arab, $)
Palazzo del Freddo di G. Fassi
(Gelato, $)

San Pietro
Cantina Tirolese (Mittel Europe, $$)
Da Benito e Gilberto (Fish, $$)
Dante Taberna de' Gracchi
(Roman, $–$$)
Il Matriciano (Roman, $$)
La Veranda (Creative Italian, $$$)

Teatro Marcello
Da Giggetto (Jewish Roman, $$)

Testaccio
Al Regno di Re Ferdinando II
(Neapolitan, $$–$$$)
Checchino dal 1887 (Roman, $$)

Trastevere
Checco er Carettiere (Roman, $$)
Ferrara (Creative Italian/Winery, $$$)

Ivo (Pizza, $)
Osteria Ponte Sisto (Roman, $)
Ouzerie (Greek, $$)
Sora Lella (Roman, $$)
Surya Mahal (Indian, $$$)

Trevi

Gelateria Trevi (Gelato, $)
Il Gelato di S. Crispino (Gelato, $)

La Taverna Trevi da Tarquinio
(Abbruzzese/Roman, $)
Presidente (Fish, $$$)
Quirino (Roman, $$)

Via Veneto

Al Forno della Soffitta 1 (Pizza, $)
Cesarina (Roman/Bolognese, $$$)
Regno di Napoli (Neapolitan/Pizza,
$$–$$$)

Index of Establishments by Cuisine

Abruzzese

La Taverna Trevi da Tarquinio
(Trevi, $)

Arab

Oriental Express (Repubblica, $)

Bolognese

Bolognese (Piazza del Popolo, $$)
Cesarina (Via Veneto, $$$)

Caribbean

Macondo (Prati, $$)

Creative Italian

Arcangelo (Prati, $$)
Enoteca Capranica (Navona/
Pantheon, $$$)
Ferrara (Trastevere, $$$)
Gusto (Piazza Del Popolo, $$)
La Pergola (Monte Mario, $$$$)
La Veranda (San Pietro, $$$)

Creative Roman

Il Convivio Troiani (Navona/
Pantheon, $$$–$$$$)
La Casina Valadier (Piazza del
Popolo, $$$–$$$$)

Creative Sicilian

Trattoria (Navona/Pantheon, $$)

Fish

Al Regno di Re Ferdinando II
(Testaccio, $$–$$$)
Arcangelo (Prati, $$)
Da Benito e Gilberto (San Pietro, $$)
Filetti di Baccalà (Campo de' Fiori, $)
Presidente (Trevi, $$$)

French

Bric (Campo De' Fiori, $)

French Colonial

Eau Vive (Navona/Pantheon, $$)

Gelato

Gelateria alla Scala (Trastevere, $)
Gelateria Trevi (Trevi, $)
Giolitti (Navona/Pantheon, $)
Il Gelato di S. Crispino (Trevi, $)
Palazzo del Freddo di G. Fassi
(Repubblica/Colosseo, $)
Pica (Campo de' Fiori, $)

Greek

Ouzerie (Trastevere, $$)

Indian

Il Guru (Colosseo, $$)
Surya Mahal (Trastevere, $$$)

Japanese
Hamasei (Piazza di Spagna, $$)
Hasekura (Colosseo, $$)

Jewish Roman
Da Giggetto (Teatro Marcello, $$)

Mediterranean
Bric (Campo De' Fiori, $)

Mittel Europe
Birreria Viennese (Piazza di Spagna, $$)
Cantina Tirolese (San Pietro, $$)

Neapolitan
Al Regno di Re Ferdinando II
(Testaccio, $$–$$$)
Regno di Napoli (Via Veneto, $$–$$$)

Pizza
Al Forno della Soffitta 1 (Via
Veneto/Repubblica, $)
Al Forno della Soffitta 2 (Porta Pia, $)
Baffetto (Navona/Pantheon, $)
Da Maciste al Salario (Parioli, $)
Grillpoint (Porta Pia, $)
Gusto (Piazza Del Popolo, $$)
Ivo (Trastevere, $)
Opera (Repubblica/Colosseo, $)
Pizza Forum (Colosseo, $)
Pizza Re (Piazza del Popolo, $)
Regno di Napoli (Via Veneto, $$–$$$)

Roman
Arcangelo (Prati, $$)
Bric (Campo De' Fiori, $)
Cesarina (Via Veneto, $$$)
Checchino dal 1887 (Testaccio, $$)
Checco er Carettiere (Trastevere, $$)
Da Maciste al Salario (Parioli, $)
Dante Taberna de' Gracchi (San
Pietro, $–$$)
Grillpoint (Porta Pia, $)
Hostaria L'Archeologia (Appian
Way, $$)
Hostaria Nerone (Colosseum, $)
Il Matriciano (San Pietro, $$)
La Taverna Trevi da Tarquinio
(Trevi, $)
Maccheroni (Navona/Pantheon, $)
Osteria Ponte Sisto (Trastevere, $)
Pasqualino al Colosseo Antica
Trattoria (Colosseo, $$)
Quirino (Trevi, $$)
Sora Lella (Trastevere, $$)

Sardinian
Il Drappo (Campo De' Fiori, $)

South American
Baires (Navona/Pantheon, $$)

Vegetarian
Naturist Club CMI (Piazza di
Spagna, $)

Index of Establishments by Price

$
Al Forno della Soffitta 1 (Pizza, Via
Veneto/Repubblica)
Al Forno della Soffitta 2 (Pizza,
Porta Pia)
Baffetto (Pizza, Navona/Pantheon)
Bric (Roman/French/Mediterranean,
Campo De' Fiori)

Da Maciste al Salario (Roman/Pizza,
Parioli)
Dante Taberna de' Gracchi (Roman,
San Pietro)
Filetti di Baccalà (Fish, Campo de'
Fiori)
Gelateria alla Scala (Gelato, Trastevere)
Gelateria Trevi (Gelato, Trevi)
Giolitti (Gelato, Navona/Pantheon)

Grillpoint (Roman/Pizza, Porta Pia)
Hostaria Nerone (Italian, Colosseum)
Il Drappo (Sardinian, Campo De' Fiori)
Il Gelato di S. Crispino (Gelato, Trevi)
Ivo (Pizza, Trastevere)
La Taverna Trevi da Tarquinio
(Abbruzzese/Roman, Trevi)
Maccheroni (Roman, Pantheon)
Naturist Club CMI (Vegetarian, Piazza
di Spagna)
Opera (Pizza, Repubblica/Colosseo)
Oriental Express (Arab, Repubblica)
Osteria Ponte Sisto (Roman,
Trastevere)
Palazzo del Freddo di G. Fassi (Gelato,
Repubblica/Colosseo)
Pica (Gelato, Campo de' Fiori)
Pizza Forum (Pizza, Colosseo)
Pizza Re (Pizza, Piazza del Popolo)
Regno di Napoli (Neapolitan/Pizza,
Via Veneto)

$$

Al Regno di Re Ferdinando II
(Neapolitan/Fish, Testaccio)
Arcangelo (Roman/Creative
Italian/Fish, Prati)
Baires (Southamerican,
Navona/Pantheon)
Birreria Viennese (Mittel Europe,
Piazza di Spagna)
Bolognese (Bolognese, Piazza del
Popolo,)
Cantina Tirolese (Mittel Europe, San
Pietro)
Checchino dal 1887 (Roman, Testaccio)
Checco er Carettiere (Roman,
Trastevere)
Da Benito e Gilberto (Fish, San Pietro)
Da Giggetto (Jewish Roman, Teatro
Marcello)
Dante Taberna de' Gracchi (Roman,
San Pietro)
Eau Vive (French Colonial,
Navona/Pantheon)

Gusto (Creative Italian/Pizza, Piazza
Del Popolo)
Hamasei (Japanese, Piazza di Spagna)
Hasekura (Japanese, Colosseo)
Hostaria L'Archeologia (Roman, Appian
Way)
Il Guru (Indian, Colosseo)
Il Matriciano (Roman, San Pietro)
Macondo (Caribbean, Prati)
Ouzerie (Greek, Trastevere)
Pasqualino al Colosseo (Roman,
Colosseo)
Quirino (Roman, Trevi)
Regno di Napoli (Neapolitan/Pizza,
Via Veneto)
Sora Lella (Roman, Trastevere)
Trattoria (Creative Sicilian,
Navona/Pantheon)

$$$

Al Regno di Re Ferdinando II
(Neapolitan/Fish, Testaccio)
Cesarina (Roman/Bolognese, Via
Veneto)
Enoteca Capranica (Creative
Italian/Winery/Navona/Pantheon)
Ferrara (Creative Italian/Winery,
Trastevere)
Il Convivio Troiani (Creative Roman,
Navona/Pantheon)
La Casina Valadier (Creative Roman,
Piazza del Popolo)
La Veranda (Creative Italian, San
Pietro)
Regno di Napoli (Neapolitan/Pizza,
Via Veneto)
Surya Mahal (Indian, Trastevere)

$$$$

Il Convivio Troiani (Creative Roman,
Navona/Pantheon)
La Casina Valadier (Creative Roman,
Piazza del Popolo)
La Pergola (Creative Italian, Monte
Mario)

Part IV
Exploring Rome

The 5th Wave   By Rich Tennant

"It says, children are forbidden from running, touching objects, or appearing bored during the tour."

In this part . . .

Whether you're an architecture buff, an amateur archaeologist, an art aficionado, a devout Catholic, or simply
a lover of the world's great cities, you'll be delighted with all
that the Eternal City has to offer. In this part, we tell you about
Rome's best attractions, both inside and outside the city walls.

Rome is a veritable "who's who" of famous monuments,
museums, and ruins, and we cover them all in Chapter 11,
along with tips on how best to enjoy them. And although
Rome isn't as well known for fashion and shopping as some
other Italian cities, it has some fabulous shopping areas specializing in Roman- and Italian-made goods, which we tell you
about in Chapter 12. In Chapter 13, we've done some of your
planning ahead of time, putting together a choice of the five
best itineraries you can take, depending on your interests.
And although it has been said that even a lifetime is not enough
to visit Rome, in Chapter 14 we suggest five side trips — easy
excursions from Rome to unique sights as absorbing as the
great city itself.

Chapter 11

Discovering Rome's Best Attractions

- -

In This Chapter
▶ Exploring Rome's most famous attractions
▶ Enjoying the Vatican's artistic riches
▶ Checking out other fun things to see and do
▶ Taking a guided tour

- -

*T*he seven hills of Rome have been continuously inhabited for the past 3,000 years or so, resulting in a melting pot that laid the foundation for a cosmopolitan European culture, of which Rome remained the heart for centuries and in which it still plays a central role. The **Vatican** — the small city-state that is the official seat of the Catholic faith — still leads the Catholic world from its location in the center of the city.

With such a history, it's not surprising that nowhere else will you find such a cultural density and layering of periods and styles. For instance, the 913 churches in Rome's *il centro* range in period from the 8th to the 18th century, many lavishly decorated with masterpieces. The Vatican is a vast complex of museums, apartments, chapels, and gardens filled with artistic riches. What's more, the Papal Jubilee in 2000 was the impetus to make many much-needed renovations to the entire city, as well as efforts to reduce congestion and pollution. These changes have had a big impact on the city, and ever-increasing numbers of appreciative tourists are pouring in.

The Eternal City may have an exalted history, but Rome is no lifeless museum of the past. A couple million people live and work in this place, where the thoroughfares were designed for chariots instead of cabs. Romans walk on ruins from the days of Caesar, turn along the same alleyways trod by masters of the Renaissance, and thrill to the same lighted fountains that were reflected in the eyes of Fellini's beautiful debauchers.

Rome wasn't built in a day or even a millennium, so don't think you can *see* it all in a day: Set aside several days to do the city right.

Don't pass up these deals

If you're planning to do a lot of sightseeing in Rome, you may want to purchase discount cards offered by various museums and attractions.

The four branches of the **Museo Nazionale Romano (National Roman Museum)** — Palazzo Altemps, Palazzo Massimo, Terme di Diocleziano, and Cripta Balbi — offer a three-day pass good for a single visit to each of the sights; it costs 7€ ($9), a savings of 10€ ($13), and is sold at each of the four branches.

The complex of the **Musei Capitolini (Capitoline Museums)** also offers a cumulative ticket; it is valid seven days and includes admission to the two Capitoline Museums, in addition to the Tabularium and the Centrale Montemartini, for 9.90€ ($13), a savings of 5.20€ ($6.80).

The **Park of the Appia Antica** also offers a cumulative ticket to visit its major monuments; 6€ ($8) gets you into the Baths of Caracalla, the Mausoleum of Cecilia Metella, and the Villa of the Quintili. The pass is valid for seven days, and you can purchase it from any of the three sites.

If you're planning an extensive visit of Ancient Rome, the best deal is the seven-day **Roma Archeologia Card:** for 20€ ($26), you can access the four sites of the **National Roman Museum** (Palazzo Altemps, Palazzo Massimo, Terme di Diocleziano, and Cripta Balbi) and the three paying sites of the **Appian Way** (the Baths of Caracalla, the Mausoleum of Cecilia Metella, and the Villa of the Quintili), plus the Colosseum and the Palatino. You can purchase card at the participating sites (except for the Via Appia locations) or at the main Visitor Center of the Tourist Board of Rome (APT), at Via Parigi 5 (☎ **06-36004399**).

 For a service fee of 1.50€ ($1.95), you can make reservations for a number of attractions — and even buy your tickets online — by contacting **Pierreci** (☎ **06-39967700;** www.pierreci.it), the official agency that manages reservations for many Roman attractions. Pierreci will send you a voucher by e-mail, and you pick up your tickets at a special desk directly at the attraction entrance, skipping the waiting line. Pierreci's hours are Monday through Saturday 9 a.m. to 1:30 p.m. and 2:30 to 5 p.m. The official agent for reservations and tickets for other attractions — such as the Galleria Borghese — is **Ticketeria** (☎ **06-32810;** Fax: 06-32651329; www.ticketeria.it). Just as with Pierreci, Ticketeria sends you a voucher by e-mail, and you pick up your tickets at a special location at the attraction entrance, thereby avoiding lines.

 The **Vatican** is a separate state, and you make reservations for the attractions there at its visitor office (see "The Vatican," later in this chapter).

To accommodate its tourists, the city of Rome continues to expand opening hours for museums and other attractions, especially during holidays and the summer months. Check with a local tourist office for changes that may occur during your visit (see Chapter 8 for locations).

To fully appreciate the Roman Forum, the Colosseum, and other ruins, pick up a copy of the small book *Rome Past and Present,* sold in bookstores or at stands near the Forum for approximately 10€ ($13). Its plastic overleaves show you how Rome looked 2,000 years ago.

Rome's Top Sights

Where do you begin? If you're an archaeology buff, Rome's ancient sights could keep you going for days, weeks, months, and even years. But the city is also loaded with famous museums, impressive monuments, and awe-inspiring churches. In this treasure trove of possibilities, you have to make some decisions. The sights in this section are our roster of the most important Roman attractions. For their locations, see the "Rome Attractions" map on p. 148.

 Remember that as a rule, ticket booths close half an hour to an hour before the stated closing time of a given attraction.

Rome's attractions tend to be busy at any time of day or year, crowded with both foreign and local visitors. April and May are the worst for the large groups of schoolchildren who flock into Rome from all over the world for their field trips; June and July are almost as bad for the huge numbers of tourists from everywhere. If you want to avoid throngs of people, the best time of year to visit is from late January to early March, when the bad weather keeps tourist crowds at bay. In general, weekends tend to be uncrowded in summer, when most locals head for the beach; weekdays are a good choice the rest of the year, when locals are at work. Mondays are tricky, because most galleries and some museums are closed, so people flock to those other attractions that remain open. Usually, early morning, lunch recess, and late evening are good times to visit; midmorning and midafternoon are the peak visiting hours.

For the Capella Sistina (Sistine Chapel) and Basilica di San Pietro (St. Peter's Basilica), see "The Vatican," later in this chapter.

 ### Musei Capitolini (Capitoline Museums)
Teatro Marcello

The **Capitoline Museums** are housed in the two palaces — Palazzo Nuovo and Palazzo dei Conservatori — that open onto the beautiful **Piazza del Campidoglio,** designed by Michelangelo. The oldest public collections in the world, the museums hold a treasury of ancient sculpture and an important collection of European paintings from the 17th and 18th centuries. Among the masterpieces of the museums is the original second-century bronze **equestrian statue of Marcus Aurelius.** (The one you see standing in the middle of the square is a copy.) The statue was saved only because early Christians thought it was the first Christian emperor, Constantine. The Palazzo Nuovo houses the famous *Capitoline Venus* and such other famous sculptures as the *Dying Gaul,* a Roman copy of a Greek original,

Rome Attractions

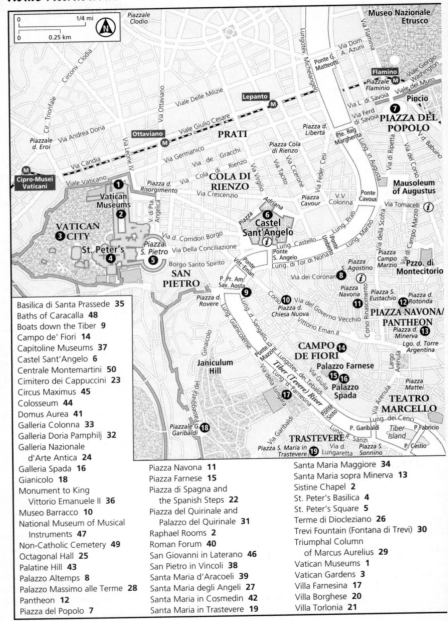

Basilica di Santa Prassede **35**
Baths of Caracalla **48**
Boats down the Tiber **9**
Campo de' Fiori **14**
Capitoline Museums **37**
Castel Sant'Angelo **6**
Centrale Montemartini **50**
Cimitero dei Cappuccini **23**
Circus Maximus **45**
Colosseum **44**
Domus Aurea **41**
Galleria Colonna **33**
Galleria Doria Pamphilj **32**
Galleria Nazionale
  d'Arte Antica **24**
Galleria Spada **16**
Gianicolo **18**
Monument to King
  Vittorio Emanuele II **36**
Museo Barracco **10**
National Museum of Musical
  Instruments **47**
Non-Catholic Cemetery **49**
Octagonal Hall **25**
Palatine Hill **43**
Palazzo Altemps **8**
Palazzo Massimo alle Terme **28**
Pantheon **12**
Piazza del Popolo **7**

Piazza Navona **11**
Piazza Farnese **15**
Piazza di Spagna and
  the Spanish Steps **22**
Piazza del Quirinale and
  Palazzo del Quirinale **31**
Raphael Rooms **2**
Roman Forum **40**
San Giovanni in Laterano **46**
San Pietro in Vincoli **38**
Santa Maria d'Aracoeli **39**
Santa Maria degli Angeli **27**
Santa Maria in Cosmedin **42**
Santa Maria in Trastevere **19**

Santa Maria Maggiore **34**
Santa Maria sopra Minerva **13**
Sistine Chapel **2**
St. Peter's Basilica **4**
St. Peter's Square **5**
Terme di Diocleziano **26**
Trevi Fountain (Fontana di Trevi) **30**
Triumphal Column
  of Marcus Aurelius **29**
Vatican Museums **1**
Vatican Gardens **3**
Villa Farnesina **17**
Villa Borghese **20**
Villa Torlonia **21**

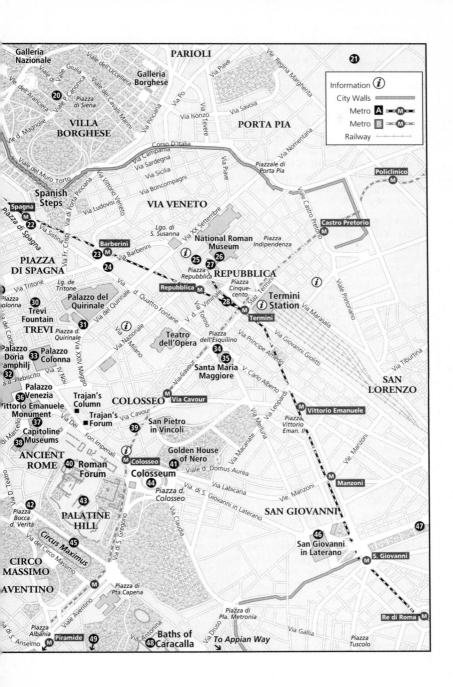

and *The Amazons* (under restoration at press time), two statues of female warriors that were originally in Hadrian's Villa in Tivoli (see Chapter 14).

In the courtyard of the Palazzo dei Conservatori are the much-photographed dismembered pieces of an ancient 40-foot **statue of Constantine II** — huge head, hands, foot, kneecap, and so on. Inside the Palazzo dei Conservatori, you find the famous *Lupa Capitolina,* the wolf suckling Romulus and Remus, a fifth-century-B.C. bronze that is the symbol of Rome. Another famous work is the bronze of the **boy removing a thorn from his foot.** Children, including toddlers, are often drawn to these two sculptures — our 2-year-old was particularly fascinated by the bronze of the boy. On the top floor is the **Pinacoteca Capitolina** (picture gallery), a superb collection including such famous paintings as Caravaggio's *Fortune Teller* and *John the Baptist;* Titian's *Baptism of Christ;* and works by Veronese, Rubens, and others.

Between the Palazzo Nuovo and the Palazzo dei Conservatori, bordering Piazza del Campidoglio to the south, is the **Palazzo Senatorio (Senatorial Palace).** This palace was used for administrative purposes until recently, when it was included in the Capitoline Museums to provide additional exposition space and show the results of the recent excavations underneath it. The palace was built in the Middle Ages over the **Tabularium,** an imposing Roman building that housed the public archives of the Roman Republic. The Tabularium was built of massive stone blocks with Doric columns in the facade. You can clearly see its remains from the Forum (3 of the original 11 arcades remain). It's now part of the museum complex, and its admission is included in the ticket.

You can spend several hours in these museums if you want an in-depth visit, but you can see the highlights in three hours or less, depending on your interests.

See map p. 148. Piazza del Campidoglio 1, off Piazza Venezia. ☎ *06-67102475.* www.museicapitolini.org. *Bus: Minibus 117. Admission: 6.20€ ($8); 1.60€ ($2) extra for special exhibits. Audio guides: 4€ ($5.20). Open: Tues–Sun 9 a.m.–8 p.m. Ticket booth closes 1 hour earlier. Closed Jan 1, May 1, Oct 28–29, and Dec 25.*

Castel Sant'Angelo (St. Angelo Castle)
San Pietro

This "castle" is a perfect example of practical Roman reuse: It began as a mausoleum to house the remains of Emperor Hadrian and other important Romans, later became a fortress, and is now a museum. Built in A.D. 123, it may have been incorporated into the city's defenses as early as 403; it was attacked by the Goths (one of the barbarian tribes that pillaged Rome in its decline) in 537. Later, the popes used it as a fortress and hideout, and, for convenience, connected it to the Vatican palace by an elevated corridor — which you can still see near Borgo Pio, stretching between St. Peter's and the castle. Castel Sant'Angelo houses a museum of arms and armor; you can also visit the elegant papal apartments from the Renaissance, as well as the horrible cells in which political prisoners were kept (among them sculptor Benvenuto Cellini). Count about three hours for a full visit.

See map p. 148. Lungotevere Castello 50. ☎ *06-6819111. Bus: 62 or 64 to Lungotevere Vaticano. Admission: 5€ ($6.50). Audio guides: 4€ ($5.20). Open: Tues–Sun 9 a.m.–8 p.m. Ticket booth closes 1 hour earlier. Closed Jan 1 and Dec 25.*

Catacombe di San Callisto (Catacombs of San Callisto)
Park of Appia Antica

Although there are several places to visit the catacombs in Rome (including the catacombs of St. Sebastian at Via Appia Antica 136, ☎ 06-7850350, and those of Ste. Domitilla, Via delle Sette Chiese 282; ☎ 06-5110342, www.catacombe.domitilla.it), the catacombs of St. Callisto are among the most impressive, with 20km (12½ miles) of tunnels and galleries underground, and organized on several levels. (It's cold down there at 18m/60 ft., so bring a sweater.) The catacombs began as quarries outside Ancient Rome where travertine marble and the dirt used in cement were dug. Early Christians, however, hid out, held mass, and buried their dead in the catacombs. The Catacombs of St. Callixtus (Callixtus III was an early pope, elected in 217) have four levels, including a crypt of several early popes and the tomb where St. Cecilia's remains were found. Some of the original paintings and decoration are still intact and show that Christian symbolism — doves, anchors, and fish — was already well developed. You can tour the catacombs in about one hour.

See map p. 176. Via Appia Antica 110. ☎ *06-51301580.* www.catacombe.roma.it. *Metro/Bus: Colli Albani (on Sun to Arco di Travertino); then Bus 660 to Via Appia Antica. Admission: 5€ ($6.50). Open: Thurs–Tues 8:30 a.m. to noon and 2:30–5 p.m. (in summer to 5:30 p.m.). Closed Feb.*

Terme di Caracalla (Baths of Caracalla)
Aventino

Built by the Roman Emperor Caracalla, these baths were completed in A.D. 216 and operated until 537. They are the best-preserved large thermal baths in Rome, with some of the internal decoration still visible, making it possible to imagine what it must have been like: richly decorated with enormous columns, hundreds of statues, colored marble or mosaic floors, and marble or stucco and frescoes on the walls. The baths in Roman times were much more than just a place to wash; people also came here to relax and to exercise. After entering the building from the porticos on the northeast side, Romans would access the dressing rooms and then could move through the deep-cleansing area, a sort of sauna similar to Turkish baths, starting in the *calidarium* (hot room) and proceeding to the *tepidarium* (first cooling down), the *frigidarium* (complete cooling down), and *natatio* (swimming pool). The baths also house two gymnasiums (exercise rooms), where trainers used to be on duty, and gardens for reading and relaxing. Plan to spend about an hour here.

See map p 148. Via delle Terme di Caracalla 52. ☎ *06-39967700.* www.pierreci.it. *Metro: Circo Massimo. Admission: 6€ ($8). Includes admission to Mausoleum of Cecilia Metella, and Villa of the Quintili. Open: Mon 9 a.m.–2 p.m., Tues–Sun 9 a.m. to 1 hour before sunset. Ticket booth closes 1 hour earlier. Closed Jan 1 and Dec 25.*

Colosseo or Anfiteatro Flavio (Colosseum)

Colosseo

The Colosseum, along with St. Peter's Basilica, is Rome's most recognizable monument. However, "Colosseum" isn't its official name. Begun under the Flavian Emperor Vespasian, it was named the Amphiteatrum Flavium and was finished in A.D. 80. The nickname came from the colossal statue of Nero that was erected nearby in the second century A.D. Estimates are that the Colosseum could accommodate up to 73,000 spectators. The entertainment included fights between gladiators and battles with wild animals. In the labyrinth of chambers beneath the original wooden floor of the Colosseum, deadly weapons, vicious beasts, and gladiators were prepared for the mortal combats. (Contrary to popular belief, the routine feeding of Christians to lions is a legend.) The Colosseum was damaged by fires and earthquakes, and eventually abandoned; it was then used as a marble quarry for the monuments of Christian Rome until Pope Benedict XV consecrated it in the 18th century. Next to the Colosseum is the **Arch of Constantine,** built in 315 to commemorate the emperor's victory over the pagan Maxentius in 312. Pieces from other monuments were reused, so Constantine's monument includes carvings honoring Marcus Aurelius, Trajan, and Hadrian.

In the summer of 2000, for the first time in centuries, the Colosseum was brought to life again with performances under the aegis of the Estate Romana (see Chapters 2 and 15); now it also houses special exhibitions.

We strongly recommend that you reserve your tickets to avoid the long lines; you can do so at the number or Web site in the following listing information. Plan to spend about an hour here.

See map p. 148. Via dei Fori Imperiali. ☎ *06-39967700.* www.pierreci.it. *Metro: Colosseo. Bus: Minibus 117. Admission: 8€ ($10) plus 2€ ($2.60) for exhibitions. Advance reservation 1.50€ ($1.95). Ticket price includes admission to the Palatine Hill. Audio guides: 4€ ($5.20). Open: Daily 9 a.m. to 1 hour before sunset. Ticket booth closes 1 hour earlier. Closed Jan 1 and Dec 25.*

Domus Aurea (Golden House)

Colosseo

The complex of Domus Aurea (Golden House) was the brainchild of the infamous Emperor Nero. Built after the great fire of A.D. 64 (which is traditionally but perhaps incorrectly blamed on him), it once covered more than 200 acres, with buildings scattered over a park landscaped to look like romantic countryside with an artificial lake, pastures, and vineyards. The lavishly decorated main reception building — the Golden House itself — was abandoned after Nero's fall in 68 and buried under the thermal baths of the emperors Titus and Trajan. Completely forgotten, it was stumbled upon in the 18th century when Romans digging in the "hill" across from the Colosseum found caves that turned out to be ceilings of ancient rooms decorated with Roman frescoes. Only since 2000, however, have tourists been allowed to visit these cavernous spaces, some of which still show the elegant interior paintings that decorated the walls. Often done in red tones, they tend to show mythological scenes surrounded by fine traceries and flourishes, of which you can see some fragments. *Note:* You need to reserve a ticket at the number or Web site in the following listing information. The visit lasts about an hour.

See map p. 148. Viale della Domus Aurea 1, off Via dei Fori Imperiali. ☎ *06-39967700. www.pierreci.it. Metro: Colosseo. Bus: Minibus 117. Tram: 3. Admission: 5€ ($6.50) plus 1.50€ ($1.95) for required advance reservation. Audio guides: 2€ ($2.60). Open: Wed–Mon 9 a.m.–7:45 p.m. Ticket booth closes 1 hour earlier. Closed Jan 1, May 1, and Dec 25.*

Galleria Borghese (Borghese Gallery)
Parioli

The Galleria Borghese is housed in the splendid building inside the Villa Borghese (now a large public park; see "Finding More Cool Things to See and Do," later in this chapter) that Cardinal Scipione Borghese created in 1613 for his art collection. Closed for restoration for 13 years, the building and site are now an attraction in themselves; the art inside is probably the most stunning smaller collection on view in Italy. The ground floor focuses on sculpture, including Canova's sensual reclining *Paulina Borghese as Venus Victrix* (Paulina was Napoleon's sister) and breathtaking marble carvings by the young Gian Lorenzo Bernini. His *David,* captured in the middle of a slingshot windup, is full of charmingly boyish concentration; *Apollo and Daphne* freezes in marble the moment when Daphne turns into a laurel tree, her fingers bursting into leaves and bark enveloping her legs. In the *Rape of Proserpine,* a sculpture Bernini executed in collaboration with his father, the god's fingers uncannily seem to press into her marble flesh. The extensive painting collection contains many masterpieces: Caravaggio's haunting self-portrait as *Bacchus* and his *St. Jerome Writing,* Antonello da Messina's subtle and mysterious *Portrait of a Man,* a young Raphael's *Deposition,* and Tiziano's *Sacred and Profane Love.* Andrea del Sarto, Coreggio, Lucas Cranach, Bronzino, Lorenzo Lotto, and many other artists are also represented in this dazzling display of genius.

The Galleria Borghese can accommodate only so many people, so reservations are required for admission, and your visit must be limited to two hours. (The astounding number of true masterpieces will make you long for a second visit.)

See map p. 148. Piazzale del Museo Borghese. ☎ *06-8417645. Reservations required (call* ☎ *06-328101 or visit www.ticketeria.it). Bus: 52, 53, or 910 to Via Pinciana behind the villa; 490 to Viale San Paolo del Brasile inside the park; or Minibus 116 to the Galleria Borghese. Metro: Line A to Spagna; take the Villa Borghese exit, and walk up Viale del Museo Borghese. Admission: 6.50€ ($8.45) plus 2€ ($2.60) booking fee. Open: Tues–Sun 9 a.m.–7 p.m.*

Ancient Rome

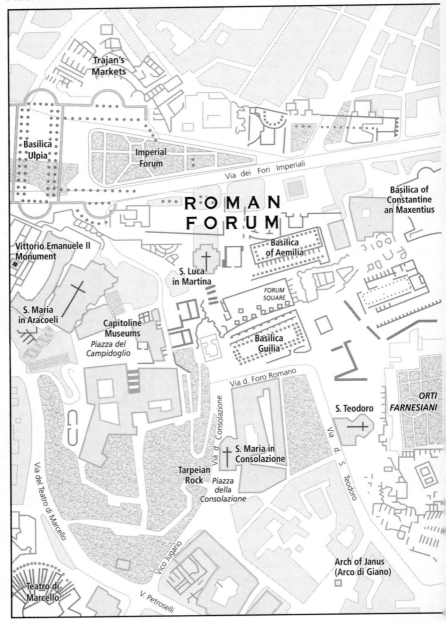

Trajan's Markets

Basilica Ulpia

Imperial Forum

Via dei Fori Imperiali

ROMAN FORUM

Basilica of Constantine an Maxentius

Vittorio Emanuele II Monument

Basilica of Aemilia

S. Luca in Martina

FORUM SQUARE

S. Maria in Aracoeli

Capitoline Museums
Piazza del Campidoglio

Basilica Guilia

Via d. Foro Romano

Via d. Consolazione

S. Teodoro

ORTI FARNESIANI

Via d. S. Teodoro

S. Maria in Consolazione

Tarpeian Rock

Piazza della Consolazione

Via del Teatro di Marcello

Vico Lugario

V. Petroselli

Arch of Janus (Arco di Giano)

Teatro di Marcello

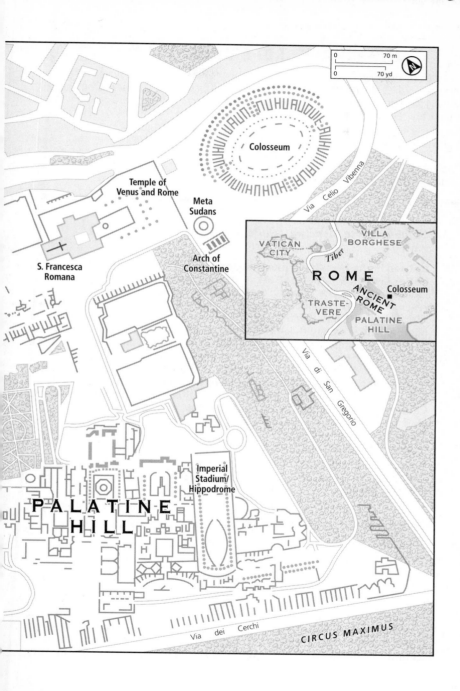

Colosseum

Temple of
Venus and Rome

Meta
Sudans

S. Francesca
Romana

Arch of
Constantine

Via Celio Vibenna

VATICAN
CITY

VILLA
BORGHESE

Tiber

ROME

TRASTE-
VERE

ANCIENT
ROME

Colosseum

PALATINE
HILL

Via di San Gregorio

Imperial
Stadium/
Hippodrome

PALATINE
HILL

Via dei Cerchi

CIRCUS MAXIMUS

0   70 m
0   70 yd

The etiquette of standing in line

Roman rules for lining up at museums — or even at the ice cream counter, for that matter — take some getting used to. You may think that people are packed together, trying to push their way through, but each person is more or less aware of who was there first. Even if the mass of people doesn't look like a line, it's sort of structured like one. If you want not to be regarded as another one of those pushy and arrogant Americans, pay attention to who's already there when you arrive, and be ready to modify your posture slightly so the person behind you knows that *you* know when it's your turn, and you know that he knows that you know, and so on. (*Remember:* Body language is important in Italy!)

Galleria d'Arte Moderna (Gallery of Modern Art)
Parioli

Housed in the beautiful, Liberty-style (Italian Art Nouveau) **Palazzo delle Belle Arti,** this important art museum preserves a rich collection of modern art from the 19th and 20th centuries. Italian artists are largely represented, but the collection includes works by all sorts of great artists. The two sections dedicated to the 19th century hold a great selection of paintings by artists of the *Macchiaioli* movement and a number of works by French modern artists such as **Rodin, Van Gogh,** and **Monet,** but the real riches are in the two sections dedicated to the 20th century, where you can admire a profusion of artwork by **De Chirico, Giorgio Morandi, Marino Marini, Lucio Fontana,** and **Giò Pomodoro,** to name some highlights. The collection also includes international names such as **Pollock, Calder,** and **Tápies,** among others. Schedule at least two hours for your visit. The museum is building a new pavilion nearby — the ex-Caserme Montello (Via Reni, off Piazza Apollodoro) — to house its 21st-century collection; it is scheduled to open sometime in 2006.

Viale delle Belle Arti 131. ☎ *06-322981; reservations 06-3234000.* www.gnam. arti.beniculturali.it. *Tram: 3, 19. Admission: 6.50€ ($8). Open: Tues–Sun 8:30 a.m.–7:30 p.m.*

Galleria Nazionale d'Arte Antica in Palazzo Barberini
(National Art Gallery of Palazzo Barberini)
Via Veneto

Completed in 1633, the Palazzo Barberini is a magnificent example of a baroque Roman palace. Bernini decorated the rococo apartments in which the gallery is now housed, and they're certainly luxurious. Also preserved in the Palazzo Barberini is the wedding chamber of Princess Cornelia Costanza Barberini and Prince Giulio Cesare Colonna di Sciarra, exactly as it was centuries ago. Although the structure itself is an attraction, the collection of paintings that make up the Galleria Nazionale d'Arte Antica is most impressive, including Caravaggio's *Narcissus;* Tiziano's *Venus and Adonis;* and Raphael's *La Fornarina,* a loving, informal portrait of the bakery girl who was his mistress (and the model for his Madonnas). Other artists represented are the great Sienese painters Il Sodoma and Simone Martini, and also Filippo Lippi. The galleria's **decorative-arts collection** contains not only Italian pieces, but also fine imported objects, including some from Japan. In addition to the permanent collections, the gallery regularly houses special exhibits. Two-and-a-half hours should be enough for a complete visit.

See map p. 148. Via Barberini 18. ☎ 06-4824184. We recommend that you book the visit to the apartments in advance at ☎ 06-328101. Metro: Barberini. Admission: 5€ ($6.50). Open: Tues–Sun 9 a.m.–7 p.m.

Museo Nazionale Etrusco di Villa Giulia (National Etruscan Museum of Villa Giulia)
Parioli

This splendid papal villa, built by the most prominent architects of the 16th century, houses the world's most important Etruscan collection. Originally from Asia Minor, the Etruscans were a mysterious people who dominated Tuscany and Lazio, including Rome, up to the fifth century B.C. Many of the objects in this museum came from Cerveteri, an important Etruscan site northwest of Rome. One of the most spectacular objects is the **bride-and-bridegroom sarcophagus** from the sixth century B.C., upon which two enigmatic figures recline. You can also see a fairly well-preserved **chariot** and impressive sculptures. Some of the most amazing works are the tiniest: The Etruscans made **intricate decorative objects** from woven gold. (Their goldsmithing techniques remain a mystery today.) In the summer, the garden is the site of musical events (see Chapter 15). Consider about three hours for a full visit.

Piazzale di Villa Giulia 9. ☎ 06-3226571. www.ticketeria.it. Tram: 3 or 19 to last stop and then walk down Viale delle Belle Arti to Piazzale di Villa Giulia, or 225 to Via di Villa Giulia. Admission: 4€ ($5.20). Open: Tues–Sun 8:30 a.m.–7:30 p.m. Closed Jan 1 and Dec 25.

Palatino (Palatine Hill)
Colosseo

If you find the ruins in the Roman Forum confusing, you'll find those on the Palatino behind it sometimes incomprehensible. We definitely recommend a guided tour. Huge blocks of brick surrounded by trees and greenery testify mutely to what was once an enormous residential complex of patrician houses and imperial palaces, built with the grandiose ambitions of the emperors. The throne room of the **Domus Flavia** was approximately 30m (100 ft.) wide by 39m (131 ft.) long. Although Augustus began the development of the Palatine residences, they were vastly expanded under Domitian, a notoriously cruel emperor.

The Palatino is also where the first Roman developments started and where Romulus drew the original square for the foundation of Rome. Excavations in the area uncovered remains that date back to the eighth century B.C. **Casa di Livia (Livia's House)** is one of the best-preserved homes. During the Middle Ages, the site was transformed into a fortress, and during the Renaissance, it again became the residence of the aristocracy, who built large villas (the **Horti Palatini,** erected by the Farnese on top of the palaces of Tiberius and Caligula, for example). From the hill, you can look down behind to the **Circus Maximus.**

Do not miss the **Museo Palatino (Palatine Museum),** housed in what was the Palace of Caesar and later transformed into a convent. This is where the most precious artwork recovered from the archaeological excavations of the Palatino is conserved, including frescoes and sculptures. Admission is included in your ticket. Depending on your pace and whether you visit the museum, you should consider between one-and-a-half and two-and-a-half hours for your visit.

See map p. 148. Via di San Gregorio 30 or Piazza Santa Maria Nova 53, off Piazza del Colosseo. ☎ *06-39967700. Metro: Colosseo. Bus: Minibus 117. Admission: 8€ ($10); includes admission to the Colosseum. Guided tour 3.50€ ($4.60). Open: Daily 8:30 a.m. to 1 hour before sunset. Ticket booth closes 1 hour earlier. Closed Jan 1 and Dec 25.*

Palazzo Altemps (Altemps Palace)
Navona/Pantheon

Situated behind Piazza Navona, the Palazzo Altemps was begun sometime before 1477; continued by the cardinal of Volterra, Francesco Soderini, from 1511 to 1523; and finished by Marco Sittico Altemps, who enlarged it at the end of the 1500s. The palace was restored in such a way that you can see the layers of medieval, Renaissance, and later decoration. Inside is the **Ludovisi Collection,** one of the world's most famous private art collections, particularly strong in Greek and Roman sculpture as well as Egyptian works.

The most important piece from the Ludovisi Collection is the **Trono Ludovisi,** a throne thought to be the work of a fifth-century-B.C. Greek sculptor brought to Rome from Calabria. One side depicts Aphrodite Urania rising from the waves; another shows a female figure offering incense; and another side features a naked female playing a flute. The remarkable *Dying Gaul,* depicting a man apparently committing suicide with a sword, was commissioned by Julius Caesar and placed in his gardens to commemorate his victories in Gaul. The *Ares Ludovisi,* a statue restored by Bernini in 1622, is believed by art historians to be a Roman copy of an earlier Greek work and shows a warrior (possibly Achilles) at rest. The colossal **head of Hera** (also known as Juno) is one of the best-known Greek sculptures; Goethe wrote of it as his "first love" in Rome and said it was like "a canto of Homer." It has been identified as an idealized portrait of Antonia Augusta, mother of Emperor Claudius. Plan to spend at least one hour here.

See map p. 148. Piazza Sant'Apollinare 46. ☎ *06-39967700. Bus: Minibus 116 to Via dei Coronari; then walk away from Piazza Navona. Admission: 5€ ($6.50). Audio guides: 4€ ($5.20). Open: Tues–Sun 9 a.m.–7.45 p.m. Ticket office closes 1 hour earlier. Closed Jan 1 and Dec 25.*

Palatine Hill

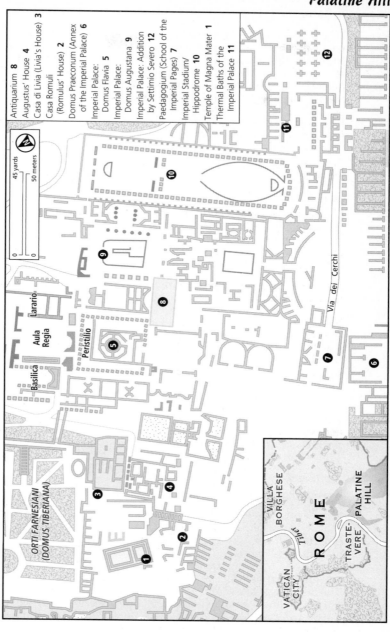

Antiquarium **8**

Augustus' House **4**

Casa di Livia (Livia's House) **3**

Casa Romuli
(Romulus' House) **2**

Domus Praeconum (Annex
of the Imperial Palace) **6**

Imperial Palace:
Domus Flavia **5**

Imperial Palace:
Domus Augustana **9**

Imperial Palace: Addition
by Settimio Severo **12**

Paedagogium (School of the
Imperial Pages) **7**

Imperial Stadium/
Hippodrome **10**

Temple of Magna Mater **1**

Thermal Baths of the
Imperial Palace **11**

45 yards

50 meters

ORTI FARNESIANI
(DOMUS TIBERIANA)

Basilica

Aula
Regia

Larario

Peristilio

Via dei Cerchi

VATICAN
CITY

Tiber

VILLA
BORGHESE

ROME

TRASTE-
VERE

PALATINE
HILL

Palazzo Massimo alle Terme (Massimo Palace by the Terme)

Repubblica

Founded in 1889, this museum was recently completely restored and reorganized. It holds a fantastic collection of Ancient Roman art put together from decades of excavations in Rome and Rome's environs. Among the most striking works are a **satyr pouring wine,** a Roman copy of the original by Greek sculptor Praxiteles; *Daughter of Niobe,* from the Gardens of Sallust; and an *Apollo* copied from an original by Phidias, one of the greatest Ancient Greek sculptors. These few examples are only highlights — the museum's collection includes literally hundreds of statues, including an interesting series showing how the style of representation changed under various emperors, and even discussing the family resemblances of the Claudians, Flavians, and other dynasties. The upper level holds a magnificent collection of **floor mosaics,** including many large ones that once graced some of the most elegant villas in Ancient Rome. But the part that really took our breath away the first time is the separate section holding the **fresco collection:** Entire rooms from the **Villa of Livia** on the Palatine Hill have been reconstructed here, and you can enjoy the frescos as they were meant to be. *Note:* You can visit the fresco collection by guided tour only — you will be assigned a time when you enter the museum — and it is best to make a reservation.

The basement of the museum contains a huge and fascinating **numismatic display,** with coins dating from the origin of the monetary system in the 8th century B.C. through the 21st century and the introduction of the euro (much of the collection once belonged to the king of Italy). The exhibit explains, among other things, the economy of Ancient Rome and of Renaissance Italy. Also in the basement are the Roman jewelry collection of the royal house of Savoy and many items from burial sites, such as a **rare Roman mummy** of a child buried with her most precious belongings. The whole visit, including the tour of the fresco collection, will take you a minimum of two hours.

See map p. 148. Largo di Villa Peretti 1. ☎ 06-39967700. Metro: Line A, B to Termini. Bus: 64 or 70. Admission: 6€ ($8). Audio guides: 4€ ($5.20).Open: Tues–Sun 9 a.m.–7:45 p.m. Ticket office closes 1 hour earlier. Closed Jan 1 and Dec 25.

Pantheon

Navona/Pantheon

Rome's best-preserved monument of antiquity, the imposing Pantheon was rebuilt by the Emperor Hadrian in A.D. 125 over the smaller original temple built by Marcus Agrippa in 27 B.C. as a temple for all the gods (from the ancient Greek *pan theon,* meaning "all gods"). It was eventually saved from destruction by being transformed into a Christian church in A.D. 609. The adjective that all descriptions of the Pantheon should contain is *perfect:* The building is 43m (142 ft.) wide and 43m (142 ft.) tall. The portico is supported by huge granite columns, all but three of which are original, and the bronze doors weigh 20 tons each. Inside, the empty niches surrounding the space once contained marble statues of Roman gods; most of the marble floor is also original. Animals were once sacrificed beneath the beautiful **coffered dome,** whose 5.4m (18-ft.) hole *(oculus)* lets in the light (and sometimes rain) of the Eternal City. An architectural marvel, this dome inspired Michelangelo when he was designing the dome of St. Peter's, though he made the basilica's dome 0.6m (2 ft.) smaller. Inside, you'll find the tombs of the painter Raphael and of two of the kings of Italy. Crowds always congregate in the square in front, **Piazza della Rotonda** (Piazza del Pantheon to Romans), one of the nicest squares in Rome; it is graced by a fountain by Giacomo della Porta. Cafes — as well as a McDonald's, an addition much opposed by the locals — line the square; the fast-food eatery is detectable from the plastic tablecloths and, unfortunately, the smell. A half-hour should be enough to take in the highlights of the monument, plus another hour to soak in the atmosphere from the terrace of one of the cafes.

See map p. 148. Piazza della Rotonda. ☎ *06-68300230. Bus: Minibus 116. Admission: Free. Open: Mon–Sat 8:30 a.m.–7:30 p.m., Sun 9 a.m.–6 p.m, holidays 9 a.m.–1 p.m.*

Piazza di Spagna and Scalinata di Spagna (Spanish Steps)
Piazza di Spagna

The Piazza di Spagna and the Scalinata di Spagna (Spanish Steps) rising from the piazza are the meeting place of Rome. In spring, the steps are decorated with colorful azaleas, but in any season, the square is atmospheric — though you can hardly see it when it's covered with wall-to-wall tourists, lovers, backpackers, Roman youth, and so on. The atmosphere is festive and convivial, though. The piazza's name comes from the 16th century, when the Spanish ambassador made his residence here. In those days, the piazza was far less hospitable. (People passing through the piazza at night sometimes disappeared, because it was technically Spanish territory, and the unwary could be press-ganged into the Spanish army.) The area's most famous resident was English poet John Keats, who lived and died in the house to the right of the steps, which is now the **Keats–Shelley Memorial House** (☎ **06-6784235;** open Mon–Fri 9 a.m.–1 p.m. and 3–6 p.m., Sat 11 a.m.–2 p.m. and 3–6 p.m.; admission: 3€/$3.90). And by the way, the real name of the steps isn't the Spanish Steps but the Scalinata della Trinità del Monte, because they lead to the **Trinità del Monte church,** whose towers loom above. At the foot of the steps, the **boat-shaped fountain** by Pietro Bernini, father of Gian Lorenzo, is one of the most famous in Rome.

See map p. 148. Via del Babuino and Via dei Condotti. Metro: Line A to Spagna. Bus: Minibus 117 or 119 to Piazza di Spagna.

Piazza Navona
Navona/Pantheon

One of Rome's most beautiful *piazze* and also one of its most popular hangouts, Piazza Navona was built on the ruins of the **Stadium of Domitian** from the first century A.D., where chariot races were held (note the oval track form). Between the 17th and 19th centuries, the bottom of the square was flooded for carnival-float parades. The twin-towered facade of **Santa Agnese in Agone** is a baroque masterpiece by Borromini, who renovated and rebuilt the original church, which had been constructed on the site between the 8th and the 12th centuries. The interior was also redecorated in the 17th century, but in the lower level, you'll find vestiges of Domitian's stadium, with an Ancient Roman mosaic floor. The square's other great baroque masterpiece is Bernini's **Fontana dei Quattro Fiumi (Fountain of the Four Rivers),** with massive figures representing the Nile, Danube, della Plata, and Ganges — the figure with the shrouded head is the Nile, because its source was unknown at the time. Built in 1651, it is crowned by an **obelisk,** a Roman copy from Domitian's time. This fountain came as a monumental addition to the two simple fountains already existing at each end of the square. Created in 1576 by Giacomo della Porta, they were decorated with figures only later. Bernini also designed the **Fontana del Moro (Fountain of the Moor)** at the piazza's south end, which was finished in 1654 (the tritons and other ornaments are 19th-century copies made to replace the originals, which were moved to the garden of Villa Borghese lake), whereas the figures of the **Fontana di Neptuno (Fountain of Neptune),** at the piazza's north end, were added in the 19th century to balance the Fountain of the Moor.

On the east side of the square is the famous **Palazzo Braschi,** which opened its doors in May 2002 after 15 years of closure and an $8 million restoration. It houses the **Museo di Roma,** covering the cultural, social, and artistic life of the city from the Middle Ages to the first half of the 20th century. Interesting temporary exhibitions are often on display as well. The *palazzo* is an attraction in itself, a baroque palace with a grand staircase (Via di San Pantaleo 10; ☎ 06-67108346; www.museodiroma.comune.roma.it; open: Tues–Sun 9 a.m.–7 p.m.; admission: 6.20€/$8).

See map p. 148. Just off Corso Rinascimento. Bus: 70 or 116 to Piazza Navona.

Foro Romano (Roman Forum)
Colosseo

The **Roman Forum,** the original forum used as market and meeting place, was gradually expanded by the various emperors and remained the heart of public life in Ancient Rome for over a thousand years. The ruins lie in the valley between the Capitoline Hill, site of the great Jupiter Temple, and the Palatine Hill, where the royal palace, and later the palaces of other noble families, were located. The forum was built at the end of the seventh century B.C., after the existing marshes were drained by the **Cloaca Massima,** the huge drainage and sewer canal under the forum. The forum is crossed by the **Via Sacra,** the "sacred street," so called because it led to the main temples on the Capitoline Hill (today, Piazza del Campidoglio). A stone discovered under the forum in 1899 bears an inscription from the sixth century B.C., the time of the Roman kings. The forum has many ruins (some, like the sanctuary of the sewer goddess Venus Cloaca, are just a mark on the ground), as well as a few standing buildings. The most important structure is the square **Curia,** where the Senate once met; many of the walls were heavily restored in 1937, but the marble-inlay floor inside is original from the third century A.D. Also well conserved is the **Temple of Antoninus and Faustina** (the Emperor Antoninus Pius, who succeeded Hadrian in A.D. 138), because it was turned into a church and given a baroque facade (as the Chiesa di San Lorenzo in Miranda).

Near the Curia is the **Arch of Septimius Severus,** built in A.D. 203 to commemorate this emperor's victories. The arch originally mentioned his two sons, Caracalla and Geta, but after Caracalla murdered Geta, Geta's name was removed. At the other end of the forum is the **Arch of Titus.** Titus reigned as emperor from A.D. 79 to 81. Nearby is the hulking form of the fourth-century **Basilica of Constantine and Maxentius,** which occupies the site of what was Rome's law courts. The **Temple of the Dioscuri,** dedicated to the twins Castor and Pollux, is immediately recognizable by its three remaining columns joined by a piece of architrave. Against the Capitoline Hill, you see the **Temple of Saturn,** which housed the first treasury of Rome. It was also the site of the feast that was the pagan ancestor of Christmas.

If you buy a map of the forum when you enter, you can identify the sometimes faint traces of a host of other structures (also see the map "The Roman Forum and Imperial Forums," p. 164).

Note: At press time, the **Antiquarium Forense,** which contains materials from the excavations of the forum, was closed for restoration. No date was set for the reopening, but check for updates at the ticket booth or with the tourist office.

 As with any archaeological site, things often make much more sense if you take a guided tour. The tour in English is at 10:30 a.m. daily and lasts about an hour. Ask at the ticket booth or, even better, make a reservation.

See map p. 148. Piazza Santa Maria Nova 53, off Piazza del Colosseo; and Largo Romolo e Remo 5, off Via dei Fori Imperiali. ☎ *06-39967700. Metro: Colosseo. Bus: Minibus 117. Admission: Free. Guided tours: 3.50€ ($4.60). Audio guides: 4€ ($5.20). Open: Daily 9 a.m. to 1 hour before sunset.*

San Giovanni in Laterano (St. John in Laterano) and Cloister Colosseo

Built in A.D. 13 by Constantine, this cathedral of the diocese of Rome (St. Peter's Basilica is in the separate city-state of the Vatican) suffered many indignities, including being sacked by the Vandals (a barbarian tribe whose name has given us the word *vandalism*), burned, and then damaged in an 896 earthquake. The basilica was restored and rebuilt at various times by different architects. The facade, designed and executed by Alessandro Galilei in 1735, is crowned by **15 giant statues** (7m/22 ft. tall) representing Christ, St. John the Baptist, John the Evangelist, and other doctors of the Church; you can see them from many parts of Rome. Outside is an **Egyptian obelisk,** the tallest in Rome (32m/105 ft.), consecrated in the fourth century as a symbol of Christianity's victory over pagan cults.

The Roman Forum and Imperial Forums

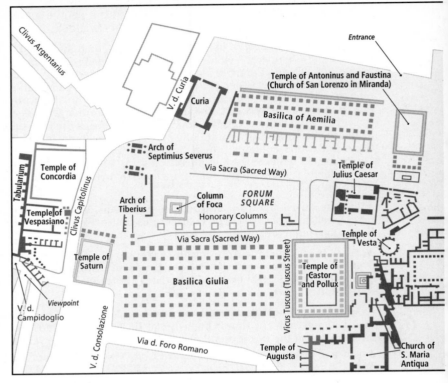

Clivus Argentarius

Entrance

V. d. Curia

Curia

Temple of Antoninus and Faustina
(Church of San Lorenzo in Miranda)

Basilica of Aemilia

Arch of
Septimius Severus

Tabularium

Temple of
Concordia

Via Sacra (Sacred Way)

Temple of
Julius Caesar

Clivus Capitolinus

Arch of
Tiberius

Temple of
Vespasiano

Column
of Foca

FORUM
SQUARE

Honorary Columns

Via Sacra (Sacred Way)

Temple of
Vesta

Temple of
Saturn

Basilica Giulia

Vicus Tuscus (Tuscus Street)

Temple of
Castor
and Pollux

V. d.
Campidoglio

Viewpoint

V. d. Consolazione

Via d. Foro Romano

Temple of
Augusta

Church of
S. Maria
Antiqua

The interior of the basilica as you see it today was redesigned by Borromini in the 17th century. The **papal altar** — under a beautiful 14th-century *baldacchino* (canopy) — conserves an important relic: the wooden altar on which Peter and the other paleo-Christian popes after him are said to have celebrated mass in Ancient Rome's catacombs. In the left transept is the altar of the **Santissimo Sacramento,** decorated with four giant, gilded-bronze columns that are the only remains of the original basilica. Under the *baldacchino* of this altar is another important relic, said to be the table of Christ's Last Supper. The apse was redone during the 19th century, and its mosaics are copies of the original medieval mosaics. However, the fresco fragment depicting Pope Boniface VIII, who declared the first Papal Jubilee in 1300, is from the 14th century. The **Baptistry** was built by Constantine in the fourth century, making it the first of the Western world. (The walls are original, although the interior was restored several times, and the present form was designed by Borromini.) From a side door, you can access the delightful 13th-century **cloister,** which was designed by Vassalletto and is a showcase for carvings and other art pieces from the older basilica, including paleo-Christian inscriptions. Set aside at least an hour for your visit.

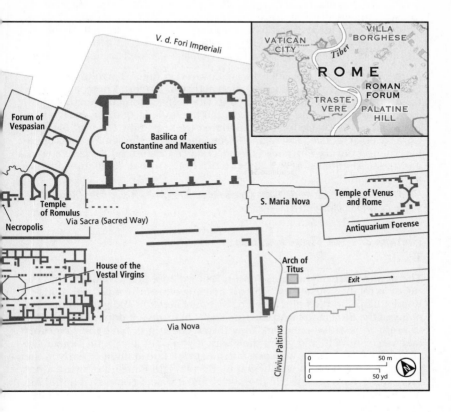

See map p. 148. Piazza di San Giovanni in Laterano. ☎ *06-69886433. Metro: San Giovanni. Bus: 81, 85, 850, or Minibus 117. Tram: 3. Admission: Basilica free; cloister 2€ ($2.60). Open: Basilica and cloister daily 7 a.m.–6 p.m. (in summer to 6:45 p.m.); Baptistry daily 9 a.m.–1 p.m.*

Mercati Traianei and Foro di Traiano (Trajan's Market and Trajan's Forum)
Colosseo

During the first century A.D., each Roman emperor added luxurious public constructions to the original Roman Forum (see listing earlier in this chapter), and each new forum was named after the emperor who built it. Emperor Trajan added the most splendid of them all, an elegant open space — **Trajan's Forum** — overlooked by a tall curved building — **Trajan's Markets.** Unfortunately, many of the temples and decorations were dismantled during the Middle Ages and the Renaissance, when the marble was used for other construction, but the archaeological remains are still fascinating. Walking north along the Via dei Fori Imperiali from the Colosseum, you can see the archaeological site from the outside (to your right), but obviously, a visit to the impressive brick complex itself affords an irreplaceable experience. This second-century structure housed stalls and small boutiques — sort of an ancient mall — as well as meeting places.

Note: Most of the Imperial Fori were covered in the 1920s to build Via dei Fori Imperiali, a major transportation artery of modern Rome, and today, the whole area is being excavated in the largest Roman archaeological excavation to date. The plan is to exhibit the findings of these excavations in the Trajan Markets. To accommodate the excavation, the visit has temporarily been reduced to Trajan's Forum and part of the semicircular building; the temporary entrance is from Trajan's Column off Piazza Venezia, and reduced admission is 3.20€ ($4.20). Count about 40 minutes for the reduced visit.

Via 4 Novembre 94. ☎ *06-6790048. Admission: 3.20€ ($4.20). Open Tues–Sun 9 a.m.– 4:30 p.m. winter, until 6:30 p.m. in summer.*

Fontana di Trevi (Trevi Fountain)
Trevi

The massive Trevi Fountain, fronting its own little piazza, existed for centuries in relative obscurity before it became one of the must-see sights of Rome, thanks to the film *Three Coins in the Fountain.* Today, it seems that many of the thousands who clog the space in front of it don't take the time to *really* look at it — instead, they throw coins in it, have their pictures taken in front of it, and go on their way. If you want a tranquil moment to actually appreciate the artwork, you must visit late at night or early in the morning. The fountain was begun by Bernini and Pietro da Cortona, but there was a 100-year lapse in the works, and it wasn't completed until 1751 by Nicola Salvi. The central figure is Neptune, who guides a chariot pulled by plunging sea horses. *Tritons* (mythological sea dwellers) guide the horses, and the surrounding scene is one of wild nature and bare stone.

Of course, you have to toss a coin in the Trevi, something all kids love to do. To do it properly (Romans are superstitious), hold the coin in your right hand, turn your back to the fountain, and toss the coin over your left shoulder. According to tradition, the spirit of the fountain will then see to it that you return to Rome one day.

A pocketful of change

In many of Rome's churches, fragile paintings are kept in semiobscurity, but you'll often find a light box nearby. When you insert a coin or two, a light pops on to illuminate a painting, fresco, or sculpture for a limited amount of time. Carrying a pocketful of coins is always a good idea.

See map p. 148. Piazza di Trevi. Bus: 62 or Minibus 116 or 119. Take Via Poli to the fountain.

The Vatican

In 1929, the Lateran Treaty between Pope Pius XI and the Italian government recognized the independent state of the Holy See, with its physical seat in Vatican City (St. Peter's Basilica and adjacent buildings). Politically independent from Italy, the Vatican is the world's second-smallest sovereign state, with its own administration, post office, and tourist office. The Vatican comprises St. Peter's Basilica, the Vatican Museums, and the Vatican Gardens, all reviewed in this section.

Making the **Vatican Information Office** (☎ **06-69884466;** open Mon–Sat 8:30 a.m.–7 p.m.) the first stop on your visit is a good idea — it's just to the left of the entrance to St. Peter's. In the tourist office, you can get a plan of the basilica — very useful, given the sheer size of the thing — and make a reservation for a tour of the Vatican Gardens. You can also find the **Vatican Post Office** — nice stamps and reliable service — and public restrooms.

Consider that at the Vatican, even the men wear ankle-length gowns, and the most popular color is black. Bare shoulders, halter tops, tank tops, shorts, and skirts above the knee will *definitely* result in your being turned away from the basilica. This is, after all, the center of a world religion, not just a tourist extravaganza.

Piazza San Pietro (St. Peter's Square)
San Pietro

The entrance to the Vatican is through one of the world's greatest public spaces — Bernini's **Piazza San Pietro (St. Peter's Square).** As you stand in the huge piazza (no cars allowed), you're in the arms of an ellipse partly enclosed by a majestic Doric-pillared colonnade, atop which stand statues of some 140 saints. Straight ahead is the facade of **Basilica di San Pietro (St. Peter's Basilica);** the two statues flanking the entrance represent St. Peter and St. Paul, Peter carrying the Keys to the Kingdom. To the right, above the colonnade, are the ochre buildings of the **papal apartments** and the **Musei Vaticani (Vatican Museum).** In the center of the square is an **Egyptian obelisk,** brought from the ancient city of Heliopolis on the Nile delta. On either side are 17th-century **fountains** — the one on the right by Carlo Maderno, who designed the facade of St. Peter's, was placed here by Bernini himself; the one on the left is by Carlo Fontana. The piazza is particularly magical at night during the Christmas season, when a *presepio* (nativity scene) and a large tree take center stage.

See map p. 148. Bus: 62 or 64 to Via della Conciliazione, and follow it to the end. Metro: Ottaviano/San Pietro; take Via di Porta Angelica, and follow it to the end.

How to attend a papal audience

Many Catholics come to Rome to attend a *papal audience,* during which the pope addresses a crowd of people gathered in the Vatican (but of course, you don't have to be Catholic to attend). To attend a papal audience (Wed only; entrance between 10 and 10:30 a.m.), you must get free tickets from the **Prefecture of the Papal Household** (☎ **06-69883114**) at the bronze door under Piazza di San Pietro's right colonnade (Mon–Sat 9 a.m.–1 p.m.). To get tickets in advance, write to the Prefecture of the Papal Household, 00120 Città del Vaticano, indicating your language, the dates of your visit, the number of people in your party, and (if possible) the hotel in Rome to which the office should send your tickets the afternoon before the audience.

Basilica di San Pietro (St. Peter's Basilica)

San Pietro

In 324, Emperor Constantine commissioned a sanctuary to be built on the site of St. Peter's tomb. The first apostle was thought to have been buried here under a simple stone, and excavation and studies commissioned by the Vatican have produced additional proof that the tomb is indeed St. Peter's. You can find the tomb in the present basilica's central nave, under the magnificent altar by Bernini.

The original basilica stood for about 1,000 years. After a millennium of remodeling, pillaging, sacking, and rebuilding, it was on the verge of collapse. The basilica you see today, mostly High Renaissance and baroque, began with the renovation begun in 1503 following designs by the architects Sangallo and Bramante. Michelangelo was appointed to finish the magnificent dome in 1547 but wasn't able to do so; he died in 1564, and his disciple Giacomo della Porta completed the job.

The inside of the basilica is almost too huge to take in; walking from one end to the other is a workout, and the opulence will overpower you. On the right as you enter is Michelangelo's exquisite *Pietà,* created when the master was in his early 20s. (Because of an act of vandalism in the 1970s, the statue is kept behind reinforced glass.) Dominating the nave is Bernini's 29m-tall (96-ft.) *baldacchino* (canopy), supported by richly decorated twisting columns. Completed in 1633, it was criticized for being excessive and because the bronze was supposedly taken from the Pantheon. The canopy stands over the papal altar, which in turn stands over the **tomb of St. Peter.** A **bronze statue of St. Peter** (probably by Arnolfo di Cambio, 13th century) marks the tomb; its right foot has been worn away by the millions of pilgrims kissing it in the traditional devotional gesture to salute the pope. By the apse, above an altar, is the **bronze throne** sculpted by Bernini to house the remains of what is, according to legend, the chair of St. Peter.

To visit Michelangelo's dome and marvel at the astounding view, you have to climb some 491 steps. Make sure that you're ready and willing to climb, however, because after you've started up, you're not allowed to turn

The Vatican

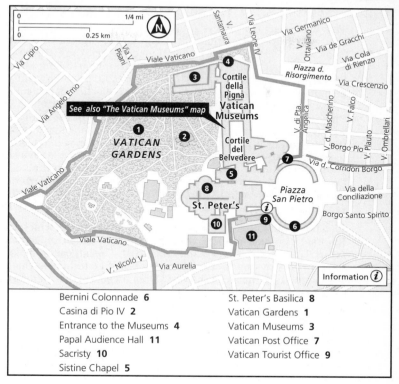

Bernini Colonnade **6**	St. Peter's Basilica **8**
Casina di Pio IV **2**	Vatican Gardens **1**
Entrance to the Museums **4**	Vatican Museums **3**
Papal Audience Hall **11**	Vatican Post Office **7**
Sacristy **10**	Vatican Tourist Office **9**
Sistine Chapel **5**	

around and go back down. If you want to take the elevator as far as it goes, it'll save you 171 steps. You have to make a reservation for the elevator when you buy your ticket to enter the dome (you'll pay an additional 1†/$1.30). On busy days, expect to wait in line to get a lift.

Beneath the basilica are **grottoes,** extending under the central nave of the church. You can visit them and wander among the tombs of popes. The excavations proceed farther down, to the **paleo-Christian tombs** and **architectural fragments of the original basilica** that have been found here, but you need to apply in writing at least three weeks beforehand to arrange for a visit.

Plan on at least three hours to see the entire basilica.

See map p. 148. Piazza San Pietro, ☎ 06-69884466. Bus: 62 or 64 to Via della Conciliazione. Metro: Ottaviano/San Pietro. Take Viale Angelico to the Vatican. Admission: Basilica and grottoes free; dome 4€ ($5.20), with elevator 5€ ($6.50). Open: Oct–Mar basilica daily 7 a.m.–6 p.m., dome daily 8 a.m.–4:45 p.m.; Apr–Sept basilica daily 7 a.m.–7 p.m., dome daily 8 a.m.–5:45 p.m.; grottoes daily 8 a.m.–5 p.m.

Musei Vaticani (The Vatican Museums)
San Pietro

This enormous complex of museums could swallow up your entire vacation, with its tons of Egyptian, Etruscan, Greek, Roman, paleo-Christian, and Renaissance art. Four museums house the art: the **Gregorian Egyptian Museum,** a fantastic collection of Egyptian artifacts; the **Gregorian Etruscan Museum,** a beautiful collection of Etruscan art and jewelry; the **Ethnological Missionary Museum,** a large collection of artifacts from every continent, including superb African, Asian, and Australian art; and the **Pinacoteca (picture gallery),** the most famous of the Vatican Museums, which contains works by medieval and Renaissance masters. In Room 9 of the Pinacoteca is Leonardo da Vinci's *St. Jerome,* which has been pieced back together — one piece had ended up as a stool seat in a shoemaker's shop; the other, as a tabletop in an antiques shop. In Room 2 is Giotto's luminous *Stefaneschi Triptych;* in Room 8, Raphael's *Transfiguration.* Other highlights include works by Beato Angelico, Perugino, Bernini, and Caravaggio (a single but great painting, the *Deposition from the Cross*).

Also part of the museums are the **Stanze di Raffaello,** which translates as **Raphael's Rooms,** although they are in fact the private apartments of Pope Julius II, which were frescoed by the artist. The largest of the four rooms is the room of **Constantine,** painted between 1517 and 1524, which illustrates key moments in the life of the first Christian emperor, including his triumph over Maxentius and his vision of the cross. Along the way, you'll come across the **Appartamento Borgia (Borgia Apartments),** designed for Pope Alexander VI (the infamous Borgia pope), and the **Cappella di Nicola V (Chapel of Nicholas V),** with floor-to-ceiling frescoes by Fra Angelico.

But of course, it is the **Cappella Sistina (Sistine Chapel),** Michelangelo's masterpiece, that is the crowning glory of the museums. Years after their restoration, conflict continues over whether too much paint was removed, flattening the figures. On the other hand, the brilliant color has been restored. Whether you like the colors of the drapery or not, Michelangelo's modeling of the human form is incredible. The *Creation of Adam* and the temptation and fall of Adam and Eve are the most famous scenes. Michelangelo also painted a terrifying and powerful *Last Judgment* on the end wall.

 Binoculars or even a hand mirror will help you appreciate the Sistine ceiling better; your neck tires long before you can take it all in. Just think how poor Michelangelo must have felt while painting it flat on his back atop a tower of scaffolding!

Visiting the whole museum complex in one day is impossible. If you don't want to take a guided tour, you can follow one of the **four color-coded itineraries** (A, B, C, or D), taking you to the highlights of the museums. They range from one-and-a-half to five hours, and all end at the Sistine Chapel. We recommend that you pick and choose according to your personal taste: Perhaps you're fascinated by Ancient Egypt and are only marginally interested in paintings; maybe you prefer to view African and Asian art and the

The Vatican Museums

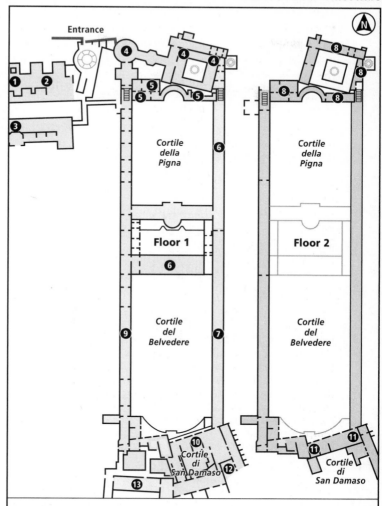

Borgia Apartments **10**

Chapel of Nicholas V **12**

Chiaramonti Museum (Antiquity) **6**

Epigraphy **7**

Ethnological Missionary Museum **1**

Gallery of Candelabra (Antiquity) **9**

Gregorian Egyptian Museum **5**

Gregorian Etruscan Museum **8**

Gregorian Roman
 and Greek collection **2**

Pio-Clementino Museum (Antiquity) **4**

Picture Gallery (Pinacoteca) **3**

Raphael's Rooms (Stanze di Raffaello) **11**

Sistine Chapel **13**

frescoed apartments. Whatever you do, we recommend the audio guide (rental: 5.50€/$7.15) to avoid the "Stendhal syndrome" of sensory overload (see "Seeing Rome by Guided Tour," later in this chapter). The guide discusses over 300 artworks; select what you want to hear by pressing a work's label number.

 The museums charge no admission on the last Sunday of each month, but the crowds are unbelievable, especially in the good season. We recommend paying a visit during a less busy time; after all, you don't know whether you'll have time to come back.

See map p. 148. Viale Vaticano, to the northeast of St. Peter's basilica. ☎ *06-69883332. Reservations for guided tours 06-69884676.* www.vatican.va. *Admission: 12€ ($16) adults, 8€ ($10) children; free last Sun of each month. Open: Jan 7–mid Mar and Nov 2–Dec 24 Mon–Sat 8:45 a.m.–1:45 p.m.; mid-Mar–Oct and Dec 27–Jan 6 Mon–Fri 8:45 a.m.–4:45 p.m. and Sat 8:45 a.m.–1:45 p.m. Entrance closes 85 minutes before closing. Closed Catholic holidays.*

Giardini Vaticani (Vatican Gardens)
San Pietro

People often think that the Vatican is made up of only the basilica and the museums, but behind those walls lies a busy town surrounding a huge — and splendid — park. You can catch a glimpse of the park from the windows of the Vatican Museums, revealing groomed grounds, fountains, and elegant Renaissance buildings. Although normally, you need a special permit to enter the Vatican grounds, you can sign up for the special guided tours that take small numbers of visitors to the gardens. Tours last two hours and start by bus. If you forgot to ask for a reservation (by phone or fax — see the following paragraph), try to sign up directly at the Vatican Information Office (see contact information at the beginning of this section) — it may be able to fit you in an upcoming tour.

See map p. 148. Piazza San Pietro. ☎ *06-69884676. Fax: 06-69885100. Bus: 62 or 64 to Via della Conciliazione. Metro: Ottaviano/San Pietro. Take Viale Angelico to the Vatican. Guided tours: Tues, Thurs, and Fri 10 a.m. Admission: 9€ ($12).*

Finding More Cool Things to See and Do

Rome has so many famous attractions that many lesser-known sights are often overlooked, yet many of them are also first rate and well worth a visit. Here are a few of our favorites, organized by type.

For museum buffs

If you love museums, Rome is the perfect city for you; the problem, if anything, is that there are too many to take in on a single visit unless you're staying for weeks or months. The advantage is that you can find a museum to satisfy the taste and special interests of everyone. Here are a few suggestions in addition to such famous choices as the Capitoline

Use these handy Post-It® Flags to mark your favorite pages.

Museums, the National Roman Museums, and the Vatican Museums, which we describe in the previous sections.

Centrale Montemartini (Montemartini Plant)
Testaccio

When the **Capitoline Museums'** Palazzo Nuovo was restored, the Greek and Roman sculpture collection was permanently moved to this new site, the first electrical plant built in Rome, dating from 1912. An intriguing and beautiful setting for the art collection, it contains over 400 sculptures; among the most important pieces is a huge **mosaic with hunting scenes** (6m x 12m/20 x 40 ft.) recovered from one of the Ancient Roman imperial residences. Plan to spend about an hour here.

See map p. 148. Via Ostiense 106. ☎ *06-5748038.* www.centralemonemartini. org. *Metro: Line B to Pyramide; walk down Via Ostiense. Bus: 23 to Via Ostiense. Tram: 3 to Piazza di Porta San Paolo (Stazione Ostiense, Piramide). Admission: 4.20€ ($5.50). Open: Tues–Sun 9:30 a.m–7 p.m. Closed Jan 1, May 1, Oct 28–29, and Dec 25.*

Museo Barracco (Barracco Museum)
Navona/Pantheon

This wonderful small museum was the private collection of Baron Giovanni Barracco, which he donated to the city at his death. Housed in a 16th-century *palazzo,* the collection was conceived as a panoramic history of ancient sculpture and includes superb examples of Assyro-Babylonian, Egyptian, Greek, and Roman sculpture. *Note:* The museum was being restored at press time and should reopen in 2006. You'll need about one-and-a-half hours for an in-depth visit.

See map p. 148. Corso Vittorio Emanuele II 168. ☎ *06-68806848. Bus: 62, 64. Open: Tues–Sat 9 a.m.–7 p.m. and Sun 9 a.m.–1 p.m. Admission 3€ ($3.90); 2€ ($2.60) extra for special exhibits.*

Museo della Civiltá Romana (Museum of Roman Civilization)
EUR

Located south of *il centro,* in a modern neighborhood well connected by public transportation, this interesting museum focuses on the history of Ancient Rome and the spread of its civilization throughout the world. The big attraction, and a favorite with kids, is an impressive model of Imperial Rome, a perfect reconstruction in 1:250 scale. You'll see all the great buildings intact, which helps you make sense of all the broken columns and holes in the ground. Other models display facets of daily life in antiquity — a good complement to your visit of Ancient Rome. You could easily spend two hours here.

Piazza Giovanni Agnelli 10. ☎ *06-5926141. Metro: EUR Fermi. Admission: 6.20€ ($8). Open: Tues–Sat 9 a.m.–6:15 p.m. and Sun 9 a.m.–1:30 p.m.*

Museo Nazionale degli Strumenti Musicali (National Museum of Musical Instruments)
Colosseo

This wonderful museum is great to visit (even if you aren't a musician) for the incredible variety of instruments, some of them true works of art. Created in 1974 to house the private collection of famous Italian tenor Evan Gorga (he was the first Rodolfo in Puccini's *Boheme* back in 1896), it counts over 3,000 pieces stretching from antiquity to the 19th century. Among the showstoppers are a superb piano built in 1722, a beautiful harpsichord built in Leipzig in 1537, and a trumpet from 1461. If you're a fan of musical instruments, schedule at least an hour for your visit.

See map p. 148. Piazza Santa Croce in Gerusalemme 9a. ☎ *06-7014796.* www. museostrumentimusicali.it. *Bus: 117. Tram: 3, 13. Admission 2€ ($2.60); more for special exhibits. Open: Tues–Sun 8:30 a.m.–7:30 p.m.*

For serious antiquity lovers

Rome was the cradle of the Roman Empire, and mementoes from the Ancient Roman civilization are everywhere, in various levels of repair. Ruins are so numerous that you would need months to explore them all; you can use the **Archeobus** (see "Seeing Rome by Guided Tour," later in this chapter) to move from one to the other or to get an overview. Besides the "biggies" — Baths of Caracalla, Colosseum, Domus Aurea, Roman Forum, Pantheon, Palatine, and Trajan Markets — which are reviewed in the previous sections, a number of others are well worth a visit if you're interested in archaeology or the ancient world.

Parco Archeologico dell'Appia Antica (Appian Way Archaeological Park)

This beautiful archaeological park starts beyond the Baths of Caracalla, near the Aventino, and stretches for several miles to the south. Here, you can walk over an original section of what was the first and most important Roman consular road, called the **Regina Viarum (Queen of Roads).** Started in 312 B.C. as the highway to Capua, the road was progressively extended to reach Benevento (233km/146 miles to the southeast), then Taranto (an extra 281km/176 miles), and finally all the way to Brindisi (another 70km/40 miles). It was on this road that St. Peter, in flight from Rome, had his vision of Jesus (a church stands where Peter asked, *"Domine quo vadis?"* or "Lord, where are you going?") and turned back toward his martyrdom. The street is still paved with the original large, flat basalt stones and lined with the remains of villas, tombs, and monuments against the background of the beautiful countryside. The whole area is now a park, which you can visit via the hop-on/hop-off **Archeobus** (see "Seeing Rome by Guided Tour," later in this chapter) or by bicycle — you can rent one at the park visitor center **Cartiera Latina** (via Appia Antica 42) or at the **Bar Caffe dell'Appia Antica** (Via Appia Antica 175); bikes rent for 3€ ($3.90) per hour for the first three hours and 10€ ($13) for the whole day. Among the archaeological attractions are the **Circo di Massenzio (Maxentius Circus), Mausoleo di Romolo (Mausoleum of Romulus), and Residenze Imperiali (Imperial Residences),** where you can see the ruins of the arena built by the Emperor Maxentius in honor of his son Romulus and his mausoleum (Via Appia Antica 153; ☎ 06-7801324; open: Tues–Sun winter 9 a.m.– 5 p.m., summer 9 a.m.–1 p.m.; admission: 2.60€/$3.40). Another famous attraction is the **Mausoleo di Cecilia Metella (Mausoleum of Cecilia Metella)** (Via Appia Antica 161; ☎ 06-39967700; open: Tues–Sun 9 a.m. to 1 hour before sunset; admission: 2€/$2.60). Metella was a first-century-B.C. gentlewoman whose mausoleum was integrated into the fortification of a medieval castle — Castrum Caetani — in 1303. Also on the Via Appia are two sets of catacombs: the Catacombs of San Callisto (see listing earlier in this chapter) and the **Villa dei Quintili** (see listing in this section).

See map p. 176. Via Appia Antica. ☎ *06-5130682.* www.parcoappiaantica.org. *Bus: Archeobus, 118, 218. Admission: Free.*

Circo Massimo (Circus Maximus)
Aventino

A quarter-million Romans once watched chariot races in this oblong arena, a huge, evocative space overlooked by the dramatic heights of the Palatino and its soaring pines. Although the structures once flanking the arena have almost disappeared, having been plundered for their stone in the Middle Ages and Renaissance, the Circus Maximus has not lost its majesty and is still a preferred destination for Roman joggers and tourists looking to give their kids a place to expend some energy.

See map p. 148. Tram: 3. Admission: Free.

Aula Ottagona (Octagonal Hall)
Repubblica

Part of the Diocletian Baths (see listing later in this section), this is a beautiful example of Ancient Roman architecture, completely preserved, including its roof. Adapted into a planetarium in 1928, it is now accessible from a separate entrance from the rest of the complex. Inside is an important sculpture collection originating from several of the bath complexes in Rome, including some famous statues, such as the two bronzes, one of a Roman general of the second century and another of a **sitting fighter** of the first century (in the last phase of restoration at press time and about to be re-exhibited to the public). A staircase leads to the original level of the floor, under which have been discovered remains of buildings on which the baths were constructed.

See map p. 148. Via G. Romita 8. ☎ *06-39967700. Metro: Line A to Repubblica; Bus: 60, 62, or Minibus 116T to Piazza della Repubblica. Admission: Free. Open: Tues–Sat 9 a.m.–2 p.m. and Sun and holidays 9 a.m.–1 p.m.*

Appian Way Archaeological Park

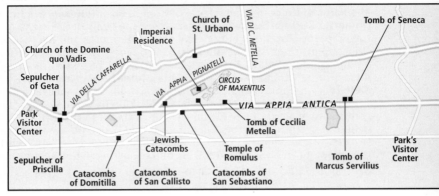

Church of St. Urbano
VIA DI C. METELLA
Tomb of Seneca
Imperial Residence
Church of the Domine quo Vadis
Sepulcher of Geta
VIA DELLA CAFFARELLA
VIA APPIA PIGNATELLI
CIRCUS OF MAXENTIUS
Park Visitor Center
VIA APPIA ANTICA
Tomb of Cecilia Metella
Park's Visitor Center
Jewish Catacombs
Temple of Romulus
Tomb of Marcus Servilius
Sepulcher of Priscilla
Catacombs of Domitilla
Catacombs of San Callisto
Catacombs of San Sebastiano

Terme di Diocleziano (Diocletian Baths)
Repubblica

This grandiose Roman bath complex was built between A.D. 298 and 305 and covered a surface area of almost 1.5 million square feet! Part of the thermal baths are occupied by **Santa Maria degli Angeli,** the church that opens on Piazza della Repubblica (☎ **06-4880812;** free admission). **Piazza della Repubblica** itself was part of the baths and covers the imprint of what originally was the main *esedra* (semicircular exercise area) at the back of the complex, which should give you an idea of how enormous the baths were. The church occupies the central monumental halls and what was the *tepidarium* (warming halls), which was placed between the original *frigidarium* (cooling area) and *calidarium* (sauna). The original Renaissance plan — yet another example of Roman "creative reuse" — included a church and an attached monastery with two cloisters, and was realized in the 16th century by Michelangelo, who conserved much of the original structures. In the 18th century, the church was enlarged and redecorated to its present state by Luigi Vanvitelli. The monastery, with its beautiful main cloister, has been converted into a museum holding a very rich collection of epigraphy: inscriptions that have been found in the various archaeological sites in Rome, mostly carved in stone.

See map p. 148. Viale E. de Nicola 78. ☎ *06-39967700. Metro: Line B to Repubblica. Admission: 5€ ($6.50). Open: Tues–Sun 9 a.m.–7:45 p.m.*

Colonna di Marco Aurelio (Triumphal Column of Marcus Aurelius)
Navona/Pantheon

At the center of beautiful Piazza Colonna, this commemorative column is an imposing sight, 25m (83 ft.) tall and completely decorated with bas-reliefs. The column was erected in honor of Marcus Aurelius, the enlightened emperor who ruled from A.D. 161 to 180, and the reliefs recount his exploits in battles against the German tribes. A statue of the emperor once adorned

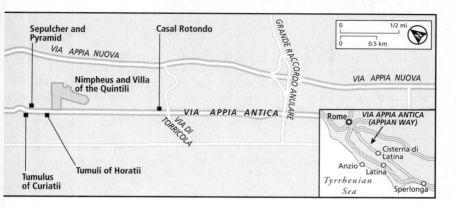

the top, but in the 16th century, Pope Sixtus V replaced it with the statue of St. Paul that you see today. The **Palazzo Chigi** on one side of the piazza is the residence of the Italian prime minister, so don't be surprised if you see intense guys standing around with submachine guns.

See map p. 148. Piazza Colonna, off Via del Corso at Via del Tritone. Bus: 62, 85, or Minibus 116, 117, or 119 to Piazza Colonna.

Villa dei Quintili (Quintili's Villa)
Park of the Appia Antica

Recently opened after lengthy excavations (still ongoing), this was the largest private villa in the Roman suburbs. It was the property of the two brothers Quintili, who were consuls in A.D. 151. The structure was enlarged when it became the property of the Emperor Commodus, who loved the quiet and the villa's thermal baths. For centuries, it was a mine of statuary for treasure hunters; much of it is now on display in many of the great museums of the world. For its sheer size — it extends between the Appia Antica and the Appia Nuova — the site is quite impressive and affords beautiful views of the Roman countryside.

Via Appia Nuova 1092. ☎ 06-39967700. Admission: 6€ ($8). Includes admission to the Baths of Caracalla and the Mausoleum of Cecilia Metella. Open: Tues–Sun 9 a.m. to 1 hour before sunset.

For families with kids
Kids of all ages love imagining lost civilizations and treasure hunts, and as Rome is essentially one big archaeological site, children will find much to love about the city. Throughout this chapter, we use the Kid Friendly icon to indicate what we believe are the best attractions for children. Here, we give you a few more suggestions of places and activities that are particularly suited for children or teens.

Boats down the Tiber
Trastevere

Sailing down the Tiber is a wonderful way to experience Rome. The **Compagnia di Navigazione Ponte San Angelo** operates boat service between **Ponte Duca d'Aosta** and **Isola Tiberina.** Boats have 50 seats and leave every hour from 8 a.m to 2 p.m. and 4 to 7 p.m.; check for the latest schedule, because it changes often. You can also catch a boat at one of the intermediary stops at the following bridges: **Risorgimento, Cavour, Sant'Angelo, Sisto, Isola Tiberina,** and **Ripa Grande.** The ride is not only idyllic, but also a convenient and inexpensive means of transportation, provided that where you need to go is along the Tiber. The same company also organizes special tours (see "Seeing Rome by Guided Tour," later in this chapter), including a wonderful cruise to Ostia Antica, which allows you to get to Rome's ancient seaport in much the same way as the Ancient Romans (see Chapter 14).

See map p. 148. Ponte d'Aosta, off Piazza della Rovere. ☎ *06-6789361 for info and reservations. E-mail:* info@battellidiroma.it. *Fare: Single trip 1€ ($1.30); daily pass 2.30€ ($3).*

Cimitero dei Cappuccini (Capuchins Cemetery)
Via Veneto

In the crypt of the **Chiesa dell'Immacolata Concezione** is a fascinating, if ghoulish, sight. A Capuchin monk used the bones of 4,000 of his brothers to create a monument that reminds us — literally — that "in the midst of life, we are in the midst of death." Skeletal pieces decorate the ceilings and walls of five underground chapels, creating interesting patterns and designs (for example, rows of spinal vertebrae trace the vaults). *Note:* This might be a "kid-friendly" sight if you have a teenager, but it would disturb and frighten smaller children.

See map p. 148. Via Veneto 27, not far from the U.S. embassy; ☎ *06-4871185. Metro: Barberini. Bus: 62 or Minibus 116 or 119 to Largo Tritone. Admission: Donation. Open: Fri–Wed 9 a.m. to noon and 3–6 p.m.*

Villa Borghese
Parioli/Piazza del Popolo

Just above Piazza del Popolo and extending north beyond the city walls is one of Rome's most beautiful parks, formerly belonging to the aristocratic Borghese family, who donated it to the city. Famous for the **Galleria Borghese** (see listing earlier in this chapter), it is also beloved by Romans, who come here to enjoy the greenery on weekends and the splendid panorama over Rome from the **Pincio.** Maybe the most romantic spot of Rome, this terrace above Piazza del Popolo offers a beautiful view that is particularly striking at sunset. Inside the park is also the **Piazza di Siena,** a picturesque oval track surrounded by tall pines, used for horse races and particularly for the **Concorso Ippico Internazionale di Roma** (Rome's international horse-jumping event), held in May (see Chapter 3). This park is perfect for a family picnic, especially in summer, when its beautiful Roman pines offer relief from the heat.

See map p. 148. Piazza Porta Pinciana. Bus: Minibus 116, or 116T. Open: Park daily from sunrise to sunset; Pincio terrace always open. Admission: Free.

For religious-architecture lovers: More great churches

 ### Basilica di Santa Prassede *(St. Prassede Basilica)*
Repubblica

One of the oldest churches in Rome, Santa Prassede already existed in the fifth century A.D. but was restored in the Middle Ages; the current entrance dates back to that time. Inside are some splendid Byzantine **mosaics,** on the arch over the main altar, in the apse, and in the splendid chapel of **San Zenone** — Rome's most important Byzantine monument. The church is full of other works of art, including a bust of Bishop G. B. Santoni from 1614, an early work by Gian Lorenzo Bernini (located by the third column to the right of the main nave).

See map p. 148. Via Santa Prassede 9, off Piazza Santa Maria Maggiore. ☎ *06-4882456. Metro: Termini. Walk south on Via Cavour. Bus: 70. Admission: 2€ ($2.60). Open: Daily 7:30 a.m.–7:30 p.m.*

San Pietro in Vincoli *(St. Peter in Chains)*
Colosseo

Vincoli means *chains,* and this church is named after the chains, on display in a bronze urn in the crypt, that held St. Peter in Jerusalem and in Rome. According to Catholic Church legend, the chains were miraculously welded together when they were brought into contact in this church. This ancient basilica, which was built in A.D. 439 over an older church and was partially redecorated in the 18th century and then again in the 19th century, also contains one of Michelangelo's masterpieces, his famous *Moses,* part of the majestic funeral monument he designed for Pope Julius II.

See map p. 148. Piazza San Pietro in Vincoli 4. ☎ *06-4882865. Metro: Colosseo or Cavour. Admission: Free. Open: Daily 8 a.m. to noon and 3:30 a.m.–6 p.m.*

Santa Maria Maggiore
Repubblica

This church's history stretches back 1,600 years, and though it has undergone many changes over the centuries, Santa Maria Maggiore remains one of the city's four great basilicas. Ordered constructed by Pope Sisto III, it was built as a sanctuary for Mary (mother of Jesus) and was originally referred to as Santa Maria della Neve (St. Mary of the Snow) because its outline was drawn in the snow that had miraculously fallen in the summer of A.D. 352. The current baroque facade was designed by Ferdinando Fuga, who sandwiched it between two palaces that had been built in the meantime (one in the 17th and the other in the 18th century). The walls, though, are original, as are the mosaics of the apse and side walls. Although restored, the floors are the original 12th-century Cosmatesque-style (mosaic in marble and colored stones), and the 15th-century coffered wooden ceiling is richly decorated with gold (said to be the first gold brought back from the New World and donated by the Spanish queen). One of the church's main attractions is in the loggia: the **13th-century mosaics** preserved from the old facade. Look carefully to the right side of the altar for the **tomb of Gian Lorenzo Bernini,** Italy's most important baroque sculptor/architect. In the crypt are relics of what are said to be pieces of Jesus's crib. Inside the church is a little-known architectural masterpiece by Michelangelo (he designed but did not complete it), the **Cappella Sforza;** the small space is elegantly decorated and artificially enlarged by the clever disposition of its angular columns.

See map p. 148. Piazza di Santa Maria Maggiore. ☎ *06-4881094. Metro: Termini; then walk south on Via Cavour. Bus: 70. Admission: Free. Open: Daily 7 a.m.–7 p.m.*

Santa Maria d'Aracoeli
Teatro Marcello

Next to Piazza del Campidoglio (just by the Capitoline Museums), Santa Maria d'Aracoeli dates from 1250 and is reached by a soaring flight of steps (you can't miss them as you approach the Campidoglio). It stands on the site of an Ancient Roman temple. The exterior of the church is austere but is punctuated by two rose windows, and inside are a number of interesting works of art. The floor is an excellent example of **Cosmati marblework** (the Cosmati were Roman stoneworkers of the Middle Ages). The **Cappella Bufalini (Bufalini Chapel)** is decorated with Pinturicchio masterpieces, frescoes depicting scenes from the life of St. Bernardino of Siena and St. Francis receiving the stigmata.

See map p. 148. Piazza d'Aracoeli. ☎ *06-6798155. Bus: Minibus 117 to Campidoglio; then walk to the right around the Vittorio Emanuele II Monument. Admission: Free. Open: Daily 7 a.m. to noon and 4–7 p.m.*

Santa Maria sopra Minerva
Pantheon

The construction of this church started in the eighth century A.D. on the foundation of an ancient temple to Minerva (goddess of wisdom), but the present structure dates from 1280. This is the only Gothic church in Rome (though you wouldn't know it from the facade, due to a 17th-century revision, one of many), with its elegant pointed arches and blue starred ceiling. The treasures inside include Michelangelo's **Cristo Portacroce** in the sanctuary, as well as frescoes by Filippino Lippi. Under the altar are the **relics of St. Catherine of Siena.** The church also houses the **tomb of the painter Fra Angelico.** On the square in front of the church is the much-photographed Bernini **elephant sculpture** that serves as the base for a sixth-century-B.C. Egyptian obelisk.

See map p. 148. Piazza della Minerva. ☎ *06-6793926. Bus: 62 or 64 to Largo Argentina, or Minibus 116 to Piazza della Minerva. Admission: Free. Open: Daily 7 a.m.–7 p.m.*

Santa Maria in Trastevere
Trastevere

Opening on a square graced by an early baroque fountain, this is believed to be the first Roman church to be officially opened to the public. Founded by Pope Saint Callixtus in the 3rd century A.D., it was later enlarged and given its present look in the 12th century with materials from the Baths of Caracalla (see listing earlier in this chapter). The facade is decorated with its original mosaic, but the portico is a later, baroque addition. Inside, you can admire the Cosmatesque floor; the richly decorated wooden ceiling (designed by Domenichino in the 17th century); and the star of the show: the beautifully preserved original **mosaics** decorating the apse. Over the main altar is another famous artwork: the *Madonna della Clemenza,* a unique painting from the sixth century.

See map p. 148. Piazza Santa Maria in Trastevere. ☎ *06-5814802. Bus: 23. Tram: 8. Admission: Free. Open: Daily 7:30 a.m.–8 p.m.*

Santa Maria in Cosmedin and Bocca della Verità
(St. Mary in Cosmedin and Mouth of Truth)
Aventino

Although this Orthodox church is very pretty inside and outside — it's one of the few Roman churches to have escaped baroque "restoration" — the real attraction is the famous **Bocca della Verità (Mouth of Truth),** a Roman marble relief of a head with an open mouth that sits against the wall under the porch outside the church. The round marble piece was in fact a Roman manhole cover, but legend has it that if you put your hand inside the mouth while lying, it will bite off your hand. (Remember the scene with Gregory Peck and Audrey Hepburn from *Roman Holiday?*) Kids get a kick out of putting their hands in the mouth. The church opens on **Piazza Bocca della Verità,** one of the nicest squares in town — at its best during off hours — with two small Roman temples still standing, the round one believed to be dedicated to the goddess Vesta and the other to the twins of Greek mythology, Castor and Pollux.

See map p. 148. Piazza Bocca della Verità. ☎ *06-6781419. Bus: 81. Admission: Free. Open: Daily 7 a.m.–6:30 p.m.*

Basilica di San Paolo Fuori Le Mura (St. Paul's Basilica)
San Paolo (outside *il centro*)

This basilica, second in size and importance only to St. Peter's, was built well outside the city walls in what was then the countryside, along the road that leads from Rome to the Ancient Roman seaport of Ostia (Via Ostiense). San Paolo is now a modern neighborhood of Rome, well connected to the city center by public transportation. According to tradition, the body of St. Paul was buried here after his martyrdom. As early as the time of Emperor Constantine in the fourth century A.D., a church was built around St. Paul's tomb (still below the high altar). Consecrated in A.D. 324 but later vastly enlarged, this magnificent church was almost destroyed by fire in

1823 and rebuilt with marble salvaged from the original structure. The apse and triumphal arch are original, and the mosaic in the apse is a faithful copy of the 13th-century one, reconstructed with parts of the original damaged by the fire. The *baldacchino* (canopy) — a masterpiece by Arnolfo di Cambio from 1285 — miraculously escaped the fire. Under the altar is the **sepulchre of St. Paul,** the tomb containing the saint's remains; it's accessible via a staircase. The interior is vast and impressive (divided by 80 granite columns), regardless of its age; the windows may look like stained glass, but they're actually made of translucent alabaster. The **cloisters** are original, and you'd have to go to Sicily to find such distinctively carved and decorated columns of so many diverse patterns.

Via Ostiense 184. ☎ *06-5410341. Metro: Basilica di San Paolo. Bus: 23. Admission: Free. Open: Church daily 7 a.m.–6:30 p.m.; cloister daily 9 a.m.–1 p.m. and 3–6 p.m.*

For secular-architecture lovers: More delightful Roman piazze and palaces

Piazza del Quirinale and Palazzo del Quirinale
Trevi

Now the home of Italy's president, the Palazzo del Quirinale was the residence of the king up until the end of World War II, and earlier in history, the pope lived here — or hid, in the case of Pius VII, who locked himself in after excommunicating Napoleon (it didn't help: soldiers broke in and carted him off to Fontainebleau for the duration of the Napoleonic era). The royal family of Savoy substituted some gaudy and second-rate 19th-century art for earlier decoration, but the palace is still impressive and has some spectacular rooms. The private gardens enclosed by the palace are gorgeous, especially in spring. *Note:* Bring your passport — you'll need to pass through an identity and security check in order to gain admission.

On the square, the **fountain (Fontana di Monte Cavallo)** has two giant statues of Castor and Pollux, the founders of Rome. The **Egyptian obelisk** adorning the square was taken from the Mausoleum of Augustus by Pius VI in 1793. Across from the palace's entrance on the same side of the square are the smaller buildings that were the **Scuderie del Quirinale (Palace Stables),** today the setting of many fine-art exhibits (check with the tourist office for the current schedule).

See map p. 148. Piazza del Quirinale off Via del Quirinale, the continuation of Via XX Settembre. ☎ *06-46991.* www.quirinale.it. *Metro: Barberini. Bus: Minibus 116 or 117 to Via del Quirinale. Admission: 5€ ($6.20). Open: Sun and June 2 8:30 a.m. to noon. Closed July, Aug, and major holidays.*

Piazza del Popolo
Piazza del Popolo

The "piazza of the people" really lives up to its name: Romans like to meet here to talk, have a drink, hang out, and people-watch. You can do the same, though be warned that the two cafes fronting the piazza gouge you unmercifully if you sit at an outdoor table (or even an indoor one) instead of taking your coffee at the counter like a Roman. **Santa Maria del Popolo** (☎ 06-3610836) stands by the gate leading out to busy **Piazzale Flaminio** (where you can catch lots of buses). Founded in 1099, the church contains magnificent Caravaggios as well as a Pinturicchio. The brace of baroque churches directly across the square are the work of Carlo Rainaldi, Bernini, and Carlo Fontana. In the center is an **Egyptian obelisk,** one of Rome's most ancient objects, dating from 1200 B.C. It came from Heliopolis and had been placed there by Ramses II, but was brought to Rome during Augustus's reign (it stood in the Circo Massimo until one of the popes, in their nearly endless reshuffling and meddling with monuments, moved it here). When you leave the piazza, head up the steps into the trees on the east side. This path leads to the Pincio, the park overlooking the square, which is one of the best places to see the sun set over Rome.

See map p. 148. Off Via del Babuino, Via del Corso, and Via de Ripetta. Metro: Flaminio. Bus: 490 to Piazzale Flaminio. Bus: Minibus 117 or 119. Tram: 2.

Piazza Farnese
Campo de' Fiori

This delightful piazza is dominated by the **Palazzo Farnese,** surely one of Rome's most dramatic buildings, designed by Sangallo and Michelangelo. The cleaning completed in 1999 turned its somber gray a startling pale yellow and brought out the delicate decorations. Currently the seat of the French embassy, it can be visited on selected Sundays; call the French embassy at ☎ **06-686011.**

See map p. 148. Off Via dei Baullari, near Campo de' Fiori. Bus: 116.

Villa Torlonia
Porta Pia

The Torlonia were — and still are — a noble Roman family (no less than princes), and this was their family residence until the early 20th century, when they donated the entire villa and the surrounding park to the city. In the park are the main residence and the beautiful conservatory (both in ruins, but plans are in process to restore the conservatory), as well as two smaller buildings that have been fully restored and can be visited. One is the **Casina delle Civette (Cottage of the Owls),** an Art Nouveau jewel with whimsical architecture and beautiful stained-glass windows. Back in the 19th century, the prince allowed his artistic son to build this cottage as a bachelor apartment; it now houses a museum of Art Nouveau glasswork. On the other side of the park is the **Casino dei Principi (Cottage of the Princes),** an elegant outbuilding that was the residence of Mussolini when he was in power and that now preserves some of the collected artworks of the Torlonia family. The beautiful grounds of the villa are a popular place for Romans to exercise, meet, and relax. You can make a reservation for a guided tour of the Casina delle Civette, which we recommend.

See map p. 148. Via Nomentana 70; ☎ *06-8207304. Open: Tues–Sun summer 9 a.m.– 7 p.m., winter 9 a.m.–5 p.m. Admission: Park free; Casina delle Civette 2.60€ ($3.40); Casino dei Principi 2.60€ ($3.40).*

For art-gallery rats

Galleria Spada
Campo de' Fiori

This gorgeous 16th-century *palazzo* houses the State Council, but it has recently been opened to the public, and you can now admire part of the riches inside. From the elegant inner courtyard, you can access the beautiful library and admire the famous and unique **Galleria della Perspettiva** designed by **Borromini** (Borromini's Perspective) — a magnificent corridor in trompe-l'oeil style, which appears to be very long but is actually made of diminutive columns that fool the eye (the sculpture at the end is only waist high). Inside the palace, you can also visit the rich picture gallery, a collection of works focusing mostly on 17th-century artists, including **Guido Reni, Guercino,** and **Tiziano.** It is hung in Renaissance style, just as it was when Cardinal Bernadino Spada acquired many of the works. The paintings hang against walls that are still richly decorated, gilded, and painted. We find particularly interesting some works by women: **Lavinia Fontana** (1552–1614) and **Artemesia Gentileschi** (1593–1652). The collection also includes two beautiful large globes from this period by **Willem Blaeu,** one containing a small portrait of his friend, astronomer Tyco Brahe.

See map p. 148. Piazza Capo di Ferro 13, off Piazza Farnese. ☎ *06-6832409. Bus: 116. Admission:5€ ($6.50). Open: Tues–Sun 9 a.m.–7 p.m. Ticket office closes at 6:30 p.m.*

Galleria Colonna
Trevi

Reopened after a long closure and completely restored, this is the palace housing the private gallery of the noble Roman family Colonna. The visit includes the actual apartments. The splendid 15th-century wing — the **Appartamento Principessa Isabelle** — is richly decorated with frescoes by Pinturicchio (Sala della Fontana) and a picture collection of Flemish masters, including such artists as Jan Brueghel the Elder. The 17th-century wing — the **Appartamento Galleria Colonna** — is a baroque extravaganza of works of art and precious furnishings, including a picture collection with masterpieces by Ghirlandaio, Veronese, Tintoretto, and Guercino, among others.

See map p. 148. Piazza Santi Apostoli 66. ☎ *06-6784350.* www.galleriacolonna.it. *Bus: 61, 62, 63, 80 to Piazza San Silvestro. Admission: 7€ ($9). Open: Sat 9 a.m.–1 p.m. Closed Aug.*

Galleria Doria Pamphili
Navona/Pantheon

This is the place to come if you want to know what it was like to live in an 18th-century Roman palace. Residence of the Roman aristocratic Doria Pamphili family, it houses one of Rome's most important private art collections. The *palazzo*'s lavish apartments are filled with tapestries, beautiful furnishings, and art. The gallery includes paintings by Filippo Lippi, Raphael, Caravaggio, Tiziano, and others. One of the greatest highlights is Velázquez's portrait of Pope Innocent X.

See map p. 148. Piazza del Collegio Romano 2, off Via del Corso. ☎ *06-6797323.* www.doriapamphili.it. *Bus: Minibus 117 or 119. Admission: 8€ ($10) including audio guides. Open: Fri–Wed 10 a.m.–5 p.m.*

Villa Farnesina
Trastevere

Not exactly a picture gallery, this gorgeous villa holds a wonderful **collection of frescoes by Raphael** and other artists in a suite of rooms. Built along the river Tiber in the early 16th century by the architect Baldassarre Peruzzi — who also decorated with frescoes part of the interior — and surrounded by a pleasant garden, it is a splendid example of Roman architecture. It was unfortunately mutilated in 1884 when the Lungotevere (the riverside road) was built, destroying part of the gardens and a loggia overlooking the river that was probably designed by Raphael. The villa was built for the Chigi family; later passed to the Farnese; and is today the seat of the Accademia dei Lincei, a major Italian cultural institute, and of the National Print Gallery, the largest print collection in Italy. The frescoes in the first room — the *Loggia di Psiche* — were done by Raphael's assistants from cartoons by Raphael, whereas the great fresco of Galatea in the *Sala di Galatea* is by Raphael himself. The *Camera da Letto* on the second floor was frescoed by Siennese artist Il Sodoma.

See map p. 148. Via della Lungara 230. ☎ *06-68027268.* www.lincei.it. *Bus: 23. Tram: 8. Admission: 5€. Open: Mon–Sat 9 a.m.–1 p.m. Closed on holidays.*

For history buffs

Campo de' Fiori
Campo de' Fiori

Surrounded by cafes, restaurants, and bars, the lovely square of Campo de' Fiori boasts many attractions. Its **fruit-and-vegetable market** is one of the city's best and certainly one of the liveliest. Though popular with working people as a lunch spot, the campo is even more popular with young people (both Romans and foreigners) at night. The **central statue of the hooded Giordano Bruno** hints at the more sinister parts of the campo's history — it was the site of executions in the Middle Ages and the Renaissance, and Bruno was burned at the stake here in 1600. Bruno was a philosopher who championed the ideas of early scientists like Copernicus and maintained such heretical ideas as that the Earth revolved around the sun.

See map p. 148. Off Via dei Giubbonari, near Largo Argentina. Bus: 116.

Gianicolo (Janiculum Hill)
Trastevere

Overlooking Trastevere, this is one of the two best places to see the panorama of Rome, the other being the **Pincio** (see the listing for Villa Borghese, earlier in this chapter). On the hill is a monument to Giuseppe Garibaldi, perhaps the most beloved figure of the 19th-century Italian struggle for self-determination, and a little farther down is a unique equestrian statue of his wife, Anita, likewise a hard-charging revolutionary. Anita's tomb is located under the statue.

See map p. 148. Bus: 119, or take a cab up and stroll down.

Vittoriano aka Altare della Patria (Monument to King Vittorio Emanuele II)
Colosseo

This controversial monument — called "the typewriter" by detractors because of its shape — was built to honor the memory of the first king of Italy, who unified the country. The construction took place between 1885 and 1911, and employed the most talented Italian artists of the time. Since 1921, it has also housed the *Tomba del Milite Ignoto* **(Tomb of the Unknown Soldier).** Closed to the public for decades, it was recently completely restored, and it is now possible to admire the beautiful decorations. Also, you can climb the stairs and enjoy one of the most beautiful views over Rome, particularly at sunset. The lower floors house excellent art exhibits; check with the tourist office for the current schedule.

See map p. 148. Piazza Venezia. ☎ 06-6991718. Metro: Colosseo. Bus: 64, 62, 63. Admission: Free. Open: 9:30 a.m.–4:30 p.m.

Cimitero Acattolico (Non-Catholic Cemetery)
Testaccio

A pilgrimage site for fans of poets **John Keats** and **Percy Bysshe Shelley,** who are buried here, this is a very pretty small cemetery. Among other famous eternal occupants is the anti-Fascist Antonio Gramsci, who died in 1937 after 11 years in prison. The cemetery has a prestigious next-door neighbor: the **pyramid of Caius Cestius,** a Roman praetor and tribune who died in 12 B.C.

See map p. 148. Via Caio Cestio. ☎ 06-5741141. Metro: Line B to Piramide. Bus: 23 or Tram 3 to Via Marmorata. Admission: Free. Open: Tues–Sun 9 a.m.–5 p.m.

Seeing Rome by Guided Tour

The French writer Stendhal once wrote, "As soon as you enter Rome, get in a carriage and ask to be brought to the Coliseum [sic] or to St. Peter's. If you try to get there on foot, you will never arrive: Too many marvelous things will stop you along the way."

Taking a bus tour of this complicated city when you first arrive still is an excellent idea. Doing so helps you get the general feeling of the place and gives you an idea of what you'd like to see in depth. After you decide what you want to see, you can take a walking tour of the area or areas that interest you most and then do the rest by yourself.

Bus tours

We like the hop-on/hop-off formula: You can stay on to have the complete tour and get an idea of what's where and what it looks like, and then start again and get down off the various stops. Here are some recommended options:

✔ Rome's public transportation authority, **ATAC,** gives the best bus tour of Rome (☎ **06-46952252** daily 9 a.m.–8:30 p.m. for reservations and info; www.trambus.com/servizituristici.htm); you can't beat the price or the options. The tourist **line 110** "open" decker buses leave from Piazza dei Cinquecento in front of Stazione Termini every 15 minutes; you can stay on the bus for the whole itinerary (the tour lasts about 2 hours and covers over 80 sites) or hop on and off along the way at one of 10 stops. Tickets cost 13€ ($17) per person; children under 6 ride free. The buses are new, and the tour guides are professionals. It's a great way to see many of the major sights of Rome. You can buy tickets at the ATAC bus information booth in front of Stazione Termini or on the bus (in which case you need the exact fare in cash).

✔ Also run by ATAC, the **Archeobus** tour (☎ **06-46952252** daily 8:30 a.m.–8 p.m. for reservations and info; www.trambus.com/servizituristici.htm) is another hop-on/hop-off itinerary (if you decide to stay onboard, the whole tour takes just under 2 hours) taking in 15 historic sites of Ancient Rome. The small, 16-seat electric buses leave every hour from Piazza dei Cinquecento (in front of Termini train station) between 9:45 a.m. and 4:45 p.m.; tickets cost 8€ ($10) and can be purchased on board (with exact change).

✔ **Stop 'n' Go** (Via Ezio 12; ☎ **06-48905729;** www.romecitytours.com) offers eight departures daily for 12€ ($16) per person. The tour starts in Piazza dei Cinquecento (in front of Stazione Termini) at the corner of Via Massimo d'Azeglio and makes 14 stops; you can get on or off at your leisure. (You can buy the ticket directly on the bus; try to have exact change, but it's not required.) If you prefer to spend more time at the sights, Stop 'n' Go offers two- and three-day tickets for 18€ ($23) and 24€ ($31), respectively.

If you prefer a more traditional bus tour instead, several formulas are available. Tours usually depart around 9 a.m., 3 p.m., and 8 p.m. — with possible pickup from your hotel included — and cost about 28€ ($36) for a three-hour tour. Here are the three best operators: **Appian Line** (Piazza dell'Esquilino 6; ☎ **06-487861;** www.appianline.it), **Green Line** (Via Farini 5/A; ☎ **06-483787;** www.greenlinetours.com), and **Vastours** (Via Piemonte 34; ☎ **06-4814309;** www.vastours.it).

Walking tours

Enjoy Rome (Via Varese 39, 3 blocks north off the side of Stazione Termini; ☎ 06-4451843; www.enjoyrome.com; Metro: Termini) offers a variety of three-hour walking tours, including a night tour that takes you through *il centro* and its sights, and a tour of Trastevere and the Jewish Ghetto. All tours cost 21€ ($27) adults and 15€ ($20) for those under 26, including the cost of the tour and admission to sights. The office is open Monday through Friday from 8:30 a.m. to 2 p.m. and 3:30 to 6:30 p.m., and Saturday from 8:30 a.m. to 2 p.m. Enjoy Rome also organizes a bike tour with English-speaking guides. Reserve at least two weeks in advance, and you can arrange special-interest tours such as "Fascist Rome: The Urban Planning of Mussolini" and "Caravaggio in Rome" (prices quoted upon request).

For **Scala Reale** (Via Varese 52; ☎ **888-4671986** or 06-44700898; Metro: Termini), American architect Tom Rankin organizes small-group walking tours with an architectural twist for as little as 20€ ($26) per person. Discounts are available for groups of four; children under 12 are free.

Boat tours

Besides its regular boat service on the Tiber (see "Finding More Cool Things to See and Do," earlier in this chapter), the **Compagnia di Navigazione Ponte San Angelo** (☎ 06-6789361; info@battellidiroma.it) offers a number of **day cruises** on the river leaving at 10 a.m., 11:30 a.m., 3:30 p.m., and 5 p.m., and two dinner-cruises — one leaving at 8 p.m. and a more exclusive **candlelight dinner cruise** leaving at 9 p.m.

Our preferred morning cruise is the special ride down the river all the way to the Tiber mouth, which includes a two-hour stop at **Ostia Antica** to visit the archaeological area. Prices range from 10€ ($13) for a one-way cruise to Ostia Antica to 45€ ($59) per person for the candlelight dinner cruise.

Società Tourvisa (☎ **06-448741**; www.tourvisaitalia.com) organizes three-hour weekend dinner cruises from March to December for 45€ ($59) per person; boats leave from the pier at Ponte Umberto I, off Piazza Cavour at 8:30 p.m.

Air tours

Created as a temporary attraction, the **hot air balloon** in Villa Borghese — the largest anchored aerostatic balloon in the world — has become a permanent feature. It takes off from the vicinity of the **Galoppatoio** and is operated by **Aerophile Italia** (☎ 06-32111511; www.aerophile.it; bus: 88, 490, 495, or Minibus 116; admission: Mon–Fri 15€ [$20] for adults and 11€ [$14] youth age 12–18, Sun and holidays 18€ [$23] adults and 12€ [$16] youth age 12–18, daily 6€ [$8] children 6–12, and 3€ [$3.90] children under 6).

Chapter 12

Shopping the Local Stores

A lot of people say Rome isn't good for shopping, at least not compared with Florence and Milan (the latter is the fashion capital of Italy). That may be true, but there are certainly a vast array of goods for sale in the capital city and a selection of some items — antique prints, for instance — that other Italian cities cannot match. You'll also find bargains here when you know where to look — and you'll have a great time browsing in the process!

Surveying the Scene

Shopping in Rome is great, if only because of the splendid setting of the major shopping areas — right in the heart of the city, among Roman ruins, medieval streets, and Renaissance palaces. Italy's largest city and also the seat of government, Rome is full of elegant and fashionable shops both for apparel and housewares, and the city is almost as good as Milan for all the big names of Italian fashion, which you'll find at great discounts during the official sales period in January and again in July.

Rome was also once the center of a large artisan community, but here as elsewhere, many historical trades have been lost, and in terms of crafts, the city isn't as rich as it was in ages past. Alas, very few workshops still practice traditional arts. On the other hand, because this is the capital of the country, you can find shops selling all the specialty items from around the country. Thus, you can also shop for famous products from places that you may not have time to visit, including Florence, Venice, and Sicily.

Needless to say, Rome has been and still is a center for the arts. If you had a euro for every picture that's been drawn of the Forum, you would be rich enough to buy your own Roman villa. Rome has been a magnet for artists for centuries, and views of the city's Ancient and baroque monuments have been endlessly reproduced, especially in prints. Rome is the best place in Italy to find this specialized kind of artwork, as well as modern, high-quality prints from antique plates.

Shopping hours are generally 9 or 9:30 a.m. (later for boutiques, which may open as late as 10:30 or 11 a.m.) to about 1 or 1:30 p.m. and then from 3:30 or 4 p.m. to 7:30 p.m. Many shops close Monday mornings, and most are closed all day Sunday. In *il centro,* however, quite a few shops now stay open during the lunchtime break and on Sundays.

Italy's **value-added tax** (known as the IVA) is a steep 19 percent, but you can get a refund for purchases costing more than 155€ ($178). This means that if you spend that much or more with one merchant, regardless of the number of items (three pairs of shoes, or five shirts, or whatever), you can get the rebate. If you buy the three pairs of shoes at three different stores, however, even if they add up to 155€, that doesn't help you, because they're three different purchases.

The value-added tax is included in all the prices that you're quoted. Stores displaying a "TAX FREE" insignia can give you an invoice that you can cash at the airport's Customs office as you leave Italy. Otherwise, you have to take the invoice from the store; have it stamped at the airport by Customs; and then mail it back to the store, which will then send you a check or credit your charge account.

When shopping for clothes or shoes, keep in mind that Italian sizes are different from those in the United States. Use Table 12-1 to find your Italian size.

Table 12-1 — **Size-Conversion Chart**

Clothes

Italy	40–42	44–46	48–50	52–54	56–58
U.S. women	S 4–6	M 8–10	L 12–14	XL 16	XXL 18
U.S. men	XS	S	M	L	XL

Men's shirts

Italy	36	37	38	39	41	42	43	44	46
U.S.	14	14½	15	15½	16	16½	17	17½	18

Shoes

Italy	35	35½	36	37	37½	38	38½	39	40	41
U.S. women	5	5½	6	6½	7	7½	8	8½	9	10
U.K. women	2½	3	3½	4	4½	5	5½	6	6½	7½
Italy		40	41	42	43	44	45	46		
U.S. men		7	8	8½	9½	10	11	11½		

Shoes									
U.K. men		6½	7½	8	9	9½	10½	11	
Italy	26	27	28	29	30	31	32	33	34
U.S. girls	9.5	10.5	11.5	12.5	13	1	2	2.5	3.5
U.S. boys			11.5	12	13	13.5	1	2	
U.K.	8	9	10	11	11.5	12.5	13	1	2

Checking Out the Department Stores

Italians are not as big on department stores as Americans are, and in Rome, you'll find only three major ones, but they are ubiquitous, with a number of locations scattered around the city:

✔ **La Rinascente** is an elegant department store carrying mainly clothes and accessories, with a larger selection for women and a smaller one for children and men. It also carries a nice cosmetics section on the ground floor and a smallish housewares selection. It has two major locations in Rome: Piazza Fiume 1 (☎ **06-8416081**) and Piazza Colonna (☎ **06-6784209**), both open daily from 9 a.m. to 7:30 p.m.

✔ **COIN** is another upscale department store, with a trendier and younger image, carrying a good selection of clothes and accessories for women, men, and children, and some interesting housewares. Its major locations are Via dei Gracchi (☎ **06-36004298**), Piazzale Appio 7 near San Giovanni Basilica (☎ **06-77250177**), and Viale Trastevere 60 (☎ **06-5816036**). It's open daily from 9 a.m. to 7:30 p.m.

✔ **UPIM** is a cheaper department store with a good selection of housewares and a rather inexpensive (and sometimes tacky) line of clothes for women, men, and children, as well as a modest selection of toys, stationery, and odds and ends. You'll find it in Via del Tritone 172 (☎ **06-6783336**), Piazza di Santa Maria Maggiore (☎ **06-4465579**), and Via Giovanni Giolitti 10 (☎ **06-47825909**) by Termini station. All are open Monday through Saturday from 9 a.m. to 7:30 p.m.

Going to Market

The most colorful of the **food markets** — and the most famous in Rome — is in the lively and picturesque **Campo de' Fiori** (Bus: 62 or 64 to Largo Argentina), where you'll find fresh fruit and vegetables, fish, meat, cheese, and cured meats, each sold by specialized vendors. It is surprising that the market hasn't become touristy, given the site; the vendors still keep selling all kinds of great goodies that Romans eat, from artichokes to anchovies, at good prices. It starts early in the morning — some vendors arrive as early as 6 — and ends around 2 p.m. Another historical food market, and also a great one, is in **Piazza San Cosimato** in the heart of Trastevere (Tram: 8), with a great variety of vendors and excellent quality and prices; it observes the same hours as Campo de' Fiori. The noisiest and most exuberant food market of them all is in **Piazza Vittorio,** not far from Termini Station, in an area of Rome that has been taken over by Asian and African immigrants, leading to an exotic choice of merchandise. In addition to food, you'll find stands selling cheap clothes and accessories.

There are a lot of other things to buy at market besides food. The **antiquarian book and print market** on Piazza Fontanella Borghese in the Navona/Pantheon neighborhood (Bus: 81 or Minibus 117 or 119 to the Corso at Via Tomacelli) is a historic small market and a great place to browse if you know your stuff — otherwise, *caveat emptor* (let the buyer beware), to use a Roman (or at least Latin) phrase.

For a truly uproarious market where you'll see average Romans searching for every conceivable item, visit the most famous of **flea markets** in Rome, at **Porta Portese.** Extending over several streets in Trastevere, this market is organized by type of merchandise: antiques, automotive, clothes, house fabrics, and so on. You never know what you're going to find, from oil paintings to tube socks. It's a fun place to go, and you're likely to find something you like, but go early to have a good selection before the mobs have picked over the merchandise. It's open only on Saturday and Sunday from about 7 a.m. to 2 p.m.

Another famous but smaller operation is the market in **Via Sannio** (off Piazza San Giovanni, near Colosseo and Aventino), with interesting clothes, accessories, and camping equipment. It's open daily from 7 a.m. to 1 p.m. Pickpockets are absolutely dreadful on weekends, when it gets most crowded. In both these markets, a small amount of dickering over the price is usual, so you can practice your bargaining skills.

In these bustling markets, particularly the flea markets, be very aware of pickpockets, who take advantage of the crowds.

Discovering the Best Shopping Neighborhoods

If you don't want to spend any money as you window-shop in the following shopping neighborhoods, you should leave your purse at home, because you'll see plenty of goodies tempting you to open your wallet wide.

Il Corso

The best shopping area in Rome is right in *il centro* — the triangle of medieval and Renaissance streets running between Piazza del Popolo, Piazza Venezia, and Piazza di Spagna. This area actually includes **Via del Corso** itself — now restricted to pedestrians (except for buses and taxis) — which is the area's main artery. The exclusive shopping area around **Piazza di Spagna** with **Via Frattina** and **Via dei Condotti** also falls within this part of *il centro*. Here is where the **big names** of Roman shopping concentrate; along these streets are the best designer bou- tiques and all the stars of Italian fashion (Bulgari, Ferragamo, Valentino, Armani, and so on), with prices so high you may get a nosebleed. But you'll also find small shops specializing in items ranging from stylish Italian housewares to antiques. With more variety and lower prices, the Corso is lined with shops selling everything from clothing to shoes to CDs. Some are fashionable; some are touristy; others are just trendy (and a few are rather tacky). On the Corso, you're more likely to see average Romans buying things that real people wear and at prices they can afford. You can find **Fendi** (Via Borgognona 39; ☎ 06-696661), **Valentino** (Via dei Condotti 13; ☎ 06-6739420), **Gucci** (Via Condotti 8; ☎ 06-6793888), **Armani** (Via dei Condotti 77; ☎ 06-6991460), and **Emporio Armani** (Via del Babuino 140; ☎ 06-36002197) nearby. **Battistoni** (Via dei Condotti 61/a; ☎ 06-697611) and **Testa** (Via Frattina 104, ☎ 06-6791294) are both men's clothing specialists.

Don't forget that Italy is famous for its leatherwork. For leather acces- sories, head for **Via dei Condotti;** beautiful leather gloves can also be found around **Piazza di Spagna.** For leather bags and wallets (if money isn't an issue), go to **Prada** (Via dei Condotti 88/90; ☎ **06-6790897;** Metro: Line A to Spagna). For shoes, try **Dominici** (Via del Corso 14; ☎ **06-3610591**), **Ferragamo** (Via dei Condotti 73–74; ☎ **06-6798402**), and **Ferragamo Uomo** (Via dei Condotti 75; ☎ **06-6781130**).

For more relaxed and youthful shopping, head for the newly opened **Galleria Alberto Sordi,** across from Piazza Colonna (it's also right next to La Rinascente, the department store mentioned earlier in this chapter). This mall has many nice shops and two bars, one near each entrance: Bar Tritone and Bar Trevi.

Via del Babuino and **Via Margutta** are the traditional locations of some of the best — and priciest — antiques shops in town. Among the anti- quarian and artwork shops in this area that merit a mention are **Alinari** (Via Alibert 16/a; ☎ **06-6792923;** Metro: Line A to Spagna) and **Fava** (Via del Babuino 180, ☎ **06-3610807;** Metro: Line A to Spagna), both selling artistic prints, the former specializing in Roman and the latter in Neapolitan scenes. At these shops, you can be sure that the antique you're buying is really an antique.

Navona/Pantheon

The intricate medieval streets on the west side of the Corso hide a great trove of elegant and original boutiques, and some of the oldest establish- ments in Rome. Here, you find even more variety of goods, from old prints to exclusive fashions, from books to antique furniture. The foot traffic is often less heavy here than on the Corso, which on major shopping days and holidays looks like New York's Fifth Avenue around Christmastime.

In these smaller shops, you can buy something that you'd never find at home. Big Italian designer labels often turn up at U.S. discount stores, so why not check out a smaller Roman designer store that you'll never see on the other side of the Atlantic? An elegant men's store, **Davide Cenci** (Via Campo Marzio 1–7; ☎ 06-6990681; bus: Minibus 116 to Pantheon), is popular with locals. Just a stone's throw away is **Tombolini** (Via della Maddalena 31/38; ☎ 06-69200342), which carries handsome clothes and shoes for women and men, with an emphasis on timelessly classic styling rather than chic. However, if you really want to make your friends green with envy, have a pair of shoes custom-made by **Listo** (Via della Croce 76; ☎ 06-6784567). For leather bags and wallets, **Bottega Veneta** (Piazza San Lorenzo in Lucina 9; ☎ 06-68210024; bus: 81 or minibus 116 to Piazza San Lorenzo) is famous for its beautiful woven leather designs, often in rich and startling colors.

For high-quality prints, well-known shops are the famous **Nardecchia** (Piazza Navona 25; ☎ 06-6869318; bus: Minibus 116) and **Antiquarius** (Corso Rinascimento 63; ☎ 06-68802941; bus: Minibus 116), a nice shop just across the street from the Palazzo Madama. At these shops, you find higher-quality — and somewhat more reliable — articles than at the nearby **antiquarian book and print market** (see earlier in this chapter).

Local Roman crafts do survive here and there, especially in the medieval area around **Piazza Navona.** Here, you can find *vimini* (basketry) on **Via dei Sediari,** ironwork on **Via degli Orsini,** and even reproductions of Roman and Pompeian mosaics. For beautiful ceramic work, try the **Compagnia del Corallo** (Via del Corallo 27; ☎ 06-6833697), and for elegant wrought iron, head to **Nicola Arduini** (Via degli Specchi 12; ☎ 06-68805537). For handmade quality jewelry, check out the **Bottega Mortet** (Via dei Portoghesi 18; ☎ 06-6861629). For plasterwork, including reproductions of antique designs (some objects are small enough to take home; others can be shipped), visit the **Laboratorio Marani** (Via Monte Giordano 27; ☎ 06-68307866).

Rome's most special source of intoxicants is **Ai Monasteri** (Corso Rinascimento 72; ☎ 06-68802783; bus: Minibus 116), off the east side of Piazza Navona. Here, you can find the liqueurs, elixirs, and other alcoholic concoctions that Italian monks have been making since the Middle Ages. Another great place for wines and spirits is **Trimani** (see Chapter 16), which also has a cafe where you can sit and imbibe.

Of course, it's not always the case that you're looking for something Italian; the **English Bookshop** (Via di Ripetta 248; ☎ 06-3203301; bus: Minibus 117 or 119 to Piazza del Popolo) stocks a wide variety of books in — you guessed it — English. The **Libreria Babele** (Via dei Banchi Vecchi 116; ☎ 06-6876628; bus: Minibus 116 to Via dei Banchi) is Rome's most central gay/lesbian bookstore. In addition, many of the larger newsstands in the *centro* have English-language newspapers and magazines as well as bestsellers in fiction and some classics.

Paper in various forms — colored, marbled, deckle-edged — is an Italian specialty and can be found all over Rome. This is one of the most popular, portable, and affordable gifts for the folks back home. For especially refined stationery and paper, go to **Pineider,** founded in 1774 (two locations: Via Fontanella Borghese 22, ☎ **06-6878369,** bus: Minibus 117 or 119 to the Corso at Via Tomacelli; and Via dei Due Macelli 68, ☎ **06-6795884,** bus: Minibus 116, 117, or 119 to Via Due Macelli).

If you're interested in antiques, Rome is *the* place to go, and **Via dei Coronari** is Rome's antiquarian headquarters. This street — and it's not short — is lined with antiques dealers, one shop after another on both sides of the street. Whether it's furniture, glass, lamps, armoires, or paintings, you'll find it here. And even if you aren't planning on lugging home a count's antique bureau or a trestle table from a convent, the street is basically like a museum where you can (if you have the money) buy the exhibits.

Other shops in this area specialize in religious objects and attire (naturally, shops selling similar fare are located in the Vatican area, near Cola di Rienzo, discussed in the following section). Although you probably don't want to buy a cardinal's outfit, you may want to choose among the huge selection of figurines, bronzes, candleholders, paintings, crèches, and other religious objects. Two good stores are **Ghezzi** (Via de Cestari 32; ☎ **06-6869744**) and **Salustri** (Via de Cestai 11; ☎ **06-6791587**) nearby.

Cola di Rienzo

Although this area on the San Pietro side of the Tevere doesn't boast the luxury shops of Via dei Condotti, you can still find big names of Italian fashion, and what's more, it may even be affordable. This area is best for clothes and is also excellent for shoes, with shops catering to every level of price and style. Stores line both sides of **Via Ottaviano** and **Via Cola di Rienzo.**

Although this is not a traditional area for artistic crafts, a handful of very nice workshops here turn out high-quality goods, including the jewelry at **Carini** (Piazza dell'Unitá 9; ☎ **06-3210715**) and handmade lace at **Ricami Italia Garipoli** (Borgo Vittorio 91; ☎ **06-68802196**).

Proceeding farther toward the Vatican, near St. Peter's Basilica itself, you'll find one of the largest religious-items shops in the city, **Savelli,** with one location specializing in mosaics in Via Paolo VI 27 (☎ **06-68307437**) and another location right off the square, with a huge variety of other objects (Piazza Pio XII; ☎ **06-68806383**).

Via Nazionale

Off Piazza della Repubblica near Stazione Termini and running down toward Piazza Venezia, Via Nazionale used to be an elegant shopping area, but the traffic noise — the street was a main connecting artery between the train station and the *centro* — had driven away many customers. Fortunately, Via Nazionale is now open only to buses and taxes, which has reduced the deafening noise. The shops are varied, some good and others less so. The revived area has attracted some big names (perhaps fleeing the ridiculous rents of the Corso), but it is still frequented more by Italians than by tourists. Known especially for leather goods, this may be the best place to find that sleek number you really want without going to Florence.

Trastevere

This romantic medieval area of Rome is mostly known for its restaurants and night spots, but it's also rich in workshops of artists and craftspeople. Among the many great little shops and showrooms — some of them have been there for decades, and others are new ventures — you can find woodcarving at **Laboratorio Ilaria Miani** (Via degli Orti di Alibert 13/A; ☎ 06-6861366), stringed instruments at **Mohesen** (Vicolo del Cedro 33; ☎ 06-5882484), ceramics at **Ceramica Sarti** (Via Santa Dorotea 21; ☎ 06-5882079), and jewelry at **Elisabeth Frolet** (Via della Pelliccia 30; ☎ 06-5816614).

Via della Scala is almost wall-to-wall showrooms and workshops, from the goldsmiths **Massimo Langosco di Langosco** (Via della Scala 77; ☎ 06-5896375) and **Ferrone** (Via della Scala 76; ☎ 06-5803801) to the dressmakers **Scala Magica** (Via della Scala 66; ☎ 06-5894098) and **Scala 14** (Via della Scala 14; ☎ 06-5883580). It also has some great stores offering craft items from other Italian regions, such as the **Officina della Carta** (Via Benedetta 26; ☎ 06-5895557), selling paper and leather goods in the best Italian tradition; **Pandora** (Piazza Santa Maria in Trastevere 6; ☎ 06-5895658), which carries a great selection of Murano glass and Italian designer goods; **Modi e Materie** (Vicolo del Cinque; ☎ 06-5885280), with ceramics from the island of Sardinia; and **Ciliegia** (Via della Scala 5; ☎ 06-5818149), specializing in fashions from Positano, from handmade sandals and dresses to curios. You'll even find a nice English bookshop, **The Corner Bookshop** (Via del Moro 48; ☎ 06-5836942), and a shop selling sundials and other ancient time-measuring instruments, **Guaytamelli** (Via del Moro 59; ☎ 06-5880704).

Index of Stores by Merchandise

Antique Prints and Artworks
Alinari (Il Corso)
Antiquarian book and print market (Navona/Pantheon)
Antiquarius (Navona/Pantheon)
Fava (Il Corso)
Nardecchia (Navona/Pantheon)

Books and Magazines
The Corner Bookshop (Trastevere)
English Bookshop (Il Corso)
Libreria Babele (Piazza Navona/Pantheon)

Crafts

Ceramica Sarti (Trastevere)
Ciliegia (Trastevere)
Compagnia del Corallo
(Navona/Pantheon)
Elisabeth Frolet (Trastevere)
Laboratorio Ilaria Miani (Trastevere)
Laboratorio Marani (Navona/Pantheon)
Modi e Materie (Trastevere)
Mohesen (Trastevere)
Nicola Arduini (Navona/Pantheon)
Pandora (Trastevere)

Designer Clothing

Armani (Il Corso)
Battistoni (Il Corso)
Bulgari (Il Corso)
Davide Cenci (Navona/Pantheon)
Emporio Armani (Il Corso)
Fendi (Il Corso)
Ferragamo (Il Corso)
Gucci (Il Corso)
Scala 14 (Trastevere)
Scala Magica (Trastevere)
Testa (Il Corso)
Tombolini (Navona/Pantheon)
Valentino (Il Corso)

Flea Markets

Porta Portese (Trastevere)
Via Sannio (near Colosseo/Aventino)

Food Markets

Campo de' Fiori (Campo de' Fiori)
Piazza San Cosimato (Trastevere)
Piazza Vittorio (Termini)

Jewelry

Bottega Mortet (Piazza Navona/
Pantheon)

Carini (Cola di Rienzo)
Elisabeth Frolet (Trastevere)
Ferrone (Trastevere)
Massimo Langosco di Langosco
(Trastevere)

Lace

Ricami Italia Garipoli (Cola di Rienzo)

Leather Clothing and Accessories

Bottega Veneta (Il Corso)
Officina della Carta (Trastevere)
Prada (Il Corso)

Religious Items

Ghezzi (Navona/Pantheon)
Salustri (Navona/Pantheon)
Savelli (Cola di Rienzo)

Shoes

Ciliegia (Trastevere)
Dominici (Il Corso)
Ferragamo (Il Corso)
Ferragamo Uomo (Il Corso)
Listo (Navona/Pantheon)
Tombolini (Navona/Pantheon)

Stationery

Officina della Carta (Trastevere)
Pineider (Navona/Pantheon)

Sundials

Guaytamelli (Trastevere)

Wine

Ai Monasteri (Navona/Pantheon)
Trimani (Navona/Pantheon)

Chapter 13

Following an Itinerary: Five Great Options

- -

In This Chapter

▶ Hitting Rome's highlights in three days
▶ Seeing Rome in five days
▶ Taking in Rome's architectural highlights
▶ Admiring Michelangelo's Rome
▶ Enjoying Rome's many outdoor attractions

- -

*I*n the following five itineraries, we make recommendations on how best to spend your time in Rome and give you a few possible themes to give your vacation focus. You may have limited time, or maybe you just hate museums and being closeted indoors for hours, or perhaps you have special interests that you'd like to satisfy during this visit. No matter what your time restrictions or desires, we've got you covered in this chapter!

Rome in Three Days

So much to see, so little time! Here, we put together an itinerary for seeing the best Rome has to offer without suffering total exhaustion. This itinerary is a great introduction to a city for which, in the words of the great Italian writer Silvio Negro, a lifetime is not enough to know.

Day 1

Start with an overview of the city to get your bearings and get a sense of the flavor by taking the excellent **ATAC bus tour** (see guided tours in Chapter 11). This tour will leave you hungry for more, but if you started early, you still have time to take in a major sight before lunch. Make it the beautiful **Piazza del Popolo,** and drop into **Santa Maria del Popolo** to see the magnificent paintings by Caravaggio (see Chapter 11). Afterward, head for **Bolognese** (see Chapter 10), an outstanding restaurant on the square.

After lunch, stroll to nearby **Piazza di Spagna** for the famous **Spanish Steps** (see Chapter 11). Along the way, check out the shops on Via del

Babuino — a street lined with high-fashion and antiques stores — as well as the other elegant shops of *il Corso* area, as in Via Margutta and Via Frattina (see Chapter 12). Make your reservations for the **Galleria Borghese** (see Chapter 11), and after your visit, walk through **Villa Borghese** to the Pincio — it's a beautiful walk, with a beautiful panorama of Rome that lights up with gold at sunset. Have dinner — or at least an *aperitivo* (predinner drink) — at the newly reopened **La Casina Valadier** (see Chapter 10); then stroll to **Fontana di Trevi** (see Chapter 11), which is beautifully lit at night. Have dinner at one of the many restaurants in the area.

Day 2

Start your day with a visit to the **Roman Forum,** the **Colosseum,** and another sight in the core area of Ancient Rome, such as the **Trajan Markets,** the **Palatine,** the **Capitoline Museums,** or the **Domus Aurea** (see Chapter 11). Have lunch in the area at the **Hostaria Nerone** or at **Pasqualino al Colosseo** (see Chapter 10).

In the afternoon, cross the Tiber, and head for **St. Peter's Basilica.** See as much as you can there, including **Castel Sant'Angelo** and even part of the **Vatican Museums,** although we recommend a minimum of three hours for this museum. (You can always run swiftly through this mind-boggling array of artworks directly to the **Sistine Chapel,** a do-not-miss attraction.) If you have time before dinner, take a shopping break down the **Via Cola di Rienzo** (see Chapter 12). You'll be famished afterward; luckily, the charming traditional tavern **Dante Taberna de' Gracchi** is not far away; even closer is the inventive **La Veranda.** Or head for the picturesque nearby neighborhood of **Trastevere,** and dine at **Checco er Carettiere** (see Chapter 10). Be sure to have a stroll to get a sense of this delightful neighborhood.

Day 3

Start your third day with a visit to the **Palazzo Massimo alle Terme** (make a reservation to see the Roman frescoes). When you're finished, take a bus to the *centro,* and visit the **Pantheon** (see Chapter 11); have lunch in the Navona/Pantheon area (see Chapter 10).

In the afternoon, relax with a stroll and some shopping through the area around **Piazza Navona** (don't forget to look at what special exhibits are on at the **Museo di Roma**), stopping for an espresso at **Antico Caffè della Pace** (see Chapter 16) or a gelato at **Giolitti** (see Chapter 10). Crossing Corso Vittorio Emanuele II, you come to one of the most atmospheric squares in Rome, the **Campo de' Fiori** (see Chapter 11). Eat dinner at the nearby **Bric,** where you can savor imaginative versions of Mediterranean cuisine, or try something different: **Da Giggetto,** in the old Jewish quarter of the city. Or choose a truly special restaurant for your last dinner in Rome (see Chapter 10). If you still have steam (or if you're a night owl), see the Colosseum lit up at night as a final, indelible memory of Rome.

Rome in Five Days

If you have five days in Rome, you can spend time absorbing or even pondering the sights rather than just seeing them and moving on. You also don't have to make as many painful choices. You can begin with **Day 1** as in the "Rome in Three Days" itinerary, earlier in this chapter, but then take the second day of that itinerary and divide it into two days, so that you can visit more attractions. Concentrate on the Rome of antiquity on Day 2, and give the Vatican the attention that this massive sight deserves on Day 3. Visit the **Colosseum,** the **Roman Forum,** and the **Palatine** in the morning of **Day 2;** then have lunch at one of the suggested restaurants for that day. Afterward, continue with the **Domus Aurea,** the **Trajan Markets,** and the **Capitoline Museums** — where you can also have a great break at the beautiful terrace restaurant–cafe inside. For dinner, head to the Testaccio, the most Roman of Roman neighborhoods, and treat yourself to a lavish meal at **Checchino dal 1887** or **Al Regno di Re Ferdinando II,** two fine restaurants that occupy caverns dug out of the Monte Testaccio (see Chapter 10 for more on these restaurants and the hill made of pot shards). If you feel like burning the midnight oil, you can stop in at **Club Picasso,** one of Testaccio's hottest clubs (see Chapter 16).

But make sure you're ready to head for the **Vatican Museums** early on **Day 3,** when you can linger over the spectacular collection of art and visit the **Sistine Chapel** as well. Have lunch in one of our recommended restaurants in the area (see Chapter 10), and,\ once refreshed, resume your visit with **St. Peter's Basilica** and **Castel Sant'Angelo.** Those who finish early can take a shopping break down the **Via Cola di Rienzo** (see Chapter 12). For dinner, make it a panoramic treat at the elegant **La Pergola** — you deserve it after an intense day of sightseeing.

For **Day 4,** follow Day 3 in the "Rome in Three Days" itinerary, earlier in this chapter, which takes in the **Palazzo Massimo** and other sights. On **Day 5,** head for the **Appia Antica** (see Chapter 11), or for something even more out of the ordinary, take a boat on the Tiber early in the morning to **Ostia Antica** (see Chapter 14). Have lunch near the attractions you choose. In the afternoon, return to Rome, and pick one of the attractions you're interested in but didn't have time to visit. Leave time in the late afternoon for some last-minute shopping and strolling in the Eternal City. Toward evening, head for **Trastevere,** where you can find not only excellent restaurants and nightlife (see Chapters 10 and 16, respectively), but also great shopping (see Chapter 12).

Rome for Architecture Lovers

The Renaissance completely changed the face of Rome, leaving few mementoes of Byzantine and medieval times, and shaping the city as we see it today. The center of Rome has been little touched in later centuries, because most modern development has taken place outside the city walls — and of course, virtually everything in the center is now a historic site. Splendid palaces and buildings await you at every street corner, while large and tiny squares — sudden openings in the fabric of narrow streets — surprise you with their beauty. If you love architecture, Rome has more to offer than can be related in a few lines, but here are the highlights.

Start with Michelangelo's masterpiece the **Piazza del Campidoglio,** defined by the three palaces that house the **Capitoline Museums** (see Chapter 11) — surely one of the great architectural monuments of Rome. Proceed to **Piazza Navona,** perhaps Rome's most beautiful square, lined by palaces and churches (keeping in mind that the shape recalls the chariot-racing oval that was here millennia ago). Take a break in one of the cafes in the square, or if you prefer something more solid, head toward Campo de' Fiori for lunch at **Il Drappo** for excellent Sardinian fare (see Chapter 10).

After lunch, continue to nearby **Piazza Farnese,** graced by the superb **Palazzo Farnese,** with its serene facade and gorgeous courtyard (visible only through a gate at the back). From there, you can easily reach the **Galleria Spada,** a little-known but gorgeous palace, still decorated in Renaissance style and especially famous for housing Borromini's Perspective, a unique architectural trompe l'oeil (see Chapter 11). Cross the Tiber over **Ponte Sisto** — an elegant Renaissance bridge rebuilt in the 15th century with part of the ruined preexisting Roman bridge — to reach the neighborhood of **Trastevere.** There, you'll find the **Villa Farnesina,** another lesser-known architectural marvel, graced by a garden over the river (magnificent frescoes are displayed inside the villa, too). You can finish your day with a stroll through Trastevere, a wonderful neighborhood rich in medieval buildings and churches, where the various architectural strata are often seen superimposed on one another in buildings that have been built, adapted, and rebuilt again. Be sure to see **Santa Maria** in Trastevere, a church begun in the third century and one of the oldest in Rome. The neighborhood has great shops and artist showrooms (see Chapter 12), as well as excellent restaurants and nightlife (see Chapters 10 and 16, respectively).

Rome for Michelangelo Lovers

A splendid sculptor, an exquisite painter, and a masterly architect, Michelangelo was extremely active in Rome, where the pope and other wealthy families largely exploited his many talents.

Start with **St. Peter's Basilica,** surmounted by the beautiful dome Michelangelo designed but didn't see finished — he died almost 30 years before its quite-faithful completion by architect Giacomo Della Porta. The basilica also houses the splendid *Pietà,* the sculptural masterpiece of Mary and Christ, which Michelangelo carved between 1498 and 1500. Continue to his crowning achievement and one of the most important works in the history of Western culture: the **Sistine Chapel,** the pictorial masterpiece at which he worked on and off for decades (between 1508 and 1512 for the ceiling and between 1535 and 1564 for the wall behind the main altar). After taking in this awe-inspiring sight, cross the Tiber, and head to **Campo de' Fiori** for lunch (see Chapter 10).

After your break, stroll to nearby **Piazza Farnese,** where you can admire the facade of Palazzo Farnese, which Michelangelo finished after the death of the original architect, Sangallo the Younger. You can then proceed to **Piazza del Campidoglio,** the square behind the monument to King Vittorio Emanuele II, a great architectural achievement in large part following Michelangelo's design (the 12-pointed star pattern set in the pavement of the square signifies the 12 apostles). Today, the beautiful palaces fronting the square house the **Capitoline Museums.** From here, it is only a few bus stops to **San Pietro in Vincoli,** where you can admire the artist's monument to Pope Julius II, decorated with his famous sculpture of Moses. You can then stroll up the hill — or take a couple of bus stops — to **Santa Maria Maggiore,** where you'll find a little-known architectural marvel, the **Cappella Sforza,** designed and begun by Michelangelo but completed well after his death. You can finish your tour with **Santa Maria degli Angeli,** the church that Michelangelo created by reorganizing, with great skill and respect for the original architecture, the well-preserved ruins of the **Terme di Diocleziano (Diocletian Baths).** (See Chapter 11 for all the preceding attractions.) After seeing the sights, grab a pizza in the neighborhood at **Opera** or **Al Forno della Soffitta,** or for a more substantial reward, visit **Cesarina,** another excellent restaurant not far away (see Chapter 10).

Rome for Outdoors Lovers

If you love sports and outdoor activities, and you hate the very idea of spending hours in an enclosed space such as a museum or a church, don't worry. Rome will surprise you, as it has done with her visitors century after century.

Start your day bright and early by going to the **Appian Way** visitor center (see Chapter 11) and renting bicycles there. Now you can proceed on your exploration on wheels. You can take in some of the attractions along the park of the Appian Way, or you can just enjoy the views of the countryside — one of the last undeveloped places where it still looks as the Ancient Romans must have seen it. Alternatively, you can hike through antiquity, covering a couple of miles of ruins by crossing what was the heart of Ancient Rome. Start with the **Roman Forum** and the **Colosseum;** then climb the **Palatino** — ancient Rome's most exclusive residential hill — and come out on the other side at the **Circo Massimo** (see Chapter 11), where you'll see Romans jogging around what was a chariot-racing track. Continue on (at this point, you'll have covered a lot of ground), and finish your day of sightseeing with the **Caracalla Baths.** By this time, you should have worked up a hearty appetite; have lunch in one of our recommended restaurants (see Chapter 10).

In the afternoon, tackle Renaissance Rome. Descend to the Tiber, where you can take a **boat ride** and view the heart of Rome from the water; then walk to **Piazza di Spagna,** where you can climb the **Spanish Steps,** and head for the **Pincio** and **Villa Borghese** (see Chapter 11), enjoying expansive vistas over the city. From here, you can rent a bicycle to explore the park, row a boat on the small romantic lake — complete with ruined temple — and even see Rome from a hot air balloon. Make sure to be back on the Pincio at sunset to admire Rome's gilded skyline of cupolas and domes, and reward yourself with an excellent dinner (see Chapter 10).

Chapter 14

Going Beyond Rome: Five Day Trips

● ●

In This Chapter

▶ Traveling back in time to Ostia Antica

▶ Visiting the fountains of Tivoli

▶ Dining with the Romans in the Castelli

▶ Discovering Etruscan marvels in Tarquinia

▶ Taking in the great outdoors at Lago di Vico

● ●

*L*azio, the region surrounding Rome, is rich in beautiful and fascinating sites only a short drive from the capital. If you have the time, stay a couple extra days in Rome and branch out from there for some enjoyable day trips.

Ostia Antica: Rome's Ancient Seaport

 Southwest of Rome, toward the sea, is **Ostia Antica,** the archaeological site of ancient Rome's commercial harbor. This is a destination not to miss — especially if you're keen on antiquity. It is also an excellent outing for kids, particularly if you get there by the very pleasant boat cruise along the Tiber (see "Taking a tour," later in this section). The ruins are particularly attractive early in the morning or at sunset, when many Romans like to come for an evening *passeggiata* (stroll). It's popular also on weekends for picnics, but most popular are the shows — music and theater — held in the Roman Theater, the **Teatro Romano,** in July.

The ancient city of Ostia served as a shipyard, a gathering place for the fleet, and a distribution center for Ancient Rome. Founded in the fourth century B.C. as a military colony for the defense of the river Tevere, Ostia flourished for about eight centuries before being progressively abandoned as a result of the silting up of the river and the spread of malaria in the region (no longer a concern, fortunately).

Rome and Environs

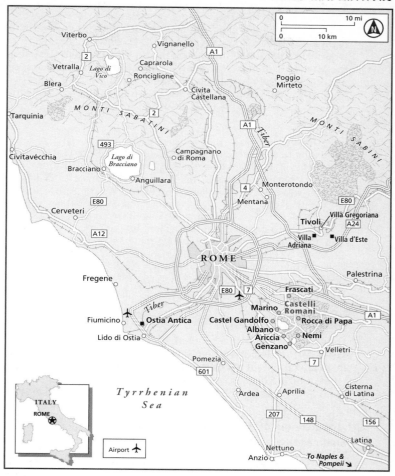

 Keep in mind that the ruins are incredibly hot in summer. They're spread across a flat plain, and shade is hard to come by. If you don't like heat, come early, end your visit just before lunch, and head elsewhere to dine.

Getting there

Ostia Antica is about 28km (16 miles) from Rome. It's linked by **train** from Stazione Ostiense (take Metro Line B to the Piramide stop, and follow the signs for Ostia to your platform), with trains departing every half-hour and costing about 1€ ($1.30) for the 25-minute trip. You can easily reach the site on foot from the train station, which is across the street.

By far the most interesting way to get to Ostia Antica is by **boat,** as the Ancient Romans would have done. The **Compagnia di Navigazione Ponte San Angelo** (☎ **06-6789361** for reservations; info@battellidiroma.it) runs morning cruises down the Tiber, with a two-hour stop in **Ostia Antica,** for 10€ ($13) one-way, 11€ ($14) round-trip, and 35€ ($46) round-trip plus buffet lunch during the return trip. Boats for Ostia Antica leave the Marconi bridge at 9:15 a.m. Tuesday through Sunday. *Important note:* A guided tour of the ruins is not included in the boat trip — you must book your tour in advance directly with the office at the Archaeological Area of Ostia Antica (see the following section).

Taking a tour

By far the best and most economical tour is offered by the Archaeological Area of Ostia itself, led by licensed guides and art historians. You can book a tour by calling or faxing the Archaeological Area at ☎ **06-56352830** Tuesday through Sunday. You'll meet your tour guide at the entrance to the excavations.

If you prefer a commercial excursion, including transportation by bus from Rome and entrance to the sights, we like **Stop n Go/C.S.R.** (Via Ezio 12; ☎ **06-3217054**; e-mail: csr@gisec.it). It organizes half-day tours of Ostia Antica leaving Tuesday through Sunday at 9:30 a.m. from the Stop n Go Terminal of Via Giolitti in Rome (on the side of Termini train station) for 12€ ($16).

Seeing the sights

Ostia Antica includes a small medieval village, the **Borgo Medievale di Ostia Antica.** Inside is the **Castello di Giulio II (Julius II's castle),** built in 1483 and one of the first examples of modern military architecture (Piazza della Rocca; ☎ **06-56358024**; open Wed, Fri–Sun 9 a.m.–12:45 p.m.; Tues and Thurs also 2:30–4:15 p.m.; free admission and guided tour).

Archaeological Area of Ostia Antica
Ostia Antica

The archaeological site covers the impressive excavations of the ancient town of Ostia. The main streets of the town have been unearthed, as have some of the principal monuments. After entering the site, on the right you'll find **Via delle Corporazioni,** leading to the **Roman Theater (Teatro Romano).** Be sure to take note of the mosaics indicating the nature of the businesses that once were housed along this street. The theater is still in use today for performances of works by modern and ancient authors during July as part of the **Estate Romana** (you can find details on the Web at www.estateromana.comune.roma.it or by calling ☎ **06-68809505**; Mon–Sat 10 a.m.–5 p.m.).

Returning to the main street and continuing ahead, you'll find on your left the **Forum** and behind it the **Terme (thermal baths).** Two temples are on the left, and the **Capitolinum** is on the right. The site also includes many interesting houses and buildings. The tourist office in Rome has a relatively good map of the park. Allow a minimum of three hours for the visit, more if you visit the museum. The **Museum (Museo Ostiense)** — conserving all the material found during the excavations of the site — just opened its doors after a restoration that lasted several years. The huge collection is exhibited now in a modern and rational way, making it a pleasure to visit. The entrance to the museum is within the excavations.

We definitely recommend taking an official guided tour; you'll learn a lot of interesting details, and what's more, the guide can take you into areas of limited access you couldn't visit on your own. There are a new restaurant cafeteria and a gift shop by the museum.

Viale dei Romagnoli 717, off Via Ostiense. ☎ *06-56358099. For guided tours call* ☎ *06-56352830.* www.itnw.roma.it/ostia/scavi. *Admission: 4€ ($5) including the museum. Open: Excavations: Tues–Sun Jan–Feb and Nov–Dec 8:30 a.m.–5 p.m.; Mar 8:30 a.m.–6 p.m.; April–Oct 8:30 a.m.–7:30 p.m. Last admission 1 hour before closing Nov–Mar and 90 minutes before closing Apr–Oct. Museum: Tues–Sun Jan–Feb and Nov–Dec 9 a.m.–4:30 p.m.; Mar 9 a.m.–5:30 p.m.; Apr–Oct 9 a.m.–1:30 p.m. and 2:15–6:30 p.m.*

Dining locally

With the reopening of the museum, the Ostia excavation site has also gained a nice **restaurant cafeteria,** where you can get a simple meal at a reasonable price, as well as beverages and ice creams, right inside the exhibit area. This is a great solution, because there aren't many dining options near to hand.

Otherwise, the environs of the archaeological area hold only a small restaurant and a bar in the village of Ostia Antica. You can do much better in the nearby town of Ostia, where there are some excellent restaurants overlooking the sea — or do as many Romans do, and bring a picnic lunch.

Capannina
$$$ Ostia   SEAFOOD

Very popular with the locals — and Romans who come here on weekends — this is a typical seaside restaurant, offering a variety of excellent fish dishes and more. The menu depends on the daily market, but you'll usually find *insalata di mare e di polpo* (cold octopus, squid, and fish salad), *rigatoni ai gamberi rossi* (pasta with large shrimp sauce), and a choice of the now-fashionable *crudi* (raw fish).

Lungomare A. Vespucci 156. ☎ *06-56470143. Reservations recommended on weekends. Secondi: 12€–21€ ($16–$27). AE, DC, MC, V. Open: Summer, daily noon to 3 p.m. and 7:30–11p.m.; winter Tues–Sun noon to 3 p.m. and 7:30–11 p.m.. Closed 3 weeks in Nov.*

Vecchia Pineta

$$$ Ostia   SEAFOOD

This classic restaurant might appear a bit serious in its décor, but its cuisine is the best in Ostia. Try the perfect *risotto alla pescatora* (seafood risotto) or the *spaghetti alle vongole veraci* (spaghetti with clams), followed by one of the daily specials prepared grilled, baked, or *in guazzetto* (light herb and tomato broth).

Piazza dell'Aquilone 4, on the Lungomare. ☎ 06-56470282. Reservations recommended on weekends. Secondi: 12€–22€ ($16–$29). AE, DC, MC, V. Open: Summer daily noon to 3 p.m. and 7:30–10:30 p.m; winter daily noon to 3 p.m. and Mon and Wed–Sat 7:30–10:30 p.m.

Tivoli and Its Trio of Villas

Tivoli, a small town on a hill 32km (20 miles) northeast of Rome, is the single best day trip from Rome in the summertime. The resort town enjoys a cooler climate during the hot months of summer and has been a traditional getaway for the wealthy and famous of Rome since ancient times. Its three famous villas — one Ancient Roman, one baroque, and one from the romantic period — reveal Rome's architectural history as it played out over almost 2,000 years.

Getting there

Trains leave Rome's Stazione Tiburtina for Tivoli about every hour. The ticket costs 2.50€ ($3.25) for the 40-minute trip. The Tivoli train station is located outside the town center, and although the walk is not too long, it is completely uninteresting because it crosses the new part of town. You can as easily take a taxi — available just outside the train station — to get to your destination; the fare to the center of town is about 4€ ($5.25). You will definitely need a taxi to visit Villa Adriana (see later in this chapter), because it is out of town.

Buses are also a good way to get to Tivoli. The bus company **Linee Laziali** (☎ 0774-11137) offers frequent service from Ponte Mammolo in Rome. You can also take **Metro Line B** to the last stop, Rebibbia (a 15-minute trip); at the bus terminal outside the Rebibbia metro station, switch to a **COTRAL** (☎ 0774-720096) bus for Tivoli. Buses depart about every 20 minutes for the 30-minute trip, and tickets cost $6€ ($8). *Beware:* Buses operate less frequently on Saturday and quite infrequently on Sunday. If you want to travel by bus on a Sunday, check the schedule in advance to ensure that you'll have a bus at a convenient time for your return.

A **short drive** — only 31km (20 miles) — from the capital, Tivoli lies at the end of a very busy consular road, the Via Tiburtina, running northeast of Rome and east of the Via Nomentana. Tivoli is like a suburb of Rome, and many people commute to and from the city daily, so traffic at peak hours can be horrible. And of course, when you get there, parking is at a premium and can be quite costly. This makes driving to Tivoli an unappealing proposition.

Taking a tour

If you sign up with a tour from Rome, you can avoid both the hassle of driving and the trouble of dealing with transportation in a foreign language. A reliable agency that organizes excursions to Tivoli is **Argiletum Tour Operator** (Via Madonna dei Monti 49, off Via Cavour; ☎ **06-47825706;** www.argiletumtour.com). It runs a four-hour tour leaving Tuesday through Sunday — in the afternoon in summer and in the morning in winter — for 49€ ($64); price includes admission to Villa Adriana, Villa d'Este, and Villa Gregoriana, and pickup from centrally located hotels.

Seeing the sights

The **tourist office in Tivoli** is in the central square of Largo Garibaldi (☎ **0774-334522**); summer hours are Monday through Saturday 9 a.m. to 6 p.m. and Sunday 9 a.m. to 2 p.m. (in winter, it closes one hour earlier).

Although visiting the three villas will likely be the focus of your jaunt, be sure to have a look at the town of Tivoli itself. The highlights are the second-century-B.C. **Tempio della Sibilla,** on the Roman Acropolis (on the other side of the Aniene River); the 12th-century churches of **San Silvestro** (southwest of the Villa d'Este) and **Santa Maria Maggiore;** and the 1461 **Rocca Pia,** Pope Pius II's castle, which was turned into a prison after 1870.

Villa Adriana

Hadrian, one of Rome's "good" emperors, had this villa built between A.D. 118 and 138 as his holiday home. He spent the last three years of his life here. The villa, placed on the site of a Roman villa from Republican times, is magnificent, though it has lost its marbles, so to speak — many of its sculptures are now conserved in Roman museums. Much of the marble once covering the structures has gone because the estate was used as a "quarry" during the Renaissance, as were many other Roman buildings, like the Colosseum. In his villa, Hadrian wanted to be surrounded by the architectural marvels he'd seen during his trips across the Empire: On the 300 acres of this self-contained world for his vast royal entourage, he constructed replicas of famous buildings of antiquity, such as the **Canopus** (the Egyptian round canal ringed with statues) and the **Lyceum** (the school of Aristotle), as well as temples and theaters, monumental thermal baths, fountains and gardens, and a library. Although most of the monuments are today in ruins, the effect is still impressive, and the atmosphere that Hadrian cultivated is still intact in a mysterious way. For a glimpse of what the villa looked like in its heyday, see the reconstruction at the entrance. Kids love both the model and exploring the ruins of the park.

Like any ruin in Italy, the villa gets very hot at midday during summer, so the best times to visit are early in the morning or late in the afternoon.

Via di Villa Adriana, 5km (3½ miles) from the center of Tivoli. ☎ *0774-530203. Bus: 4 and 4X from Largo Garibaldi (the main square of Tivoli) to Villa Adriana. Admission: 6.50€ ($8). Open: Daily Nov–Jan 9 a.m.–5 p.m.; Feb 9 a.m.–6 p.m.; Mar and Oct 9 a.m.–6:30 p.m.; Apr and Sept 9 a.m.–7 p.m.; May–Aug 9 a.m.–7:30 p.m. Ticket booth closes 1½ hours before close.*

Villa d'Este

Built in 1550 by Cardinal Ippolito d'Este of Ferrara — the son of the notorious Lucrezia Borgia and Alfonso I d'Este — this would be just another beautiful 16th-century villa if it weren't for its gardens. Designed by architect Pirro Ligorio, they are graced by a complex system of fountains — a true masterpiece of hydraulic engineering. Using an underground spring and the natural slope of the land, Ligorio managed to have naturally feeding fountains, two of which are *sonorous* (the fountains are a sort of water organ that makes "music"). The work is really magnificent and is enhanced by the sculptural work of the fountains themselves: the **Fontana dell'Organo (Fountain of the Organ),** by Claude Veanard; the **Fontana del'Ovato (Ovato Fountain),** by Ligorio; and the **Fontana del Bicchierone (Fountain of the Big Glass),** by Bernini himself. With all that water and foliage, the gardens are incredibly refreshing in summer and a perfect spot to be at midday on your visit to Tivoli. You can pick up an audio guide for 4€ ($5.25) at the entrance.

Piazza Trento, just west of Largo Garibaldi, the main square in the center of Tivoli. ☎ *199-766166 within Italy and 0424-600460 from abroad.* www.villadeste tivoli.info. *Admission: 6.50€ ($8). Open: Daily Oct 8:30 a.m.–6:30 p.m.; Nov–Jan 8:30 a.m.–5 p.m.; Feb 8:30 a.m.–5:30 p.m.; Mar 8:30–6:15 p.m.; Apr 8:30–7:30 p.m.; May–last Sat in Sept 8:30 a.m.–7:45 p.m. Ticket booth closes 1 hour before close.*

Villa Gregoriana

Villa Gregoriana, the latest of the three famous villas of Tivoli, was built in the 19th century — but it isn't a villa at all. In reality, it's a beautiful garden made to enhance the natural beauty of the gorges of the Aniene — the river that meets the Tiber in Rome, where it makes some scenic waterfalls and disappears underground for a short while (creating the grottoes, the Grotti de Nettuno e Sirene). Pope Gregory XVI had a path carved all the way down to the bottom of the ravine to allow him to admire the 90m (300-ft.) waterfall, grottoes, and ponds. The deep slopes are covered with vegetation and mighty trees, making it a magical spot, especially in summer, when it is a wonderful refuge from the heat. The park was closed for a lengthy restoration, which has brought it back to its original splendor, and has just reopened its doors.

Largo San Angelo, just north of Largo Garibaldi, the main square in the center of Tivoli. ☎ *0774-334522. Admission: 4€ ($5.25). Open: Mon–Sat 9 a.m.–1:30 p.m. and 2:30–5 p.m.*

Dining locally

Tivoli has a number of trattorie and restaurants that are Sunday favorites for Romans on outings.

Antica Hostaria de' Carrettieri
$$ Villa Gregoriana   ROMAN/SARDINIAN

This old-fashioned restaurant serves excellent — and intriguing — food. The menu places Sardinian specialties side by side with dishes true to the strictest Roman tradition — that's because the chef is originally from Sardinia. The *rigatoni all'amatriciana* (pasta in a spicy tomato and bacon sauce) is excellent, and so are the *gnocchetti in salsa di formaggio piccante* (little potato dumplings with a spicy cheese sauce) and the *tortino ai porri* (leek quiche).

Via D. Giuliani 55. ☎ *0774-330159. Reservations recommended on weekends. Secondi: 8€–15€ ($10–$20). AE, DC, MC, V. Open: Thurs–Tues 12:30–3 p.m. and 7:30–10:30 p.m. Closed 2 weeks in Aug.*

Le Cinque Statue
$$ Villa Gregoriana   ROMAN

Decorated with marble statues — the five statues in the restaurant's name — this reliable family-run restaurant offers typical Roman cuisine, such as *rigatoni all'amatriciana* (pasta in a spicy tomato and bacon sauce) and *agnello alla scottadito* (grilled lamb cutlets), which you can enjoy with a choice of local wines, mostly from the nearby Castelli region. The staff is very welcoming to children and will accommodate their special needs.

Via Quintilio Varo 8, just off the entrance to the Villa Gregoriana. ☎ *0774-335366. Reservations recommended on weekends. Bus: Near the last stop of the COTRAL bus from Rome. Secondi: 9€–14€ ($12–$18). AE, DC, MC, V. Open: Sat–Thurs noon to 2:30 p.m. and 7:30–10:30 p.m. Closed the second 2 weeks in Aug.*

Ristorante Adriano
$$$ Villa Adriana   ROMAN

"Countryside elegance" describes this tree-surrounded villa offering well-prepared Roman specialties. Everything is homemade and delicious, from the delicious pastas — try the cannelloni or the excellent fettuccine, ravioli, and *tortelli* — to the desserts. For *secondo,* the local specialty is *agnello con le patate* (roasted lamb with thyme and rosemary and new potatoes), which is prepared to perfection, but the *galletto alla diavola* (spicy charbroiled chicken) — a favorite of the movie director Federico Fellini on his visits here — is also delicious. Hadrian's Banquet, a sumptuous brunch, is offered daily but is especially spectacular on Sunday. The restaurant is located in the Alberto Adriana (see "Spending the night," later in this section), and it also has a cooking school with great classes.

Via di Villa Adriana 194, near the ticket booth to Villa Adriana. ☎ *0774-382235.* www . hoteladriano.it. *Reservations not necessary. Bus: 4 and 4X to Villa Adriana. Secondi: 10€–18€ ($13–$23). Prix-fixe brunch Mon–Sat 20€ ($26); Sun 25€ ($33). AE, DC, MC, V. Open: Daily noon to 3 p.m. and 7–10:30 pm.*

Spending the night

Although you can visit Tivoli in a day trip from Rome, it's also a nice spot to spend the night.

Albergo Adriano
$$$ Villa Adriana

Housed in a villa surrounded by a park just by the entrance of Villa Adriana, this is a small, family-run hotel offering countryside elegance and welcoming service. The few guest rooms are very nicely appointed, with some antiques. Bathrooms are good size and modern. Suite 14, with a splendid view over Hadrian's Villa, was where the writer Marguerite Yourcenar stayed for a while, perhaps getting ideas for her famous novel *Memoirs of Hadrian.*

Via di Villa Adriana 194, near the ticket booth to Villa Adriana. ☎ *0774-382235. Fax: 0774-535122.* www.hoteladriano.it. *Bus: 4 and 4X to Villa Adriana. Rack rates: 115€ ($150) double; 140€–200€ ($182–$260) suite. Rates include breakfast. AE, DC, MC, V.*

Grand Hotel Duca d'Este
$$$ Tivoli Terme

This very modern hotel offers luxurious accommodations and a spa. Surrounded by a park with a beautiful swimming pool, it will impress you with the grandiose elegance of the interior public spaces. Guest rooms are equally elegant, with classic modern furniture, carpeting and fine fabrics, and beautiful marble baths. The hotel's spa — using the nearby thermal springs — is a haven of pleasure, with a great thermal swimming pool and offering a variety of beauty and health treatments.

Via Tiburtina Valeria 330, in Tivoli Terme by Bagni di Tivoli, about 6km (4 miles) west of Tivoli toward Rome. ☎ *0774-3883. Fax: 0774-388101.* www.siriohotel.com. *Rack rates: 160€ ($208) double; suites 200€ ($260) and up. Rates include breakfast. AE, DC, MC, V.*

The Castelli Romani and Their Wines

The hill towns surrounding Rome to the southeast are a favorite destination for locals — including the pope, who enjoys a magnificent villa in Castel Gandolfo — to escape the summer swelter and enjoy excellent wine and foodstuffs. Each town is dominated by its own castle — the smallest is called a *rocca* — and is surrounded by fertile countryside, the produce of which is masterfully prepared and served in the many trattorie.

Each of the Castelli towns — Albano Laziale, Ariccia, Castel Gandolfo, Frascati, Genzano, Grottaferrata, Lanuvio, Lariano, Marino, Monte Compatri, Monte Porzio Catone, Nemi, Rocca di Papa, Rocca Priora, and Velletri — could be a pleasant day trip on its own, but you might also consider taking an overview tour of the area.

Getting there

The best way to visit the Castelli is by **car.** Driving allows you to visit more than one of these attractive small towns. If you decide to rent a car, take the Tuscolana out of Rome and follow it to Frascati; then continue with the local road — almost a loop — to Marino on one side and Rocca di Papa on the other. This route will take you through all the other Castelli. You can also reach Marino from the Appia Nuova, taking a 4½-mile detour to the north. From the Appia, you can take another side road for Castel Gandolfo. The Appia then continues to Albano, Ariccia, and Genzano.

If you don't care for driving, a good alternative is taking an **organized tour** (see the following section).

Some of the Castelli are also connected by **train.** Trains leave from Rome's Stazione Termini toward Albano Laziale, with stops in Marino and Castel Gandolfo; separate lines run from Stazione Termini in Rome to Frascati and to Velletri (the latter also stops in Lanuvio). They make several runs per day and cost 3€ ($3.90). The trip from Rome takes about 30 minutes to Lanuvio, Marino, or Frascati; 40 minutes to Castel Gandolfo; 50 minutes to Albano Laziale; and 1 hour to Velletri.

You can also take a **COTRAL bus** (☎ **800-431784** toll free within Italy for schedules). Buses leave from the Subaugusta and Anagnina (the last two) stops on metro Line A for Albano every 20 minutes or so. Albano is the hub for further service among each of the Castelli; you can catch COTRAL buses from Albano to Nemi, Ariccia, Genzano, Marino, Grottaferrata, and Frascati. Of course, the length of the trip will vary depending on your destination, but all of the trips are under an hour. The price ranges from 3€ to 6€ ($3.90–$7.80).

Taking a tour

Argiletum Tour Operator (Via Madonna dei Monti 49, off via Cavour. ☎ **06-47825706;** www.argiletumtour.com) organizes four-hour afternoon tours in summer on Tuesday and Saturday for 37€ ($48); price includes pickup from centrally located hotels.

Seeing the sights

The **central tourist office** for the Castelli Romani is in Albano (Viale Risorgimento 1; ☎ **06-9324081**). Another large office is in Frascati (Piazza Marconi 1; ☎ **06-9420331**). Both are open Monday through Friday 8 a.m. to 2 p.m. and 3:30 to 6:30 p.m., and Saturday 8 a.m. to 2 p.m. Some of the villages and small towns of the Castelli have little more than a charming central square and a few good places to eat. In the rest of this section, we describe the towns that are the most interesting.

Albano Laziale

Though it's the most built up of the Castelli, Albano maintains its unique charm. It's the center of the area producing the table wine Colli Albani, a pleasant white you often find in trattorie around Rome. Albano was the site of an Ancient Roman town built along the Appian Way — Ancient Rome's *Regina Viarum* (the queen of all roads) — around Emperor Domitian's villa. Later, Emperor Septimius Severus housed Roman legions here. The little town remained a village all throughout the Middle Ages and the Renaissance, when wealthy Romans again started building elegant villas in its countryside to enjoy the beautiful views over the volcanic lake called **Lago di Albano.** During the 19th century, it became a regular stop on the Grand Tour, the extended cultural pilgrimage through Europe that well-to-do young men and women traditionally took at that time. Roman ruins abound — the **Sepolcro degli Orazi e dei Curiazi (Roman tomb),** the **Villa di Pompeo** inside the **Villa Comunale,** and the **Nimpheus** of the Villa di Domitziano — but the great attraction is the volcanic lake formed by two craters, where you can enjoy a variety of watersports.

Ariccia

One of the most ancient towns in Latium, Ariccia was the seat of a sanctuary dedicated to Diana, the hunting goddess, and was already active before Rome became a republic. Ariccia originally lay along the Appian Way, but it was moved to its current location at the top of the rocky cliff during the Middle Ages. Unfortunately, quite ugly modern buildings have been built around the historic center, but splendid treasures await those who push through.

Ariccia became a key stop on the Grand Tour of Italy in the 18th century, especially for artists, who came to enjoy the beauty of the place. Particularly striking is **Locanda Martorelli,** in Piazza di Corte, which is decorated with a cycle of paintings by the Polish painter Taddeo Kuntze. Also on the square is Ariccia's most famous attraction, the 17th-century **Palazzo Chigi.** This grandiose villa belonged to the Chigi family until 1988, when it passed to the town, which started lengthy restorations. Surrounded by a splendid garden, it was transformed into a baroque marvel by Gian Lorenzo Bernini and now houses the **Museum of the Baroque,** which can be visited daily from 10 a.m. to 7 p.m. (Piazza di Corte 14; ☎ **06-9330053;** www.palazzochigiariccia.it; admission: 4€/$5.20). Across from the *palazzo* is the **church of the Assunta,** the last achievement of the great master. Bernini designed and built it with Carlo Fontana, his pupil, who was also destined for much glory as an architect. Inspired by the Pantheon in Rome, the round church was completed in 1664. The great viaduct over the valley to the historic center was built in 1854 but destroyed by the Germans during their retreat in 1944; it was rebuilt in 1948.

Another important reason to visit Ariccia is the *fraschette* (small taverns), often with outdoor dining areas, where you can sample local wine and the town's specialty: *porchetta*. Not to be missed, *porchetta* is a whole (deboned) pig carefully roasted with herbs, and then sliced and served with peasant bread. A *porchetta* sandwich is one of the best "fast foods" you'll ever have.

Castel Gandolfo

On the slopes of the beautiful Lago di Albano, Castel Gandolfo has a great beach — bring your suit if you want to swim; your kids will love it — and a very pleasant promenade along the lake. The town grew around the 12th-century castle built by the Roman family of the Gandolfi. Since the 17th century, it has been the official summer residence of the pope. The pope's palace and villa (originally Villa Barberini, surrounded by an enormous garden and built atop the villa of the Roman Emperor Domitian), are still part of Vatican territory. The villa also houses the Vatican Observatory, the oldest astronomical research institution in the world. Obviously, you can't visit the papal villa, but you can enjoy the rest of the town, including Bernini's **San Tommaso di Villanova church** and his **fountain** on the main square, Piazza della Libertà. Just out of town is the **Villa Torlonia,** in neoclassical style and decorated with sculptures by B. Thorvaldsen.

Frascati

Frascati may be the most familiar of the Castelli towns for the famous white wine produced in the surrounding countryside. Romans come here to visit the various *cantine* (cellars), where you can sample the wine and eat simple fare, such as *porchetta* and *pecorino* (sheep's-milk cheese), or a sandwich made with local bread and salami. The town is dominated by the imposing 16th-century **Villa Aldobrandini,** set atop a steep slope overlooking the main square. You can visit its gardens daily from 9 a.m. to 1 p.m. by getting a free ticket from the **tourist office** on Piazza Marconi 1 (see "Seeing the sights," earlier in this section).

Genzano

Picturesquely situated above the Lago di Nemi, another crater of an extinct volcano, Genzano is a charming small town surrounded by beautiful countryside. Its famous wine is not the only attraction in town; among the highlights are the 17th-century **Palazzo Sforza-Cesarini** and the nearby **cathedral.** Genzano's main event is the *Infiorata* (literally, "flowering") — held one Sunday in spring when the main street is covered with a carpet of flowers. The wine is good here, and you'll find a few nice trattorie.

Marino

The closest of the Castelli to Rome (only 15 miles), Marino is a pleasant small town, though the surroundings are modern and bland. The town is most famous for its red wine, particularly enjoyable when it's fresh. On the occasion of the **harvest celebration** in October, the two main Baroque fountains in town pour wine instead of water, to the great delight of all. The rest of the time, you can sample it in the various *osterie* and *cantine* in town — just look for the sign VINO!

Nemi

Nemi is a jewel of a small town. It has its own lake, the **Lago di Nemi,** on the slopes of which are cultivated some of the best strawberries in the world and certainly the best in Italy. Kids will love the opportunity to go for a swim or a boat ride. Nemi also specializes in the production of salami, sausages, *pancetta* (Italian bacon), and other mouthwatering items. Alas, you can't bring meat products back into the States, but that's just one more reason to sample them here. They keep quite well, and you can include them in a future picnic during your trip.

Rocca di Papa

The town of Rocca di Papa, named after its castle, dominates the Lago di Albano and enjoys breathtaking views of the surrounding hills. It's worth climbing the hill above the town to see the great vista; it's now a park, and all that's left here is the ruin of an old *albergo* (hotel) where people once came to eat and enjoy the pure air. The town below is quite picturesque. The **Chiesa dell'Assunta** is a baroque church that was reconstructed after an 1806 earthquake. Children will love the climb and the ruins, as well as the chance to swim in the lake.

Velletri

This town was an important agricultural center in 63 B.C., when Emperor Augustus was born here, and it remains so today. The historical center of town is very pretty, with many baroque attractions, including the elegant Piazza Cairoli. But the biggest attraction in town is in the cloister of Velletri's Cathedral, which houses the **Diocesan Museum** (Corso della

Repubblica 347; ☎ **06-9627217;** www.museovelletri.com; open: Daily 10 a.m.–1 p.m. and 3–7 p.m.; admission: 2€/$2.60), a valuable collection that includes precious objects and paintings by Gentile da Fabriano, Antoniazzo Romano, and others.

Dining locally

The Castelli contains a procession of trattorie and *ristoranti*. They're all quite reliable, but keep in mind the rule of "trust the locals": If it's dinnertime, and nobody is eating in a place, there must be a reason. We give you some safe bets in this section, but just follow your nose to find some of the other great places on your own.

The food in the Castelli is typically Roman, including fresh pasta and grilled meats. People come to sample the variety of local salami and cheeses, usually served as antipasto. *Porchetta* is a specialty of Ariccia (see "Ariccia," earlier in this chapter) but is prepared to some extent everywhere in the Castelli. The wine of the Castelli is probably the best in Lazio; particularly famous are the Frascati and the Marino (white and red, respectively).

Antica Abazia
$$ **Albano Laziale   CREATIVE LATIUM**

In the rustic atmosphere of this down-to-earth restaurant, you'll discover the work of an excellent chef serving traditional recipes with a personal twist. The menu changes often, following the seasons, and the service is friendly. Among the best dishes are the *spaghetti con moscardini e pecorino* (pasta with baby squid and pecorino cheese), the *fettuccine al ragù di capretto* (homemade fresh pasta with tomato and kid-meat sauce), the *stinco di maiale con castagne e mele* (pork shank with apples and chestnuts), and the *tagliata di manzo con pomodoretti e finocchio selvatico* (beefsteak with cherry tomatoes and wild fennel). Save room for one of the homemade desserts, which are excellent.

Via San Filippo Neri 19, off via Murialdo, 1 block north of Piazza del Duomo and Piazza Sabatini. ☎ *06-9323187. Reservations recommended on weekends. Secondi: 8€–12€ ($10–$16). AE, DC, MC, V. Open: Tues–Sun noon to 2:30 p.m. and 7:30–10:30 p.m.*

Antico Ristorante Paganelli
$$$$ **Castel Gandolfo   ROMAN/SEAFOOD**

This restaurant, serving a variety of classic Roman food and seafood, has upscale leanings and impeccable service. You can choose among the á la carte menu or one of the prix-fixe offerings. The menu changes periodically but may include such local specialties as *cannelloni* (oven-cooked, filled tubes of homemade fresh pasta), *agnello arrosto con le patate* (herbed lamb with roasted potatoes), and *fritto misto* (deep-fried small fish, calamari, and shrimp).

Via Gramsci 4. ☎ *06-9360004. Reservations recommended on weekends. Secondi: 14€–25€ ($18–$33). AE, DC, MC, V. Open: Wed–Mon 12:30–3 p.m. and 7:30–10:30 p.m.*

Briciola
$$ Grottaferrata ROMAN

This small restaurant is a real find, offering friendly service and great cuisine in the best Roman–Jewish tradition. All the vegetable *contorni* (side dishes) are delicious, and if the *misticanza con alici al tartufo* (greens sautéed with anchovies and truffle) is on the menu, trust us and order it. Also good are the *insalata tiepida di moscardini e fagioli* (warm salad of baby squid and beans), the *ravioli ricotta e pecorino con salsa di fave* (ricotta and pecorino cheese ravioli with a fava sauce), and the *fagottini di vitella alla provola* (veal rolls filled with provola cheese).

Via G. D'Annunzio 12. ☎ *06-9459338. Reservations recommended. Secondi: 9€–13€ ($12–$17). AE, DC, MC, V. Open: Tues–Sun 12:30–3 p.m and Tues–Sat 7:30–10:30 p.m. Closed 3 weeks in Aug.*

Cacciani
$$$ Frascati ROMAN

The renowned Cacciani is family run and serves some of the best food and wine in the area — and that's high praise. The large dining room — subdivided so to afford a feeling of privacy at each table — opens on a beautiful terrace from which you can enjoy a great view over the surrounding hills and where meals are served in the good season. The typical Roman specialties are wonderfully prepared; go for the *rigatoni alla carbonara* (pasta with an egg, onion, and bacon sauce) or the *fettuccine alle regaglie di pollo* (homemade fresh pasta with a chicken-liver and wine sauce). The meat dishes, such as the *abbacchio alla cacciatora* (lamb cooked with white wine and rosemary), are also excellent.

Via Armando Diaz 13, off Piazza Roma. ☎ *06-9420378. Reservations required on weekends. Secondi: 12€–21€ ($16–$28). AE, DC, MC, V Open: Tues–Sun noon to 2:30 p.m. and 7:30–10:30 p.m. Closed 10 days in Jan and 10 days in Aug.*

Cantina Comandini
$ Frascati WINE/TAVERN

Not a restaurant but a "cellar," this family-run business is the outlet of one of Frascati's vineyards. Here, you'll be able to sample the famous Frascati wine and accompany it with a sandwich or a choice of local cold cuts and cheese. You can also buy wine to take away, but you'll probably want to drink it before you go home.

Via E. Filiberto 1. ☎ *06-9420915. Reservations recommended. Secondi: 5€–11€ ($7–$14). MC, V. Open: Mon–Sat 7:30–11 p.m.*

Enoteca Frascati
$$ Frascati WINE/LATIUM

An excellent choice of wines — not just local varieties — accompanied by excellent food; what more can you ask for? This welcoming enoteca offers very well-prepared food, including some of the less-usual traditional dishes. The menu is seasonal, but you may find the *strozzapreti al sugo di cinghiale* (homemade spaghetti with a wild-boar sauce), the *fettuccine al nero di seppia con zucchine in fiore e scampi* (homemade fresh pasta with baby zucchini and prawns in squid-ink sauce), or the delicious *maialino alla finocchiella con patate speziate al forno* (wild fennel suckling pig with roasted spicy potatoes).

Via A. Diaz 42, off Piazza Roma. ☎ 06-9417449. Reservations recommended on weekends. Secondi: 8€–12€ ($10–$16). MC, V. Open: Mon–Sat 7:30–10:30 p.m. Closed Aug.

Spending the night
Although the Castelli towns make for pleasant day trips from Rome, you might decide to use one of the following hotels as your base from which to explore the countryside.

Castelvecchio
$$ Castel Gandolfo

Tucked between the pope's summer residence and the lake, this luxurious hotel offers elegance and beautiful views. Housed in a Liberty-style palace from the end of the 19th century, it has a roof garden with swimming pool, affording gorgeous views of the surroundings. Guest rooms are tastefully appointed with classic furnishings, fine fabrics, and modern bathrooms.

Viale Pio XI 23. ☎ 06-9360308. Fax: 06-9360579. www.hotelcastelvecchio.com. *Rack rates: 160€ ($210) double; 200€ ($260) junior suite. Rates include buffet breakfast. AE, DC, MC, V.*

Grand Hotel Villa Tuscolo
$$ Frascati

Housed in Villa La Rufinella, one of the famous villas built on Mount Tuscolo between the 16th and 17th centuries, this gorgeous hotel is surrounded by a great park with a swimming pool and offers professional and friendly service. Guest rooms are spacious and bright, with splendid views over the countryside, and are furnished with simple elegance: a few antiques, wooden floors, and plaster walls and moldings. Bathrooms are good size and modern. The hotel also offers a shuttle to the center of Frascati, and a restaurant with panoramic views over Rome.

Via del Tuscolo at km 1.5. ☎ 06-942900. Fax: 06-9424747. www.villatuscolana.com. *Rack rates: 180€ ($230) double. Rates include buffet breakfast. AE, DC, MC, V.*

Hotel Culla del Lago
$ Castel Gandolfo

This quiet, small hotel sits in the middle of a garden right on the shore of the lake across from the pope's residence. Public spaces are welcoming, and guest rooms are large and bright — many have views of the lake — and are simply but tastefully furnished, with good-size bathrooms. The hotel's private beach is perfect to enjoy the lake, and the garden is a great spot for relaxing.

Via Spiaggia del Lago 38. ☎ *06-93668231. Fax: 06-93668243.* www.culladellago. com. *Rack rates: 120€ ($160) double. Rates include breakfast. AE, DC, MC, V.*

Hotel Flora
$$ Frascati

This splendid hotel is housed in a picturesque 19th-century palace surrounded by a park, near the historical center of Frascati. Guest rooms are . . . well, palatial — some have frescoed ceilings — and are furnished with antiques, and decorated with plaster moldings and parquet wooden floors. The marble baths are modern and good size. The hotel also offers glorious garden terraces, where breakfast is served in the good season, as well as cuisine classes and babysitting.

Via Vittorio Veneto 8. ☎ *06-9416110. Fax: 06-9416546.* www.hotel-flora.it. *Rack rates: 180€ ($230) double. Rates include buffet breakfast. AE, DC, MC, V.*

Tarquinia

The mother town of the Etruscan civilization, **Tarquinia** is famous for its Etruscan archaeological remains, including well-preserved frescoes, but it also holds a pretty medieval town with a pleasant seaside resort nearby, **Tarquinia Lido.** You can easily visit its attractions in one day, but you won't be bored if you spend the night, especially during the good season, when you can also go to the beach.

Getting there

About 90km (56 miles) north of Rome, Tarquinia is only about 10km (6 miles) north of the town and bustling port of Civitavecchia, near the coast. You can easily reach it by one of the **trains,** which depart every hour on the hour from Termini station to Tarquinia; the trip takes 1 hour and 24 minutes, and costs about 6€ ($8).

You can also reach Tarquinia **by car** from Rome in about 50 minutes by taking the Via Aurelia, although we do not recommend it: The road is narrow and winding, and people drive like maniacs. (It's a route to Tuscany and points north.)

Taking a tour

The tour operator **Dock&Discover** (☎ 0766-581574; www.dockdiscover. com) offers guided tours to Tarquinia starting from Civitavecchia. For a personalized visit of Tarquinia, book a tour with one of the licensed local guides in Tarquinia itself; contact the Tarquinia tourist office for a complete list (**IAT**; Piazza Cavour 23; ☎ 0766-849282; www.tarquinia.net).

Seeing the sights

Tarquinia was the most important town of the Etruscan kingdom and an important commercial and artistic center that dominated central Italy until the third century B.C., when it was taken over by the Romans. Tarquinia is actually comprised of two towns: the original Etruscan settlement and modern-day Tarquinia, which was rebuilt on the neighboring hill to the west of the ancient town in medieval times, leaving the Etruscan archaeological site to await future exploration. The remains of the ancient town are few but monumental, and the necropolis gave an incalculable wealth of material for the understanding of the Etruscan civilization. In the "new" town, the **Castle of Matilde di Canossa** is still in good repair, and the **Duomo** has some nice frescoes from 1508. Lining the main street in the historical center of town, you find artists' and craftsmen's showrooms, particularly fine local goldsmiths and potters who produce jewels and ceramics with an Etruscan flavor and design (excellent gifts for others or souvenirs for yourself). Three miles out of town to the west is the beautiful **Lungomare** of Lido di Tarquinia, Tarquinia's seaside resort, with pleasant restaurants overlooking the sea, neat little shops, and a good beach.

Archaeological Area of the Civita

First settled around the ninth century B.C., the city was greatly enlarged by the Etruscans, who built the **acropolis** in the seventh century B.C. The Archaeological Area is partially surrounded by the original powerful **city walls** from the fifth century B.C., of which you can still see several miles, and including one of the main gates. The acropolis is graced by an important temple from the fourth century B.C.: the **Ara della Regina (Altar of the Queen),** the largest Etruscan temple in Italy. It measures 77m by 35m (253 by 115 ft.) and was built over a temple. The base was decorated with terra-cotta figures, including the famous **winged horses** that are now preserved in the National Museum of Tarquinia.

Pian della Civita, Montarozzi, 7km (3.5 miles) east of Tarquinia on the road to Monte Romano. Free admission. Open: Sunrise to sunset.

Museo Nazionale Tarquiniense (National Museum)

One of the most important Etruscan museums in Italy, the National Museum houses not only the extremely rich collection from the thousands of tombs of the nearby necropolis, but also artifacts and remains from more-archaic nearby sites, including some Villanovian burial sites that predate the Etruscan period. The museum occupies the elegant Renaissance Palazzo Vitelleschi from the 15th century, which would be worthy of a visit even if it didn't contain Etruscan treasures. Among the huge collection of unique Etruscan objects — artwork, religious and everyday objects, bronze artifacts, sculptures — the jewels and the ceramics are truly outstanding. However, the stars of the show are the four tombs from the nearby necropolis, which have been completely reconstructed with the original frescoes. The freshness of the paintings is extraordinary; you'll find the Tomb of the Olympic Games, the Tomb of the Ship, the Tomb of the Triclynium, and the Tomb of the Racing Chariots, all from between the fifth and fourth centuries B.C.

Palazzo Vitelleschi. ☎ *0766-856036. Admission: 3€ ($3.90). Open: Tues–Sun 8:30 a.m.–7:30 p.m.*

Etruscan Necropolis

The necropolis, with its thousands of tombs, is located at the doors of the Etruscan town, the Archaeological Area of the Civita. The tombs, some of which are in outstanding condition and are considered to be the quintessential examples of Etruscan tombs, date from between the sixth and first centuries B.C. Fascinating frescoes, alive with color, decorate the tombs, which are named for the subjects of the paintings; the most famous are the tombs of the Panther, the Bulls, Hunting and Fishing, the Lioness, the Jugglers, and the Ogre. The beautiful portrait of Velia Velcha, an Etruscan woman, is justly considered a great work of Etruscan art.

Montarozzi, 7 km (3.5 miles) east of Tarquinia on the road to Monte Romano. ☎ *0766-856308. Admission: 3€ ($3.90). Open: Tues–Sun 8:30 a.m.–7:30 p.m.*

Dining locally

Don't pass up an opportunity to sample Tarquinian cuisine, often featuring wild game and truffles from the countryside, seafood, and excellent goat cheese. Don't forget to order a bottle of Tarquinian wine to accompany your meal.

Chalet del Pescatore
$ Foce del Marta   TARQUINIAN/SEAFOOD

Right on the seaside, this is a great place to relax and tuck into some fresh, delicious seafood. The menu includes all kinds of fresh homemade pasta, excellent *risotto alla pescatora* (spaghetti with seafood), and plenty of local fish.

Foce del Marta, Tarquinia Lido. ☎ *0766-864565. Reservations recommended. Secondi: 10€–18€ ($13–$23). AE, DC, MC, V. Open: Tues–Sun noon to 3 p.m. and 7:30–10:30 p.m.*

La Cantina dell'Etrusco
$$ Tarquinia   TARQUINIAN

You can taste local specialties and traditional dishes of the interior at this cantina, located in the historic center of Tarquinia. Choices include *pappardelle al sugo di cinghiale* (homemade fresh pasta with wild-boar ragout), *ragout di lepre* (hare ragout), and *pollo in salmì* (savory chicken with a tomato-and-wine sauce), all of which are very well prepared. The wine list features all the best local vintages, including the famous Est!Est!Est!, as well as Cerveteri, Orvieto Classico, and Vignanello. Do not miss the *tozzetti* (biscotti made with local hazelnuts) with Aleatico di Gradoli (a muscat wine) for dessert.

Via Menotti Garibaldi 13. ☎ *0766-848418. Reservations recommended. Secondi: 11€–18€ ($14–$23). AE, DC, MC, V. Open: Tues–Sun 12:30–3 p.m. and 7:30–11:30 p.m.*

La Cantinetta
$ Tarquinia   TARQUINIAN

This pleasant restaurant in the historic center of Tarquinia offers excellent food and a welcoming atmosphere. The seasonal menu might include superb *fettuccine ai ferlenghi* (homemade pasta with local wild mushrooms), *zuppa ceci e castagne* (thick soup with chickpeas and chestnuts), and *lepre in salmì* (savory hare with a tomato-and-wine sauce), as well as some fish dishes.

Via XX Settembre 27. ☎ *0766-856810. Reservations recommended. Secondi: 9€–16€ ($12–$21). AE, DC, MC, V. Open: Fri–Wed 12:30–3 p.m. and 7:30–10:30 p.m.*

Spending the night
Be sure to pack your swimsuit if you plan to spend the night in the seaside resort town of Tarquinia Lido.

Hotel La Torraccia
$$ Tarquinia Lido

This nice, family-run hotel is surrounded by umbrella pines and is only steps from the sea. Guest rooms are well appointed, with quality modern furniture and bright carpeting; most have a private balcony. In the good season, breakfast is served on the delightful garden terrace.

Viale Mediterraneo 45. ☎ *0766-864375. Fax: 0766-864296.* www.torraccia.it. *Rack rates: 120€ ($156) double. Rates include breakfast. AE, DC, MC, V.*

Hotel Ristorante Pizzeria all'Olivo
$ Tarquinia

You'll be pampered at this freshly renovated, family-run hotel located in the modern part of Tarquinia but near the historic center of town. Accommodations are simple but comfortable and welcoming. Guest rooms are large, furnished with simple modern furnishings, tiled floors, and good-size modern bathrooms. The hotel's restaurant is very good and also serves excellent pizza.

Via Palmiro Togliatti 15. ☎ ***0766-857318.*** *Fax: 0766-840777.* www.hotel-allolivo. it. *Rack rates: 80€ ($104) double. Rates include breakfast. AE, DC, MC, V.*

Hotel San Marco
$ Tarquinia

This is our place of choice in town, right across from the Museo Nazionale (see review earlier in this section) in the historical center of Tarquinia. The hotel is housed in the splendid cloister of the 16th-century convent Agostiniano, which has housed some kind of hostelry since 1876. Guest rooms are large and nicely furnished, with some antiques.

Piazza Cavour 18. ☎ ***0766-842234.*** *Fax: 0766-842306.* www.san-marco.com. *Rack rates: 70€ ($91) double. Rates include breakfast. AE, DC, MC, V.*

Nature Reserve of the Lago di Vico

Only 65km (40 miles) from Rome, the splendid Lago di Vico has escaped the development afflicting other volcanic lakes near the capital. Tucked among the scenic southern slopes of the Monti Cimini (Cimini Mountains), the lake offers a perfect respite from the bustle of Rome. Fortunately, Romans had the foresight to create a regional park with a nature reserve to protect the area, and Lago di Vico is now the best preserved of the volcanic lakes in central Italy. Nature isn't the only attraction, though; if you just aren't satisfied unless you've gotten a cultural fix, you can visit the beautiful Gothic Abbey of San Martino al Cimino near the park. Together, both attractions will fill one day.

Getting there
We recommend renting a car to visit these sights. Public transportation is available to the town of San Martino al Cimino, and you could hire a taxi to take you around to the park, but it would be a cumbersome journey. The nature reserve is located on the north shore of the lake. Coming by car from Rome, take Via Cassia (S.S. 2) toward Viterbo, and turn onto Strada Provinciale (S.P.), following the signs for Ronciglione and then Caprarola, where you'll begin to see signs for the Riserva Naturale Parco

di Vico. Take S.P. 39, the Strada Provinciale Lago di Vico, a road circling around the lake and the nature reserve. From the nature reserve, take S.P. 81 another 16km (10 miles) to the small town of **San Martino al Cimino,** located just north of the lake.

Taking a tour

Contact the tourist office **APT** (Palazzo Doria Pamphili, San Martino al Cimino; ☎ 0761-291000; www.tusciainforma.it) for a list of licensed private guides to the park. Guides will design a tour appropriate to your party's interests.

Seeing the sights

The Cimini Mountains offer many surprises, not least of which are the unspoiled blue waters of the Lago di Vico and the elegant and sober architecture of the Cistercian Abbey of San Martino al Cimino. Be sure to wear sturdy shoes for a hike in the park to take in the natural beauty, and don't forget your swimsuit for a dip in the lake afterward. If you're feeling more adventurous, you can rent mountain bikes and boats at La Bella Venere, a resort on the beach of the lake doubling as hotel and restaurant (see the listing later in this section).

Regional Park of Lake Vico

The park, established in 1982, covers over 3,300 hectares (82,000 acres) and stretches along the slopes of the extinct volcano that form the lake. Gorgeous beech woods, oaks, and chestnut trees of unusual height and majesty (producing some of the best chestnuts in the world) complete the splendid landscape of the lake. You can hike several trails through the park, which are very popular, especially with bird- and wildlife-watchers.

Strada Provinciale (S.P.) Lago di Vico. ☎ *0761-647444. Admission: Free.*

Cistercian Abbey of San Martino al Cimino

The splendid baroque town of San Martino al Cimino is noted for its Gothic abbey, a large monastery that serves as the mother house of the Cistercian order in Italy. A small monastery existed on the site beginning before the ninth century and was a Benedictine house dependent on the Abbey of Farfa to the south. When the Cistercians — a French religious order — took it over in the 12th century, they enlarged it according to a grandiose design, which was completed in 1305. Inside, you can still see the splendid cloister, two libraries, the abbot's apartment, and the monks' cells, as well as the church, all in the sober and more austere Gothic style imported from France.

San Martino al Cimino, in the center of town, near Palazzo Doria Pamphilij. ☎ *0761-379803. Admission: Free. Open: Daily sunrise to sunset.*

Dining locally

Viterbese cuisine is tasty and hearty, made from the local produce of the mountains, particularly chestnuts and wild mushrooms, which are added to soups and stew for a unique flavor.

Baita La Faggeta
$ La Faggeta   VITERBESE

Near the summit of Monte Cimino, at 1,056m (3,500 ft.) altitude, this is a great stop for famished hikers or those simply looking for a leisurely break. The views are superb, and so is the homemade cuisine. You might find such local favorites as *zuppa ai ceci e castagne* (thick soup with chickpeas and chestnuts), *pollo a bujone* (savory chicken stewed with herbs), and the legendary *patate arrosto coi funghi porcini* (oven-roasted potatoes and porcini mushrooms). The restaurant doubles as a pizzeria, and the pizza is very good too. The local wine is excellent.

Strada Provinciale Cimina, La Faggeta, on Monte Cimino. ☎ *0761-747120. Reservations recommended. Secondi: 8€–16€ ($10–$21). MC, V. Open: Wed–Mon 12:30–3 p.m. and 7:30–10:30 p.m.*

Ristorante Pizzeria La Bella Venere
$ Scardenato   VITERBESE

This large, welcoming restaurant sits in a hotel complex right on the lake, offering paddleboat, bicycle, and inline-skate rentals. You can take in superb views of the lake while you dine on excellent cuisine from a seasonal menu that includes surf and turf as well as pizza. Selection might include homemade *tortelloni ai funghi porcini e tartufo* (large round ravioli with porcini mushroom filling and seasoned with truffles) and the local fish stew known as *sbroscia*.

Strada Provinciale (S.P.) Lago di Vico at km 15.5, Scardenato. ☎ *0761-612342. Reservations recommended. Secondi: 8€–15€ ($10–$20). MC, V. Open: Tues–Sun noon to 3 p.m. and 7–10:30 p.m.*

Trattoria Pizzeria Zi' Catofio
$ Caprarola   VITERBESE

This traditional trattoria on the outskirts of the town of Caprarola is a great place to taste all the local specialties in a down-to-earth atmosphere. You'll find great *pappardelle col sugo di lepre* (homemade fresh pasta with hare ragout), delicious *polenta con le spuntature* (polenta with a pork-ribs sauce), *agnello arrosto colle patate* (roasted lamb with potatoes), and *coniglio alla cacciatora* (rabbit with wine, olives, and tomatoes), as well as very well prepared fresh fish from the nearby lake. The restaurant also serves good pizza.

Strada Provinciale (S.P.) Cimina, Caprarola. ☎ *0761-646111. Reservations recommended. Secondi: 8€–15€ ($10–$20). MC, V. Open: Tues–Sun noon to 3 p.m. and 7–10:30 p.m.*

Spending the night

Hotel Il Cardinale
$ Lago di Vico

This welcoming and comfortable hotel, which was recently renovated, is well situated near the lake, the mountains, and the major attractions in the area. Guest rooms are tastefully furnished, with good-quality furnishings, tiled floors, and good-size bathrooms. All rooms afford splendid views over the lake and mountains. From the hotel, you can hike in the woods nearby.

Strada Provinciale (S.P.) Cimina, near Ronciglione and Lago di Vico at km 19. ☎ *0761-624051. Fax: 0761-612377.* www.hotelilcardinale.com. *Rack rates: 90€ ($117) double; 110€ ($143) triple. Rates include breakfast. AE, DC, MC, V.*

Hotel La Bella Venere
$ Scardenato

Right on the lake in the heart of the park, this small hotel is a perfect base for all the excursions in the area. The welcoming guest rooms are roomy and comfortable, with nice furnishings and modern bathrooms; many have lovely views over the lake. The hotel also offers tennis, rollerblading, a playground, and a nice beach on the lake; you can rent bicycles and *pedalò* (pedal boats) right at the hotel. The hotel's restaurant is famous in the area for its local traditional cuisine.

Strada Provinciale (S.P.) Lago di Vico at km 15.5, Scardenato. ☎ *0761-612342. Fax: 0761-612344.* www.labellavenere.it. *Rack rates: 90€ ($117) double; 110€ ($143) triple; 125€ ($163) quad. Rates include breakfast. AE, DC, MC, V.*

Part V
Living It Up after Dark: Rome's Nightlife

The 5th Wave
By Rich Tennant

"Funny I just assumed it would be Carreras too."

In this part . . .

Still got some energy after a full day of sightseeing? Then this part is for you! Here we offer suggestions for filling those marvelous evenings in Rome, when the air is sweet and soft and everything seems so romantic. Whether you want to attend a performance or show (see Chapter 15) or take in the atmosphere at Rome's many bars and discos (see Chapter 16), we've got your evening covered.

Chapter 15

Applauding the Cultural Scene

● ●

In This Chapter

▶ Finding out what's going on around town

▶ Reserving tickets

▶ Attending the symphony, opera, and dance performances

● ●

*R*ome offers some splendid opportunities for lovers of the performing arts. All major performers pass through Rome, and the city has traditionally been the hot spot for theater production in Italy. Of course, a moderate knowledge of Italian is required for theatergoing.

Getting the Inside Scoop

Rome's cultural scene is very hot year-round, with top-notch performers making tour stops here on a regular basis. The scene positively burgeons in summer, though, when a mind-boggling range of performances is staged throughout the city in various indoor and outdoor venues for the famous **Estate Romana (Roman Summer),** discussed later in this section.

The newly opened **Parco della Musica** (Viale Coubertin 34; ☎ **06-8082058;** www.auditorium.com; bus: M from Piazza del Popolo) — a daring, modernistic complex almost ten years in the making — is now the principal venue for music in Rome, with several halls and a number of other attractions. Designed by the famous architect Renzo Piano, this grand, ambitious project is probably the largest addition to the Roman cultural and architectural landscape in decades. Located 2km (1¼ miles) from **Piazza del Popolo** and connected by a special bus line to the center (Bus M, for music), the entire site takes up 55,000 square meters (13.6 acres). It has three concert halls as well as other structures, including **La Cavea,** a 3,000-seat outdoor concert space reminiscent of a classical amphitheater. In addition to classical, pop, and contemporary music, theater and dance performances take place here. Restaurants, stores, lecture halls, and a host of other activities and services are located on site.

Most other performance venues in Rome are in or near the city center. The newly restored **Teatro dell'Opera** (Piazza Beniamino Gigli 1, just off Via Nazionale; ☎ **06-48160255;** www.opera.roma.it; metro: Line A to Repubblica; bus: Minibus 116 to Via A. Depretis) — a beautiful venue built at the end of the 19th century — hosts opera as well as ballet and classical concerts. The **Teatro Olimpico** (Piazza Gentile da Fabriano; ☎ **06-3265991;** www.teatroolimpico.it; tram: 225 from Piazzale Flaminio), another great space, hosts musical performances of all kinds.

From June through September — during the off season of many venues in Rome — Roman nights come alive with **Estate Romana (Roman Summer),** a series of musical, theatrical, and other cultural events (see also Chapter 16). These often take place in some of the most picturesque locations and monuments in Rome, lit up especially for the event, which transforms the show into a multidimensional treat. Among the most impressive settings for the festival is the **Colosseum,** which opened its doors to the public again in 2000 after 15 centuries (don't expect blood sports and severed limbs, however; civilization has changed somewhat in the interim). Also very dramatic is the **Theatre of the Caracalla Baths** (Teatro delle Terme di Caracalla, Viale delle Terme di Caracalla 52; contact the Teatro dell'Opera at ☎ 06-48160255 for information), where the **Teatro dell'Opera** holds some of its summer season. To hear Verdi's *Requiem* resounding at night through these cavernous, massive ruins is a truly remarkable musical experience. Other unique venues for summer events are the **Roman Forum** (Via dei Fori Imperiali; ☎ 06-70393427); **Villa Borghese** (Largo Aqua Felix, entrance at Piazzale delle Ginestre; ☎ 06-82077304 Mon–Thurs 9 a.m.–4 p.m. and Fri 9 a.m.–1 p.m.); the elegant **Chiostro del Bramante** (Via della Pace; ☎ 06-7807695); the suggestive **Archeological Park of Teatro Marcello** (Via del Teatro Marcello; ☎ 06-87131590); the mausoleum–cum–fort **Castel Sant'Angelo** (Lungotevere Castello 50; ☎ 06-32869 or 06-32861); and, outside Rome, the **Teatro Romano of Ostia Antica** (Viale dei Romagnoli 717, Ostia Antica; ☎ 06-56352850). You can find details on the festival online at www.estate romana.comune.roma.it (also in English) or get information by calling ☎ 06-68809505 Monday through Saturday from 10 a.m. to 5 p.m.

The opera, classic concerts, and ballet always call for elegant dress, as do the most famous theaters and even the best jazz clubs. More-casual attire is okay for other venues and shows.

The curtain is usually right on time, and if you miss yours, you'll usually have to wait for the intermission to gain your seat; it's also customary to give a small tip to your usher.

Shows are usually late enough so that you can have a regular dinner; because most venues are in the center of Rome, you can pick a restaurant in the area (see Chapter 10) and still make it to the show on time. For after-theater restaurants, see the "After-theater dining" sidebar, later in this chapter.

Finding Out What's Playing and Getting Tickets

Rome's tourist office publishes an excellent monthly review of what is going on in Rome called *The Happening City;* you can pick up an English- or Italian-language copy at any of the tourist info points listed in Appendix A and in Chapter 8, or you can request that it be e-mailed to you before you leave (which would be the smart thing to do if you want to order tickets in advance). Indeed, if you're coming for only a short vacation, you'll do a lot better by ordering your tickets from home, especially for big performances that will be sold out or booked well before your feet touch Italian soil.

We recommend using an Italian ticket service. **TicketOne** (☎ 02-392261 for an English-speaking operator; www.ticketone.it) and **HellòTicket** (☎ 800-907080 toll free within Italy or 06-48078400 from abroad and cellphones; www.helloticket.it) sell tickets for just about everything in the country. You can make reservations and purchase your tickets online through both services' Web sites, but note that they are only in Italian. **Charta** (www.charta.it) — an Italy-wide Internet-based agent for theater, concerts, and dance — is also a good resource; its parent site, **Viva Ticket** (www.vivaticket.it), is user friendly but again, only in Italian so far, unfortunately.

Global Edwards & Edwards (☎ 800/223-6108 in the U.S.) is a good ticket agency that's based in England. And you'll find that many U.S.-based agencies offer advance-sale tickets for events in Rome, but none of them is as comprehensive as the Italian services, and they add a steep service fee over the actual price of the event. Nonetheless, if you want to use a U.S.-based company, a good one is **Culturalitaly.com** (☎ 800/380-0014; fax: 928/639-0388; www.culturalitaly.com), a Los Angeles–based Web company where you can get tickets for a nice selection of events.

After-theater dining

At least a couple of restaurants near each theater in Rome specialize in after-dinner service. Showtime is usually late enough so that you can easily have an early dinner anywhere, but if you want to do like the Romans (when in Rome . . .), try to resist until after the show and check out one of the late-night spots.

Restaurants that stay open late among those we suggest in Chapter 10 are **Bolognese, Checchino dal 1887, Enoteca Capranica, Ferrara,** and **Gusto.** You can also try **Il Boscaiolo** (Via degli Artisti; ☎ 06-4884023), a very nice pizzeria behind the Teatro Sistina; **L'Archetto** (Via dell'Archetto; ☎ 06-6789064), a good *spaghetteria* only steps from the Teatro Quirino; and **Il Cantuccio** (Corso Rinascimento 71; ☎ 06-68802982), a restaurant serving good Roman fare not far from the Teatro Valle and the Teatro Argentina.

Once in Rome, you'll find detailed listings of events for the day in daily newspapers, and in the weekly publication *Roma C'è* — available in all newsstands (it comes out on Wed) — which has a section in English. You can also find information in the **daily newspapers.** Other sources are the fortnightly magazine *Wanted in Rome* (www.wantedinrome.com), which specializes in the city, and the monthly magazine *The American* (www.theamericanmag.com), which covers all of Italy; both are in English and have an online version as well. You'll find them at most newsstands in the historical center of the city. You can also pick up a copy of *The Happening City* — or view it online at www.romaturismo.it; then click Events in Rome and then Happening in Rome — an excellent review of events published by Rome's tourist board. For the events of the **Estate Romana** festival, you can get details at the tourist points in town and also online at www.estateromana.comune.roma.it (also in English) or by calling ☎ 06-68809505 Monday through Saturday from 10 a.m. to 5 p.m. Besides the resources listed in this section, your concierge at your hotel will always be able to help you find out what's on and purchase tickets.

Many venues offer reduced-price tickets and matinees on one specific day of the week, often Thursday. For last-minute theater tickets at a discount of up to 50 percent, you can go to the booth of Via Bari 20, off Piazza Salerno (☎ 06-44180212; bus: 61, 490, 491, 495; metro: Line B to Policlinico; open: Tues–Sat 2–8 p.m.).

Raising the Curtain on the Performing Arts

Any given day in Rome, you'll have a variety of shows to choose among. Here, we highlight the main categories. During the summer, remember to check with the tourist office for the special events of the **Estate Romana** festival.

Symphony

A variety of classical concerts is organized in Rome on a daily basis; you can check out programs with the tourist office and in the publications we recommend (see the preceding section) or directly with each of the following associations. The most important orchestras and associations are the **Accademia Nazionale di Santa Cecilia** (Parco della Musica, Viale Coubertin 34; ☎ 06-8082058; www.santacecilia.it), one of Italy's premier musical groups, offering classical concerts and events and holding a summer season during the **Estate Romana** (see earlier in this chapter); the **Opera di Roma** (Teatro dell'Opera, Piazza Beniamino Gigli 1; ☎ 06-48160 or 800-016665 toll free within Italy; www.opera.roma.it); and the **Filarmonica di Roma,** also called Accademia Filarmonica Romana (Teatro Olimpico, Piazza Gentile da Fabriano; ☎ 06-3265991; www.teatroolimpico.it).

Other important associations include the **Amici della Musica Sacra** (Via Paolo VI 29; ☎ **06-6830 1665;** www.amicimusicasacra.com), **Il Tempietto** (☎ **06-8720 1523;** www.tempietto.org), the **Orchestra di Roma e del Lazio** (☎ **06-9766711;** www.orchestradellazio.it), and the **Fondazione Arts Academy Roma** (☎ **06-4425 2303;** www.artsacademy. it). In addition to regular performance spaces, classical concerts are held in churches and various halls all over the city. A particularly pleas-ant series is the concerts of the **Musici Veneziani** in the Anglican church of San Paolo entro le Mura (Via Nazionale 16 at the corner of Via Napoli; ☎ **06-4826296**), with a repertoire of operatic arias — Verdi, Puccini, Bizet, and Mozart, among others — with performers dressed in baroque costumes. Concerts usually start at 8 p.m., and tickets range between 15€ and 30 € ($20–$40). Check with the tourist office for a complete schedule of events.

Tickets prices vary according to the performance and, in the largest the-aters, the quality of the seat, with prices ranging from free to 50€ ($65).

Opera

Opera is pretty much limited to the great national theater of the **Teatro dell'Opera** (Piazza Beniamino Gigli 1; ☎ **06-48160;** www.opera.roma.it). Its season runs from January to June, but it also has a not-to-be-missed summer season during the famous **Estate Romana** (see earlier in this chapter), with performances held at the **Teatro delle Terme di Caracalla,** the theater situated amid the picturesque scenery of the **Caracalla Baths.** Ticket prices range between about 30€ and 120€ ($40–$160), depending on the seat and performance.

Dance

Ballet and dance performances are quite numerous in Rome and are often of world-class quality. The **Rome Opera Ballet** performs classical and modern ballet at the Teatro dell'Opera (see the preceding section for con-tact information); international performers often stage their shows at the **Teatro Olimpico** or the **Parco della Musica** (see earlier in this chapter).

Ticket prices vary according to the performance, the venue, and — in large theaters — the quality of the seat, ranging between 10€ ($13) for a performance at the Parco della Musica all the way up to 120€ ($160) for the best seat at the Teatro dell'Opera.

Theater

Rome is famous for theater, and some of the best companies in the coun-try and the world perform here. Italy has produced such playwrights as Goldoni, Pirandello, and recent Nobel Prize winner Dario Fo. Of course, if you don't understand Italian, you won't get much out of Roman theater — but if you do know the language, you'll be delighted by the number of performances, from classical to contemporary. Fortunately, some shows are in English, especially in the summer during the **Estate Romana** festival (see later in this section).

The best theaters in Rome are the **Teatro Argentina** (Largo Argentina 52; ☎ **06-684000345;** www.teatrodiroma.net), **Teatro Brancaccio** (Via Merulana 244, off Piazza Santa Maria Maggiore; ☎ **06-47824893;** www.politeamabrancaccio.it), **Teatro Ghione** (Via delle Fornaci 37; ☎ **06-6372294;** www.ghione.it), **Teatro Quirino** (Via delle Vergini 7, near Fontana di Trevi; ☎ **06-6794585;** www.teatroquirino.it), **Teatro Valle** (Via del Teatro Valle 21, near Piazza Navona; ☎ **06-68803794;** www.teatrovalle.it), and **Teatro Sistina** (Via Sistina 129, off Via del Tritone; ☎ **06-4200711;** www.ilsistina.com), but there are a great number more, all quite good.

During the summer, many theater performances move outdoors for the **Estate Romana** festival. One of the highest rated for tourists is the English company **The Miracle Players** (☎ **06-70393427;** www.miracleplayers.org) performing in English at the **Roman Forum** (Via dei Fori Imperiali; ☎ **06-70393427**). As the name suggests, the **Toti Globe Theatre** in **Villa Borghese** (Largo Aqua Felix, entrance at Piazzale delle Ginestre; ☎ **06-82077304;** www.globetheatreroma.com) is a replica of the famous theater of Shakespeare in London, where the Toti performs Shakespeare as well as other productions. The **Teatro Romano of Ostia Antica** (Viale dei Romagnoli 717, Ostia Antica; ☎ **06-56358041**), a bit farther afield, is well worth the trip. It always offers a summer season in the highly atmospheric Roman theater within the archaeological site of the ancient seaport of Ostia.

The newly opened **Centrale RistoTheatre** (Via Celsa 6, off Piazza del Gesu; ☎ **06-6780501;** www.centraleristotheatre.com) is an ultramodern restaurant–cabaret–theater hall presenting musical and theatrical performances that you can enjoy over an *aperitivo* (predinner drink) and a light snack or dinner. The dinner — with a weekly menu based on Tuscan fare — is at 7:30 p.m., and the live show is at 10:30 p.m.

Ticket prices vary according to the performance and venue, but they usually range from 12€ to 26€ ($16–$34).

Chapter 16

Hitting the Clubs and Bars

*R*oman nights keep on being sweet no matter what the season and the set you move in. If you aren't too pooped from treading through the sites, come join *la dolce vita* and the ancient and modern pleasures of Rome.

Finding Out What's on Where

You can pick up or download a copy of *The Happening City,* an excellent review of events published by Rome's tourist board at www.romaturismo. it (see Appendix A). You can also find extensive listings in the **daily newspapers** and in the weekly publication *Roma C'è,* which is available at any newsstand (it comes out on Wed) and has some listings in English. Other sources are *Wanted in Rome,* a fortnightly magazine published by Società della Rotonda (Via dei Delfini 17; ☎ 06-6790190; www.wantedin rome.com), and *The American* (www.theamericanmag.com), a 48-page monthly covering all of Italy, with extensive listings for Rome. Both are available at newsstands in the historic center of the city and at selected newsstands elsewhere, and both have an online version.

For the events of the **Estate Romana** festival, you can get details at the tourist points in town and also online at www.estateromana.comune. roma.it (also in English) or by calling ☎ 06-68809505 Monday through Saturday from 10 a.m. to 5 p.m.

All That Jazz

Romans love jazz, and the city is home to many first-rate jazz venues featuring excellent local musicians as well as all the big names of the international scene. Most clubs are in Trastevere and in Prati, and open their doors around 10 p.m. and close around 3 a.m. Cover charges vary depending on the event and the club, but they usually range between 7€ ($9) for a regular night all the way up to 30€ ($39) for special concerts.

The most famous jazz clubs are the **Alexanderplatz** (Via Ostia 9, just off the Musei Vaticani; ☎ 06-39742171; www.alexandreplatz.it; metro: Line A to Ottaviano/San Pietro; bus: 23 to Via Leone IV), where reservations are recommended; **Big Mama** (Vicolo San Francesco a Ripa 18 in Trastevere; ☎ 06-5812551; www.bigmama.it; metro: Piramide; tram: 8), which attracts both small and big names in jazz and blues, and is somewhat more expensive, depending on how bright the star is; and the **Fonclea** (Via Crescenzio 82/a, behind Castel Sant'Angelo; ☎ 06-6896302; www.fonclea.it; bus: 23 to Via Crescenzio), where the emphasis is on jazz, but it also has some excellent ethnic and other concerts. Another great place for jazz, a bit out of the city center, is the **La Palma Club** (Via Giuseppe Mirri 35; ☎ 06-43599029; www.lapalmaclub.it), not far from the Tiburtina train station, seat of the popular **Fandango Jazz Festival** in June and July.

In addition to jazz and contemporary music, you may hear traditional Italian songs at **Arciliuto** (Piazza Montevecchio 5; ☎ 06-6879419; bus: 62 or 64 to Corso Vittorio Emanuele), located in the maze of streets behind Piazza Navona. Unfortunately, it's closed most of the summer, but then you can enjoy the many jazz events of the **Estate Romana** (discussed earlier in this chapter), usually including **Fiesta!** (Ippodromo delle Capannelle, Via Appia Nuova 1245; ☎ 06-7182139), with Latin American jazz, and the concerts of **Villa Celimontana** (Via della Navicella; ☎ 06-7182139).

Historic Cafes

Rome boasts many famous old cafes that have never lost their glamour. Although some are protected historical sites, they still operate as regular bars (Rome-style; see Chapter 10), opening early in the morning — usually by 7 — and closing around 9 or 9:30 p.m. They are all in the historical center of town.

Very pleasant, if a little expensive, the **Antico Caffè della Pace** (Via della Pace 3–7; ☎ 06-6861216; bus: Minibus 116 to Piazza Navona) is one of the most popular cafes in the city, where you can linger at outdoor tables opening onto a romantic little square. Another sought-after spot is the beautifully furnished **Caffè Greco** (Via Condotti 84; ☎ 06-6791700; metro: Line A to Spagna); among its customers were famous writers like Stendhal, Goethe, and Keats. Also noteworthy is the **Caffè Rosati** (Piazza del Popolo 4–5; ☎ 06-3225859; bus: Minibus 117 or 119), which retains its 1920s Art Nouveau décor. **Tre Scalini** (Piazza Navona 30; ☎ 06-6879148; bus: Minibus 116) is a perfect spot for people-watching while having a drink or an ice cream. It's famous for *tartufo* — ice cream coated with bittersweet chocolate and topped with sour cherries and whipped cream — but the regular gelato is nothing to rave about.

Wine Bars and Pubs

Rome has many a fine *enoteca* (wine shop), a very popular hangout place for young and not-so-young Romans. Some of them are regular wine shops that turn into wine bars–cum–restaurants after 8 p.m. (and sometimes also at lunch, between 1 and 3 p.m.). Others are wine bars that open exclusively in the evening, usually from 8 p.m. to 1 a.m. but sometimes even later. They're scattered everywhere in Rome, with some of the most popular located in the *centro,* in particular the Pantheon/Navona, Colosseo, Trastevere, and Campo de' Fiori areas.

The granddaddy of Roman wine stores, **Trimani** (Via Goito 20; ☎ 06-4469661; www.trimani.com; bus: 60 or 62; closed Sun and Aug) has been run by the same family since 1821 and is lodged in the old residential neighborhood behind the Terme di Diocleziano. In addition to selling thousands of bottles of wine, Trimani is a happening wine bar. Across town, the exceedingly popular but old-fashioned wine bar called **Vineria** (Campo de' Fiori 15; no phone) still holds its own amid the nightly crowds swarming this trendy piazza, popular with all age groups. For something calmer, try the wine bar at **Gusto** (see Chapter 10), which has an intimate, romantic atmosphere.

Not an enoteca but an American-style bar with a DJ, the **Drunken Ship** (Campo de' Fiori 20; ☎ 06-68300535) is often jammed with people. This is the place where every American student doing his or her year abroad will eventually turn up — be warned or informed, as the case may be.

The European Economic Union has had a very definite impact on nightlife: The Italian craze for Irish pubs has hit Rome very hard. These are among the nicest ones: **Mad Jack** (Via Arenula 20, off Largo Argentina; ☎ 06-68808223; tram: 8) is the place for Guinness and a choice of light food; it also features live music on Wednesday and Thursday. The **Abbey Theatre Irish Pub** (Via del Governo Vecchio 51–53, near Piazza Navona; ☎ 06-6861341; bus: 62 or 64 to Corso Vittorio Emanuele II) is in the oldest part of town, and features authentic décor and souvenirs from the famous theater of Yeats, J. M. Synge, and Lady Gregory. The **Albert** (Via del Traforo 132, off Via del Tritone, before the tunnel; ☎ 06-4818795; bus: Minibus 116, 117, or 119 to Largo del Tritone) is not an Irish pub at all but deserves mention: It provides a real English-pub atmosphere and beer, with everything from the furnishings to the drinks imported from the old country.

Dance Clubs

Romans, especially the younger set, love dancing, and clubs abound. You can hear a mixture of live and recorded music at **Alpheus** (Via del Commercio 36, near Via Ostiense; ☎ 06-5747826; bus: 23, but best to take a cab). Several halls offer different kinds of music, from jazz to Latin to straight-ahead rock, so if you don't want to dance, you can actually find comfortable places to sit and have a drink while listening. **Alien**

(Via Velletri 13–19; ☎ 06-8412212; www.aliendisco.it; bus: 490 to Piazza Fiume) continues to work at its reputation as Rome's clubbiest club — with mirrors, strobe lights, and a New York–style atmosphere appealing to a frenetic twentysomething crowd. Not to be outdone in the club-as-phenom category is **Gilda** (Via Mario de Fiori 97; ☎ 06-6797396; www.gildadiscoclub.it; metro: Line A to Spagna), which caters to an older crowd and plays classic rock as well as some newer stuff.

In **Testaccio,** clubs come and go, but the neighborhood remains one of the preeminent Roman hot spots. **Club Picasso** (Via Monte Testaccio 63; ☎ 06-5742975; metro: B to Piramide) has blasting music — from rock to blues — for most of the night.

During the summer, the **Estate Romana** festival (see earlier in this chapter) provides additional dancing venues, including on a barge on the Tiber and on the terraces and gardens of monuments around town.

Cover charges hover between 10€ and 20€ ($13–$26) for the most elegant and hippest venues. They usually open around 10:30 p.m. and close around 4 a.m.

Gay and Lesbian Bars

Rome has a lively gay scene, which becomes positively sizzling in summer with **Gay Village** (☎ 340-5423008; www.gayvillage.it), a special section of the **Estate Romana** festival that includes music and theater performances, as well as disco dancing and other entertainment.

Gay clubs are scattered around the city, although lately, the area between San Giovanni and the Colosseo has been developing as a gay enclave; they observe the same hours as other clubs and discos in town, from around 10 p.m. to around 4 a.m. Cover charge usually runs about 10€ ($13).

The hottest gay club in Rome is **Alibi** (Via di Monte Testaccio 40–44; ☎ 06-5743448; www.alibionline.it; nus: 23 or tram 3 to Via Marmorata and then walk down Via Galbani, though taking a cab is best), with a rotating schedule of DJs and a great summer roof garden. The gay disco **Angelo Azzurro** (Via Cardinale Merry del Val 13 in Trastevere; ☎ 06-5800472; tram: 8 to Viale Trastevere at Piazza Mastai) welcomes all ages and offers an eclectic mix of music. Admission is free, and Friday night welcomes ladies only.

The leading lesbian club is **New Joli Coeur** (Via Sirte 5; ☎ 06-86215827; bus: 56 or 88 to Piazza Sant'Emerenziana); it's nonexclusive and welcoming too. The club is only for women on Saturday nights, but all are welcome at other times.

Part VI
The Part of Tens

The 5th Wave   By Rich Tennant

"He had it made after our trip to Italy. I give you Fontana di Clifford."

In this part . . .

*H*ere we add some special details that we hope will make your vacation even more successful and memorable.

Think you can make do in Rome knowing only ten Italian words? Believe it or not, it's possible, and we get you started in Chapter 17. In Chapter 18, we list ten of the greatest Roman artists and point you to where you can find their art and architecture. In Chapter 19, we suggest ten great purchases to serve as a beautiful reminder of your visit to the Eternal City.

Non Capisco: The Top Ten Expressions You Need to Know

● ●

In This Chapter
▶ Using salutations
▶ Asking questions
▶ Memorizing some lifesavers

● ●

*T*raveling in a country where you don't know the language can be intimidating, but trying to speak the language can be amusing at the very least. Although you can get by in Rome without knowing Italian, locals often appreciate it if you at least make an effort to speak to them in their native tongue. And we think you'll find that Italian is a fun language to speak.

Per Favore

Meaning **"please,"** *per favore* (*per* fa-*voe*-ray) is the most important expression you can know. With it, you can make useful phrases such as *Un caffè, per favore* ("A coffee, please") and *Il conto, per favore* ("The bill, please"). There's no need for verbs, and it's perfectly polite!

Grazie

Grazie (*gra*-tziay) means **"thank you"**; if you want to go all out, use *grazie mille* (*mee*-lay), meaning "a thousand thanks." Say it clearly and loudly enough to be heard. Saying *grazie* is always right and puts people in a good mood. *Grazie* has other uses as well: Italians often use it as a way to say goodbye or mark the end of an interaction. It's particularly useful when you don't want to buy something from an insistent street vendor: Say *"Grazie,"* and walk away.

Permesso

Meaning **"excuse me"** (to request passage or admittance), *permesso* (per-*mess*-ow) is of fundamental importance on public transportation. When you're in a crowded bus and need to get off, say loudly and clearly, *"Permesso!"* People will clear from your path (or feel less irritated as you squeeze your way through). The same thing applies in supermarkets, trains, museums, and so on. Of course, you may be surrounded by non-Italians, and the effect may be a little lost on them.

Scusi

Scusi (*scoo*-sy) means **"excuse me"** (to say you're sorry after bumping into someone) and is more exactly *mi scusi,* but the shortened form is the one more people use. Again, it's a most useful word in any crowded situation. You'll note that Italians push their way through a narrow passage with a long chain of *"Scusi, permesso, mi scusi, grazie, permesso. . . ."* It's very funny to hear. *Scusi* has another important use: It's the proper beginning to attract somebody's attention before asking a question. Say *"Scusi?"*, and the person will turn toward you in benevolent expectation. Then it's up to you.

Buon Giorno and Buona Sera

Buon giorno (bwon *djor*-know), meaning **"good day,"** and its sibling *buona sera* (*bwon*-a *sey*-rah), meaning **"good evening,"** are of the utmost importance in Italian interactions. Italians always salute one another when entering or leaving a public place. Do the same, saying it clearly when entering a store or restaurant. Occasionally, these words can also be used as forms of goodbye.

Arrivederci

Arrivederci (ah-rree-vey-*der*-tchy) is the appropriate way to say **goodbye** in a formal occasion — in a shop, in a bar or restaurant, or to friends. If you can say it properly, people will like it very much: Italians are aware of the difficulties of their language for foreigners.

You'll hear the word *ciao* (chow), the familiar word for goodbye, used among friends (usually of the same age). Note that using the word *ciao* with someone you don't know is considered quite impolite!

Dov'è

Meaning **"where is,"** *dov'è* (doe-*vay*) is useful for asking for directions. Because the verb is included, you just need to add the thing you're looking for: *Dov'è il Colosseo?* ("Where is the Colosseum?") or *Dov'è la stazione?* ("Where is the train station?"). Of course you need to know the names of monuments in Italian, but don't worry! We always give you the Italian names in this book. It makes things much easier when you're there!

Quanto Costa?

Meaning **"how much does it cost?"**, *quanto costa?* (*quahnn*-tow *koss*-tah) is of obvious use all around Italy for buying anything from a train ticket to a Murano glass chandelier.

Che Cos'è?

Meaning **"what is it?"**, *che cos'è?* (kay *koss*-ay) will help you identify something before you buy it. It is particularly useful in restaurants and grocery stores, but it also may come in handy in museums and other circumstances. But then the tricky part begins: understanding the answer. If you don't understand the answer, you can get the person to repeat it by saying the next phrase on our list. . . .

Non Capisco

Non capisco (nonn kah-*peace*-koh) means **"I don't understand."** There's no need to explain this one: Keep repeating it, and Italians will try more and more imaginative ways to explain things to you.

Chapter 18

Ten Great Roman Artists

. . . .

In This Chapter

▶ Identifying Rome's great sculptors, painters, and architects

▶ Discovering great women artists

. . . .

lthough hundreds of books have been written about the great figures of Italian art, few have focused specifically on Roman artists.
However, most great Italian artists spent time in this great city, at least
for a time, because so much art was — and still is — produced here.
Moreover, Rome gave birth to a number of important artists and, what is
most interesting, to some of the first professional *women* artists in the
Renaissance. These women's work is all over the city, decorating some
of the most important monuments you'll see, but their names are often
obscure except to art historians because of the overshadowing reputa-
tions of the great names from the rest of the country.

We chose ten of the best Roman artists — men and women — and list
them in order of chronology, but we left behind many whose names
you'll encounter over and over during your visit, such as Giuseppe
Chiari (1654–1727), Giovanni Odazzi (1663–1731), Michelangelo Cerruti
(1663–1748), and Marco Benefial (1684–1764) for the Renaissance and
baroque, as well as the internationally known modern painters Giuseppe
Capogrossi (1900–1972) and Toti Scaloja (1914–1998).

Pietro Cavallini

Considered the Roman Giotto for medieval painting, Pietro Cavallini
(c. 1250–1344) was a very active painter and mosaic designer of great skill.
A marvelous artist, his documented and still extant work includes the
splendid mosaic in the apse of Santa Maria in Trastevere (see Chapter 11).
Although many of his frescoes have been lost — as is the case for Giotto —
we know he decorated the inner facade of St. Peter's and the main nave of
San Paolo Fuori Le Mura. In that basilica, you can still admire his mosaic
on the facade, as well as the Christ in the main nave and the crucifix in
the Cappella del Santissimo. Among his other works in Rome, some of
the best are the *Giudizio Universale* (Last Judgment) on the inner facade
of Santa Cecilia in Trastevere, and the frescoes and decorations of the
Cappella Savelli in Santa Maria in Aracoeli, which are unfortunately partially ruined (see Chapter 11).

Jacopo Torriti

Active during the same period as Cavallini (see the preceding section), Jacopo Torriti was also a great mosaic designer and painter, although much less innovative than his colleague. We can still admire the mosaics in the apse of Santa Maria Maggiore and the *Enthroned Virgin* in the chapel dedicated to Santa Rosa in Santa Maria in Aracoeli (see Chapter 11).

Antoniazzo Romano

Antonio di Benedetto Aquilio degli Aquili (c. 1430–1512) rapidly became the leading painter of the Roman school in the 15th century. He developed a highly refined painting technique, especially for tempera. Indeed, some of his work is exhibited in major international museums, including his *Madonna di Leone IX* in the National Gallery in Dublin, his *Madonna* at the Detroit Institute of Arts, and his triptych in the Prado of Madrid. He was very active in Rome, where you can see his splendid frescoes in the *Camera di Santa Caterina* in the church of Santa Maria sopra Minerva; his *Nativity* in the Galleria Nazionale d'Arte Antica in Palazzo Barberini; his *Madonna del Tribunale della Sacra Rota* in the Pinacoteca Vaticana at the Vatican Museums; and his *Madonna* in San Paolo Fuori Le Mura (see Chapter 11).

Giulio Pippi

Also known as Giulio Romano (c. 1492–1546) because of his Roman birth and training, Pippi worked with Raphael in the Vatican and was deeply influenced by the greater painter but quickly developed his own personal style. He was often called on to finish and complement some of Raphael's work, such as the frescoes in the Villa Farnesina in Trastevere and the *Sale di Costantino* in the Vatican. He also worked extensively in Mantova for the Gonzaga family. His work is all over Rome; in addition to his frescoes in the Vatican and the Villa Farnesina, you can see his *Virgin with Child and St. John* in the Galleria Borghese (see Chapter 11).

Cavalier d'Arpino

Also known as Giuseppe Cesar (1568–1640), this artist's Roman birth is not certain — some think he may have been born in Arpino, near Frosinone, where he spent some of his childhood. In any case, he was back in the city at the age of 14 to work as a painter helper in the Vatican, and was quickly promoted and started getting his own commissions, gaining increasing fame. He worked mostly in Rome but also in Naples, where he frescoed the choir in the Carthusian Monastery of Saint Martin. His elegant Mannerist style modernized with naturalistic elements made him a favorite painter in 16th-century Rome, and he was often called in by Pope Clement VIII. You can see many of his works around the city, including the frescoes in the Palazzo dei Conservatori (Capitoline Museums), the transept of San Giovanni in Laterano, the lunettes over the main altar and in the cupola of the Cappella Paolina in Santa Maria Maggiore, and the vault of the Cappella degli Olgiati in Santa Prassede. Some of his best paintings are in museums in Rome, such as his *Annunciazione* in the Pinacoteca Vaticana (Vatican Museums), his *Diana* in the Pinacoteca Capitolina (Capitoline Museums), and his frescoes at the Galleria Borghese (see Chapter 11).

Artemisia Gentileschi

Born into a life of art — she was the daughter of Orazio, a painter of the Caravaggio school — Artemisia Gentileschi (1593–1652) started in the profession working with her father but soon obtained her own commissions in Rome and elsewhere in Italy — churches in Naples; paintings in Rome, Florence, and Venice — and even abroad, including in England for King Charles I. She is a great figure both in art and in the history of women. A professional painter at a time when women painters were rare and confined by rigid convention to doing portraits and still-lifes, she tackled mythological and religious subjects, producing work that holds its own in comparison with that of other artists of her period. She has been the subject of many books, most recently *Artemisia: A Novel,* by Alexandra La Pierre.

Among her work in Rome, you can see her *Cecilia* and a *Madonna and Child* at the Galleria Spada and self-portraits at the Galleria Nazionale d'Arte Antica in Palazzo Barberini (see Chapter 11).

Plautilla Bricci

Lesser known, Plautilla Bricci (1616–1690) has her place in history as being the first woman architect in Rome and in the Western world. She practiced mostly in Rome, both in secular and religious architecture. Among her remaining work in the capital, you can admire the chapel dedicated to San Luigi in the church of San Luigi dei Francesi, near the Pantheon, where she also painted the great San Luigi IX over the altar.

Pietro Bracci

Considered the greatest sculptor of the 18th century and of the baroque period, Pietro Bracci (1700–1773) produced work of powerful expression and grace. He became a master in the use of colored marble, which he used to highlight and provide background for his figures. Among his best works in Rome are the Neptune and the Tritons in the Trevi fountain; the monumental tomb of Benedict XIII in the church of Santa Maria sopra Minerva; the statues of angels over the portico of Santa Maria

Maggiore; the tomb of Benedict XIV; and the monument to Maria
Clementina Sobieski (wife of James Francis Stuart, who would have
been James III of England if the Jacobites had had their way) in
St. Peter's Basilica (see Chapter 11).

Giuseppe Valadier

A great architect and urbanist, Giuseppe Valadier (1762–1839) made an
important contribution to the reshaping of the Eternal City in the early
19th century. He is considered one of the greatest neoclassical architects; he also was an archaeologist and was responsible for the restoration of several monuments in Rome. His greatest work is the
transformation of Piazza del Popolo, crowned by the elegant building
named after him, La Casina Valadier (now a restaurant; see Chapter 10).
Among his other works are the Teatro Valle (see Chapter 15), the reorganization of Piazza San Giovanni in Laterano (see Chapter 11), and the
retracing of Via Flaminia.

Duilio Cambellotti

A multifarious artist, Duilio Cambellotti (1876–1960) is one of the greatest figures of the modern style of Art Nouveau. He began his career as an
illustrator and in that field produced much work of great expressional
intensity — such as his famous illustrations for the Alinari edition of
Dante's *La Divina Commedia* in 1901, in perfect Liberty (Italian Art
Nouveau) style. He also was a scenographer, a landscape designer, and
an interior decorator and designer, and he tackled most other artistic
media at one time or another — his artistic glass windows are beautiful.
It is, however, as a sculptor that we love him the most. The majority of
his work is in private collections and buildings, but you can admire his
frescoes on the vaults of the two small halls in Castel Sant'Angelo off the
Sala delle Colonne and some of his glasswork in the Museum of the
Casina delle Civette in Villa Torlonia (see Chapter 11).

Chapter 19

From Antique Prints to Cardinal Socks: The Best Roman Souvenirs

In This Chapter

▶ Enjoying Rome's finest art galleries and antiques shops
▶ Shopping for fashion, jewelry, and fine lace
▶ Finding unique religious souvenirs

*Y*ou won't have to look very long to find fabulous things to buy in Rome — not only those special items with a century-long tradition in the city, but also the best crafts and art produced elsewhere in Italy. Whether you plan to spend $8 or $8,000, you'll have no problem finding something that'll remind you of your trip and bring beauty to your home or to the home of a relative or friend (see Chapter 12 for store addresses).

A little note: We've excluded food specialties from this list because of the many Customs exclusions on foodstuffs and because most packaged edible Italian specialties are sold in gourmet specialty stores worldwide.

Antique Prints

Rome is known for its beautifully executed prints and engravings, usually of classic subjects such as monuments, landscapes, and ruins. Whether you're in the market for valuable antique prints or less-expensive newer prints from antique engraving plates, you won't have any trouble finding a wide selection. If purchased without a frame, prints can be easily transported and make excellent gifts.

Art

Rome is not only a great city in which to *view* art, but also a great city in which to *buy* art. Numerous young artists and well-established pros have showrooms and studios in Rome, and welcome visitors to browse — and purchase — their works. Even if you decide to go out empty-handed, you'll have a lot of fun just looking.

Crafts

Il centro served as a headquarters for craftsmen for centuries, and although high rents and other factors have greatly reduced the number of artisans, you can still find some who learned their trade the traditional way: from their fathers. Among the traditional items are wrought iron, basketry, and ceramics.

Fashion

Of course, you could fill your suitcases with designer fashions almost anywhere you go in Italy, but Rome has all the great names of Italian *pret-a-porter*, as well as lesser-known (and, thus, less expensive) designers producing unique and fashionable clothes. And the great thing about Rome is that it isn't only for girls; a great number of splendid shops are completely devoted to men's fashion needs.

Gold Jewelry

Goldsmiths have an ancient tradition in Rome, and you'll find — especially in the medieval streets of Trastevere, but also elsewhere in the city — skilled artisans who have been at their work for decades. Some follow the inspiration of antiquity and produce Roman- or Etruscan-styled jewels; others have chosen modernity and explore aesthetics from another end. No matter what your tastes, you'll certainly find something to your liking.

Handmade Paper Goods

Romans have a true love for stationery, and the city boasts a sophisticated selection of wonderful and sophisticated paper. Even if you use e-mail for most of your correspondence, you may find yourself yearning to put pen to paper when you see the thick, cream-colored, handmade stationery or agendas and scrapbooks lined with handmade marbleized paper (a technique, by the way, that was invented either in Florence or Venice). Whether shopping for yourself or someone else, stationery makes a fine Roman souvenir.

Lace and Embroideries

Although Rome is not the most famous Italian source for laces and embroideries (that title belongs to Venice), and the craft has almost disappeared from the city, a few stores keep the tradition alive. Popular items include exquisite handkerchiefs, tablecloths, bedsheets, and children's clothing.

Murano Chandeliers and Sardinian Pottery

If you can't find enough Rome-made specialties to satisfy your needs, a number of showrooms in town showcase the best arts and crafts Italy has to offer. All the greatest specialties are represented, from artistic Venetian glass to brightly colored hand-painted Positano ceramic. What better place than Rome, the heart and marketplace of the Italian peninsula for over 2,000 years, to find an Italian souvenir?

Plaster Reproductions

Because so many artworks and so many artists concentrate in Rome, and because Rome is also the seat of a great number of art schools, the traditional art of plaster reproductions has been maintained over the centuries, and you can still find specialized laboratories selling the perfect copy of Michelangelo's *Pietà* or of a Roman bust. Smaller reproductions make great gifts and souvenirs, and if you decide you can't live without a copy of the *Pietà* or some other large statue, you can always have it shipped to your home.

Religious Paraphernalia

Even if you're not religious, you may be drawn to the many faith-based souvenirs available in Rome, from beautifully bound Bibles to religious paintings, carvings, and figurines — some truly exquisite. And if you don't feel too blasphemous, religious attire has a quaint attraction: You can purchase beautiful red socks (made for cardinals) and superbly embroidered items.

Quick Concierge

Fast Facts

American Express

The office is at Piazza di Spagna 38 (☎ 06-67641; Metro: Line A to Spagna); it's open Mon–Fri 9 a.m.–5:30 p.m.; Sat 9 a.m.–12:30 p.m.; closed major local holidays.

Area Codes

The area code for Rome and surroundings is **06**; the area code for Tivoli and surroundings is **0774**; the area code for Civitavecchia and Tarquinia is **0766**; and the area code for the Lago di Vico area is **0761**. Cellphone area codes, which are all three digits, always begin with a 3, such as 340, 338, and so on. Toll-free numbers start with **800** or **888** (don't add a 1 to them; they won't work). Some paying services use three-digit codes beginning with 9. In addition, some companies have their own special numbers that don't conform to any of the preceding standards and that are local calls from anywhere in Italy.

ATMs

ATMs are available everywhere in the centers of towns. Most banks are linked to the Cirrus network. If you require the Plus network, your best bet is BNL (Banca Nazionale del Lavoro), but ask your bank for a list of locations before leaving on your trip.

Automobile Club

Contact the Automobile Club d'Italia (ACI) at ☎ 06-4477 for 24-hour information and assistance. For **road emergencies** in Italy, dial ☎ **116**.

Baby Sitters

Hotels in Rome usually don't offer structured activities for children but use professional agencies to provide their guests babysitting services on request. Good providers are Giorgi Tiziana (Via Cavour 295; ☎ 06-4742564) and GED (Via Sicilia 166/b; ☎ 06-42012495; www.gedonline.it).

Business Hours

Shops are usually open Monday through Saturday from 8:30 a.m. to 1 p.m. and again from 4 to 7:30 p.m. Groceries and other food shops are traditionally closed Thursday afternoons and other shops on Monday mornings. Businesses are usually open Monday through Friday from 8:30 a.m. to 1 p.m. and again from 2:30 to 5:30 p.m., and sometimes also Saturday mornings. Banks are open Monday through Friday from 8:30 a.m. to 1:30 p.m. and again from 2:30 to 4 p.m. or 3 to 4:30 p.m., depending on the bank. A few banks are open Monday through Friday from 8:30 a.m. straight through to 4 p.m. and Saturday from 8:30 a.m. to 12:30 p.m.

Camera Repair

A good shop is Dear Camera (Via G. Manno 3; ☎ 06-77073770; www.dearcamera.com; Metro: Furio Camillo).

Credit Cards

If your card is lost or stolen, contact these offices: American Express (☎ 06-7220348, 06-72282, or 06-72461; www.americanexpress.it); Diners Club (☎ 800-864064866 toll-free within Italy; www.dinersclub.com); MasterCard (☎ 800-870866 toll-free within Italy; www.mastercard.com); or Visa (☎ 800-819014 toll-free within Italy; www.visaeu.com).

Currency Exchange

You can find exchange bureaus (marked CAMBIO/CHANGE/WECHSEL) everywhere in the center of Rome and at points of entry such as major train stations; the cambio/change/wechsel at Fiumicino airport usually offers the best rates in town.

Customs

U.S. citizens can bring back $800 worth of merchandise duty free. You can mail yourself $200 worth of merchandise per day and $100 worth of gifts to others — alcohol and tobacco excluded. You can bring on the plane 1 liter of alcohol and 200 cigarettes or 100 cigars. The $800 ceiling doesn't apply to artwork or antiques (antiques must be at least 100 years old). You're charged a flat rate of 10 percent duty on the next $1,000 worth of purchases — for special items, the duty is higher. Make sure that you have your receipts handy. Agricultural restrictions are severely enforced: no fresh products, no meat products, and no dried flowers; other foodstuffs are allowed only if they're canned or in airtight sealed packages. For more information, contact the U.S. Customs Service, 1301 Pennsylvania Ave. NW, Washington, DC 20229 (☎ 877/287-8867), and request the free pamphlet "Know Before You Go," which is also available for download on the Web at www.customs.gov.

Canadian citizens are allowed a CAN$750 exemption and can bring back duty free 200 cigarettes, 2.2 pounds of tobacco, 40 imperial ounces of liquor, and 50 cigars. In addition, you're allowed to mail gifts to Canada from abroad at the rate of CAN$60 a day, as long as they're unsolicited and don't contain alcohol or tobacco (write on the package "Unsolicited Gift, Under $60 Value"). Declare all valuables on the Y-38 form before your departure from Canada, including serial numbers of valuables that you already own, such as expensive foreign cameras. You can use the $750 exemption only once a year and only after an absence of seven days. For more information, contact the Canada Border Services Agency (☎ 800-461-9999 from within Canada, or 204-983-3500 or 506-636-5064 from outside Canada; www.cbsa-asfc.gc.ca).

There's no limit on what U.K. citizens can bring back from an EU country, as long as the items are for personal use (this includes gifts) and the necessary duty and tax have already been paid. However, Customs law sets out guidance levels. If you bring in more than these levels, you may be asked to prove that the goods are for your own use. Guidance levels on goods bought in the European Union for your own use are 800 cigarettes, 200 cigars, 1 kilogram of smoking tobacco, 10 liters of spirits, 90 liters of wine (of this, not more than 60 liters can be sparkling wine), and 110 liters of beer. For more information, contact HM Customs and Excise, Passenger Enquiry Point, 2nd Floor, Wayfarer House, Great South West Road, Feltham, Middlesex, TW14 8NP (☎ 0845/010-9000; from outside the U.K. ☎ 44/208-929-0152), or consult its Web site at www.hmce.gov.uk.

Australian citizens are allowed an exemption of A$400 or, for those under 18 years of age, A$200. Personal property mailed back home should be marked "Australian Goods Returned" to avoid payment of duty. On returning to Australia, you can bring in 250 cigarettes or 250 grams of loose tobacco and 1.125 milliliters of alcohol. If you're returning with valuable goods you already own, such as foreign-made cameras, you should file Form B263. A helpful brochure, available from Australian consulates or Customs offices, is "Know Before You Go." For more information, contact Australian Customs Services, GPO Box 8, Sydney NSW 2001 (☎ 02/9213-2000 or 1300/363-263 within Australia or 612/6275-6666 from outside Australia; www.customs.gov.au).

New Zealand citizens have a duty-free allowance of NZ$700. If you're over 17, you can bring in 200 cigarettes, 50 cigars, or 250 grams of tobacco (or a mix of all three if their combined weight doesn't exceed 250 grams), plus 4.5 liters of wine and beer or 1.125 liters of liquor. New Zealand currency doesn't carry import or export restrictions. Fill out a certificate of export, listing the valuables you're taking out of the country. (That way, you can bring them back without paying duty.) You can find the answers to most of your questions in a free pamphlet available at New Zealand consulates and Customs offices: "New Zealand Customs Guide for Travelers, Notice no. 4." For more information, contact New Zealand Customs, The Custom House, 17–21 Whitmore St. Box 2218, Wellington (☎ 04-473-6099; www.customs.govt.nz).

Doctors

Contact your embassy or consulate to get a list of English-speaking doctors or dentists. You can also ask the concierge at your hotel. For any emergency, go to the emergency room of any nearby hospital (see "Emergencies," later in this appendix).

Electricity

Electricity in Rome is 220 volts. To use your appliances, you need a transformer. Remember that plugs are different too: The prongs are round, so you also need an adapter. You can buy an adapter kit in many electronics stores before you leave.

Embassies and Consulates

Rome is the capital of Italy and, therefore, the seat of all the embassies and consulates, which maintain a 24-hour referral service for emergencies: United States (☎ 06-46741), Canada (☎ 06-445981), Australia (☎ 06-852721), New Zealand (☎ 06-4402928), United Kingdom (☎ 06-7482441), Ireland (☎ 06-6979121).

Emergencies

For an **ambulance,** call ☎ **118;** for the **fire department,** call ☎ **115;** for the **police,** call ☎ **113** or **112;** for any **road emergencies,** call ☎ **116.**

Hospitals

The major hospitals in the historic center are the Santo Spirito (Lungotevere in Sassia 1; ☎ 06-68351 and 06-68352241 for first aid), and the Fatebenefratelli on the Isola Tiberina (Piazza Fatebenefratelli 2; ☎ 06-68371 or 06-6837299 for first aid).

Hotlines

For drug intoxication, call ☎ 06-3054343 or 06-490663. The Children Hotline (Telefono Azzurro) is ☎ 19696 toll-free for children; adolescents and adults can call at 199151515. The tourist information hotline at ☎ 06-36004399 will provide round-the-clock information on just about anything in four languages, including English.

Information

See "Where to Get More Information," later in this appendix.

Internet Access and Cybercafes

The ever-expanding Easy Everything has a big Internet access point at Piazza Barberini 2, open 24 hours a day 7 days a week, and with 350 computers. Internet Train has several locations, including Via Pastini 125, near the Pantheon; Via delle Fornaci 3, near San Pietro; Via Merry del Val 20, in Trastevere; and Via in Arcione 103 by Fontana di Trevi. Netgate (www.thenetgate.it) has several locations around Rome, and more are on the way; the most central are Piazza Firenze 25 (☎ 06-6893445) and Via in Arcione 103 (☎ 06-69922320). Near Termini, behind the Terme di Diocleziano, is Freedom Traveller (Via Gaeta 25; ☎ 06-47823862; www.freedom-traveller.it).

Language

Romans speak Italian, and although many know a bit of English, it isn't widely understood. Luckily, you can survive in Rome with very little knowledge of the Italian language (see Chapter 17 for a few choice terms), especially because Romans tend to be very friendly and ready to help foreigners in difficulty. However, you'll greatly enhance your experience if you master a dozen or so basic expressions. Good places to start your studies are the glossary in Appendix B and, if you're really serious, the excellent *Italian For Dummies* (Wiley).

Liquor Laws

There are no liquor laws in Italy. However, there are laws against disturbing the *quiete pubblica* (public quiet) — getting drunk and loud in bars, streets, and so on. There are also laws against littering — and drinking a can of beer while sitting on a bit of Ancient Roman wall is considered littering. Romans consider public drunkenness disgraceful, and though they love wine, they very much frown upon drinking to excess. You can buy alcohol in all supermarkets and grocery stores, as well as in specialized wine stores;

all are open usually from 9 a.m. to 1 p.m. and 4 to 7 p.m. (Groceries are closed Thurs afternoons.)

Mail

Mail in Italy used to be notoriously unreliable, and many tourists still prefer to use the Vatican post office (by the entrance to the Vatican Museums) while they're visiting St. Peter's in Rome; it's the same price as Italian post offices but somewhat faster. Note, though, that you can mail letters with Vatican stamps only from the blue mailboxes in the Vatican.

Italian mail has gotten a lot better with the introduction of *Posta Prioritaria* (express/priority). A letter to the United States costs 0.80€ ($1.05) and can take as little as four to five days to get there. Be aware, though, that postcards are always sent via the equivalent of U.S. third-class mail and will take a long time to arrive; if you want your postcards to arrive fast, slip them in an envelope and send them letter rate. Also, make sure you put your mail in the right mailbox: The ones for international mail are blue, whereas the red ones are for national mail, and sorting will take longer. The new priority mail also applies to packages; however, it's expensive, and you may be better off using a private carrier like UPS or DHL, which will guarantee your delivery, especially for valuables.

Maps

You can find free maps at the tourist information points (see "Where to Find More Information," later in this appendix). If you want something more detailed, you can buy maps at newsstands and kiosks around Rome. Get a map with a *stradario* (street directory); one of the best, albeit a bit bulky, is *Tutto Città*, which costs about 8€ ($10) and is a largish booklet with a full street directory.

Pharmacies

Pharmacies are usually open Monday through Friday from 8:30 a.m. to 1 p.m. and again from 4 to 7:30 p.m. A few pharmacies are open all night: Piazza dei Cinquecento 49, at Termini Station (☎ 06-4880019); Via Cola di Rienzo 213 (☎ 06-3244476); Piazza Risorgimento 44 (☎ 06-39738166); Via Arenula 73 (☎ 06-68803278); Corso Rinascimento 50 (☎ 06-68803985); Piazza Barberini 49 (☎ 06-4871195); and Viale Trastevere 229 (☎ 06-5882273).

Police

To call the **police**, dial ☎ **113** or **112.**

Post Office

The central post office in the historic center is located at Piazza San Silvestro 19, not far from Piazza di Spagna. You'll also find post offices in Via di Porta Angelica 23, near San Pietro, and in Viale Mazzini 101 in the Cola di Rienzo area. They're open Monday through Friday from 8:30 a.m. to 6:30 p.m. and Saturday from 8:30 a.m. to 1 p.m. For information, call ☎ 800-160000 toll free within Italy.

Restrooms

Some public toilets are scattered around town, but not many. You can find one outside the Colosseum across the road toward Via Labicana and another one halfway up the steps from Piazza del Popolo to the Pincio, on the left side. Facing San Pietro, you can find toilets under the colonnade on the right. Make sure you have some change to tip the attendant. Your best bet may be to go to a nice-looking cafe (though you have to buy something, like a cup of coffee, to use the restroom).

Safety

Rome is a very safe city except for pickpockets. Pickpockets concentrate in tourist areas, on public transportation, and around crowded open-air markets like the Porta Portese. One area that gets somewhat seedy at night is behind the main rail station Termini.

If you're a pretty young woman traveling alone, you'll attract men's attention — some may even approach you and try to charm you. However, it's unlikely that someone will touch you, let alone harm you. Still, it's a good idea to ignore and avoid eye contact with anyone who approaches you. The way you dress sometimes has an effect. Romans have a stricter dress code than Americans do, and people tend to dress more conservatively. You can either dress however you feel like dressing (and steel yourself for the occasional look of disapproval or suggestive remark) or adapt your mode of dress to fit in with local traditions — the choice is yours.

Smoking

In 2005, Rome passed a law outlawing smoking in most public places. Smoking is allowed only where there is a separate, ventilated area for nonsmokers. If you want to smoke at your table, call beforehand to make sure the restaurant or cafe you'll be visiting offers a smoking area.

Taxes

Refer to Chapter 12 for VAT information.

Taxis

If you need a taxi, call ☎ 06-88177, 06-6645, 06-4994, 06-5551, or 06-6545 for radio taxi service; you can also go to the many stations scattered around town at major squares and stations.

Telephone

To call Italy from the United States, dial the international access code, 011; then Italy's country code, 39; then the area code for the place you're calling (06 for Rome, 0774 for Tivoli, and so on); and then the regular phone number. Note that cellphone numbers do not begin with a 0, nor do special phone numbers such as toll-free numbers (mostly starting with 800) and paying services.

To make a call within Italy, remember to dial area codes (including the 0) for every call, even local calls. All public pay phones in Italy take a *carta telefonica* (telephone card), which you can buy at a *tabacchi* (tobacconist, marked by a sign with a white *T* on a black background), bar, or newsstand. The cards can be purchased in different denominations, from 2.58€ to 7.74€ ($3.35–$10). Tear off the perforated corner and stick the card in the phone, and you're ready to go. A local call in Rome costs 0.10€ (13¢).

To call abroad from Italy, dial the international access code, 00; then the country code of the country that you're calling (1 for the U.S. States and Canada, 44 for the U.K., 353 for Ireland, 61 for Australia, 64 for New Zealand); and then the phone number. Make sure that you have a high-value *carta telefonica* before you start; your 5€ won't last long when you call San Diego at noon. Lower rates apply after 11 p.m. and before 8 a.m. and on Sunday. The best option for calling home, though, is using your own calling card linked to your home phone. Some calling cards offer a toll-free access number in Italy; others do not, and you must put in a *carta telefonica* to dial the access number (you're usually charged only for a local call or not at all). Check with your calling-card provider before leaving on your trip. You can also make collect calls. For AT&T, dial ☎ 800-1724444 and then your U.S. phone number area code first; for MCI, dial ☎ 800-905825; and for Sprint, dial ☎ 800-172405 or 800-172406. To make a collect call to a country other than the United States, dial ☎ 170. Directory assistance for calls within Italy is a free call: Dial ☎ 12. International directory assistance is a toll call: Dial ☎ 176.

Remember that calling from a hotel is convenient but usually very expensive.

Time Zone

In terms of standard time zones, Italy is six hours ahead of eastern standard time in the United States: When it's 6 a.m. in New York, it's noon in Italy. Daylight saving time goes into effect in Italy each year from the last Sunday in March to the last Sunday in October.

Tipping

Tipping is customary as a token of appreciation as well as a polite gesture on most occasions. A 10 to 15 percent service charge is usually included in your restaurant bill (check the menu when you order — if the service is included, *servizio incluso* will be marked at the beginning or at the end), but it is customary to leave an additional 5 to 10 percent if you appreciated the meal; if the service is not included, leave 15 to 25 percent. In bars, leave a 5 percent tip at the counter and a 10 to 15 percent tip if you sit at a table. Bellhops who carry your bags will expect about 1€/$1.30 per bag, and you may want to leave a small tip for the maid in your hotel; cab drivers will expect 10 to 15 percent of the fare.

Transit Info

The local public transportation authority (bus, tram, and subway) is ATAC (☎ 800-431784 or 06-46952027; www.atac.roma.it). For railroad information, call Trenitalia (☎ 892021; www.trenitalia.it).

Weather Updates

Before you go, you can check a local Web site such as http://meteo.tiscalinet.it or one of the U.S.–based ones, such as www.cnn.com. When you're in Italy, your best bet is to watch the news on TV (there's no telephone weather number as there is in the U.S.).

Toll-Free Numbers and Web Sites

Airlines that fly to Rome and around Italy

Air France
☎ 800/237-2747
www.airfrance.com

Air New Zealand
☎ 800/737-000
www.airnewzealand.com

Air One
☎ 199-207080 in Italy
☎ 06-488800 from abroad
www.air-one.it

Air Sicilia
☎ 06-650171046

Alitalia
☎ 1478-65643 toll-free within Italy or 06-65643
☎ 800/223-5730 in the United States
☎ 800/361-8336 in Canada
☎ 0990/448-259 in the United Kingdom
☎ 020/7602-7111 in London
☎ 1300/653-747 or 1300/653-757 in Australia
www.alitalia.it or in the United States www.alitaliausa.com

American Airlines
☎ 800/433-7300
www.aa.com

British Airways
☎ 800/247-9297
☎ 0345/222-111 or 0845/77-333-77 in Britain
www.british-airways.com

Cathay Pacific
☎ 131-747 in Australia
☎ 0508-800454 in New Zealand
www.cathaypacific.com

Continental Airlines
☎ 800/525-0280
www.continental.com

Delta Air Lines
☎ 800/221-1212
www.delta.com

Lufthansa
☎ 800/645-3880 in the United States
www.lufthansa-usa.com

Meridiana
☎ 199-111333 within Italy
☎ 0789-52682 from abroad
www.meridiana.it

Northwest Airlines
☎ 800/225-2525
www.nwa.com

Qantas
☎ 800/227-4500 in the United States
☎ 612/9691-3636 in Australia
www.qantas.com

United Airlines
☎ 800/241-6522
www.united.com

US Airways
☎ 800-428-4322
www.usairways.com

Major car-rental agencies

AutoEurope
☎ 800-334440 in Italy
☎ 800/223-5555 in the United States
www.autoeurope.com

Avis
☎ 06-41999 in Italy
☎ 800/331-1212 in the United States
www.avis.com

Europe by Car
☎ 800/223-1516 in the United States
www.europebycar.com

Europcar
☎ 800/014410 or 06-65010879 in Italy
www.europcar.it

Hertz
☎ 199-112211 in Italy
☎ 800/654-3001 in the United States
www.hertz.com

Kemwel
☎ 800/678-0678 in the United States
www.kemwel.com

National/Maggiore
☎ 1478-67067 in Italy
☎ 800/227-7368 in the United States
www.maggiore.it

Sixt
☎ 888/749-8227 in the United States
☎ 199-100666 in Italy
www.e-sixt.it and
www.sixtusa.com for U.S. citizens

Major hotel chains

Best Western
☎ 800/780-7234 in the United States
and Canada
☎ 0800/39-31-30 in the
United Kingdom
☎ 131-779 in Australia
☎ 0800/237-893 in New Zealand
www.bestwestern.com or
www.bestwestern.it

Hilton Hotels
☎ 800/HILTONS
www.hilton.com

Holiday Inn
☎ 800/HOLIDAY
www.holiday-inn.com

ITT Sheraton
☎ 800/325-3535
www.sheraton.com

Jolly Hotels
☎ 800-017703 in Italy
☎ 800/221-2626 in the United States
☎ 800/247-1277 in New York state
☎ 800/237-0319 in Canada
☎ 0800/731-0470 in the
United Kingdom
www.jollyhotels.it.

Sofitel
☎ 800-SOFITEL in the United States
and Canada
☎ 020/8 283-4570 in the
United Kingdom
☎ 02-29512280 in Italy
☎ 800/642-244 in Australia
☎ 0800/44-44-22 in New Zealand
www.sofitel.com or www.accor-
hotels.it/sofitel.htm.

Where to Get More Information

As in any other metropolis, getting the proper info is essential in Rome.
Here, you'll find the best sources around.

Visitor information

The national tourist board, ENIT (www.enit.it), maintains a Web site
where you can find all kinds of cultural and practical information —
including hotel listings and the mail and Web addresses of local tourist
offices. It also maintains the following liaison offices abroad where you

can get brochures and other info (all offices are open Mon–Fri 9 a.m.–
5 p.m. local time):

✔ **New York** (630 Fifth Ave., Suite 1565, New York, NY 10111;
☎ **212/245-5618** or 212/245-4822; Fax: 212/586-9249; E-mail:
enitny@italiantourism.com)

✔ **Chicago** (500 N. Michigan Ave., Suite 2240, Chicago, IL 60611;
☎ **312/644-0996** or 312/644-0990; Fax: 312/644-3019; E-mail:
enitch@italiantourism.com)

✔ **Los Angeles** (12400 Wilshire Blvd., Suite 550, Los Angeles, CA
90025; ☎ **310/820-9807** or 310/820-1898; Fax: 310/820-6357;
E-mail: enitla@earthlink.net)

✔ **Toronto** (175 Bloor St., Suite 907, South Tower Toronto M4W3R8
Ontario; ☎ **416/925-4822**; Fax: 416/925-4799; E-mail: enit.canada@
on.aibn.com)

✔ **London** (1 Princes St., London, WIB 2AY; ☎ **0207/399-3562**; Fax:
0207/493-6695; E-mail: italy@italiantouristboard.co.uk)

✔ **Sydney** (Level 26, 44 Market St. NSW 2000 Sydney; ☎ **02/9262-1666**;
Fax: 02/9262-1677; E-mail: enitour@ihug.com.au)

You can also write to (or visit, after you're there) the separate tourist
boards of Rome and the Vatican:

✔ **APT Roma** (Via Parigi 5, 00100 Roma; ☎ **06-36004399**; www.
romaturismo.it; Open: Mon–Sat 9 a.m.–7 p.m.).

✔ **Vaticano — Ufficio Informazioni Turistiche** (Piazza San Pietro,
00163 Roma; ☎ **06-69884466**; Open: Mon–Sat 8:30 a.m.–6 p.m.).

When you're in Rome, you can get detailed and up-to-date cultural and
practical information, including a calendar of events, info on special
exhibits, and hotel information at the many tourist information kiosks
about town:

✔ **Fiumicino Airport** (Terminal B; ☎ **06-65956074**; Open: Daily
8 a.m.–7 p.m.) and several information kiosks around the city
near major attractions (Open: Daily 9 a.m.–6 p.m.)

✔ **Castel Sant'Angelo,** Piazza Pia, to the west of the Castel Sant'Angelo
(☎ **06-68809707**; Metro: Ottaviano–San Pietro)

✔ **Largo Goldoni,** on Via del Corso at Via Condotti (☎ **06-68136061**;
Metro: Piazza di Spagna)

✔ **Piazza delle Cinque Lune,** off Piazza Navona to the north (☎ **06-
68809240**; Bus: Minibus 116)

- **Fori Imperiali,** Piazza Tempio della Pace on Via dei Fori Imperiali (☎ 06-69924307; Metro: Colosseo)

- **Santa Maria Maggiore,** Via dell'Olmata, on the southeastern side of the church (☎ 06-4740955; Metro: Termini)

- **Stazione Termini,** Piazza dei Cinquecento, in front of the railroad station (☎ 06-47825194; Metro: Termini)

- **Stazione Termini,** inside the gallery (☎ 06-48906300; Metro: Termini)

- **Trastevere,** Piazza Sonnino (☎ 06-58333457; Tram: 8)

- **San Giovanni,** Piazza San Giovanni in Laterano (☎ 06-77203535; Metro: San Giovanni)

- **Fontana di Trevi,** Via Minghetti, off Via del Corso (☎ 06-6782988; Bus: Minibus 117, Minibus 119)

- **Palazzo delle Esposizioni,** Via Nazionale (☎ 06-47824525; Bus: 64)

Also, you can call the 24-hour tourist information hotline at ☎ 06-36004399; it will provide you information in four languages, including English.

Newspapers

A few papers are printed, at least in part, in English:

- *The Happening City* (www.romaturismo.it) is an excellent monthly magazine that covers all cultural events in the Eternal City. It's published by the Roman tourist board in Italian and in English.

- *Roma C'E* (www.romace.it) is a weekly paper with extensive listings of all that is going on in Rome, from markets to art exhibits and concerts. A section of it is in English and lists all the special events that are of particular interest to tourists and expatriates living in Rome. It comes out on Wednesdays and costs 1.20€ ($1.60); an online version is available at www.romace.it.

- *Wanted in Rome* is an English-language magazine published every two weeks. It's sold at newsstands in the historical center of the city and at selected newsstands elsewhere; it can also be accessed online at www.wantedinrome.com.

Other sources of information

For great suggestion on walking itineraries in Rome, check out *Memorable Walks in Rome,* a very portable Frommer's edition (published by Wiley).

You can also find excellent information on a number of Web sites:

- ✔ **Ciao Italy** (www.ciao-italy.com) provides links to a variety of other Web sites, from museums to local news.

- ✔ **Dolce Vita** (www.dolcevita.com) is all about style — as it pertains to fashion, cuisine, design, and travel. Dolce Vita is a good place to stay up to date on trends in modern Italian culture.

- ✔ **In Italy Online** (www.initaly.com) provides information on all sorts of accommodations in Italy (country villas, historic residences, convents, and farmhouses) and includes tips on shopping, dining, driving, and viewing art.

- ✔ The **Italian Tourist Web Guide** (www.itwg.com) provides new itineraries each month for art lovers, nature buffs, wine enthusiasts, and other Italophiles. It features a searchable directory of accommodations, transportation tips, and city-specific lists of restaurants and attractions.

- ✔ **Welcome to Italy** (www.wel.it) is a good source for all kinds of visitor information about Italy, from the cultural (monuments and history) to the practical (hotels and restaurants), with some curiosities thrown into the mix.

- ✔ **Virtual Rome** (www.virtualrome.com) provides information on hotels, as well as other travel-oriented suggestions and tips on topics from shopping to sightseeing.

- ✔ **Rome City** (www.romecity.it) provides excellent historical and cultural information, as well as a variety of practical information, including restaurants and hotel listings.

Appendix B

Glossary of Italian Words and Phrases

Although most Romans speak at least some English and will do their best to understand foreigners, knowing even a smidge of Italian will help you enormously. You'll feel freer and more relaxed, and Romans will appreciate your taking an interest in their language. This appendix contains some basic vocabulary to help you get around; if you are interested in learning more, *Italian For Dummies,* which comes with a CD, is a good resource.

Basic Vocabulary

English	Italian	Pronunciation
Thank you	**Grazie**	*graht*-tzee-yey
You're welcome	**Prego**	*prey*-go
Please	**Per favore**	*pehr* fah-*vohr*-eh
Yes	**Si**	see
No	**No**	noh
Good morning or Good day	**Buongiorno**	bwohn-*djor*-noh
Good evening	**Buona sera**	bwohn-ah *say*-rah
Good night	**Buona notte**	bwohn-ah *noht*-tay
How are you?	**Come sta?**	koh-may *stah*
Very well	**Molto bene**	*mohl*-toh *behn*-ney
Goodbye	**Arrivederci**	ahr-ree-vah-*dehr*-chee
Excuse me (to get attention)	**Scusi**	*skoo*-zee
Excuse me (to get past someone)	**Permesso**	pehr-*mehs*-soh
Where is . . . ?	**Dovè . . . ?**	doh-*vey*
the station	**la stazione**	lah stat-tzee-*oh*-neh
a hotel	**un albergo**	oon ahl-*behr*-goh

a restaurant	**un ristorante**	oon reest-ohr-*ahnt*-eh
the bathroom	**il bagno**	eel *bahn*-nyoh
To the right	**A destra**	ah *dehy*-stra
To the left	**A sinistra**	ah see-*nees*-tra
Straight ahead	**Avanti** (*or* **sempre dritto**)	ahv-*vahn*-tee (*sehm*-pray d*reet*-toh)
How much is it?	**Quanto costa?**	*kwan*-toh *coh*-sta
The check, please	**Il conto, per favore**	eel kon-toh *pehr* fah-*vohr*-eh
When?	**Quando?**	*kwan*-doh
Yesterday	**Ieri**	ee-*yehr*-ree
Today	**Oggi**	*oh*-jee
Tomorrow	**Domani**	doh-*mah*-nee
Breakfast	**Prima colazione**	*pree*-mah coh-laht-tzee-*ohn*-ay
Lunch	**Pranzo**	*prahn*-zoh
Dinner	**Cena**	*chay*-nah
What time is it?	**Che ore sono?**	kay *or*-ay *soh*-noh
Monday	**Lunedì**	loo-nay-*dee*
Tuesday	**Martedì**	mart-ay-*dee*
Wednesday	**Mercoledì**	mehr-cohl-ay-*dee*
Thursday	**Giovedì**	joh-vay-*dee*
Friday	**Venerdì**	ven-nehr-*dee*
Saturday	**Sabato**	*sah*-bah-toh
Sunday	**Domenica**	doh-*mehn*-nee-kah

Numbers

Number	Italian	Pronunciation
1	**uno**	*oo*-noh
2	**due**	*doo*-ay
3	**tre**	tray
4	**quattro**	*kwah*-troh
5	**cinque**	*cheen*-kway
6	**sei**	say
7	**sette**	*set*-tay
8	**otto**	*oh*-toh
9	**nove**	*noh*-vay
10	**dieci**	dee-*ay*-chee

11	undici	*oon*-dee-chee
20	venti	*vehn*-tee
21	ventuno	vehn-*toon*-oh
22	venti due	*vehn*-tee *doo*-ay
30	trenta	*trayn*-tah
40	quaranta	kwah-*rahn*-tah
50	cinquanta	cheen-*kwan*-tah
60	sessanta	sehs-*sahn*-tah
70	settanta	seht-*tahn*-tah
80	ottanta	oht-*tahn*-tah
90	novanta	noh-*vahnt*-tah
100	cento	*chen*-toh
1,000	mille	*mee*-lay
5,000	cinquemila	*cheen*-kway *mee*-lah
10,000	diecimila	dee-ay-chee mee-lah

Architectural Terms

abside (apse): The half-rounded extension behind the main altar of a church; Christian tradition dictates that it be placed at the eastern end of an Italian church, the side closest to Jerusalem.

ambone: A pulpit, either serpentine or simple in form, erected in an Italian church.

amorino or **cupido** (cupid): The personification of the mythological god of love as a chubby and winged naked child armed with bow and arrows.

atrio (atrium): A courtyard, open to the sky, in an Ancient Roman house; the term also applies to the courtyard nearest the entrance of an early Christian church.

baldacchino or **ciborio** (baldachin, baldaquin, or ciborium): A columned stone canopy, usually placed above the altar of a church.

basilica: Any rectangular public building, usually divided into three aisles by rows of columns. In Ancient Rome, this architectural form was frequently used for places of public assembly and law courts; later, Roman Christians adapted the form for many of their early churches.

battistero (baptistery): A separate building or a separate area in a church where the rite of baptism is held.

calidarium: The steam room of a Roman bath.

campanile: A bell tower, often detached, of a church.

capitello (capital): The four-sided stone at the top of a column, often decoratively carved. The Greek classic architectural styles included three orders: Doric, Ionic, and Corinthian.

cariatide (caryatid): A column carved into a standing female figure.

cattedrale (cathedral): The church where a bishop has his chair.

cavea: The curved row of seats in a classical theater; the most prevalent shape was a semicircle.

cella: The sanctuary, or most sacred interior section, of a Roman pagan temple.

chiostro (cloister): A courtyard ringed by a gallery of arches or lintels set atop columns.

cornice: The horizontal flange defining the uppermost part of a building, especially in classical or neoclassical facades.

cortile: An uncovered courtyard enclosed within the walls of a building complex.

cripta (crypt): A church's underground chapel, mostly used as a burial place, usually below the choir.

cupola: A dome.

duomo: A town's most important church, usually also a cathedral.

foro (forum): The main square and principal gathering place of any Roman town, usually adorned with the city's most important temples and civic buildings.

ipogeo: A subterranean structure; also an adjective describing any subterranean structure (such as a temple, a chamber, or a chapel), often used as *tomb*.

loggia: A roofed balcony or gallery.

navata (nave): Each of the longitudinal sections of a church or basilica, divided by walls, pillars, or columns.

palazzo: A palace or other large building, usually of majestic architecture.

pergamo: A pulpit.

piano nobile: The floor of a *palazzo* destined for the owner's use (usually the second floor), as opposed to the floors used by the house staff and for other services.

pietra dura: A semiprecious stone, such as amethyst and lapis lazuli.

portico: A porch with columns on at least one side, usually for decorative purposes.

presbiterio: The area around the main altar of a church, elevated and separated by columns or, in the oldest churches, by a screen *(transenna),* which was traditionally reserved for the bishop and the officiating clergy.

pulvino (pulvin): A typical structure of Byzantine architecture consisting of a four-sided stone, often in the shape of a truncated pyramid and often decorated with carvings of plants and animals, which connected the capital to the above structure.

putto: An artistic representation of a naked small child, especially common in the Renaissance.

stucco: A building material made of sand, powdered marble, lime, and water applied to a surface to make it smooth or used to create a decorative relief.

telamone or **atlante:** A statue of a male figure used as structural support.

terme: Thermal baths or spas, such as the Ancient Roman ones.

timpano (tympanum): The triangular wall — sometimes decorated with reliefs — between the cornice and the roof.

transenna: A screen (usually in carved marble) separating the *presbiterio* from the rest of an early Christian church.

travertino (travertine): A type of limestone that is white, pale yellow, or pale reddish and porous, commonly found in Central Italy.

Common Roman Foods

agnello: Lamb, usually grilled or baked.

agnello alla scottadito: Thin, char-broiled lamb chops (*scottadito* means literally "burn your fingers," and the name applies because they are served piping hot, and you're supposed to eat them with your hands).

amatriciana: Traditional local pasta sauce made with lard, onions, hot red pepper, and tomatoes.

animelle: Intestines of baby veal still filled with milk.

antipasto: Succulent tidbits served at the beginning of a meal (before the pasta), whose ingredients may include slices of cured meats, *insalata di mare, bruschetta,* and cooked and seasoned vegetables.

aragosta: Lobster.

baccalà: Dried and salted codfish, usually prepared as a stew.

bistecca: Steak.

bomba alla crema: A deep-fried pastry filled with cream and served for breakfast at bars.

braciola: Chop, usually lamb or pork.

brasato: Beef braised in wine with vegetables.

bruschetta: Toasted peasant-style bread, heavily slathered with olive oil and garlic, and often topped with tomatoes.

bucatini: Thick, hollow spaghetti.

calamari: Squid.

calzone: A filled pocket of pizza dough, usually stuffed with ham and cheese, and sometimes other ingredients. It can be baked or fried.

cannelloni: Tubes of fresh pasta dough stuffed with meat, fish, or vegetables and then baked with cheese, tomato sauce, and sometimes béchamel (creamy white sauce).

caprese: A salad of fresh tomatoes and fresh mozzarella, seasoned with fresh basil and olive oil.

carciofi: Artichokes.

carpaccio: Thin slices of raw beef, seasoned with olive oil, lemon, pepper, and slivers of Parmesan. Sometimes raw fish served in the same style but without the cheese.

ciambella: A deep-fried, doughnut-shaped pastry served for breakfast at bars.

coniglio alla cacciatora: Rabbit cooked in wine with olives and herbs.

cornetto: A sort of croissant served for breakfast at bars; it can be plain or filled with a dollop of pastry cream or jam.

cozze: Mussels.

fagioli: Beans.

fiordilatte: A type of mozzarella made with cow's milk.

fragaglie: Very small fish, usually served deep fried.

fresella: Whole-wheat rustic bread served as a salad with fresh tomatoes, fresh basil, salt, and olive oil. The special bread is sold in flat rounds.

frittata: Italian omelet.

fritto misto: A deep-fried medley of seafood, usually calamari and shrimp.

frutti di mare: Translated "fruits of the sea" and refers to all shellfish.

gelato (produzione propria): Ice cream (homemade).

gnocchi: Dumplings made from potatoes *(gnocchi alla patate)* or from semolina *(gnocchi alla romana)* and usually served with a tomato sauce.

granita: Flavored ice, usually with lemon or coffee.

insalata di mare: Seafood salad (usually including octopus or squid) seasoned with olive oil and lemon — sometimes vinegar — and whatever the chef fancies, usually parsley and other herbs and spices.

involtini: Thinly sliced beef, veal, pork, eggplant, or zucchini rolled, stuffed, and sautéed, often served in a tomato sauce.

maritozzo: A sweet bun studded with raisins and little bits of candied citrus fruit served for breakfast at bars.

maritozzo alla panna: *Maritozzo* (see preceding definition) that's been cut in half and filled with whipped cream.

melanzane: Eggplant.

minestrone: A rich and savory vegetable soup usually sprinkled with grated *Parmigiano.*

mozzarella di bufala: Typically from Campania, a nonfermented cheese, exclusively made from fresh buffalo milk, boiled, and then kneaded into a rounded ball and served fresh. What is called *mozzarella* in the rest of Italy and abroad is mere *fiordilatte,* a similar kind of cheese made with cow's milk.

panna: Heavy cream.

panna montata: Whipped cream.

Parmigiano: Parmesan, a hard and salty yellow cheese usually grated over pastas and soups but also eaten alone; the best is *Parmigiano-Reggiano.* A pale imitation is *Grana Padano,* still a good cheese but quite different.

peperoni: Green, yellow, or red sweet peppers (not to be confused with pepperoni, which doesn't exist in Italy).

pesce al cartoccio: Fish baked in a parchment envelope with the chef's whim of seasonings.

pesce spada: Swordfish.

pesto: Fresh basil, garlic, and olive oil, finely chopped into a paste.

piselli: Peas.

pizza: Specific varieties include *margherita* (with tomato sauce, cheese, fresh basil, and memories of the first queen of Italy, Marguerite di Savoia, in whose honor it was first made by a Neapolitan chef), *marinara* (with tomatoes and oregano), *napoletana* (tomatoes, cheese, and anchovies; quite hilariously, these are the same toppings that in Naples make the pizza *romana*).

pizzaiola: A process in which something (usually, a slice of beef or a fillet of fish) is cooked in a tomato, garlic, and oregano sauce.

polipetti: Squid.

polpo or **polipo:** Octopus.

ragù: Meat-based tomato sauce, where the chef's imagination rules.

ricotta: A soft, bland cheese served very fresh and made from sheep's milk or, in lesser-quality versions, with cow's milk.

rigatoni: Classic short pasta usually served *all'amatriciana.*

risotto alla pescatora: Rice cooked with wine, a little tomato, and lots of fresh seafood.

semifreddo: A frozen dessert, usually ice cream with sponge cake.

seppia: Cuttlefish (a kind of squid); its black ink is used for flavoring in certain sauces for pasta and also in risotto dishes.

sogliola: Sole.

spaghetti: A long, round, thin pasta, variously served; *al ragù* (with meat sauce), *all'Amatriciana* (see earlier in this list), *al pomodoro* (with fresh tomatoes), *ai frutti di mare* (with a medley of sautéed seafood), and *alle vongole* (with clam sauce) are some of the most common.

spiedini: Pieces of meat grilled on a skewer over an open flame.

tagliatelle: Flat egg noodles.

tonno: Tuna.

trippa: Tripe.

vermicelli: Thin spaghetti.

zabaglione/zabaione: Egg yolks whipped into the consistency of a custard, flavored with Marsala, and served warm as a dessert.

zuccotto: A liqueur-soaked sponge cake molded into a dome and layered with chocolate, nuts, and whipped cream.

zuppa inglese: Sponge cake soaked in custard.

Index

BUSINESS, CAREERS & PERSONAL FINANCE

0-7645-5307-0   0-7645-5331-3 *†

Also available:

✔Accounting For Dummies †
0-7645-5314-3
✔Business Plans Kit For Dummies †
0-7645-5365-8
✔Cover Letters For Dummies
0-7645-5224-4
✔Frugal Living For Dummies
0-7645-5403-4
✔Leadership For Dummies
0-7645-5176-0
✔Managing For Dummies
0-7645-1771-6

✔Marketing For Dummies
0-7645-5600-2
✔Personal Finance For Dummies *
0-7645-2590-5
✔Project Management
For Dummies
0-7645-5283-X
✔Resumes For Dummies †
0-7645-5471-9
✔Selling For Dummies
0-7645-5363-1
✔Small Business Kit For Dummies *†
0-7645-5093-4

HOME & BUSINESS COMPUTER BASICS

0-7645-4074-2   0-7645-3758-X

Also available:

✔ACT! 6 For Dummies
0-7645-2645-6
✔iLife '04 All-in-One Desk Reference
For Dummies
0-7645-7347-0
✔iPAQ For Dummies
0-7645-6769-1
✔Mac OS X Panther Timesaving
Techniques For Dummies
0-7645-5812-9
✔Macs For Dummies
0-7645-5656-8
✔Microsoft Money 2004 For Dummies
0-7645-4195-1

✔Office 2003 All-in-One Desk
Reference For Dummies
0-7645-3883-7
✔Outlook 2003 For Dummies
0-7645-3759-8
✔PCs For Dummies
0-7645-4074-2
✔TiVo For Dummies
0-7645-6923-6
✔Upgrading and Fixing PCs
For Dummies
0-7645-1665-5
✔Windows XP Timesaving
Techniques For Dummies
0-7645-3748-2

FOOD, HOME, GARDEN, HOBBIES, MUSIC & PETS

0-7645-5295-3   0-7645-5232-5

Also available:

✔Bass Guitar For Dummies
0-7645-2487-9
✔Diabetes Cookbook For Dummies
0-7645-5230-9
✔Gardening For Dummies *
0-7645-5130-2
✔Guitar For Dummies
0-7645-5106-X
✔Holiday Decorating For Dummies
0-7645-2570-0
✔Home Improvement All-in-One
For Dummies
0-7645-5680-0

✔Knitting For Dummies
0-7645-5395-X
✔Piano For Dummies
0-7645-5105-1
✔Puppies For Dummies
0-7645-5255-4
✔Scrapbooking For Dummies
0-7645-7208-3
✔Senior Dogs For Dummies
0-7645-5818-8
✔Singing For Dummies
0-7645-2475-5
✔30-Minute Meals For Dummies
0-7645-2589-1

INTERNET & DIGITAL MEDIA

0-7645-1664-7   0-7645-6924-4

Also available:

✔2005 Online Shopping Directory
For Dummies
0-7645-7495-7
✔CD & DVD Recording For Dummies
0-7645-5956-7
✔eBay For Dummies
0-7645-5654-1
✔Fighting Spam For Dummies
0-7645-5965-6
✔Genealogy Online For Dummies
0-7645-5964-8
✔Google For Dummies
0-7645-4420-9

✔Home Recording For Musicians
For Dummies
0-7645-1634-5
✔The Internet For Dummies
0-7645-4173-0
✔iPod & iTunes For Dummies
0-7645-7772-7
✔Preventing Identity Theft
For Dummies
0-7645-7336-5
✔Pro Tools All-in-One Desk
Reference For Dummies
0-7645-5714-9
✔Roxio Easy Media Creator
For Dummies
0-7645-7131-1

SPORTS, FITNESS, PARENTING, RELIGION & SPIRITUALITY

0-7645-5146-9   0-7645-5418-2

Also available:
- Adoption For Dummies
  0-7645-5488-3
- Basketball For Dummies
  0-7645-5248-1
- The Bible For Dummies
  0-7645-5296-1
- Buddhism For Dummies
  0-7645-5359-3
- Catholicism For Dummies
  0-7645-5391-7
- Hockey For Dummies
  0-7645-5228-7

- Judaism For Dummies
  0-7645-5299-6
- Martial Arts For Dummies
  0-7645-5358-5
- Pilates For Dummies
  0-7645-5397-6
- Religion For Dummies
  0-7645-5264-3
- Teaching Kids to Read
  For Dummies
  0-7645-4043-2
- Weight Training For Dummies
  0-7645-5168-X
- Yoga For Dummies
  0-7645-5117-5

TRAVEL

0-7645-5438-7   0-7645-5453-0

Also available:
- Alaska For Dummies
  0-7645-1761-9
- Arizona For Dummies
  0-7645-6938-4
- Cancún and the Yucatán
  For Dummies
  0-7645-2437-2
- Cruise Vacations For Dummies
  0-7645-6941-4
- Europe For Dummies
  0-7645-5456-5
- Ireland For Dummies
  0-7645-5455-7

- Las Vegas For Dummies
  0-7645-5448-4
- London For Dummies
  0-7645-4277-X
- New York City For Dummies
  0-7645-6945-7
- Paris For Dummies
  0-7645-5494-8
- RV Vacations For Dummies
  0-7645-5443-3
- Walt Disney World & Orlando
  For Dummies
  0-7645-6943-0

GRAPHICS, DESIGN & WEB DEVELOPMENT

0-7645-4345-8   0-7645-5589-8

Also available:
- Adobe Acrobat 6 PDF
  For Dummies
  0-7645-3760-1
- Building a Web Site For Dummies
  0-7645-7144-3
- Dreamweaver MX 2004
  For Dummies
  0-7645-4342-3
- FrontPage 2003 For Dummies
  0-7645-3882-9
- HTML 4 For Dummies
  0-7645-1995-6
- Illustrator CS For Dummies
  0-7645-4084-X

- Macromedia Flash MX 2004
  For Dummies
  0-7645-4358-X
- Photoshop 7 All-in-One Desk
  Reference For Dummies
  0-7645-1667-1
- Photoshop CS Timesaving
  Techniques For Dummies
  0-7645-6782-9
- PHP 5 For Dummies
  0-7645-4166-8
- PowerPoint 2003 For Dummies
  0-7645-3908-6
- QuarkXPress 6 For Dummies
  0-7645-2593-X

NETWORKING, SECURITY, PROGRAMMING & DATABASES

0-7645-6852-3   0-7645-5784-X

Also available:
- A+ Certification For Dummies
  0-7645-4187-0
- Access 2003 All-in-One Desk
  Reference For Dummies
  0-7645-3988-4
- Beginning Programming
  For Dummies
  0-7645-4997-9
- C For Dummies
  0-7645-7068-4
- Firewalls For Dummies
  0-7645-4048-3
- Home Networking For Dummies
  0-7645-42796

- Network Security For Dummies
  0-7645-1679-5
- Networking For Dummies
  0-7645-1677-9
- TCP/IP For Dummies
  0-7645-1760-0
- VBA For Dummies
  0-7645-3989-2
- Wireless All In-One Desk Referenc
  For Dummies
  0-7645-7496-5
- Wireless Home Networking
  For Dummies
  0-7645-3910-8